Elvis '57

Seattle, September 1, 1957. (Seattle Post-Intelligencer Collection, Museum of History & Industry, Seattle)

Elvis '57

The Final Fifties Tours

Alan Hanson

iUniverse, Inc.
New York Lincoln Shanghai

Elvis '57
The Final Fifties Tours

Copyright © 2007 by Alan R. Hanson

iUniverse books may be ordered through booksellers or by contacting:

iUniverse
2021 Pine Lake Road, Suite 100
Lincoln, NE 68512
www.iuniverse.com
1-800-Authors (1-800-288-4677)

Because of the dynamic nature of the Internet, any Web addresses or links contained in this book may have changed since publication and may no longer be valid.

The views expressed in this work are solely those of the author and do not necessarily reflect the views of the publisher, and the publisher hereby disclaims any responsibility for them.

Cover Photo: Leo Harrison/Toronto Star
Front Cover: Ticket courtesy of Marlene Moeller

ISBN: 978-0-595-43122-9 (pbk)
ISBN: 978-0-595-87465-1 (ebk)

Printed in the United States of America

Contents

Acknowledgments

The author would like to acknowledge the following people, without whose assistance this volume could never have been written.

On multiple occasions Gordon Stoker and Hugh Jarrett of the Jordanaires graciously shared their memories of being on stage with Elvis for all of his 1957 stage shows.

Disc jockeys Bob Blackburn, Bob Hough, Robin Mitchell, Pat O'Day, and Red Robinson shared the excitement of being on the front lines for the birth of rock 'n' roll and the rise of Elvis Presley.

The following shared their memories of seeing Elvis perform live in 1957: Dick Baker, Lavette Carpenter, Gordon Johnson, John Latta, Marlene Moeller, Gary Pinkley, Nancy Ramsden, Linda Stephens, and Judith Zenk.

The following provided assistance in obtaining photographs for this volume: Elizabeth Clemens of the Walter P. Reuther Library at Wayne State University, Deborah Cribbs of the St. Louis Mercantile Library at the University of Missouri–St. Louis, Hariette Fried of the City of Ottawa Archives, Brenda Galloway-Wright of the Urban Archives at Temple University, Linda Hee of the Tropic Lightning Museum at Schofield Barracks, Carolyn Marr of the Museum of History and Industry in Seattle, Susan Snyder of the Bancroft Library at the University of California–Berkeley, and Wendy Watts and Lisa Harmatuk of the Toronto Star.

In the research stage numerous librarians and curators provided much needed help in gathering far-flung information. They include Barbara Berreman, interlibrary loan clerk of the Spokane County Public Library; Betty Cagle of the Lee County Library in Tupelo; Scott Daubert of the Tropic Lightning Museum at Schofield Barracks; Peggy Hatfield of the E. H. Butler Library at Buffalo State College; Martha Hoverson, librarian of the Hawaii and Pacific Section of the Hawaii State Library; and Margaret Stallkamp of the Havre-Hill County Library in Montana.

I would also like to thank the following people for their help along the way: Bob Blackburn Jr. for introducing me to his father; Rick Bonino of *The Spokesman-Review,* for publishing the article that eventually grew into this book; Phillip Burger for giving professional advice and support to a beginning writer; Joanie Eppinga for copyediting the manuscript; George Fogelson for his research in Los Angeles; Doug Clukey for steering me in helpful directions; Sarah Loury and Kimberly Petsch of iUniverse for their help in the submission and production processes; Shirley Mott for arranging my interview with Red Robinson and for asking a hundred times, "How's your book coming?"; and Sue Walker of the Spokane Police History Project for leading me to John Latta.

Finally, I'd like to thank my wife, Christine, for allowing me to retire while I was still young enough to pursue a dream.

Introduction

There's no automobile traffic, there's no war scare, and I've never heard an Elvis Presley record.

—Valeria Sherard
Baptist missionary
September 1957

By 1957 it seemed that everyone on earth had heard of Elvis Presley and formed an opinion about him. In talking about living in a tiny Eskimo village in Alaska, Valeria Sherard revealed that Presley's controversial reputation penetrated even remote areas where his voice had never been heard.

I certainly knew who he was that year, even though I was only eight years old at the time. Growing up in Spokane, Washington, I remember at about that time asking one of my teenage aunts if she liked Elvis. When she answered no, I further inquired, "Is it because of his sideburns?" Being too young to tune into any music scene beyond what I heard on *The Mickey Mouse Club* each afternoon, I associated that trademark feature most strongly with Elvis Presley then. I knew nothing of his music and was totally unaware of his presence in my city when he appeared at Spokane's Memorial Stadium on August 30, 1957.

Eventually I did tune into him, but it wasn't until late 1962, at the age of thirteen, that I joined the legion of Elvis fans. I can't remember exactly what it was that drew me to him at that time. Certainly by then his rock 'n' roll days and his ability to affect American pop culture were well behind him. When I came into the fold, Presley's career was on cruise control, producing multiple formula-scripted movies and records that usually stalled in the middle of the pop music charts.

Given that his career was based in Hollywood, the prospect of my ever seeing Elvis in person seemed very slight. But then, unbelievably, in 1970 he went back on the road, and in November of that year, Elvis came to Seattle, where I was in the middle of my senior year at the University of Washington. For me, seeing him that evening was not the spiritual experience so many others describe after seeing an Elvis concert; it seemed more like a memorable reward for having remained a loyal fan through the dismal movie years of the 1960s. I saw him perform again in Spokane in 1976. Although his physical decline was sadly obvious then, his death a year later was still a shock. The loyalties of youth are strong, though, and I have remained an Elvis fan through the decades since his death.

Partly, then, I came to this project as a long-time Elvis Presley fan. While gathering information for this volume, I talked on the phone with Hugh Jarrett, a member of Presley's 1957 backup group, the Jordanaires. When I asked his permission to record our conversation, Jarrett hesitated a moment, then responded, "OK, but let's not make anybody look bad."[1] I assured him that, as a Presley fan myself, my purpose was not to diminish Elvis or anybody associated with him. There are other books out there that appeal to those critical of Presley.

However, my purpose was not solely to make Elvis Presley look good, either. Certainly numerous books have been written for the many Elvis worshippers. Thirty years as a history teacher tempered my vision of Elvis Presley, and I came to view him on a level quite different and separate from that of an entertainer that I had long admired. Presley was clearly a significant historical figure, whose actions, both on and off stage, had a profound effect on American culture during the mid-1950s. Uncovering that influence was primarily on my mind when I started gathering information for the story told here. As such, I let the story take me where it would. Obviously, there were thousands who witnessed the events described herein who were fanatical Elvis fans. However, in 1957 there were others who detested him just as passionately, and their view was just as much part of the Elvis Presley story then as that of those who revered him. To attain an accurate picture of the Elvis phenomenon in those days, both sides need to be understood.

I knew that if I came across information that reflected poorly on Elvis, it would have to be included to maintain historical honesty. And, in fact, in the following pages some incidents—such as the call girl in Vancouver and the snubbing of the Montana crowds—are not among Presley's finest moments. However, none of them rise beyond the level of exposing him as a young man boxed into a highly scrutinized lifestyle and subject to unreasonable expectations.

In the end, though, revealing a few personal indiscretions and misjudgments is much less damaging to Elvis Presley's legacy than the outright distortions perpetuated over the years by the Elvis mythmakers. For instance, several reputable Presley experts have reported that riots took place at all five appearances Elvis made in the Pacific Northwest in 1957. In Portland, according to several Internet and print sources, a riot caused Elvis to leave the stage after only fifteen minutes. Easily accessible press reports at the time reveal that these assertions are clearly false. The only crowd problem on the tour was in Vancouver, B.C., and that didn't rise to the level of a riot. As for the Portland concert, there were no security problems at all. Elvis completed his forty-minute show as planned, with not a single spectator leaving the seating area.

Another area of distortion has been the exaggeration of crowd sizes during the Northwest tour. Colonel Parker created false impressions by overstating the attendance in local newspapers the day after each appearance. Some Presley advocates over the years have even added to Parker's inflated numbers. For instance, in Vancouver, B.C., where 22,000 would have been a sellout in Empire Stadium, Parker reported a crowd of 25,000. Some Presley sources today list the Vancouver crowd at 26,500. In fact, Elvis didn't come close to selling out Empire Stadium. The actual number of tickets sold was closer to 17,000. The story was the same for many other Presley personal appearances in 1957.

In perpetuating such exaggerations, Elvis loyalists through the years have defeated their own purposes. In an effort to accentuate the legend of their idol, they have instead clouded the true extent of his cultural legacy. A close look at Presley's 1957 concert tours reveals one overriding and repeated truth: it is a complex story that can't be told by numbers alone. In fact, it is a story that is much greater than Elvis Presley himself. Certainly it was an important time in Presley's life. While making the transition to an acting career, he faced and extinguished rumors that his stage popularity was declining. At the same time, the specter of the military draft threatened to end his career entirely.

This, however, is the story of many others besides Elvis. It is the story of his musicians, Scotty Moore and Bill Black, and how their relationship with Elvis deteriorated. It is the story of his backup vocal group, the Jordanaires, and particularly of Gordon Stoker, who has remained fiercely loyal to Presley through the years. And it is the story of his manager, Tom Parker, who helped guide his client through a difficult professional transition in 1957.

Also involved on the story's fringes are those who were drawn into the whirlwind created by Presley's appearance in their communities. They include local promoters, like Ernie Berg in Fort Wayne and Frank Breall in Portland; disc jockeys, like Vancouver's Red Robinson and Honolulu's Tom Moffatt, whose careers would ever after be tied to Elvis; and newspaper columnists, some pro-Elvis, like Dwight Newton in San Francisco, and others anti-Elvis, like Dick Williams in Los Angeles. It's even the story of the egg-throwers in Philadelphia and the Mother Superior in Ottawa who suspended nine girls from school for attending the Elvis show there.

Ultimately, though, the story of Elvis Presley on stage in 1957 can be broken down into 250,000 individual stories, one for each person who was there to see him perform in the eighteen cities he visited that year. Most of them were teenage girls, and each had a memorable experience. There were the Elvis fan club presidents who were rewarded with the chance to meet their idol at his press conferences in their cities. There were the girls in the Pacific Northwest who went down on the stadium floors to collect handfuls of the dirt because Elvis walked on it. There were the radio station contest winners who got their pictures taken with Elvis. There were the two girls in Montreal who left home for school one morning and decided to walk to Ottawa to see Elvis instead. This is even the story of two teenage boys, Jimi Hendrix and Ricky Nelson, who were Elvis fans in 1957 before they began building their own music careers.

When I first explained the time frame for this book to Jordanaire Gordon Stoker, he replied, "You are a brave one to take on writing about something that happened this long ago. You will be lucky to find anyone that was there that will remember anything about the dates. I must warn you that this also goes for me."[2] Investigating an event that occurred fifty years ago has its advantages and disadvantages. The main benefit is that many people who participated in or attended Elvis' 1957 stage shows are still around to tell their stories. Of the eight musicians on stage then, four are still alive fifty years later. The teenagers who were in the stands are in their sixties now, and there is no shortage of them willing to talk about seeing Elvis so many years ago. However, as Gordon Stoker explained, fifty-year-old memories are often undependable. It was a revelation to me that various people who witnessed the same Presley concert in 1957 could remember it so clearly yet so differently.

When faced with the dilemma of reconciling conflicting accounts, I first attempted to confirm one version or the other through a third source. Failing that, I fell back on common sense. If some information didn't fit into the time frame or it seemed to run counter to the standard procedures Elvis used at the time, I left it out. Finally, if I could neither discount nor confirm two conflicting versions of an event, I included them both. For example, there are varying accounts of Presley's actions after leaving the stage in Vancouver, B.C., on August 31, 1957. Unable to discern which one was accurate, I included the different stories of John Kirkwood and Red Robinson, leaving it for the reader to decide which is more credible.

Finally, in describing the 1957 Presley tour events, I relied heavily on newspaper accounts of that time. The journalists who wrote them had witnessed the events they reported, usually within the previous twenty-four hours, and even allowing for the generational bias through which their observations were filtered, I concluded that their descriptions had greater potential for accuracy than memories recalled decades after the fact.

In the end, Elvis' twenty-eight stage shows in 1957 proved an uplifting, experience for Presley, and a memorable, sometimes life-altering event for those thousands who saw him perform then. It is truly an American story—what happened in those eighteen cities when Elvis Presley came calling. It's a story of conflict between the conformist, conservative values that parents of the fifties sought to pass on to their children and the yearning of a generation on the verge of adulthood to find its own way in the world. There were apprehension and fear on one side and excitement and anticipation on the other. And right in the middle of the struggle was a gyrating Elvis Presley.

—Alan Hanson

A note on spelling: In the following text, I have chosen to present all quotations from newspapers and other sources exactly as they originally appeared. This results in an apparent lack of consistency in style, particularly in the area of spelling. For example, in 1957 most journalists spelled "teen-ager" with a hyphen, which I have retained in quoting them. In my narration, however, I have used the accepted modern spelling without the hyphen. Also, in the text the reader will find multiple spellings of the term "rock 'n' roll." Newspaper writers in the 1950s usually spelled the term "rock'n'roll" or "rock and roll." Even today several different spellings are used. In my narration, I have chosen to use "rock 'n' roll," the spelling preferred by *Merriam-Webster's Collegiate Dictionary.*

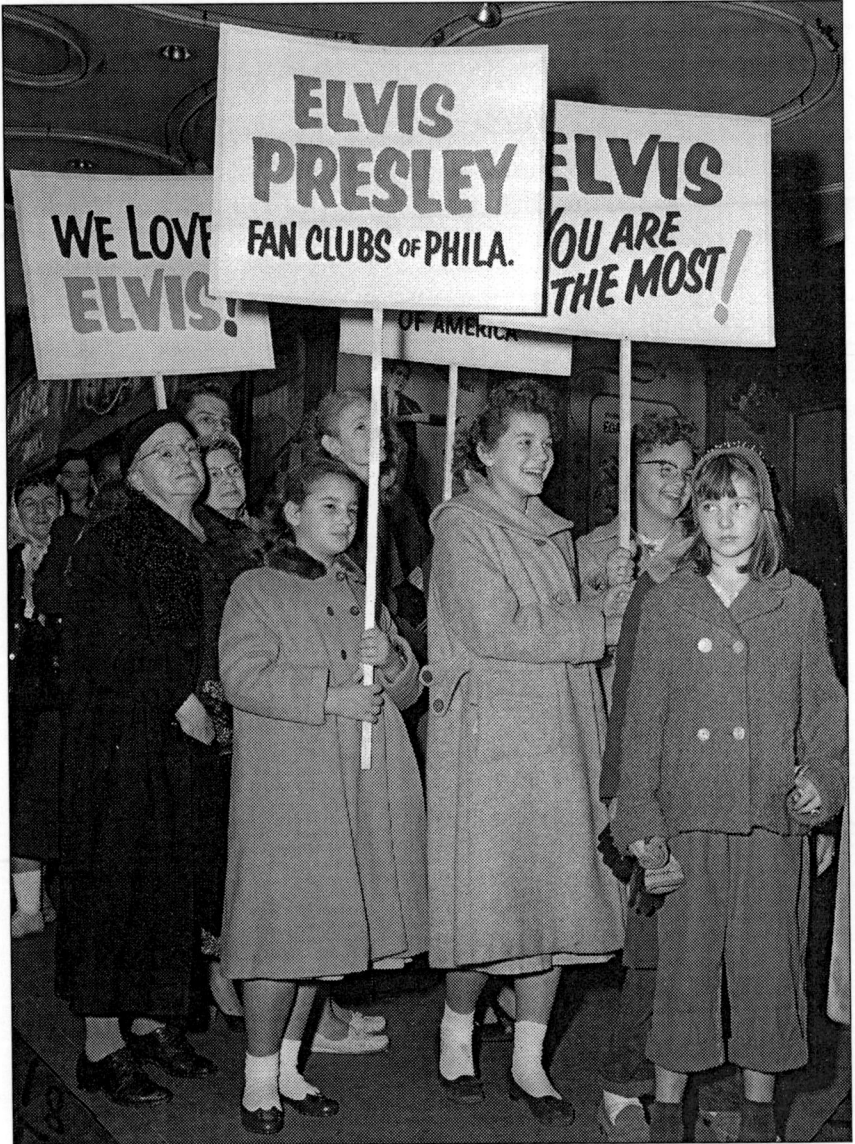

Fox Theater, Philadelphia, November 21, 1956. (Temple University
Libraries, Urban Archives, Philadelphia PA)

Chapter 1

Transition

Night had settled over Empire Stadium on August 31, 1957. It was 9:45 on a clear, warm, late-summer night in Vancouver, British Columbia. Elvis Presley had just finished his opening number, "Heartbreak Hotel," and was halfway through his second song when, looking out from the stage, he saw the far end of the stadium erupt. From where he stood on the platform a hundred yards away, it looked like excited insects spilling off an anthill as people crawled out of the stands and spread onto the grass. It grew like a wave as, from each adjoining section on both sides of the stadium, others poured onto the field to join the mass, now moving quickly toward the stage where Elvis continued his performance. "We'll never stop them now!" yelled a policeman, as he and his cohorts locked arms in a valiant effort to stem the flow.

On stage, Gordon Stoker of the Jordanaires watched the crowd collide with the cordon of cops, and fear began to take hold of him. He glanced up at Elvis and saw the fear mirrored back at him. If the boss stayed, so would he; if he ran for his life, so would he. As the crowd surged up against and pushed the security line, Stoker and the others on stage kept an eye on the man performing in front of them. If the line broke, what would he do?

Just weeks before, Elvis Presley had been enjoying a serene, untroubled summer in his hometown of Memphis. He and his family had time to adapt to life in their new home of Graceland. Elvis and his buddies—Lamar Fike, George Klein, Cliff Gleaves, Alan Fortas—along with his cousins and new girlfriend, Anita Wood, formed a pack that lived a seemingly aimless, pleasure-seeking existence. There were motorcycle outings, skating parties at the Rainbow Rollerdome, late-night movies at the Strand Theatre, and amusement rides at the Fairgrounds. Or they just hung out around the jukebox and soda fountain in the basement at Graceland. They were people of the night, with Elvis rarely rising before three o'clock in the afternoon. They rode around in Cadillacs or sometimes, when Elvis didn't want to be recognized, in an old panel truck.

During that summer of 1957, the same Elvis Presley who often pulled into Chenault's Drive-in on hamburger runs had a greater influence on American popular culture than any other single person in the country. Whether he was aware

1

of it (and he probably wasn't), Presley was in the vanguard of a gang of rock 'n' rollers who were winning the war with parents for the hearts and minds of their adolescent children. By this time, the church leaders, politicians, and community leaders who had preached the virtues of conformity in the post-war years could only hope that Presley's act was just a fad that would soon pass. In a whirlwind campaign the year before, Presley's pervasive presence in the media, both old and new, had entered American homes and created a generational schism between teenagers and their parents.

Presley's assault, of course, was anchored in the new power of television. The effect of his music would never have had such a marked impact without the visual image of the man and the stage antics that were his trademark. Eleven times, scattered throughout 1956, Presley and his alleged sexually suggestive movements appeared on network variety shows. His popularity, and infamy, grew with each appearance.

TV alone, however, can't be credited for the meteoric rise of Elvis Presley. During the year, RCA Victor saturated the market with Presley records, including eleven single releases, eight extended plays, and two albums. Led by the chart-topping singles "Heartbreak Hotel," "Don't Be Cruel," and "Love Me Tender," Presley's records sold more than fourteen million copies during 1956. Between home record players and Presley-dominated radio playlists, Elvis' voice pervaded the pop, country, and rhythm and blues charts.

His presence was felt in two other media, as well. Building on its TV triumph, the Presley phenomenon arrived at movie theaters in November with the release of *Love Me Tender*. In its first week the film played at 575 theaters nationwide, bringing in $540,000. The new star also could be heard on the radio, appearing eight Saturday nights on *The Louisiana Hayride*, broadcast live from Shreveport, Louisiana.

When not appearing on TV or radio, or filming in Hollywood, Presley took his act straight to the people with a grueling tour schedule. On 106 days in 1956, Elvis performed 143 stage shows around the country in 79 different cities. Added to that were the 28 shows he performed in Las Vegas during his two-week engagement there in April and May.

Throw in magazine covers and articles, and all the merchandise featuring his image and name, and 1956 was a year designed for maximum exposure of Elvis Presley. Though he was virtually unknown nationally when the year began, by December nearly all Americans above the age of ten knew of Elvis and were joining the battle lines either for or against him.

Never again would Elvis put up numbers like he did in 1956. It was 1957, though, that proved to be the pivotal year in his career. His popularity solidified and his path in the entertainment business for the next decade was determined.

Rather than continue the kind of bookings that had propelled Elvis to the top of the entertainment world in 1956, his manager used a new set of priorities to guide Presley's career. It was risky to abandon the proven precepts of success, but in the end the strategy put the singer's career firmly on the track both Presley and Parker wanted.

Colonel Parker has been vilified by Presley fans through the years for steering the star's career in the wrong direction. However, Parker's career-changing strategy in 1957 was based on his client's wishes. While on the road during 1956, Presley granted interviews to dozens of disc jockeys and journalists. In those interviews he often stated his desire for a future career centered in Hollywood.

Early in 1956, even as his fame as a singer and stage performer exploded around him, Elvis knew he ultimately wanted to be an actor. On March 24, 1956, in an interview at the Warwick Hotel in New York, Robert Carlton Brown asked Elvis, "Long range, do you feel you got your eye on some objective in the future that you're headed for, or don't ya think about that?" Presley responded, "Yeah, I do. I think about it. Right now, actually I would like to learn how to act in the movies. I guess … that's … the right ambition for any young person. I think if he really tried, and he's such a hit, he'd probably do it." A little over three months later, TV talk show host Hy Gardner interviewed Elvis over the phone. "Now, if you had your choice," Gardner asked, "would you prefer to be an actor to being a singing entertainer?" Elvis answered, "If I were a good actor—of course I'm not a good singer, but if I were a good actor—I think that I would like that a little better. Although, if I ever break into acting completely, I'll still continue my singing. I'll still continue making records." In another interview the following month, Presley explained his greatest ambition.

> I know I've been lucky in an awful lot of ways. But I think the luckiest thing that ever happened to me is that I'm beginning to realize my greatest ambition.
>
> All of my life, I've wanted to be an actor, though I never was in any school plays or recited a line other than the Gettysburg address for my sixth-grade homeroom class. But always sticking in the back of my head was the idea that somehow, someday, I'd like to get the chance to act.
>
> I came out to Hollywood about three months ago, and Mr. Hal Wallis of Paramount Pictures asked me to take a screen test. When the test was over … I'd gone through the first step of realizing my life's ambition.[1]

In 1956 Presley signed two multi-picture Hollywood contracts, and when Twentieth Century Fox released *Love Me Tender* nationwide on November 16, 1956, Presley called making the movie "the biggest thrill of my life."[2]

While experiencing the excitement of making movies, Elvis voiced a growing dislike for performing on the small screen. On June 16 he appeared on Wink Martindale's show on WHBQ-TV in Memphis and told the host his thoughts on TV appearances. "I mean, on television you're limited, ya know," explained Elvis. "You can only do so much. And ... so many rehearsals. By doing only so much, I mean ... you can only do a couple of songs and by the time you get warmed up, well, they're dragging you off."

While the emphasis in 1957 was clearly on making movies, Elvis still enjoyed the excitement of a live audience. In March he told a Toronto reporter, "The only time I'm really living is when I'm out there under those spotlights ... There's more of a sense of accomplishment. There's more a sense of joy. You know that this is it when you hear them calling for you and you walk out there and they welcome you."[3]

While Presley still acknowledged the thrill of live performances, he was beginning to complain about the lack of sleep and the physical dangers posed by zealous fans during his hectic road schedule. In addition, as exciting as being on stage could be, Elvis realized that his music had become meaningless during personal appearances. The large, screaming crowds meant that few patrons were able, or cared, to hear him sing. A single word, a burp, or the twitching of a little finger inspired a sea of squealing from the crowd. The exhilaration of being on stage was still there for Elvis, but the feeling of artistic accomplishment had dissipated.

Colonel Parker knew that if Elvis' future was to be in the movies, then his income would depend on theater attendance. Parker understandably reasoned that any other public appearances by Presley—whether TV or stage show—could provide fans with an Elvis-fix that potentially could reduce movie ticket sales. The logical strategy, then, was to start making Presley's image available primarily on the movie screen.

By the end of 1957, both Parker and his client must have been convinced they had made the right choice in going to Hollywood. Three Presley movies were among the top twenty box office grossing films of the year. *Love Me Tender,* despite being released in November 1956, finished at number ten for 1957 with total sales of $4.5 million. *Jailhouse Rock,* released in October of 1957, brought in $3.7 million by the end of the year to finish as the number fifteen film of the year. Released in July, *Loving You* came in at number nineteen with another $3.7 million. On the theater owners' list of "Money Making Stars" for 1957, Elvis was number four, trailing only Rock Hudson, John Wayne, and Pat Boone. In March, after a national survey of theaters revealed that more popcorn had been sold during showings of *Love Me Tender* than any other movie, Elvis won the obscure "Popscar" award. Popcorn tycoon Jim Blevins of Nashville announced that Elvis had won the award "hands down." (In covering the story in their "News and Faces" column, the *Detroit Free Press* couldn't resist adding, "The aspirin industry will not present an award to the singer until it completes its survey of adults."[4])

The numbers show how 1957 was a transitional year for Elvis Presley. Television appearances were down to 1 from 8 the year before. There were only 28 personal appearances in 18 cities in 1957, as opposed to 143 concerts in 79 cities in 1956. The majority of Elvis' working time was spent in Hollywood filming two movies, *Loving You* and *Jailhouse Rock*. Even the dozens of individual interviews Presley granted in 1956 were replaced by a series of controlled press conferences in 1957. The message to the public was clear. You want to see Elvis Presley? Buy a movie ticket. You want to hear him sing? Buy his records.

TV exposure was the first to go. Presley's only television appearance in 1957 was the last of a set of three bookings on *The Ed Sullivan Show*. After that the Colonel set the price so high that no TV producer would meet it. Parker reasoned that if Elvis' millions of fans could see him for free on television, it would reduce the incentive for them to buy tickets to see his movies. Presley didn't appear on network TV again until after he came out of the army in 1960.

With television out of the picture, that left the question of personal appearances. Both Parker and Presley knew that touring still could be a lucrative business in 1957. Elvis could draw huge crowds, and Parker was a master at increasing the take through concession sales. In addition, between movie shoots in Hollywood, Presley had some spare time. Going on tour could be an effective way to promote his coming film releases while bringing in some income as well. So Parker made his decision. Personal appearances would stay on the schedule for 1957, but only in a limited way. There would be just three short, tightly packed tours in which Elvis would appear only in large cities with high-capacity venues to maximize attendance.

As 1957 dawned, all of Presley's personal appearance obligations came to an end. For $10,000 Colonel Parker bought Elvis out of his contract with *The Louisiana Hayride*. After appearing on a charity show in Shreveport on December 15, 1956, Presley never again performed on a live radio show. His last TV appearance of the fifties was on the January 6 Sullivan show. His only remaining commitments were his five-year recording contract with RCA and his two Hollywood contracts. In April of 1956, Elvis signed a long-term contract that Colonel Parker negotiated with Hal Wallis and Paramount Pictures. The agreement called for Presley to do one movie for Paramount Pictures, with a studio option for six more. Parker retained the right to make another picture each year with a different studio. He took that option to Twentieth Century Fox, who signed Elvis in August of 1956 for a picture and an option for two more.

Presley's 1957 schedule, then, was built around his two movies that year. Mid-January to mid-March was set aside on the calendar for filming Paramount's *Loving You*. The months of May and June were designated for work on *Jailhouse Rock*, after which Elvis would take a two-month summer break with family in friends in Memphis.

Opportunities for personal appearances in 1957, then, were limited. There was a short opportunity in March and April, between stints in Hollywood. A longer period in the fall and early winter, from Labor Day to Christmas, was also open.

With that limited framework in mind, Colonel Parker combined all of Presley's personal appearance tours for the year into one package. Parker chose businessman Lee Gordon of the Detroit promotion company Gordon and Shurgin as the promoter, with Chicago booker Al Dvorin providing the entertainers for the opening segment of The Elvis Presley Show. The terms of the agreement called for Presley to receive a guaranteed amount for each performance, regardless of gate receipts. The local promoter agreed to pay for all advertising, furnish a suitable venue, and pay all venue workers and taxes. In addition, the sponsor was to provide and pay for a specified minimum number of "police officers" to provide stage security, as well as a police escort for Presley from his hotel to the venue and back again. The contract gave Colonel Parker the exclusive right to sell souvenirs, novelties, and photos of Presley at each show. Finally, no TV or radio appearances by Elvis were allowed before or after the show.

Under this contract, Gordon booked Elvis on three personal appearance tours in 1957. The first, running from March 28 through April 6, took Presley into some of the larger cities of the upper Midwest and eastern Canada. Included were dates in Chicago, St. Louis, Fort Wayne, Detroit, Buffalo, Toronto, Ottawa, Montreal, and Philadelphia. (The planned stop in Montreal was later canceled when the town councillors passed a last-minute measure blocking Presley from performing in the city.)

Following his summer break, Elvis had a four-day, five-show tour of the Pacific Northwest over the Labor Day weekend. Performances were planned for the Washington State cities of Spokane, Tacoma, and Seattle, as well as for Vancouver, B.C., and Portland, Oregon. At the end of October, Presley would travel to California for performances in San Francisco, Oakland, and Los Angeles. (While on the West Coast, Colonel Parker was offered a performance deal in Hawaii and Elvis jumped at it. His shows in Honolulu Stadium on November 10 and at Schofield Barracks the next day would be his last live stage appearances for nearly three years.)

In addition to large, urban centers that promised substantial ticket sales, Elvis' 1957 tours targeted cities Presley had not played before. During 1956 Elvis performed in St. Louis, Detroit, Tupelo, Oakland, and Los Angeles, but the citizens of the other thirteen cities he visited in 1957 got their first look at Elvis Presley live on stage.

Although they took him to three far-flung parts of the U.S. and Canada, Presley's 1957 tours had much in common. As mentioned before, primarily large urban centers were targeted, leading to larger than average crowd sizes, even for Elvis.

Colonel Parker tightened press access to Presley at all tour stops in 1957. Gone were the dozens of interviews Elvis granted before and after appearances in 1956. Starting with the Chicago appearance on March 28, a single press conference was held in each city prior to Elvis going on stage. Of course, this frustrated many local journalists and DJs, who no longer could hope for exclusive interviews and stories. In the press conference setting, each journalist could ask only a few questions, and all the other writers present could use Presley's responses in their stories. Some indignant journalists accused Elvis of acting more like the president than a rock 'n' roll singer in his dealings with the press. At the press conferences and performances, still pictures were allowed, even encouraged, but TV film was forbidden by Colonel Parker, who cited restrictions on moving images in Presley's Hollywood contracts. In fact, it was part of Parker's new marketing strategy of limiting Elvis' exposure to the public.

For most of his 1957 appearances, Presley's stage dress revolved around elements of his new gold lamé suit. Early that year Colonel Parker commissioned Nudie Cohen of Nudie's Rodeo Tailors in North Hollywood to fashion a gold-leaf tuxedo for Elvis. When finished, the full suit cost $2,500 and included jacket, slacks, belt, shoes, and string necktie. Elvis first wore the suit during his spring tour. At the first two stops in Chicago and St. Louis, he wore the complete gold ensemble, but the next night, in Fort Wayne, he substituted black slacks for the gold ones. In Toronto on April 2, he wore the black pants again during the matinee performance, but donned the entire suit again for the evening show. Presley went back to the black slacks for the rest of the spring tour and never again wore the complete gold lamé suit on stage.

According to biographer Peter Guralnick, Elvis was embarrassed by the "clownishness" of the full gold suit. Also, apparently the gold was flaking off the pants when Elvis went to his knees on stage during the "Hound Dog" finale, causing Colonel Parker some angst. For his tour of the Pacific Northwest, Elvis dropped the gold tie and shoes as well, wearing only the gold jacket and belt for each of his five shows. In Vancouver, B.C., DJ Red Robinson says Elvis told him he didn't wear the complete gold suit because the creases made him look bad, and it was too hot anyway.[5]

(Whatever his reasons, Elvis didn't forget the bad experience he had with the gold slacks in 1957. For the 1968 "Comeback Special" on NBC, costume designer Bill Belew originally intended Presley to wear an all-gold suit, based on the Nudie suit, for one segment of the show. When he pitched the idea, Elvis said, "Billy, I have to be honest with you. I always hated that suit, and I won't wear it." After Belew dropped the gold pants in favor of black ones and showed Presley the proposed jacket fabric, Elvis said, "Fine. I'll go with that."[6])

In 1957 The Elvis Presley Show had two parts. The first was a variety show produced by Colonel Parker. This first "half" of the show ran about ninety minutes and was followed by a short intermission designed to give the crowd a final chance to purchase Presley souvenirs. Elvis took the stage for the show's second half, planned to run about forty minutes. The show included fifteen to eighteen songs, the titles changing during the year to include his new RCA record releases. He always opened with "Heartbreak Hotel" and closed with "Hound Dog." Elvis performed songs from *Loving You* for the first time during his Labor Day weekend tour of the Pacific Northwest, and *Jailhouse Rock* numbers were added for the October shows in California.

In addition to the acts, if the musicians' union required it, a local band played a couple of numbers in the opening part of the show. The day after the show these opening acts, for the most part, were ignored by local newspapers, which predictably focused almost entirely on Presley's performance. Only occasionally would reporters mention the opening acts in their reviews, and when they did, it was almost always with disdain. One Vancouver, B.C., reporter got personal, referring to the variety acts as "a mediocrity of backwoods juggling, jibes, jingles and jigs that even Sullivan wouldn't use in the summertime."[7]

The other eight performers in the troupe included Elvis, his three musicians, and a vocal quartet, all of whom were on stage for the show's second part. Presley's band consisted of guitarist Scotty Moore, bass player Bill Black, and drummer D.J. Fontana. Since Scotty and Bill had been with Elvis from the start of his career with Sun Records, a bond between the three men had formed as they shared the nightly grind of playing high school gyms, dance halls, and community centers throughout the South during 1954 and 1955. Although Scotty and Bill had backed Elvis for every personal appearance and recording session for over three years, by the summer of 1957 their professional and personal relationships with him had gradually weakened as Presley's fame grew. The parting would come just days after the Pacific Northwest tour ended. That summer Scotty was twenty-six and Bill was thirty.

When Elvis, Scotty and Bill began doing *The Louisiana Hayride* radio program out of Shreveport in late 1954, local drummer D.J. Fontana sat in for their two or three numbers each Saturday night. By the following summer, Fontana had become a permanent member of Presley's band, and, like Scotty and Bill, toured and recorded regularly with Elvis leading up to the 1957 tours. At twenty-two, D.J. was the same age as Elvis when the band headed for Chicago that March.

The Jordanaires, an established Nashville quartet, supplied Presley's vocal backing for the 1957 stage shows. The group first joined the The Elvis Presley Show on tour in Atlanta in June of 1956. From then on they were regulars in the recording studio as well, starting with the classic July 2 New York session that produced "Hound Dog" and "Don't Be Cruel." The group's leader, Gordon Stoker, 33 in 1957, was the quartet's first tenor. Other group members were second tenor Neal Matthews, 27; baritone Hoyt Hawkins, 30; and bass singer Hugh Jarrett, 27. "We fit together perfectly," Jarrett said of the group's partnership with Elvis in a 1998 interview. "We were accustomed to improvising and we blended our do-wahs, ya-yas, hand-clapping and the like with his singing."[8]

The Jordanaires had a dual role in the The Elvis Presley Show in 1957. They closed the opening half of the show, and then returned to back Elvis after the intermission. Gordon Stoker remembers what it was like.

> A comedian came on, and then, with the crowd yelling, "Bring on Elvis!" they brought us on. It was one of the hardest spots in show-biz, I can assure you. We opened with a fast pop or country song that was popular at the time. Somehow we were always able to hold our spot—they didn't throw anything at us. Then came intermission, and the crowd went wild. Then they would bring Elvis on. He would do one or two numbers and then bring us on with him.[9]

Among the songs the Jordanaires sang during their solo spot in the The Elvis Presley Show in 1957 were Buddy Knox's "Party Doll," Tab Hunter's "Young Love," and their own recently released single, "Walk Away."

While Colonel Parker dealt with the other entertainers for the year's first tour, Elvis lined up the members of his personal entourage, the boys who would travel with him, protect him, and keep him company. Four regulars who accompanied him on tour in 1957 were Gene Smith, George Klein, Cliff Gleaves, and Lamar Fike.

Gene Smith was Elvis' first cousin. Their mothers were sisters. Born just seven weeks apart, the two boys grew up together in Tupelo, Mississippi. When they were thirteen, both families moved to Memphis, where Gene and Elvis continued their close relationship through high school. Starting early in 1956, when Presley's burgeoning popularity caused him to start traveling separately from his band, Gene became his constant traveling companion. For trips to New York for television appearances, flights to Hollywood for movie work, and tour traveling, Gene Smith accompanied his famous cousin everywhere he went until Presley entered the army in 1958.

George Klein and Elvis met when they were both students at Humes High School in Memphis, where a mutual interest in show business made them good friends. Their paths crossed occasionally after high school, as Klein pursued a career in radio while Presley worked on a singing and performing career. In a 1981 fan magazine interview, Klein explained how he first became one of Presley's road companions in 1957.

> As time passed on, I got me a job with another radio station in Memphis, and at about this time, Elvis was really starting to bust open. Personally, I was becoming a pretty "hot" disc jockey in Memphis at the same time. At the station I was working for, I had the only rock'n'roll show. However … in those days, rock'n'roll wasn't very popular with the old folks. The station eventually let me go because this was the only type of music I was playing. So what happened was, I was walking the streets one day, without a job, and I bumped into Elvis. He said, "What's happening?" So I told him that the station had let me go, and he said, "Well, heck, why don't you come with me? We're going to Canada and in March we're going to Hollywood to do a film called Jailhouse Rock." So I said, "Well, man! My bags are packed." I was thrilled to death.[10]

Klein was twenty-two, like his boss, when they went out on tour together that March.

Another aspiring DJ, Cliff Gleaves, connected with Elvis while hanging around with well-known Memphis disc jockey Dewey Phillips during the summer of 1956. That fall Gleaves was among a group Presley invited to accompany him to New York for an appearance on *The Ed Sullivan Show.* From then on, Gleaves became a regular member of Elvis' road entourage. Like George Klein, Gleaves went along on all of Presley's concert tours in 1957.

While learning to be a DJ under the tutelage of George Klein in Memphis, Lamar Fike met Elvis at Sun Records studio in 1954. Three years later, finding himself out of work, Fike decided to call Elvis, who was then in Hollywood shooting *Jailhouse Rock.* At Presley's invitation, Lamar drove out to California to join the troupe. When Elvis returned to Memphis, Fike came with him, moving into his own room in Graceland. When the Pacific Northwest tour came along a few months later, the twenty-one-year-old Fike accompanied Elvis on the road for the first time.

Thus, in the early spring, the elements of The Elvis Presley Show began converging on Chicago, where the year's first tour was to open on March 28. In Nashville the Jordanaires piled into a car and set off on the 475-mile drive to Chicago. In Memphis Scotty, Bill, and D.J. loaded their instruments into the car, which they would take turns driving. In Chicago, Al Dvorin made final arrangements for the opening act performers he was supplying for the tour. Finally, late on the evening of March 27, Elvis and his entourage settled into their private car for the train ride north. With Hollywood on hold for a while, it was time to hit the road again.

Chapter 2

Chicago

Prelude

Resplendent in his full gold lamé suit, Elvis Presley knew he had something to prove as he prepared to take the stage at Chicago's International Amphitheatre on March 28, 1957. He had not been on tour for over four months, by far the longest absence from the concert stage in his three-year entertainment career. Much of the time away from touring had been spent in California making his second movie. The doubts must have been there when he opened his first 1957 tour. Could he still draw the crowds and generate the pandemonium that he had throughout the previous year?

Just six days before the tour began, a published poll seemed to indicate that the answer was no. In major newspapers around the country, the Gilbert Youth Research Company, under the banner "What Young People Think," divulged current teenage views as revealed by their weekly nationwide surveys. Their March 22 study announced, "Elvis Presley's phenomenal popularity among the Nation's teenagers seems to have taken a nosedive." The article, written by company president Eugene Gilbert, compared data collected in a recent poll with that in a similar poll from October 1956, when Presleymania was taking the country by storm.[1]

In the October survey, 35 percent of teenagers named Presley their favorite male vocalist. In the new March survey, five months later, Elvis' top approval rating had dropped to 21 percent. "That's still a hefty following—and also a remarkable decline," concluded Gilbert, who offered the comments of a few ex-Elvis fans. "He's nothing anymore," one sixteen-year-old girl noted. "Last year he was news. Today he's just another wiggler." Another high school girl said, "Last year I used to think Elvis was the sexiest male alive, but I can see now that he'll become just another commercial singer like the rest." One boy blamed the movies for Presley's slide. "Hollywood's got him," he commented. "The personal appeal he had for us teen-agers is gone forever." For some in the poll, however, Presley's acting had solidified their devotion to him. Of his first movie, *Love Me Tender,* one girl observed, "Elvis was the very end in that movie. I bet someday he gets an Academy award."

As for Presley's staying power, a third of the girls polled and 39 percent of the boys felt that the Presley obsession would flame out in less than a year. Forty-two percent of the girls and 31 percent of the boys gave him one to two years of peak popularity. Those who predicted that he would have two to four more years at the top dropped to 8.5 and 17 percent, respectively. The rest, just 16 percent of the girls and 13 percent of the boys, thought Presley's star would still be shining brightly four years in the future.

If Elvis' popularity was slipping with teenagers, who was threatening to knock him from his throne? Gilbert's poll revealed that Pat Boone was moving up in popularity as fast as Elvis was moving down. At 13 percent, Boone finished second to Presley as the nation's favorite male singer among teenagers. One girl declared, "You can take Elvis and give him back to the Indians. I'll take Pat any day." A high-schooler pronounced Boone "really quite a guy. Look at him supporting a family and going to school as well as being a singer."

The numbers all seemed to indicate that Boone's star was ascending quickly. Labeled an "easy-going rock'n'roller" by *American Weekly Magazine* that March, he already had 2,300 organized and chartered fan clubs nationwide. He received around three thousand pieces of fan mail each week, and his manager, Jack Spina, sent out free Boone photos to over a thousand fans each week. In a little more than a year in the business, three of Boone's records had sold over a million copies each. He made a movie for Twentieth Century Fox and signed a five-year, million-dollar contract with ABC-TV to host his own half-hour weekly variety program scheduled to begin in the fall of 1957.

Boone's upbringing was a model of conformity with American values espoused in the post-war years. Raised in Nashville, he began singing at prayer meetings and religious services at age ten. In high school he was a straight-A student and lettered in baseball, basketball, and track. Amidst his growing popularity, he stuck to the conservative values of his youth. He declined to appear in nightclubs because his church congregation disapproved of them.

In early 1957 Pat Boone's fan base was mounting a challenge to Presley's loyalists. His recordings were matching Elvis' on the pop charts, and by the end of the year he would finish a notch ahead of Presley on Hollywood's list of leading box office draws. However, Boone's modest gestures while performing were not creating the pandemonium that Elvis generated. Once, after Boone performed in Florida, an excited teenager pulled a shoulder strap off his leather trench coat. "It was an accident," explained Boone, "and the kid was kind enough to give it back."[2] At his modest home in Leonia, New Jersey, Boone's fans honored the small, hand-written sign on the door requesting that no one ring the bell during the afternoon when the children were asleep.

By early 1957 Pat Boone had positioned himself at the opposite end of the pop music spectrum from Elvis Presley. Deeply religious and neatly groomed in his collection of tweed sport coats, collegiate sweaters, and white ducks, Boone was the darling of many in the press who hoped his clean-cut crooning could overthrow Elvis Presley's gyrating rock 'n' roll and win back the hearts and minds of the nation's youth.

And Pat Boone was not the only threat to Elvis' supremacy on the pop music charts. By March of 1957, Harry Belafonte, riding the calypso craze, had surpassed Presley in record sales on the RCA label. Belafonte then had five records among RCA's top ten sellers, while Elvis had only one. Since Christmas, Belafonte had sold 3,500,000 singles and 800,000 albums, while Elvis had tapered off. In Cleveland, considered a good indicator of national record sales, Presley's sales had peaked near Christmas, but had dropped off considerably since then. "He's cold," said one RCA executive. "The only ones who mention him now are the television comedians."[3] Calypso and Belafonte came along to offer something new just when the market had been saturated with Presley records. Soon Elvis would have out a new single and a new album, but it remained to be seen if he could reclaim the high ground in record sales.

With Pat Boone and Harry Belafonte closing in on him, his record sales declining, and a poll saying he was slipping in popularity, Presley prepared to open a critical eight-city personal appearance tour in the spring of 1957.

Chicago, Illinois
International Amphitheatre
Thursday, March 28, 1957, 8:00 pm

A week before Elvis came to town, Mervin Block's six-part series on rock 'n' roll appeared in the *Chicago American* newspaper. Block made the rounds in Chicago, interviewing college professors, record company officials, psychiatrists, educators, students, and government officials. He even got Margaret Mead's views on the subject when the renowned anthropologist visited the city. As expected, attitudes about Presley varied widely in Chicago.

"Elvis is a musical freak," DJ Marty Faye declared. "He doesn't have a voice, period. He can't play a guitar, period. He's unmusical. But he must be an entertainer, because he's entertaining millions of people."[4]

Elvis wasn't to blame, though, according to Dr. Helen Howe, director of music for the Chicago Board of Education. "The fault isn't with Elvis," she explained. "The fault is with the low musical standards of the public who views him." Dr.

Howe didn't believe, however, that Presley had an unwholesome effect on teen-agers. "I don't think those things are in the minds of young people as much as they're in the minds of the older people who watch them."

One unexpected Presley supporter was Police Commissioner Timothy O'Connor. "I think he's a pretty good singer and a pretty good entertainer," O'Connor told Block. "I don't see anything wrong with him. Unwholesome? Definitely not. There's been no time in my whole career as a policeman where rock'n'roll or any other type of music has had an evil effect."

At O'Keefe Elementary School, the boys, not girls, went overboard on Elvis, according to seventh grader Peggy Edidin. "Some kids worship the ground he walks on," she reported. "All the boys in our room envy him. Jim ... has pictures of Elvis all over his locker. He walks like Elvis and he has his hair like Elvis. The boys all wanta act like Elvis. That's too 'hoody' for me."

Block even asked Mayor Richard J. Daley what he thought of Elvis, but he had trouble getting a straight answer. "This is the time of Lent;" said the mayor, "this is the time of good will towards men." Asked if his daughters listened to rock 'n' roll, the mayor just laughed and declined to answer.

The object of all this discussion boarded a northbound train in Memphis' Central Station just before midnight on Wednesday, March 27. On hand for his unannounced departure were just three teenage girls who had been hanging around for six hours hoping to catch sight of him. A *Press-Scimitar* photographer snapped a picture of Elvis and traveling companion George Klein as they searched for reading material at the station newsstand before boarding the train. After the overnight run, Elvis arrived at Chicago's Central Station at 9:00 AM and checked into a southside hotel.

That night he was booked for his first ever Chicago performance in the city's massive, multi-purpose International Amphitheatre, located on the east side of the Chicago Union Stock Yard at the intersection of Forty-third and Halstead Streets. Designed more for hosting conventions, the wide-open "Amp" was converted to a concert venue when needed by erecting bleacher sections, thus allowing seating capacity to be tailored to ticket sales.

Tickets for Presley's appearance, priced at what newspaper ads called "popular prices" of $3.50, $2.75, and $2.00, were available at the Amphitheatre Box Office, at Mages Sports Store downtown at 229 W. Madison, and at Hudson–Ross at 8 E. Randolph and Evergreen Plaza. As they related to Presley's payday, ticket sales were irrelevant in Chicago, as they were at all concerts he played in 1957. Colonel Parker's contract with Detroit tour promoter Lee Gordon called for Elvis to receive a guaranteed fee per performance. Parker leaked to the press that his boy would receive $25,000 for his Chicago show, but Elvis himself told reporters at his pre-concert press conference that he was guaranteed $10,000 in Chicago and $120,000 for the entire eight-city tour.

Whatever Presley's cut, promoters must have been encouraged by the initial brisk ticket sales during the week leading up to the Thursday night show. Four additional telephone lines were installed at the amphitheatre to handle ticket orders. Sales took off despite a widely reported boycott by the city's Catholic school system. Newspaper reports indicated that the Catholic Interscholastic Catholic Action (CISCA) had instructed all its students to stay away from Presley's performance. The day before the show, however, the CISCA issued a statement denying that it had banned its students from seeing Elvis.[5] It had only "suggested" that students not attend the Presley show. CISCA director Rev. Francis X. Lawler pointed out that he had merely sent a letter reminding all school moderators of Cardinal Stritch's recent statement urging Catholic youngsters "to raise their standards" and reject rock 'n' roll.

After the initial rush during the first couple of days, ticket sales tapered off for the rest of the week leading up to the concert. In his "The Town Crier" column in the *Daily News,* Tony Weitzel seemed pleased by the falloff in ticket sales. "Thursday night's Elvis Presley soiree at the Amphitheatre is suddenly turning anemic at the box office," he noted gleefully in his Tuesday column. "Don't hardly seem fair, what with Elvis buying hisself a new suit and all."[6] In the end, 13,373 fans went through the amphitheatre's turnstiles to see Elvis.

Security was always a big concern for Colonel Parker, so he called for local officials to supply a large force to protect his client and control the crowd. In Chicago from 80 to 100 policemen and 40 firemen were on scene, along with 175 amphitheatre ushers. A first-aid station stood ready to deal with fainting girls and others who might be injured during the show. Parker no doubt thought he had a large enough force in place to keep order, but he was to learn otherwise. Presley's manager was on a security learning curve. The coming crowd control problems in Chicago would send him scurrying ahead to make arrangements that he hoped would preclude such problems in other tour cities. Throughout 1957, unexpected crowd conflicts caused Parker to expand police presence and tighten security procedures as Elvis moved from city to city.

At 7:54 PM, six minutes before the announced show time, the crowd in the amphitheatre began clapping their hands and chanting, "We want Elvis!" At eight o'clock Colonel Parker came to the stage microphone and hushed the crowd. "We'll begin the show," he said, and then paused before continuing, "when everybody is seated. And Elvis isn't going to sing one, two, three songs; he's going to sing fourteen songs for you!"[7] Always the hawker, he then took the opportunity to plug Presley's new record album. "Request it of your favorite disc jockey," he commanded. "Buy it at your favorite record store."

Signaling for the show to begin, Parker announced, "With Elvis we have six tremendous acts," at which the crowd again began chanting, "We want Elvis!" But they wouldn't get him—not for an hour and a half, anyway. That was how long it took for the opening acts to file across the stage. Performing during the first half of the show on Presley's spring tour were comedian Rex Marlowe, novelty musician Jimmy James, tap dancer Frankie Trent, tenor Frankie Connors, and blues singer June Day. The Jordanaires filled the final slot before intermission.

While anticipation grew in the arena, Elvis was at a press conference, the first of eighteen such meetings that year, with reporters, DJs, photographers, fan club officers, and contest winners. In Chicago, Elvis met the press in the elegant Saddle and Sirloin Club at the Stockyards Inn. Surrounded by portraits of the city's meatpacking industry moguls, the former truck driver surprised the assembled journalists with his soft-spoken demeanor. He was dressed in a two-tone, striped jacket with dark brown slacks and a sport shirt open two buttons from the top. His shoes were gold, a hint of the full suit he would debut on stage that evening. Reporter John Berhl had come down from Toronto to scout Presley before his first Canadian show a few days later. Of Presley's appearance he noted, "His hair is not as long and unruly as it appears in pictures, although he admitted it may be as long as two months since his last haircut ... His dark eyes are soft, but not surrounded by eye shadow, as they sometimes look in photographs."8

The Chicago press conference revealed the pattern and tenor that would mark those held later in seventeen other cities. First the reporters and DJs fired their questions at Elvis. Most of the queries were trivial, revealing that those who asked them didn't realize at the time that they were facing one of the most influential cultural icons of the century. When a tough question did come up, its intent more often seemed nettling than probing. Elvis, refusing to be annoyed, usually answered calmly and courteously, sometimes with a single word, sometimes with a couple of sentences. Occasionally a question piqued his interest and he offered a twenty-or thirty-second response. Most often, though, he was short and considered in his replies. There was noticeably less humor in Presley's 1957 press conferences than there had been in many of his interviews the year before. Although he spoke calmly, he was clearly much more at ease with one-on-one interviews than the press conference format.

In Chicago, reporters seemed interested in the manifestations of the singer's material success. Presley revealed that he had earned a million dollars in the previous year and had already earned another million in the first three months of the current year. In response to another question, he listed the cars he currently owned: four Cadillacs of various colors, a Lincoln Continental, a Thunderbird, a German sports car, and a midget auto racer. "I always said, when I was growing up," Elvis explained, "I was a fiend for cars. I said if I had the money I'd get my fill of them." And they weren't just for looks, he added. "I've had them up over ninety, but you've got to know when to do it. You can't go racing around city streets or crowded highways."

On the criticism of him, Elvis responded thoughtfully, "If you let it get you mad, you'd be mad all the time. It's part of dealing with the public." He had no thought, though, of slipping back into private life where no one would bother him. "If I'd stayed in private life," he explained, "I'd still be broke." He wanted to go to college, but not for the academics. "I wanted to go to play football," he said, "but I'd be foolish to give this up now. I used to play end in high school. I ate and slept football."

Someone asked his thoughts about the teenage Catholic Action Group that objected to his performances. Hesitating, he answered, "I wish they'd come out and see for themselves. You can't judge a tree by its bark. How can they judge without seeing for themselves?" In any event, he had no thought of changing his style. "Rock 'n' roll isn't going out," he said. "It's just leveling off. But it's been around for a long time." Asked whether his own popularity was waning, he responded, "If it is, I haven't noticed it. But if it is, I have no grief. I've done all right. You can't stay on top forever."

Elvis downplayed a recent Memphis street confrontation, in which he had pulled a prop gun on a marine a couple of days earlier. "That pistol thing was just horse-play on my part. The boy thought I was serious," he explained. The incident fueled a rumor that he didn't like servicemen. "I never said that," was his abrupt response.

Presley revealed that his parents were just as amazed as he was by his success. "A couple of days ago they had to have three squad cars directing traffic around my house," he related. "The neighbors told me, 'This was the quietest street in Memphis until you moved in.'"

The questions then shifted to his looks. Of his sideburns, he explained, "I've had them about five years, since I was old enough to grow them. I always wanted sideburns and a moustache. I got the sideburns but I can't seem to grow a mous-tache." Asked about his jewelry, Elvis revealed just a four-leaf clover a fan had sent and a $300 black sapphire ring. "I've lost too much already," he explained. "Five or six watches, quite a few rings—and fingers." He said fans had sent him over 320 St. Christopher medals in the past year.

Elvis gave the reporters some real news when he announced he would be get-ting a crew cut for his next movie, *Jailhouse Rock,* to begin filming soon after his current concert tour ended. As for his favorite actor, Presley named Yul Brynner, who had just won the Oscar as best male actor for *The King and I.* Other ques-tions dealt with his reaction to what was happening around him. Did the scream-ing of his fans bother him? "I love 'em. Without them I'd be lost," he insisted

After the questions ended, it was time for autographs, photos, and kisses for the teenage girls present. Somehow a basset hound named Johnny Walker Sherlock made it into the room and was led up front to pose with Elvis. Arlene Cogan, president of the Chicago Elvis Presley Fan Club, and vice president Barbara Kabakoff got signatures in their autograph books.

Jerilynn Edwards, 14, received a kiss on the cheek for winning the "Why I like Elvis Presley" contest conducted by *Chicago American* movie editor Ann Marsters. After the kiss, Elvis asked Jerilynn, "Am I shaking, or is it you?" Edwards' letter was chosen from the "avalanche" of entries because, according to Marsters, "it seemed to express, in simple, direct prose, just how his young fans feel about Elvis Presley."[9]

> I like Elvis because he is a good and sincere man. He is a wonderful singer and I don't see anything wrong with his actions.
>
> Elvis doesn't smoke or drink which shows that he has a good religious background. My other reasons for liking Elvis are the following:
> E—is for the Enjoyment he gives us.
> L—is for the Love he has for his parents.
> V—is for his Voice that we enjoy.
> I—is for his Ideal example of religious living.
> S—is for the many Songs he sings.
>
> P—is for his wonderful Personality.
> R—is for the Rapidity with which he became famous.
> E—is for his Endurance of the misleading things said about him.
> S—is for his Soul which is good and clean.
> L—is for his Leading position among the top singers.
> E—is for the wonderful Entertainer he is.
> Y—is for the Youth that Elvis represents.

Elvis won over Marsters herself at the press conference. "When you meet him, you have to like him," she admitted. "And you think: 'This is a nice kid.'" A police captain there to guard Presley came away with the same impression. He told Marsters, "That is a sweet boy, a real sweet boy—one of the nicest people I've ever met."

Out in the arena, the Jordanaires closed the show's first part, which Marsters called a "long procession of pathetically inferior acts." After intermission, a disc jockey chosen to introduce Elvis approached the microphone. "I'll tell you something," he teased the crowd. "He's wearing gold shoes." The DJ, who had seen Presley's footwear at the press conference, was unaware that the singer had changed into his complete gold lamé suit. As Elvis carefully walked down a staircase leading to the stage, the Chicago thousands became the first ever to see him wearing in public the glittering outfit that would become legendary among rock regalia. A

Colonel Parker press agent later announced that the jacket and pants, fashioned from unborn calfskin, were completely covered with twenty-four-carat gold cloth.

Mervin Block of the *Chicago American* noted that Elvis seemed somewhat "groggy" when he took the stage shortly after 9:30 PM.[10] The screaming that began as soon as Elvis appeared on the backstage stairs rose to a crescendo as he started his show. "Assuming his provocative stance," reported Block, "he tilted the microphone, embraced it and began rotating his pelvis." When he started to sing, there was a momentary hush allowing the first two words of "Heartbreak Hotel" to be heard, but the remainder of the lyrics were indiscernible above the sudden and continuing roar of the crowd.

In the *Daily News*, Irving Sablosky described the crowd's efforts to get a clear view of Elvis.

> The shrieking crowd swept to its feet, but that wasn't enough.
>
> They stood on chairs and jumped up and down, but that wasn't high enough. One boy hopped up on his buddy's shoulders piggy back style—but that wasn't high enough.
>
> Two boys stood shoulder to shoulder and their girlfriend clambered up to their backs 'til her feet were next to their ears, and there on their shoulders she jumped up and down in screaming ecstasy.[11]

Parker had promised the throng that Elvis would sing fourteen songs, but his boy did even better, gyrating through sixteen numbers during forty-seven minutes on stage. He performed "Rip It Up" and "Paralyzed" from his new album, and his latest single, "All Shook Up." Block observed Presley's bounding across the stage: "His gyrations, which resemble a man trying to ride a bronco into the ground without the bronco, inflamed a frenzied crowd."

The relationship between Presley and his audience seemed downright primitive and base to Louise Hutchinson of the *Daily Tribune*. Calling Elvis "the sideburned Lothario of the rock'n'roll set," she likened his performance to a "tribal rite" in which "Presley was the high chieftain."[12] Indeed, the crowd, mostly young girls, seemed to throw off all self-restraint. According to Block, "Many clutched their temples, tugged at their skirts or bit their nails. Scores fell to their knees howling." Sablosky saw a girl of about four, scared by the noise and commotion, bury her tear-stained face in her father's shoulder.

The aisles between the rows of seats were filled, first by those seeking a better view, and then by girls rushing toward the stage. A three-foot iron railing with angled vertical braces had been erected around the raised stage. After attempts by the mob of girls failed to bring down the railing, dozens of arms and hands reached through the fence openings in an effort to reach Elvis. With tears rolling down her cheeks, a mother sitting in the front row with her three children extended her arm and grazed Presley's clothing with her fingers. The singer stood just out of reach, all the while leaning forward and pointing at those at the front of the stage as though encouraging their efforts.

Finally the police moved in, and it was for possession of the area around the stage railing that the battle was fought. Overwhelmed by the initial, sudden rush to the stage, the officers now tried to get the girls back to their seats. One girl hugged the iron railing with such desperation that it took three policemen to pry her loose. Dozens of others tore at the coats of ushers who were trying to keep them back. One usher was kicked in the stomach. Usher Tony Carvatta, 17, got the worst of it. He went down, stunned, when a girl swung her purse at a police-man, missed, and hit Carvatta on the chin. He was taken to the first-aid station and then to Evangelical Hospital for examination.

"This is the worst crowd," said usher manager Andy Frain Jr. "I've handled the Kentucky Derby, World Series, and All-Star games, but this is impossible. You can't even talk to these people."[13] Frain put much of the blame on Presley for egg-ing on the crowd around the stage. (Elvis himself apparently agreed with Frain's assessment of the audience. During an interview in Vancouver, B.C., five months later, he called the crowd in that Canadian city "the worst audience I ever played to. Only my first time in Chicago would compare with it."[14])

While some officers tried to hold the crowd back, others carried the wounded to the rear. Martha Shafer, a fifteen-year-old sophomore at Leyden Township High School, collapsed after touching part of the platform where Elvis stood. At the first-aid station she stood crying and shaking. In all, thirteen women fainted from the hysteria and tight quarters near the stage. Sometimes it took four officers to hoist a girl's limp body above the heads of the crowd and carry her to the first-aid station. Those who fainted ranged from preteens, like twelve-year-old Mary Morgan, to adults like Louise Polz, 28, who sobbed hysterically while police car-ried her from the amphitheatre. First-aid station attendants reported that some of the girls, once revived, jumped up and ran back into the auditorium. "I drove sev-enty miles to see him and I'm going to get a piece of his clothing before I leave," announced one weeping girl after being revived by firemen.

Finally, after flailing through his closing number, "Hound Dog," Elvis ran up the stairs behind the stage and was gone, fleeing not like a "hound dog but like a jack rabbit," according to the *Tribune's* Hutchinson. An announcer came to the microphone and said, "Thank you—and leave as quietly as possible." Most left then, but hundreds, not believing Elvis had gone, milled around the seating and stage area, despite repeated police pleas for them to leave. A disappointed fifteen-year-old girl in a clinging, low-cut, fur-trimmed outfit bemoaned, "I paid $13 for this dress to wear tonight. I hoped that maybe I could meet him—but I didn't."

It took about forty minutes for the police to herd the last of the frazzled teenagers out of the amphitheatre and into the surrounding streets. Once the job was done, one policeman relaxed and sighed, "Crazy kids. Boyoboy."

The crowd reaction also troubled Ann Marsters. In her *Chicago American* column the next day, she wrote, "The over-all reaction to Elvis was weird and goofy and frightening. The screaming itself was not alarming, if your eardrums could take it. So let them scream and shriek and squeal. But when you see teen-aged girls, who look like boys in their blue jeans and leather jackets going berserk, getting on their knees and sobbing their adoration for a boy in a cloth of gold suit and shoes to match, it makes one wonder, apprehensively, what goes on in their minds." Marsters didn't stay until the end. After two policemen, carrying a young woman in a state of "absolute hysteria," passed in front of her, Marsters felt a little sick and left.

Under the headline "Elvis, Schmelvis," Tony Weitzel of the *Daily News* condemned the show.

> This was a rough week for parents. There was, of course, the howling horror of that Elvis Presley outbreak at the Amphitheatre. Not all of the 12,000 cultural illiterates present (and unaccounted for) went into complete hysterics. But there were enough Screaming Mamies to make you wonder how far the race has progressed, and in what direction.
>
> Scratch the word "progressed." Make it "regressed," in the throes of Thursday's sequined slaverings. Elvis the Pelvis resembled nothing so much as a devil dancer leading some horrid jungle sex ritual.[15]

A week later, Weitzel had what he called a "wastebasket full of reaction" from teenagers. It didn't concern him; the kids would outgrow Presley in six months, he predicted. He was eagerly awaiting the arrival of six girls from southern Illinois, though. "As soon as they save up train fare to Chicago," he wrote, "they're coming up and 'pulverize' me for what I said about Elvis."[16]

Quickly leaving the city, Elvis headed south for his appearance in St. Louis the next night. The fallout in Chicago came as expected. In a sermon three days later on WGN-TV, a minister lamented, "Apparently we needed someone to act out our songs before we would admit that we have been wallowing in a highly suggestive type of music and in some cases downright immoral music for over twenty years."[17] One miffed parent who attended the Presley show told the *Tribune* that he would love to be Elvis' first sergeant for a couple of weeks. (Presley had been classified 1A, but it was unclear when the army would claim him.)

No matter how they judged the experience, over 13,000 in Chicago had witnessed an event they would never forget. One who drew inspiration from the excitement generated that evening was fourteen-year-old Ralph Donner. Like Elvis, Ral Donner had begun singing in church. He formed his first band the year before he saw Presley perform in his hometown of Chicago, and began touring himself the next year at age fifteen. Creating a singing style very similar to Presley's, Donner broke into the U.S. record charts in 1960 with his recording of an Elvis album track, "The Girl of My Best Friend." He went on to place four other records in the American singles charts in the early sixties. Because of his ability to mimic Presley's voice, Donner was chosen in 1981 to narrate the documentary movie *This Is Elvis*. (Like the man who inspired him, Ral Donner died young. He succumbed to lung cancer in 1984 at the age of forty-one.)

Colonel Parker learned in Chicago that just having large numbers of policemen on hand was not enough to insure security and safety when Presley performed on stage. The thirteen girls who fainted in the International Amphitheatre made Parker aware of the potential for serious injury when fans were able to pack together tightly in front of the stage. To prevent it at future shows, he envisioned an open space between the seating area and the stage across which no girl could cross. During the remainder of Presley's 1957 concerts, Parker put his vision of "no woman's land" into practice, with mixed results.

As for Elvis, his Chicago appearance was an affirmation. Irving Sablosky of the *Daily News* gave the following account of Presley's reaction in the amphitheatre after he finished his first song.

> Elvis tried to speak. But one word was enough to set off the screaming.
>
> A girl fainted and was carried out by ushers, borne high over their heads like a sacrifice.
>
> The audience pressed toward the stage.
>
> Elvis' expression changed as he watched and listened to his worshippers.
>
> He seemed for a moment a little scared, a little awed, quite a bit bewildered.
>
> Then he tossed it off with a careless gesture, smiled, enjoyed it, gave an exuberant shiver and a jump—and the screaming doubled itself.[18]

If Elvis believed the Gilbert poll's contention that his popularity was slipping, and if he doubted his ability to still electrify swarms of teenage girls following his four-month absence from the stage, it all must have vanished in the crowd's reaction during that single moment early in his first concert of 1957. From then on through the ensuing twenty-seven concerts that year, there would be no doubt, no bewilderment. As Hugh Jarrett of the Jordanaires observed of Elvis, "In 1957, my goodness, he was as hot as a firecracker."[19]

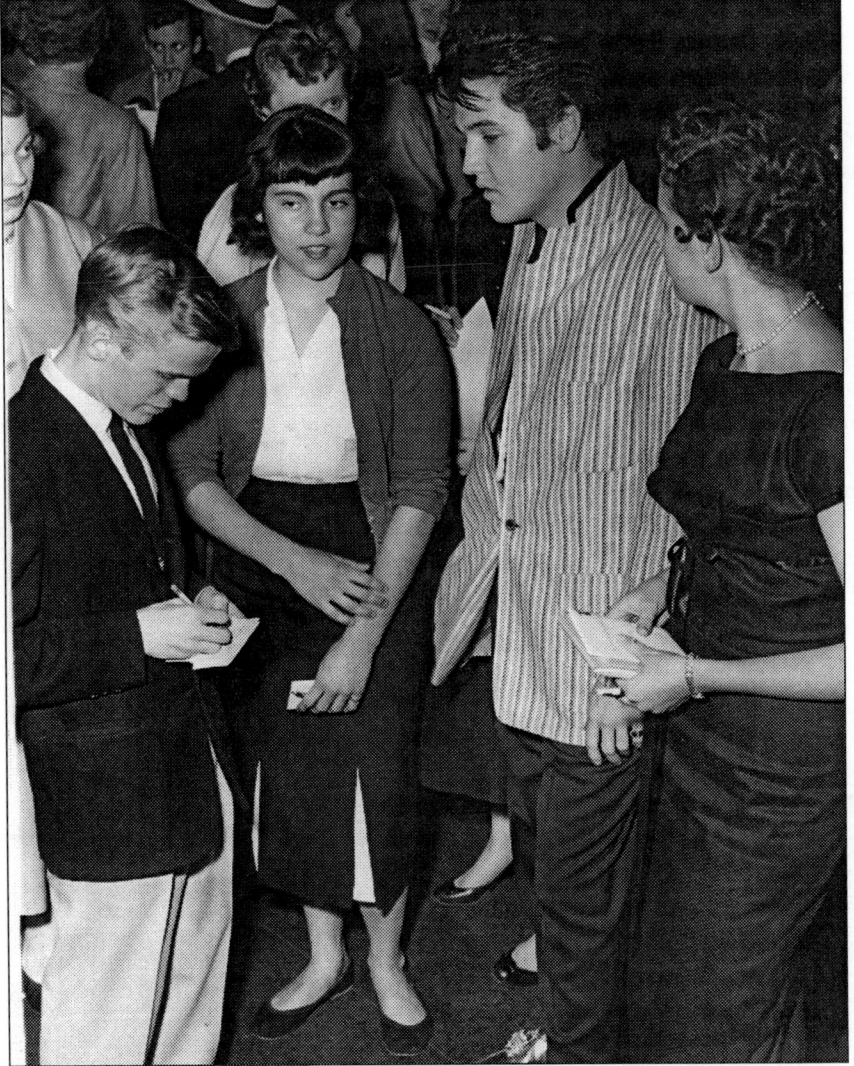

St. Louis press conference, March 29, 1957. (From The St. Louis Globe-Democrat Archives of the St. Louis Mercantile Library at the University of Missouri–St. Louis)

Chapter 3

St. Louis

St. Louis, Missouri
Kiel Auditorium
Friday, March 29, 1957, 8:00 pm

His 1957 show was not the first time Elvis had played St. Louis, but it's likely that most of the teenagers lined up to enter Kiel Auditorium that night were about to see him live for the first time. As an "extra added attraction," Presley got fourth billing in Roy Acuff's *Grand Ole Opry Stars* stage show for its three-day run at the Missouri Theater on October 21, 1955. (Just the day before, Elvis had worked with Pat Boone at a show in a Cleveland suburb. It was the only time the two had met prior to the press-generated rivalry between them in 1957.) The *St. Louis Post-Dispatch*, however, recalled Presley's earlier visit to town and still referred to him as a "singer of hillbilly songs" when it announced his return to the city in its March 17, 1957, edition.[1]

Several days before Elvis arrived in St. Louis and checked into the Hotel Chase on the morning of his March 29 performance, Colonel Parker's people were on the scene countering press reports that the singer's popularity was slipping. Kiel Auditorium's publicity representative, Virginia Davis, downplayed the notion and predicted Presley's show would be sold out by showtime. The Colonel's publicity department pointed out that Elvis had sold thirteen million records in 1956 and his new album had already passed the one million sales mark. They urged city newspapers to remind readers that Elvis had been paid $50,000 for three performances on *The Ed Sullivan Show* and that *Love Me Tender* had done well when it opened at St. Louis' Fox Theater the previous November.

Other news reports at the time seemed to indicate that Presley's influence was still being felt in areas beyond concerts and movies. The same week that Elvis started his spring tour, inventor Jacob Cohen of Chicago patented a sideburn gauge, aimed at young men who wanted to replicate Presley's famous sideburns. Fitting over the top of the head like a telephone headset, the gadget had two matching guides that slid down over graduated rulers on each side of the head.

25

The device even had a bubble in a glass tube so that the wearer could make sure it was sitting level on top of the head.

Another March news story indicated Presley's musical style had settled in with aspiring preteen singers. In his travels across the country seeking talent for Walt Disney's *The Mickey Mouse Club* TV show, mouseketeer talent scout Sid Miller reported that the country was in danger of being overrun by hordes of mini-Elvises. It disturbed Miller to find so many youngsters using songs in their auditions that weren't appropriate for their age group. "It's slightly ludicrous to see a ten-year-old with painted sideburns swinging his hips and singing about 'my kind of love,'" Miller explained.[2] From the two hundred boys who auditioned for Miller in San Francisco, he chose just two for a second look. Neither had done a Presley number in his audition.

Meanwhile, Elvis himself was in the news for the pistol incident. In Memphis on the evening of March 22, exactly a week before his appearance in St. Louis, Presley pulled a gun on Hershel Nixon, an eighteen-year-old marine from St. Louis. Elvis later said he brandished the weapon, which turned out to be a harmless Hollywood prop pistol, after Nixon tried to start a fight because Elvis had allegedly bumped into Nixon's wife two months before. The next day, the marine, who claimed he was only trying to strike up a conversation with the singer, said he thought Elvis owed him an apology. He received his apology in a long, rambling telegram from Presley, but Elvis seemed far from contrite in a *Post-Dispatch* photo showing him smiling while holding the toy pistol. It was the kind of press that rankled Presley's critics while further endearing him to his loyal base of teenage girls.

The teenage girls of Notre Dame High School, at 320 East Ripa in St. Louis, revealed that not everyone in their age group was loyal to Elvis. On the morning of his St. Louis show, the Notre Dame girls held an anti-Elvis demonstration. Reciting prayers "as public reparation for excesses committed by teen-agers," they marched toward the school incinerator to burn Presley items, including a life-sized picture of the rock 'n' roller.[3] "It was not the sort of warm welcome Presley had anticipated," concluded the *Globe-Democrat* mistakenly, for by then Elvis was quite used to such protests wherever he went.

Elvis was booked for one evening performance in the Henry W. Kiel Auditorium at the intersection of Fifteenth and Market Streets. A mayoral proclamation issued when the structure opened in 1934 could hardly have been referring to the likes of Elvis when it declared the new auditorium was "designed to enrich the peoples' lives" and would attract "cultural activities" to the city. Prior to Presley's coming, Kiel Auditorium had hosted such entertainment luminaries as Jack Benny, Duke Ellington, Judy Garland, Bob Hope, and Glenn Miller and his orchestra.

The *Globe-Democrat* and the *Post-Dispatch* broke the news of Presley's forthcoming concert in their March 17 editions. Mail-order forms appeared in both newspapers, with balcony seats priced at $2.00, $2.50, and $3.00, and lower-floor seats going for $2.50, $3.00, and $3.50. Three days later, tickets went on sale at Goldie's Ticket Agency in the Arcade Building and at the Kiel Auditorium box office.

As in Chicago, advance ticket sales in St. Louis were brisk. By March 28, the day before the concert, only tickets at the back of the auditorium were still available. By Friday's showtime, tickets for all of Kiel's 10,819 seats, even the135 marked "obstructed view," had been sold. The only previous entertainer who had been able to sell out the auditorium was Liberace.

Since Kiel was an auditorium with permanent seating, crowd management there was simpler than in Chicago's wide-open International Amphitheatre. In addition to Kiel's regular security and usher force, twenty regular city policemen and fifty auxiliary officers were on hand in the auditorium for Presley's performance. The twenty regulars were also charged with protecting the singer throughout his stay in St. Louis.

Promptly at 8:00 PM, The Elvis Presley Show got underway with Colonel Parker's six opening acts. Local maestro Benny Rader and his band provided the music. Elvis arrived at the auditorium a little before curtain time, just ahead of the Market Street traffic jam caused by his scheduled appearance. While a crowd awaited Presley's arrival at the stage door on Fifteenth Street, his police escort delivered him to an unnoticed alley entrance.

Elvis went straight to Assembly Hall 2 for his press conference. Reporters asked some questions, but the meeting was dominated by the teenage girls who had been allowed in the room due to their connections with Presley fan clubs and contests. When the girls closed in for autographs and kisses, photographers began setting up shots. On request, Elvis wrapped his arms around a pack of four girls and began kissing them for the camera. According to a *Post-Dispatch* reporter, Elvis was simply doing his duty. "He quickly disengaged himself, not with impolite haste, after each photograph," the reporter observed. "He looked like a young man being dutifully attentive to his fans, who are providing him with a life as golden as his suit."[4]

Joyce Gentry, president of the Elvis Presley Fan Club of O'Fallon, Missouri, was there and told reporters of her club's unusual symbol. "We have a rock'n'roll parakeet in our fan club as mascot," she explained. "We've taught him to roll his head and stomp his left foot and sidestep on the stick. Of course, we've named him Elvis, as he shakes his left leg like Elvis and wears a fan club button on his cage."[5]

After intermission Presley took the stage, again wearing his full, loose-fitting gold suit with a silver shirt that "shimmered when he shook and vice versa," according to *Globe-Democrat* writer Ken Beaver.[6] One jazz musician snuck in from the auditorium's adjacent opera house to watch Presley's entrance. "Man, how much do you suppose those yard goods cost him?" he asked. Tour promoter Lee Gordon said the gold suit had cost $2,500. "It's real gold, with impregnated unborn calf skin, or something of the sort," Gordon added.[7]

In his article the next morning, Beaver wrote, "The first quiver brought a two-minute flood of shrieks before you—or Elvis—could say, 'Luh-uhv Me Ten-duh.' Elvis let the crowd's screaming settle down to a roar only slightly louder than that of Niagara Falls. Then he clutched the microphone in a tender embrace, made a token slap at his guitar and sang." The Chicago audience the night before had surprised Elvis, but now he knew what to expect. "When he mouthed the opening words of his first song," according to the *Post-Dispatch*, "the uproar began again. Girls shrieked. Elvis shrieked, but he was outnumbered. His contortions were ecstatically received. His most appreciated medium of expression seemed to be burlesque's traditional hip movements."[8]

Presley went through the same sixteen-song repertoire as he had the night before. The beginning of each number was greeted with a squall of noise cascading from the back of the balcony down onto the auditorium floor. The excitement drove some girls down to the floor, while others tried to wander the auditorium aisles. The congestion in the arena, however, hindered any concerted assault upon the stage, and with the police able to mass themselves in the relatively small area where the aisles converged near the stage, a repetition of bodies crushing against the platform, which had caused so many to faint the night before in Chicago, was prevented. Although conditions worked against them, the aspirations of the girls in St. Louis were no different from those of their sisters to the north. "If I could just touch him," one girl was heard to say. "Just touch him with my finger."[9]

In keeping with the efforts of reporters everywhere who searched for some figurative language to describe the interaction between Presley and his audience, Ken Beaver of the *Globe-Democrat* came up with a unique analogy—a medical disorder.

> A sideburned virus hit 10,000 teen-agers here yesterday.
> The symptoms were alternate fever and chills, popping eyes, sore throats and uncontrollable screaming.
> The best medical opinion was that all 10,000 would survive the night but they are expected to remain in weakened condition for several days.

The virus struck with lightning speed and disappeared before scientists could isolate it.

But it was reliably identified as Hounddogus Americanus, sometimes known as Elvis Presley.[10]

As had become his practice, after Elvis finished his final number, he rushed out of the auditorium, avoiding a mass of fans who stood outside the stage door chanting, "We want Elvis." Inside, hundreds of other girls, hesitant to believe their idol had really left the building, wandered the auditorium's concourse.

One sixty-four-year-old woman standing on the fringe of the stage door crowd was doubly disappointed. She didn't get to see Elvis and her wallet was stolen. Myrtle Yoakley told police she was waiting with her daughter-in-law, Geraldine Pearson, when a young man of about twenty began talking with her about Presley. Looking down, she noticed that her billfold, containing $3.50, was missing from her open purse. The man ran away, but was later nabbed by police near the corner of Twelfth Street and Clark Avenue. The wallet, found on the sidewalk, was returned to Mrs. Yoakley.

To Colonel Parker's relief, there were no reported incidents inside Kiel Auditorium. While the setup of the arena and the distribution of security forces had much to do with keeping the crowd under control, eighteen-year-old Phyllis Van Damme thought the civility of St. Louis' young people should be recognized. She wrote a letter that was printed in the *Post-Dispatch* several days after Presley's show.

> I would like to thank the people of St. Louis for making possible the recent Elvis Presley appearance. His performance was thoroughly enjoyable, and I know that I was among those who screamed the loudest and clapped the longest …
>
> The audience should be commended on its behavior. We all participated in the hand-clapping, but there were no casualties and St. Louis can be very proud of its teenage population.[11]

Of course, not all St. Louis citizens felt such gratification after Presley's show. In another letter to the *Post-Dispatch*, a "Disgusted Musician" claimed that letting Elvis Presley perform in St. Louis should not be cause for civic pride.

> The City of St. Louis dedicated a new "mental asylum" at Kiel Auditorium where 11,000 young people gathered to witness what was classed as "entertainment" in the form of an anatomy-wiggling character known as the "King of Rock and Roll," a new low form of music.

I am thankful that I am not a parent of any writhing, wriggling, tumbling addict, such as was pictured in the *Post-Dispatch* Saturday. Screams and yells, according to what I've read, are found only in the aboriginal age. And it certainly looks like we are heading back to that state, but fast.

The sell-out house for such low-class entertainment shows where real music appreciation is today. Had any worthwhile orchestra, soloist, or production made its appearance I know very well that seat sales would have gone begging.[12]

Elvis left St. Louis to sort out the consequences of his appearance there. By the time the Saturday morning editions of the city's newspapers hit the street, Presley had already made the overnight trip to Fort Wayne, Indiana, where he was scheduled for another show that night.

Chapter 4

Fort Wayne

Prelude

Through most of the 1950s, George E. Sokolsky was an ultra-conservative syndicated newspaper columnist. In the early part of the decade, he aligned himself closely with Senator Joseph McCarthy's anti-communism campaign, and Sokolsky's articles were instrumental in the blackballing of certain actors and writers. After McCarthy's fall from grace, Sokolsky continued to fervently support traditional American values through his editorial feature in newspapers across the country. In March 1957, just as Elvis Presley hit the road on his first stage tour of the year, Sokolsky devoted two of his weekly columns to the moral implications of rock 'n' roll music and its most famous exponent.

In his March 14 article, Sokolsky responded to a letter from Charlotte Jones of Dallas, Texas. He wondered if Miss Jones would be such an Elvis worshipper if she were exposed to the music of Bach, Mozart, Beethoven, Brahms, and Tchaikovsky. "The real point of this letter is that it displays no cultural background," he continued. "The fault undoubtedly is in a school system that gives the child so little cultural background, so little basis for taste and so little understanding of beauty. Rock-N-roll, which is a musical reversion to the tom-tom of the jungle, can stir so many of our young to ecstasy only because they know no better. It is curious that in a Western country that a child could write, 'the greatest thing the world has ever known: Elvis Presley.' I used to hear them say that that title went to Jesus. How times do change!"[1]

On March 28, the same day Elvis opened his tour in Chicago, Sokolsky returned to the Presley topic after receiving several letters noting his "ignorance of things important and how a square cannot be expected to understand anything." One letter asserted that Presley was an "inspiration" because he had risen so quickly from humble beginnings to achieve such great wealth. Sokolsky responded, "It is something new in the story of man's progress that a yodler becomes an inspiration because he having been a truck driver, became a millionaire in one year. I believe that even Al Capone did not do it so quickly."

Another letter chided the columnist for not understanding that "teen-agers conform not to their parents' morals, but to the morals of their own generation." Sokolsky countered with a moral indictment against the changing values of the nation's youth.

> This is something that needs to be learned by the elders who do not understand why the world seems to be going backwards. For if civilization has any meaning at all, it must be morality—the revealed law of God to man—is eternal, universal and changeless. I do not know the age of this writer from Oradell, New Jersey, but I wonder if it ever occurred to her that such a codification of morality as the "Ten Commandments," is the symbol of man's progress up-ward from the tom-tom.[2]

In referring to his earlier characterization of rock 'n' roll as a "musical reversion to the tom-tom of the jungle," Sokolsky clearly was portraying the new music trend as a threat to long-established Christian values in America. It was on such religious grounds that Elvis Presley's stage show was condemned during his 1957 tours. As Presley came north from St. Louis to continue his tour with shows on the last two days of March, the *News-Sentinel* in Fort Wayne printed other articles that denounced his brand of rock 'n' roll music. First, the Roman Catholic archbishop of Chicago, Samuel Cardinal Stritch, issued a Lenten pastoral letter elucidating the following concerns.

> Some new manners of dancing and a throwback to tribalism in recreation cannot be tolerated for Catholic youths.
> And now I come to a matter, the very mention of which pains me. It has come to my attention that in some of our high schools and recreation centers, dancing and music are permitted which should bring the blush of shame to Catholic educators.
> When our schools and centers stoop to such things as rock'n'roll tribal rhythms, they are failing seriously in their duty. God grant that this word will have the effect of banning such things in Catholic recreation.[3]

A month later, Rhode Island Catholic Bishop Russell McVinney aimed similar criticism directly at Elvis Presley. He censured rock 'n' roll music as a fad that was leading its teenage followers "back to the jungle and animalism." Referring to Presley as the "pelvic contortionist," the bishop declared, "His stage antics are intended to arouse the lower instincts."[4]

In specifically condemning Elvis' "stage antics," Bishop McVinney focused on the thing that Presley's critics found most offensive about him. It wasn't his singing, his acting, or his lifestyle that was viewed as dangerous in the Christian community. It was his movement on stage, particularly of the pelvic area, that they feared would stimulate primitive emotions and urges in adolescent girls.

By early 1957 most newspaper reporters were referring to Presley's various stage antics under the umbrella term "gyrations," although the word's dictionary meaning of moving in a circle around a fixed point hardly summarized what the singer did on stage. When Elvis appeared in their community, the reporters of Fort Wayne seemed particularly interested in his "gyrations," including their nature, source, intent, and effect on those who watched them.

Fort Wayne, Indiana
Memorial Coliseum
Saturday, March 30, 1957, 8:30 pm

Although she was obviously not an Elvis Presley fan, Marjorie Barnhart got the assignment to cover the singer's appearance in Fort Wayne for the *News-Sentinel.* Whether she volunteered out of curiosity or had the duty dropped in her lap, she was clearly annoyed by the task, something evident in her pre-show article in the paper's March 30 edition. She couldn't resist including some sarcasm in what was otherwise a straight news article. Even though she was one of the "favored few" who would be admitted to Presley's news conference, Marjorie figuratively rolled her eyes when promoter Ernie Berg announced the ritual conditions required for admission to the interview room. "He didn't say whether we women reporters will have to wear long gloves and three feathers in our hair as for presentation to Queen Elizabeth," she grumbled.[5] In print she quoted Berg's explanation that security had to be tight because "Presley takes a terrible beating" from his fans, and then added her own observation that "the ex-truck driver ... also takes a terrible ten thousand or so for singing several songs a night."

Although her press credential earned her a front row seat at Presley's show that night, she was disappointed from the beginning. "I couldn't hear a thing," she reported the next day. "The girls never stopped screaming. I would have liked to have heard at least a snatch of something."[6] (Sixteen-year-old Kathy Bohnke tried to clarify the source of the yelling in a later letter addressed to Marjorie. "Screaming somehow fits Elvis better than mere clapping," Kathy explained.[7])

For many there, it was enough just to stare at Elvis in his "gold coat with its rhinestone lapels and rows of rhinestones down the center seam in the back," but not for Marjorie. "The sight of him brings me no special joy," she noted. "So that left his controversial gyrations," she finally concluded, "as the only reason for sitting there in the midst of all that screaming." What she saw in that area during the next forty minutes became the focal point of her *News-Sentinel* article the next day. It was the culmination of thirty days of anticipation for Marjorie and her fellow citizens after they first learned Elvis Presley was coming to their community.

Of the eight stops on Elvis' spring tour, Fort Wayne seemed the strangest choice. With a little over 150,000 inhabitants, it was by far the smallest city Presley played during his ten-day swing through the Midwest and Canada. The Indiana city may have been a last-minute addition, intended to fill an open day on the tour and chosen for its proximity to Detroit. Ernie Berg, general manager of Fort Wayne Enterprises, told the *News-Sentinel* that arrangements for Presley to appear in Fort Wayne were finalized during a phone call with Colonel Parker on the evening of March 1. Presley would come to Fort Wayne between a Friday night date in St. Louis and a Sunday date in Detroit. Parker may have hoped that a concert there would draw from the much larger cities of Indianapolis, Cleveland, and Cincinnati, all within driving distance in various directions from Fort Wayne.

Berg arranged with Parker to have Elvis do an evening performance in the five-year-old Allen County War Memorial Coliseum in Fort Wayne. The exact show time was undecided initially, another indication that the stop in Fort Wayne was an afterthought in the tour schedule. Ads for mail-order tickets began appearing in the *News-Sentinel* on March 6, with over-the-counter sales scheduled to begin March 11. The only outlet for tickets, either through the mail or in person, was the Fort Wayne Enterprises box office at 618 E. State Street. Prices were $3.50 for seats in the lower arena and $2.50 in the upper arena. The day before in-person sales began, Berg announced that mail orders had been "tremendous."[8]

Berg pitched Presley's appearance to the press as part of the singer's "farewell tour" before entering the army. From the beginning Berg predicted a full house, and he got it when the last seats sold on March 18, nearly two weeks before the concert. He hoped Elvis would break Bob Hope's Memorial Coliseum single-performance ticket sales record of 11,123, but when city officials held a meeting to formulate a plan to prevent violence at the show, they decided that no "standing room only" tickets would be sold. So Elvis had to settle for a sellout of 10,003, the exact number of seats that could be jammed into the arena. It was enough, however, to make use of the existing stage and curtain impossible. Fitting everyone into the coliseum required seating people on all sides of a temporary stage.

With Elvis completely surrounded by his audience, and mindful of the chaos in Chicago two days before, Fort Wayne officials had a tight security plan in place. Police Chief Mitchell Cleveland announced that he, along with Police Inspector

Joseph Heidenreich, Deputy Commander John Carpino, and several other officers, would be on duty in Memorial Coliseum. A force of twenty-five off-duty policemen would be called in for crowd control. "Everybody is going to stay in their seat tonight," Ernie Berg announced in a final press briefing the morning of the concert. "The only people who will be allowed to move around the floor will be six authorized photographers. Other photographers will have to take their pictures from their seats. If anyone gets out of his seat, the police and the ushers will stop him."[9] A Red Cross emergency unit with a nurse on duty would also be available.

The day before the show, Chief Cleveland revealed that he had received several letters complaining about the use of city police officers at taxpayer expense for Presley's show. The chief explained that Fort Wayne Enterprises was paying for the time of the twenty-five off-duty officers. "The 'other officers' on duty would be no more than the city offers any other celebrity or noted person as its moral obligation to the person and the citizens of Fort Wayne," the chief stated.[10] Policewomen were assigned to supervise the large number of teenage girls expected at the show.

That morning Berg was ready for Colonel Parker's arrival. "We have a certified check for $22,000, which will be the share which the show will take," he told the press. "I don't know how much Mr. Presley will get. I do know that this is one of seven dates for which he will get $75,000."[11] Despite the big payout to Elvis, the sellout left Berg's company a few thousand dollars of profit after paying the arena rental fee, security costs, and other expenses. It hardly seemed worth it to the weary Berg after a month filled with aggravating details. "I'll be glad when this is over," he said. "You'd be surprised how many headaches there are in bringing something like this to Fort Wayne."

A few days before his arrival, Elvis had been vilified at a Tuesday night meeting of the Fort Wayne City Council. Without mentioning Presley's name, Councilman John H. Robinson referred to a "certain entertainer whose exhibition is of the social quality I seriously doubt that the children of Fort Wayne ought to see." Robinson said that the city should insist that Presley "put on a decent show," adding, "When that certain character starts exhibiting himself as a 'one-man burlesque show' I think the police ought to step in and stop it."[12] None of the other council members commented on the subject during the meeting, but afterwards several of them noted that Robinson's remarks carried little weight, since the Coliseum already was sold out.

While many of his fellow councilmen chose not to comment on Robinson's tirade, several Fort Wayne citizens offered their opinions in the letters columns of local newspapers. One woman wrote to the *Journal-Gazette* in support of Robinson. "I agree Fort Wayne is a good place to stop it," she explained. "I'm a mother of a twelve-year-old daughter, a nine-year-old son, the wife of a teacher and I'm a college student. I'm a modern, but not in 'his' (Presley's) sense."13 On the other side, a letter in the *News-Sentinel* from the mother of a teenager dripped with sarcasm. "It's a fine thing to know that we have such a thoughtful man as Councilman Robinson to watch out for people to such an extent that he wants to clean up the Presley show … As to his movements while he sings, I don't know whether it's like a burlesque show or not. I never saw a burlesque show, but Councilman Robinson says so, and he should know."14

As usual, before his show Elvis held a press conference in his coliseum dressing room. "Only a well-screened group will be admitted for the interviews," Ernie Berg told reporters that morning, adding, "and no one who has been drinking will be allowed in."15

The press assembled at the 8:00 PM show time, but it wasn't until thirty minutes later that Elvis entered. Smiling, chewing gum, and wearing a two-tone brown striped coat, black trousers, tan socks, and the gold shoes from his famous suit, he jumped up on a table, and the questioning began. Someone wanted to know what kind of gum he was chewing. "Spearmint," he said. Another asked how he developed his "romantic leer," the lowering of his eyelids while raising the corner of his mouth. Pushing his cheek up with a finger, Elvis explained, "I always have smiled that way." Asked about his staying power, he responded, "I'm enjoying it while it lasts. If the people lose interest in me, I'll understand. I won't go to pieces." Of his wealth, he said, "The government gets most of it."

More significant than the actual answers he gave was the impression Presley left with his questioners. After the forty-minute press conference, William Disbsro of the *Journal-Gazette* came away describing Elvis simply as a "nice guy with a likable personality, who murders even Americanized English, but who has a money-making gimmick and is riding it for all it's worth."16 Marjorie Barnhart, unenthusiastic at best about Elvis going in, saw more depth in the man than she had imagined. "On stage Presley was what I had expected," she wrote the next day. "Elvis Presley at the press interview was a surprise. He did not have the bleary eyes, the slack mouth, or the loose-jointed, drunken demeanor of his stage appearance … Although he finds himself suddenly powerfully rich and popular, Presley does not seem at all impressed by himself. He tried very hard to answer the questions fully and honestly. With dignity he fended off some personal probes and exhibited more intelligence than I had anticipated."17 A trio of Elvis fans thought it was a sure sign of respect that everyone there addressed their idol as "Mr. Presley." They noted that Elvis obviously "wanted everyone to know that he had no prejudices. He answered all questions with great sincerity and humility, but with a touch of humor, too. It's a great pity that all of those who dislike him cannot see him as his true self."18

Soon after the press conference broke up, a different Elvis bounded onto the stage, where he was unable to say or sing a word for three minutes due to the sustained roar from the crowd all around him. He wore his gold tuxedo coat and shoes, but the accompanying gold pants seen in Chicago and St. Louis were missing, replaced by the plain black slacks he had worn at the press conference.

In these opening moments, during which Elvis could only giggle intermittently, the *Journal-Gazette's* William Disbro noticed the reaction of one girl nearby. "One distaff worshiper of the gold idol followed the entry of the pelvis with egg-shaped eyes—so wild, so hopeful, so hungry. It was the look of an Arabian washer-woman asking King Saud for a palace position." Finally, the noise subsided enough for Elvis to say, "Ladies and gentlemen …," which only caused the din to increase again. After several failed attempts to announce his first number, Presley fought his way through "Heartbreak Hotel."

The content of the concert followed the pattern of those in Chicago and St. Louis. Jerry Kelly of the *Journal-Gazette* reported that Elvis sang fourteen songs, although he wasn't sure of the exact number since the screaming made it hard for him to determine when one song ended and another began. Included were "I Was the One," "Don't Be Cruel," "All Shook Up," "I Got a Woman," "When My Blue Moon Turns to Gold Again," "One Night," and the finale, "Hound Dog." Musicians Scotty Moore, Bill Black, and D.J. Fontana did not impress Kelly. "The members of the small band playing in back of Presley," he wrote, "made noises similar to those of a raided Chinese crap game."[19]

For Kelly, the highlight of the show, and what he called "the Coliseum's finest moment in history," came when Elvis moved to the rear of the stage during a number and tenderly kissed the outstretched fingers of several adoring fans. After the show ended, one of the girls still sat in her seat, crying frantically, clasping her hand and sobbing, "He kissed it, he kissed it."

And Marjorie Barnhart? At first she marveled at the primitive scene around her. "We couldn't help but think that uneducated savages without knowledge of flashbulbs or teenage behavior in civilized countries, would have seen in this the materialization of a pagan god!" she observed. "There was the scary feeling of the supernatural about it." Then she sat back to watch the "gyrations" for which Presley was infamous. By the end of it she had come to some conclusions concerning the origin, purpose, and effect of his stage movements. She recorded her thoughts in her *News-Sentinel* article the next day.

> I can believe that, at first, the boy used his hip-swinging movements unconsciously to sell his songs. But this was not the case Saturday night where his songs could not be heard. Presley used the motions deliberately to tease the girls and to lure them into demonstrations. His con-

trol over the girls amused him, and he and the Jordanaires, his vocal quartet, exchanged many a laughing glance over the crowd reactions.

It was as if the crowd were something he could touch. Although they stretched out to the distant back wall of the Coliseum, the eagle-eyed girls seemed able to see his slightest movement. They screamed when he moved a finger. They screamed when he lifted a shoulder. And the din was deafening when he bent a knee or wiggled with vigor.

I don't know enough to trace the origins of his movements, whether from burlesque as some claim or from the native Negro snake-hips as others contend. Once I saw a tassel-twirler at the Allen County Fair do the same all-over shake he exhibited.

But I've seen sexier dances on Broadway, in the movies or even on the stage here. As a shimmy dancer, he's no great shakes. His choreography is put together as he goes along, without form or pattern. I didn't see anything specific to rise up in indignation, but the mass hysteria and sex-conscious build-up probably deserves a second look.[20]

While Barnhart saw nothing overly sexy in Presley's "gyrations" but retained a concern about its effects, another woman in the crowd that night did see a sexual element in Elvis' movements. However, she judged it as acceptable by society's standards. In a letter printed in the *News-Sentinel* a week after the Presley show, Helen Maxim of New Haven first declared herself "neutral" on the controversy surrounding Elvis. "I am not condoning the gyrations that Presley goes through," she continued. "However, why permit someone else to do nearly the same thing—and on network television—and get away with it to the applause of the critics!" She was referring to Abbe Lane, then a singer and dancer on Xavier Cugat's TV show. Maxim explained that Lane "sings a little, and then goes into some hip-swinging, wiggling contortions that are bound to stir the emotions of any 'normal red-blooded American boy' and the TV camera seems to cover all phases of the object in motion. Why on earth should this female version of 'The Pelvis' be allowed to exhibit herself and not attract the ire of the morally pure viewer when all kinds of mudslinging attacks are directed to the male version?" She answered her own question with the maxim, "What's good for the goose is good for the gander."[21]

As for Elvis, at his press conference he addressed Councilman Robinson's characterization of his performance as a "one-man burlesque" show. The singer responded, "I don't intend it to be like burlesque. It's the way I express a song. You have to give the people a show or they'll go to sleep." On the origin of his wiggling, Presley basically repeated the often-told story. He had been making his first public appearance over two years ago at a barn dance in Memphis when he first started using his unique style of "dancing." "They were screaming and liked it," Elvis recalled. "So I kept it up." He explained that he made up his own "arrangements," as well as his ad-libs.

According to Tommy Sands, a nineteen-year-old, up-and-coming teenage sensation in 1957, those "arrangements" seemed to work only for Elvis. "I wish I could do them," Sands said in a March interview. "But they've got to be natural, as they are with Elvis, for them to come off well."[22]

Elvis agreed that the gyrations that accompanied his singing came naturally, and thus could not be vulgar. "If I thought I was contributing to juvenile delinquency or causing anybody to go astray, I'd go back to driving a truck," he vowed. "When I start to sing, I'm carried away. I spread my feet apart, pick the guitar, and the rhythm carries me from there. I can't help movin' around. It's the way I sing … Just because I thrash around, just because those girls in the audience start shriekin' when I do, what's wrong with that? … Those folks who accuse me of being vulgar, they just don't understand. I'd sooner cut my throat than be vulgar. "[23]

One defense of Presley's gyrations came from an unlikely source: Rev. James H. Elder of the Mullins Methodist church in the singer's hometown of Memphis. He saw criticism of Elvis' stage antics as nothing more than harmless angst common to all generations.

> Some of the mossbacks of our city, who have apparently forgotten their own adolescence, are moaning about rock and roll music and Elvis Presley. These diehards, who haven't had a youthful thought since the Civil war, say that rock and roll music is the theme song of juvenile delinquency and that Elvis Presley is making "dead end kids" out of the whole generation. Nothing could be more idiotic.
>
> It is supposed to be perfectly all right for every bald-headed man in American to drool as Marilyn Monroe goes slithering across the pages of our time on the arm of husband number three. But the very moment that youths dance and Elvis shakes his left leg a bit, it's supposed to be juvenile delinquency of the worst sort.
>
> In the next generation some new dance will come along and the present rock and roll crowd will be mamas and papas. They will pull their hair and say, "What on earth is happening to our youth? Why can't they stick to something nice and dignified like rock and roll?"[24]

There were other reasons Elvis' appearance in Fort Wayne proved unforgettable to those who saw it. In the end the spectacle impressed Marjorie Barnhart more than the performance. She closed her April 1 *News-Sentinel* article with the prediction, "His show will long be remembered not as entertainment, but as an experience in mass reaction." For Jerry Kelly it was Presley's energy that had a lasting effect. "Elvis ... gave a wild performance that will long be remembered," he wrote. "If not for the quality of the performance than for the sheer dynamics it demonstrated."

One Fort Wayne resident had reason to remember Elvis every time her telephone rang. Figuring his fans were just having some fun at her expense, Alma Presley didn't mind so much putting up with prank calls in the days leading up to Elvis' show. "I think he's all right in his place," she noted, "but I don't care for that type of music. I like good music." So she did get a little annoyed whenever the teenager on the other end of the line asked, "Can you sing 'Hound Dog'?" Once Elvis had left town, she thought the calls would stop, but they didn't. "I wish they'd stop calling me all hours of the day and night," she said. "We just dread it when the phone rings." So Alma Presley's memories of Elvis and his fans remained unpleasant. "It isn't particularly humorous to be called by the younger element in the community who have given themselves wholeheartedly to the undulations of a truck driver," she concluded.[25]

In his room at Detroit's Sheraton-Cadillac Hotel, March 31, 1957. (Tony Spina Collection, Walter P. Reuther Library at Wayne State University)

Chapter 5

Detroit

Detroit, Michigan
Olympia Stadium
Sunday, March 31, 1957, 2:00 pm and 6:00 pm

Elvis Presley's whereabouts were unknown that Sunday morning in Detroit. By 9:00 AM teenagers had begun converging on Olympia Stadium for the afternoon show. Better known simply as the "Olympia" or by its nickname, the "Old Red Barn," Olympia Stadium had stood since 1927 at 5920 Grand River Avenue, about three miles from Detroit's central business district. It was the home of the Detroit Red Wings hockey team and was a prime boxing venue. (Sugar Ray Robinson and Jake LaMotta twice fought there in 1943.) Musical performers who appeared at the Olympia included Frank Sinatra, who preceded Elvis there, and The Beatles and The Rolling Stones, who followed him in the 1960s.

Some Detroit fans couldn't wait until 2:00 PM to see Elvis. Teenagers prowled the city's high-class hotels looking for him. The object of their search was there, at the Sheraton-Cadillac Hotel, located on the western edge of the city's downtown area at the intersection of Washington Boulevard and Michigan Avenue. After his evening show in Fort Wayne, Elvis and his entourage climbed into his pink Cadillac and made the 170-mile night drive to Detroit. Arriving around four o'clock in the morning, Elvis was able to slip into his hotel unseen.

Presley was booked at the Olympia for Sunday shows at 2:00 PM and 6:00 PM. Seats were priced at $2.50, $3.50, and $5.00, the latter being the highest price charged for seats in any of the eighteen cities Elvis played in 1957. About 85 percent of the 28,000 available tickets sold for the two shows.

One person who was relieved when March 31 finally arrived was Jean Shute, an Olympia switchboard operator who fielded what she called "impauseable" calls during the two weeks leading up to Presley's appearances. She handled calls not only from Detroit, but also from surrounding communities, including Milford, Ypsilanti, Ann Arbor, and Toledo. In a *Detroit News* article two days before Elvis' concerts, Shute shared some of her conversations with eager Elvis fans.[1]

"Uh. Mm. Uh. Well," one youngster hesitantly began. "Are there many tickets left for the Elvis Presley show? Um. Mm. Um. Well. Can you send me some?" No telephone orders, Shute told her. She'd have to come down to the Olympia box office to get them.

Next it's a boy with a high-pitched voice. "Uh. Well. What arethecheapestseats you've got for the Elvis Presley show?"

"I want some information about refunds," demanded an irate mother. "I've just discovered my daughter has bought eight seats to that Sunday show." Shute heard sobs in the background.

Then it was a giggling girl. "Um. Mm. Well, what have you got in the front row for Elvis Presley—I mean for me?" Another boy called. "How much are the box seats for Elvis Presley? Well, how much are the balcony seats?"

Some people wanted information Jean couldn't provide. "Is he going to cut that beautiful hair?" asked one. "Will he really have to go in the army?"

Despite a two-week media blitz, some seemed to have just heard the news. "Is Elvis Presley REALLY going to be here IN PERSON?" Shute confirmed it. "Well, I want a front row seat." (long pause) "They're all gone?" (long pause) "Give me anything that's left."

After the month ended and Presley had come and gone, the calls about him to the Olympia stopped. Never a Presley fan, Jean Shute didn't go to the his show in Detroit. Still, she'd always remember him from those two weeks of fielding phone calls during "Assignment Elvis" at the Olympia switchboard.

One Presley fan's hopes of seeing her idol were dashed. As soon as thirteen-year-old Linda Burell, a student at McMichael Junior High School, heard Elvis was coming to Detroit, she began pestering her mother to take her. Linda's father refused to get involved, but her mother finally agreed. But then her mother fell down the front steps and broke a leg. Still, Linda had hopes of seeing Elvis, until she, too, fell and broke a leg on March 20. When Elvis performed at the Olympia, a broken-hearted Linda was in Children's Hospital with her leg in traction.[2]

Bob Campbell was a healthy Detroit teenager, but he had no intention of going to see Elvis. In a letter to the *Detroit News,* he wanted to make it clear that there were many others like him. After reading in a *News* article that all teenagers were "crazy about Elvis," Bob countered, "Speaking as a teen-ager, I would like to deny this horrible implication. Teen-agers are not all crazy about Elvis. At the school which I attend, Royal Oak Kimball High, there are no more than 15 or 20 per cent of the kids, boys and girls alike, who even like Elvis, let alone 'are crazy about him.'"[3]

Still, there were enough to make the local promoters a few bucks. Art Shurgin was not so sure at first. If the Olympia sold out for both performances, the take would be about $65,000. Asked on March 19 how much of that would go to

Presley, promoter Shurgin responded, "I'd rather not talk about it. It hurts."[4] In fact, Colonel Parker's standard contract guaranteed Elvis $20,000 per show. As it turned out, neither show sold out, and the gate receipts came to $53,000. After paying rent on the Olympia, security costs, and other related expenses, Shurgin came out in the black. Whether it was enough to compensate for the stress and worry a promoter experienced when booking Elvis, only Shurgin could judge.

In terms of manpower, the Detroit police department was more than ready to protect Presley and control the crowd before, during, and after Sunday's shows. Plans called for a cross-precinct force of 150 men to canvass the Olympia and its environs. Three inspectors, six lieutenants, and twelve sergeants would lead the force. Cars from all five precincts were on call to patrol the area all around the stadium. At police headquarters three days before the concerts, Director of Traffic James Hoye declared his department ready.

> Yes, we're all set for the Elvis Presley show. We'll have the commando squad standing by—the commando squad with riot sticks. That's a sergeant and 14 men. Big men. There'll be a concentration of motorcycle traffic officers just in case the hot rodders think we don't love them tender, love them true. There'll be the usual complement directing traffic we use whenever Olympia has a big show.[5]

"We're not looking for trouble," announced another police official, "but it's just as well to be ready for any emergency."

Presley held his Detroit press conference before his afternoon performance. He entered the room wearing a red suede jacket with a blue shirt and blue pants. Using lots of "yes ma'ams" and "yes sirs," Elvis politely answered the questions of the assembled reporters, photographers, DJs, and fan club officers. He revealed that little girls in sufficient numbers terrified him at times, even if all they wanted to do was touch him. Asked again, as he had been at every tour stop so far, about reports that his popularity was waning, Elvis responded, "If they forget me, I'll just have to do something worth remembering." He seemed less confident, though, about continuing his singing career after serving his stint in the army. He would, he said, "if people haven't forgotten me by then."

After being told of rival singer Pat Boone's statement that he wanted Elvis to guest star on the debut of his network television program in the fall, Elvis was asked if he would accept the offer. "Sure," said Elvis, "if I am invited and it can be arranged." Speaking of future engagements, what about the army? "When I took my physical," he said, "they told me it might be three months, six months or a year." (In fact, it was eleven months after he passed his physical in January that Elvis received his draft notice in December.)

Did he plan on selling any of his eight cars? "If I wanted to sell them, I wouldn't have bought them," he replied. "I just built a new four-car garage. Guess I'll have to build another one for the other four cars." That led to a question about his home. He revealed that he was purchasing a colonial-style mansion on an eighteen-acre lot in a Memphis suburb. (Just a week before, prior to leaving on tour, Elvis had told the *Press-Scimitar* in Memphis that he was considering buying the Graceland estate, six miles south of downtown.) On request, Presley revealed his vital statistics: age, 22; height, 6 feet; weight, 180. Then the interview was cut short to give Elvis some time to meet with fan club officers, autograph his new album, and pose for some photos before showtime.

As there was no direct access to the stage, Elvis had to pass through a small section of the crowd to get there. His "security squad of four huskies," so termed by John Finlayson of the *News,* escorted the singer the short distance. The upraised, waving hands of faithful fans created an archway for him as he passed by.

As in Fort Wayne the night before, Elvis did not wear the pants from his gold lamé suit. Along with the gold coat and shoes, however, he did wear the suit's gold string tie in place of the conventional necktie he had worn in Fort Wayne. As usual when on stage, he used a guitar with "Elvis" etched in gold script above the strings. Presley put aside the instrument after finishing his first number and worked the rest of the show with microphone in hand.

The crowds for the afternoon and evening shows differed. *Free Press* reporters described the earlier crowd as consisting of "little girls, nice little girls who just adore Elvis. They wore Elvis buttons, Elvis hats, and carried Elvis pictures."[6] So loyal were they to their idol that they wouldn't allow one girl to reach her seat until she removed the "I Hate Elvis" button she was wearing. The evening crowd was just as large, but it was older and a bit more subdued, according to Finlayson. "It set up a tremendous din on occasion," he noted, "but generally it reacted to Elvis' wailings and wiggles on cue."[7]

Frank Beckman and Carter Van Lopik covered the raucous matinee show for the *Free Press.* They began their review the next morning by noting, "The trouble with going to see Elvis Presley is that you're liable to get killed. The experience is the closest thing to getting bashed on the head with an atomic bomb."[8] Elvis worked through his forty-minute show of songs, struts, and staggers as usual. The multitude present reacted similarly to the fans who had seen Elvis perform over the previous three days. "It was like a Saturday at the movies," noted Finlayson, "only a thousand times more shrill, penetrating and hysterical. His fans shrieked, sobbed, moaned and writhed in their seats, the noise reaching deafening crescendos with each intonation of the palpitating Presley voice." At times the teens swept up against the police lines in an effort to get a closer look at the singer. "Insane,

isn't it?" commented one of the officers on duty. In the end, though, security officials pronounced the crowd "fairly orderly."

After Elvis had revved up the intensity with his "Hound Dog" finale, his four
"huskies" rushed him through a police cordon out of the stadium and into a
waiting car after each show. A perilous situation arose after the afternoon show,
however, as a mass of teenagers, knowing Elvis had another show scheduled in a
couple of hours, refused to believe he had left the Olympia. Trying to find Presley's
dressing room, about a thousand of them gathered and pressed against police barricades. They eventually dispersed without damage to the stadium, the police, or
themselves.

Long after Elvis had left town, fans were still looking for him in Detroit.
Unfortunately for novelist Richard Condon (*The Manchurian Candidate*, *Prizzi's
Honor*), on Sunday night he found himself in the same Detroit hotel room that
had been assigned to Presley. It wound up being a sleepless night for Condon,
as teenagers roamed the halls looking for Elvis. "From 9 to 11 p.m. we had to
get them out," revealed Condon, "and all night after that there were whisperings
under the door."[9]

A charitable act by Elvis went awry amidst the masses entering the Olympia
that afternoon. A fundraiser event for the Macomb County Crippled Children's
Fund was scheduled at Eastgate that afternoon starting at two o'clock. Eastgate
president Hy Siegel went to the Olympia to see if Elvis would autograph a guitar
to be auctioned that afternoon. At his press conference Presley willingly signed
and added a second item for the auction by writing in one of his show programs,
"To the Crippled Children's Society" and autographing the program in two
places. Leaving the Olympia was more difficult than Siegel had envisioned, however. Fighting the incoming mob, he almost lost the guitar despite having a police
escort. So that he could wrap both hands around the prized guitar, Siegel handed
the equally precious program to someone he thought was a policeman. When he
finally cleared the crowd, the program was nowhere to be seen. A week later the
Free Press printed Siegel's futile request that the program be returned.[10]

The press revealed that Elvis had come to Detroit from Fort Wayne in a
Cadillac. That one little fact brought grief to a Plymouth woman. Mrs. Sterling
Eaton took her daughter and son to see Elvis. After the show, they were returning
to the parking lot for the drive home when Mrs. Eaton saw a group of teenagers
surrounding her car. Unfortunately, her Cadillac was pink, a color and make associated with Elvis. In his "The Town Crier" column in the *Free Press*, Mark Beltaire
described the scene.

> The idolators picked at it with their finger nails. They scraped mud
> from under the fenders and rubbed it on their clothes. They opened the

doors and tugged on fixtures inside. They scratched long gashes in the state representative sticker on the windshield. They ripped the dealers' plate off the rear ... all the while chanting the magic name. On the outskirts of the mob, feebly protesting that the Great Man was long gone, was the parking attendant. Nobody believed him. The Cadillac was pink—ergo Elvis.[11]

After Mrs. Eaton identified herself to the attendant, he had an idea for ending the disturbance. "Why don't you tell them you're Presley's mother?" he suggested. "And get myself torn limb from limb?" she answered. "I should say not." The group stood out of harm's way until the fervor subsided and the unruly pack wandered off.

As the teenagers exited the parking lot with their "souvenirs" and Mrs. Eaton examined the damage to her car, Elvis and his entourage were riding in the real thing, the singer's pink Cadillac, as it raced eastward through the night toward Buffalo and another show the next night.

Chapter 6

Buffalo

Buffalo, New York
Memorial Auditorium
Monday, April 1, 1957, 8:30 pm

By the time Elvis took the stage in Buffalo's Memorial Auditorium, Colonel Parker had staked out a position at crowd level in front of the stage. After the near disaster in Chicago four days earlier, Parker was determined to prevent fans from bunching in front of the stage. He increased his demands for local security during the rest of the tour, and to keep fans away from the stage, he was even ready and willing to use his own body as a roadblock. From in front of the stage, he could keep an eye on all aisles leading toward the platform. Should any fans elude police and find an open path to the stage, the Colonel was prepared to intercept them and send them back to their seats. The potential for such breakouts increased as the show progressed and Elvis turned up the intensity on stage.

Early in the performance that evening, while the predominately teenage crowd was content to scream and wield their cameras, Margaret Wynn saw Colonel Parker and decided to make her way to his side. Like many journalists then, Wynn was a non-Presley fan assigned to cover a Presley concert. Working the show for the *Buffalo Courier-Express*, Margaret soon realized she was in over her head. Each time Elvis opened his mouth to sing, thousands of teenagers began screaming, drowning out the song completely. Wynn decided the youngsters must have some kind of "code" that enabled them to recognize each song without hearing it, and being well beyond her teens and unfamiliar with the "code," she gravitated toward Colonel Parker for some help.

With the aisles clear for the moment, Parker was more than willing to provide song titles, each with a big number attached. "That's 'I Was the One,'" he told Wynn as Elvis started another song. "Sold several million records".[1] The writer turned her eyes toward the stage to see Elvis "strutting on the stage like the gawky teen-agers he entrances." She still couldn't hear the music, but she did see his lips move, and when he wiggled his fingers, the screaming increased. As he finished the song and started another one, Wynn gave Colonel Parker an inquiring look. "This is 'Don't Be Cruel.' Sold five million records," he announced. To Margaret's admittedly uninitiated ear, what little she could hear of the song sounded pretty much like the one before. This time, though, the stage antics were different. "Elvis demonstrated another scream-getter," she wrote the next day, "a windmill-like waving of arms. Sometimes with only one arm, sometimes with both." The song complete, Elvis announced, "Now I'd like to do another number for you," and his lips again began to move. "This is 'That's Where Heartaches Begin.' Sold a million records," Parker volunteered without being asked. Still Wynn noticed little change in rhythm between this and the previous song. The noise must have been overwhelming indeed for her not to be able to differentiate between the up-tempo "Don't Be Cruel" and the slow "Heartaches" number.

After the ballad, Presley wiped his mouth on the sleeve of his gold jacket and began to sing again. The Colonel continued his running commentary. "That's 'I've Got a Woman.' Sold two million records." Wynn may not have heard Elvis sing the song, but she continued to observe his body language on stage. "Presley's scream-getting techniques apparently are endless," she observed. "Whether he gave the appearance of snarling at the microphone, shook his over-long hair over his forehead, sneezed or grasped his abdomen like an anguished appendicitis victim, the reaction was the same. Everybody screamed."

While Margaret Wynn would have preferred hearing Elvis sing a note or two, a fellow journalist writing in the *Buffalo Evening News* came to the realization that music was not what Presley's show was about. In fact, Eylvan Fox concluded that Presley's show was less about its star than it was about his fans.

> Whether he could be heard or not didn't make too much difference. The thousands of young girls and a scattering of boys and adults had come not to hear a singer. They had come to see Elvis, to touch him if possible, and to get his signature on a piece of paper to cherish always—at least until another idol comes along....
>
> Elvis' performance is a vast, emotional catharsis for thousands of teen-agers who have found in this 22-year-old former truck driver something that answers, in a vague and ephemeral way, their longings and strivings.
>
> And much of their reaction, it might be added, is not toward Elvis directly, but toward each other. As they stand screaming and waving their arms in adoration of this unreal figure in outlandish clothing, they are together. They belong.[2]

Elvis singled out one girl in the stands for special attention. He was into his extended version of "Hound Dog" when he noticed an arm thrusting a pad and pencil toward him from the corner of the stage. Moving over and dropping to his knees, Presley momentarily took her arm in both hands, sending the crowd into a burst of shrieking. The chosen one was fifteen-year-old Montez Bellquist of Jamestown. Elvis worked his way across the stage, but when he came back again he paid Montez another visit. This time the girl was ready, and when Presley reached his arm out toward her, she fastened onto it with both hands. As Elvis pulled back, the girl refused to let go and was lifted several feet off the floor by her idol. As she held on with all her strength, a policeman came up from behind and whacked her lightly on the ankles. The frightened but uninjured girl finally let Elvis go. Standing close by, Margaret Wynn heard Montez squeal, "Look how cute he is."

Another interested observer in Memorial Auditorium that evening was Dr. Ray L. Birdwhistell. Like everyone else there he couldn't hear Presley sing, but that didn't bother him, since he had come only to see the entertainer's movements on stage. Dr. Birdwhistell, a University of Buffalo professor of anthropology, had made Presley the object of an academic study. As an expert in kinesics—the study of body movement—the professor had spent hours studying the young rock 'n' roller. "The Presley language is that of a safe rebellion of the 2-to 4-year-old child," the pipe-smoking professor explained, "and also that of the adolescent against the over-serious adult."[3]

Birdwhistell made his comments after Presley's Buffalo appearance. He left interpretation of the performer's vocal style to other experts. "I'm only interested in the motions," he said, insisting that Presley's stage antics were not sexy, but rather a "caricature of sex." He explained, "Presley joins his audience in making fun of adult emotions. His appearance and gestures are overstatements of the young adolescent's mocking attitude against the adult ... What you have is an amazingly skilled entertainer, an excellent showman with a high response rate to the audience reactions. He plays back to the audience. You never have a performer-versus-spectator situation." As a father, Birdwhistell said he found it useless for parents to disapprove of Presley's popularity. He also admitted that in the course of studying Presley as an anthropological phenomenon, he had come to enjoy him as a "delightful entertainer."

Twelve days earlier, on March 20, Elvis Presley's performance in Buffalo was first announced in a short article in the *Evening News*. While the singer had appeared before small studio audiences in New York City during his network television appearances in 1956, Buffalo would be the only place his full stage show appeared in the state of New York during the 1950s. The venue was Memorial Auditorium, located at 140 Main Street in downtown Buffalo, just a few blocks from the shores of Lake Erie. Built in 1940 as a WPA project, the "Aud" could seat around 15,000 for entertainment shows. Colonel Parker's ads ran in the Buffalo newspapers daily right up to April 1, indicating that the show did not sell out. Tickets, priced at $2.50, $2.75, and $3.50, were available by mail order or in person at the auditorium and Mathias Cigar Store. All seats were reserved for the 8:30 PM show.

While in Buffalo, Presley stayed at the Hotel Statler. As usual, once his location became known, clusters of teenagers, mostly girls, surrounded the Statler looking for Elvis. "Our mothers don't know we're here," one admitted. "But I suppose we'll have to tell them sometime."[4]

At 6:30 that evening, two hours before showtime, the auditorium doors opened and the early arrivers began filing in. The crowd consisted predominantly of teenagers, estimated at six girls to each boy. Even Sheriff Robert A. Glasser arrived at the arena with a group of teenagers in tow. When Glasser's car pulled up to the rear of the building, eight girls jumped out. One was the sheriff's fourteen-year-old daughter Donna, and the rest were her classmates from School 80. Most of the girls in the crowd were dressed in skirts, sweaters, bobby sox, and sport shoes, their ensembles augmented with Elvis hats, buttons, streamers, and programs. In the sea of youngsters, adults of various ages were scattered in little bunches. A few ladies in fur coats and armed with binoculars sat calmly together in their seats awaiting Elvis' appearance.

Outside the auditorium early that evening, police arrested a sixty-three-year-old man on drunk and disorderly charges. In court the next day, City Judge Frank A. Sodita asked the man where he had been headed when he was detained. "To the hall," the accused answered. "Aren't you a little old to be an Elvis Presley fan?" the judge asked. The defendant responded, "Presley? I don't know anything about Elvis Presley. I was looking for the Louis Armstrong hall." It turned out Armstrong was appearing at the nearby Kleinhaus Music Hall. "Well, I guess you didn't see either one," said Judge Sodita, who handed down a suspended sentence.[5]

The police also took into custody two small, sealed cardboard boxes found on Scott Street near the auditorium before the show started. The heavy boxes rattled, causing the officers to suspect bombs were inside. The packages were transported to the Franklin Station, where they were opened. Inside the police found only trash in what might have been an April Fools' prank.

The next day the *Courier-Express* estimated the crowd at 14,000, about a thousand below the arena's capacity. A caption writer for the *Evening News* set the attendance a little lower, at 13,500, while a reporter down from Toronto gave an even lower ballpark figure of 12,500. As it turned out, they all overestimated. Only Eylvan Fox of the *Evening News* took the time to check with auditorium officials. The turnstile count of the crowd was exactly 10,375. Even though the total was well short of a sellout, long-time arena concessionaire Lew Horschel said the crowd was the most enthusiastic he'd ever seen in his forty years of arena work in the city.[6]

As the fans slowly entered the auditorium and found their seats, security forces set up street barriers in some arena corridors to block off Presley's dressing room and the room set aside for his press conference. Held back by the barricades, groups of young girls alternately pleaded with and heckled the officers who wouldn't let them through.

After a short ride from the Statler, Elvis arrived with his escort and walked down a hallway to a small, crowded room where the press awaited him. He wore a red jacket, a ruffled silver shirt, dark slacks, and the gold shoes. Fox took note of the singer's "aquiline boyish features, dark eyes and the tousled hair and long side burns that have become trademarks."

As the interview progressed, it was as if the same group of reporters had followed Elvis from city to city. The questions differed only slightly from those thrown at Presley in Chicago, St. Louis, Fort Wayne, and Detroit. Again he was asked about his cars. He still had eight. Again he was asked to consider what he would do when the rock 'n' roll fad died out. "I'll try to change," he shrugged. "If I can't, I'll just figure I've had my day." No, he still didn't believe he had an adverse effect on young people. "I don't think I'm causing them to do anything wrong," he said. "They scream and yell and have fun." Asked about his Hollywood career, Elvis announced that his second movie, *Loving You,* would be out in August. He also revealed that sometime in the near future he would be getting a short haircut. "If I'm not in the army by that time," he said, "I'll have a crew cut for my next movie."

After the questions ended, Elvis posed for pictures and doled out autographs, hugs, and kisses to everyone interested. Most of those interested were teenage girls, but not all. The next day the *Evening News* ran a photo of Mrs. Paul F. Hoffman and Mrs. Edward L. Dodelin, neighbors on Brentwood Drive in Snyder, kissing Elvis on opposite cheeks.

At exactly 9:52 Presley walked around a corner and onto the floodlit auditorium stage. Those in the crowd who had cameras fired them off all at once, while everyone else screamed in unison. In a seeming wave from the front of the arena to the back, teenage girls threw their arms up and open wide. Giving a sheepish grin, Elvis grabbed the microphone and uttered an indistinguishable sound. Dick Hirsch of the *Courier-Express* described what happened next.

> For three solid minutes, like the high-pitched whines of a squadron of jet-planes, they screamed.

Elvis held up his hand for silence. He muttered something that was lost in the frenzy. Then he twitched his well-publicized pelvis.

His gargantuan mop of hair spilled over his forehead. He cuddled the mike. He snickered at the gallery behind the bunting-draped stage. Young girls squeezed their temples with their hands as if in sublime agony. Elvis himself appeared as though afflicted by a serious case of stomach cramps.

But through it all, Elvis, Tennessee's gift to teen-agers, played his part to the hilt. He is an amazing phenomenon and he had the giant audience in the palm of his hand.[7]

Except for switching out the red jacket for his gold one, Presley was dressed on stage as he had been at his press conference an hour before. David Carmichael of the *Toronto Telegram* described Elvis as "wearing a gold jacket, black zoot-suit trousers, gold shoes with silver tassels and a white silk shirt with ruffles." Moving back and forth across the stage, dragging the microphone with him, Elvis waited for the clamor to die down. When it didn't, he brought both hands together on the mike and began singing. The din increased, completely drowning out the sounds of "Heartbreak Hotel."

Both *Courier-Express* and *Evening News* reporters timed Presley's Buffalo performance at thirty minutes. If they were correct, then the singer cut at least ten minutes from the show he gave in other cities on the tour both before and after Buffalo. Since the crowd was well under control that night, there seemed no reason for Presley to cut short his performance. About 180 uniformed and plain-clothed police officers, under the command of Captain John F. Mahoney, were positioned throughout the auditorium to keep order. The overwhelming police presence caused one man to ask a turnstile attendant, "Are you sure there isn't a policeman's ball here tonight?" All teenage girls who made efforts during the show to get around the security force and reach the stage were turned back. Eylvan Fox reported that the crowd was "exuberant but orderly and dispersed without incident after the performance."

As Elvis worked through his finale, the crowd moved forward noticeably in their seats, many fans holding their arms out toward him. Others, overcome by the emotional upheaval, buried their faces in their hands. Then, with the stage exit directly behind him, Presley literally disappeared in the blink of an eye. Twenty police officers waited backstage to protect him from any fans who might try to cut off his retreat. Running full-speed down the ramp, within seconds Elvis was in a green-and-cream-colored automobile heading up the auditorium's parking incline with a police motorcycle escort on both sides.

Unaware that Elvis was long gone, hundreds of his fans, hoping for a last look at their idol, lingered in the auditorium exits for more than an hour after the show ended. Standing in tight groups in a chilling, light rain, they shared their exhilaration at having seen Elvis. "Did you touch him?" one shouted. Another pointed to a room down a hallway and said softly to no one in particular, "He was in that room." Admitting that she had cried during the show, sixteen-year-old Katherine Carlo said, "I love him. He's terrific." Having watched it all from a front row seat, ten-year-old Michele Ingrando pronounced Elvis "the coolest cat on earth." Presley had not impressed all the girls, however. One claimed she had come only out of curiosity, and added, "My boyfriend is a lot cuter anyway." She admitted screaming during Presley's show, though, "because everyone else was."

One little girl got the fright of her life after the show was over. Eleven-year-old Barbara Lewis of Niagara Falls became separated from her sister and some friends as the crowd filed out of the auditorium. Civil Defense Patrolmen Roy Schukraft and Joseph Boryszewski found the crying girl as she tried to find her group's car. As the officers helped her search the parking lots, Barbara recognized her neighbors, Mr. and Mrs. Roy Williamson, who agreed to drive the frightened girl home in their car.

Driving his own pink Cadillac, Presley was on the highway to Toronto within an hour of leaving the stage in Buffalo. Although both the *Courier-Express* and the *Evening News* ran lengthy reviews and a few pictures in their issues the next day, the Buffalo press coverage of the singer's appearance in their city was among the skimpiest provided in any community Presley played in 1957. In the two weeks leading up to the April 1 show, the two newspapers barely mentioned the coming of the country's hottest entertainment star. The *Evening News* ran only a three-inch news brief announcing the Presley visit on page seventy-five of its March 20 edition. The *Courier-Express* never heralded Elvis' coming, leaving that job to Colonel Parker's daily ads on the entertainment page. The first mention of Elvis in the *Express* came in Jerry Evarts' "As I See It" column the day before the singer's show in the auditorium. Even then Evarts made no mention of Presley's stage show, reporting instead what he had heard about the rock 'n' roller's charitable work. "Presley outfits a dozen girls and boys with clothing at Christmas time," Evarts noted, "and donates regularly to several youth groups. In addition to contributing to worthy charities, the young man who made 'Hound Dog' popular likes to stop youngsters on the street and take them for rides in one of his Cadillacs."[8]

While the *Courier-Express* put their review of Presley's show on the front page of their April 2 issue, the *Evening News* made readers turn to page fourteen for their coverage. One teenager wrote the *News,* however, to praise its meager Presley coverage. "The front page had no mention of it whatsoever," he noted, adding, "which was fine with me. The picture page showed only two photos of him. I have heard that Elvis is a 'nice kid' and fine company and also fine to talk with. He himself does not smoke and does not drink. But this doesn't condone his other actions."[9]

Another reader was upset with the *Evening News* over a brief item that ran on its editorial page on April 3. Under the title, "What Price a Monstrosity?" the paper's editors used Presley's gold lamé jacket to take a couple pokes at the singing star.

> Elvis Presley was in Buffalo the other night. We suppose even the adult members of the community know that if they read The News. Rock'n'roll—if that is what it is—doesn't inspire us to screech approval so we'll forbear critical comment.
>
> But that gold lamé and rhinestone jacket? We've read that it cost $4000; that it cost $2500; that it was a bargain at $750. Never having bought one—and having no immediate plans to do so—we wouldn't know. We'll just have to conclude that the press agent scored his biggest success when he planted the $4000 figure and that the writer who bought the top price was as overimpressed as any squealing bobbysoxer.[10]

Of course, it was a rival *Courier-Express* writer who reported the $4,000 figure, which no doubt had been fed to her by a Colonel Parker employee familiar with his boss' penchant for making big numbers even bigger. Five days later the *Evening News* ran the following letter from a reader condemning it for what the editorial writer must have thought was a harmless, tongue-in-cheek swipe at Elvis.

> It seems to me that The Buffalo Evening News owes an apology to 14,000 enthusiastic teen-agers who paid a handsome price of admission to see their Elvis Presley. They behaved themselves in a law-abiding manner and enjoyed the performance immensely only to have their faces slapped with your editorial, "What Price a Monstrosity?"
>
> The editorial was not only unkind and in very poor taste, but was actually very cruel to the young people. Ironically enough, in an editorial on the same page, The News showed great kindness and understanding to the problems of an alcoholic. But the kindness and understanding were substituted by reference to monstrosity when referring to the young people. The young people need more attention, more kindness and more understanding than all the alcoholics put together.

I am not a Presley fan, but it is sad to see the young people of this city continually take such unnecessary and unkind abuse. Let's keep the monstrosities from association with our young.[11]

With that Buffalo's press moved on. Presley had done the same, up the road into Canada. In 1972 and again in 1976, Elvis returned to perform in Buffalo's Memorial Auditorium. But things had changed—a renovated arena, a different Elvis, a different crowd. The events in the auditorium on April 1, 1957, quickly passed into history, the experience living only in the collected memories of the 10,375 who were there to see the show.

The 8:00 pm show in Toronto, April 2, 1957. (Leo Harrison/Toronto Star)

Chapter 7

Toronto

Prelude

It was 4:30 in the morning when car jockey Jack Boyle reported to work as usual at the Commonwealth garage, just across the street from the King Edward Hotel. However, it turned out to be a most unusual shift for Jack. When he arrived he was told that in the garage was a pink Cadillac hardtop with white and pink leather upholstery, Tennessee license plates 2D33502. He was to keep an eye on it and tell no one about it.

Within minutes of his getting the top-secret orders, though, three young women bounded into the garage and asked to see Elvis' car. "You should have seen them," Jack later told Wessely Hicks of the *Toronto Telegram*. "Their eyes were open like this," and he expanded his eyes so wide they nearly rolled out of their sockets.[1] Since Jack had been instructed not to tell anyone the car was there, which he hadn't, and since he hadn't been told not to show the car to anyone, he promptly escorted the women to the parked car. "They patted it," he explained. "And one of them kissed it. I never saw anyone kiss a car before, not even a Cadillac."

The car was there because train schedules could not accommodate all of Elvis Presley's transportation needs during his whirlwind ten-day tour that began in Chicago on March 28. The train took him to Chicago, then back south to St. Louis. However, no train was scheduled through Fort Wayne late Saturday night for Detroit, where Elvis was to play the next day. So his pink Cadillac was driven up from Memphis and used by him and his buddies for the 170-mile, three-hour drive to Detroit, where they arrived in the early hours of Sunday morning.

While touring in 1957, Elvis usually traveled by night and slept most of the day in his hotel room. Soon after his show ended, usually between 10:30 and 11:00 PM, he headed off to the next city by train, if possible, or by car if not. "We're operating on a weird schedule," he told reporter David Carmichael. "But despite everything I get six or seven hours of sleep a day and I don't find it too hard to keep going."[2]

After the Monday evening show in Buffalo, the Cadillac left for the short 100-mile drive to Toronto with Presley himself behind the wheel. "I drove from Buffalo to Toronto yesterday morning," he told the press in Canada. "I do most of the driving when we're on tour. I like to drive." Asked his impression of Canada's highways, Elvis responded, "I couldn't see them for the fog." He arrived in Toronto about 3:00 AM and parked his car in the garage on Colborne Street before checking into the King Edward across the street.

After Jack Boyle came on duty an hour and a half later, the vehicle became a tourist attraction. Later that morning Boyle took a break to get a cup of coffee at a nearby restaurant. "I've been going into that restaurant for years and never had a free cup of coffee," he said. "But today when I went in, the waitress comes over and says she'll give me a free cup of coffee if I'll show her the car. I say it's a deal. I show it to her, and she writes a note to leave in the car." The note read, "Dear Elvis: From one of your admiring fans." The waitress signed her name and, just in case, wrote her address on the bottom.

Throughout the morning the girls just kept coming, and finally Jack decided to hide the Cadillac. He drove it down a ramp into the bowels of the garage, parked it in a dark corner, and surrounded it with other cars. Later Hicks showed up looking for a story and Boyle took him to the car. Hicks slid between the other cars surrounding it, opened the Cadillac's driver's door and plopped down behind the wheel. Looking down, he saw the initials "E.P." in white leather sewn into the rug at his feet.

"I sat behind the wheel and dreamed I was driving down a long, golden highway," Hicks later wrote, "with trees arching over the road on either side. Instead of leaves, the trees were wearing hundred dollar bills." As if to complete his fantasy, the passenger door opened and an attractive woman crawled in beside him. "I'm an Elvis fan," she announced. "She moved around the seat," Hicks reported, "just patting the car. She moved over so far her head was almost on my shoulder. And I can't even play a guitar."

Hicks got out of the car and walked up the ramp with Boyle. Just as they got to ground level, a girl in horn-rimmed glasses came sliding around the corner. "Where's the car?" she screamed at Jack. "Where's the car?" As Hicks walked away, the valet looked like he was going to cry.

Toronto, Ontario
Maple Leaf Gardens
Tuesday, April 2, 1957, 6:00 pm and 9:00 pm

In 1956 Elvis considered bringing his live show to Canada. "I tried to get them to book a tour up here," he told Ottawa DJ Gord Atkinson, "but I wasn't well enough known ... So they figured I wouldn't make enough money." According to Colonel Parker, the sheer volume of the fan mail from Canada finally convinced him to send Elvis across the border in 1957. "I've gotten more mail from Toronto, Ottawa, and Montreal than any other place," Elvis told Atkinson. "I have been wanting to come up here. In fact, when I started looking at the tour, I said, 'By all means. I want to go to Canada.'"3

The original lineup called for Presley to play Toronto, Ottawa, and Montreal on consecutive days, starting Tuesday, April 2. But shortly before the tour opened in late March, Montreal's city fathers got cold feet. Officials had tentatively granted Presley use of the arena in nearby Verdun, but soon after the April 4 date was set on the tour schedule, permission to use the arena was withdrawn. The official word from Colonel Parker was that Montreal couldn't come up with enough policemen to provide security for Presley's show. More likely, though, Detroit columnist Mark Beltaire had it right. "They're just afraid," he wrote of elected officials in the Montreal area, "that the mere presence of Elvis might touch off a small riot, and since there's an election coming up in Quebec in April, they'd rather not take a chance."4 Elvis himself seemed unsure about the reason for the cancellation of his Montreal date. At a Canadian press conference, he said he thought the ban was a "political deal," and then added, "or maybe they just don't like me."

However, after the singer's two show dates in Ontario were announced on March 19, he was still talking about his popularity north of the border. "I'm not going to kid you that I heard all about Canada when I was growing up down in Tennessee. Course I didn't," he confessed to *Toronto Telegram* reporter Leon Kossar. "But I know that I get more mail from Canada as far as percentages go than from any other country on the face of the earth. I like to be liked, same as everybody. So I know it's going to be fun in Canada and I'm really worked up about it."5

Of Toronto specifically, he told Kossar, "I've got a tremendous following up there. Why, one girl alone collected 2,000 signatures for me to appear in Toronto." According to the *Telegram*, that one girl was Carol Vanderbleck, leader of a local fan club, who single-handedly collected 2,443 signatures and sent the petition to Elvis. (A couple of weeks later the *Daily Star* ran a photo of another Elvis fan, Shirley Harris, who also claimed "major responsibility" for Presley's coming to

Toronto. She said that on a disc jockey's show she asked Elvis fans to call her if they wanted to see him in Toronto. She got 2,000 replies.) Colonel Parker said that the 45,000 Christmas cards Elvis received from the Toronto area in 1956 was another factor that convinced him to book the star in Canada.

The Colonel's advertising hit the Toronto papers on March 19. Elvis was to play one 9:00 PM performance in Maple Leaf Gardens on Tuesday, April 2. Tickets, priced at $1.25, $1.75, $2.75, $3.00, and $3.50, were available in Toronto at the Gardens box office, the Royal York and King Edward Hotels, Moodey's, and various Plaza Ticket Service outlets. In outlying Hamilton, tickets could be purchased at the Connaught Hotel and the Maple Leaf Ticket Agency. The John Black Agency had tickets in Oakville. When the arena box office opened the morning of March 20, Toronto resident Annie Murphy was at the head of a long line and got the first ticket to the show. After all the tickets had sold out within forty-eight hours, a second Tuesday show was added at 6:00 PM, and ticket sales continued up until show time without selling out the earlier show.

The city of Toronto became "Elvisized" during the two weeks leading up to the singer's arrival there. "All Shook Up," Presley's new single, shot right to the top of the city's "10 Most Popular Records," and his "Too Much," which had fallen off the chart, suddenly climbed back into the top ten. Pollock's Shoe Stores ran ads for the "Official Elvis Presley Shoe" for women at $4.95 a pair. Disc jockeys at CHUM radio invited listeners to send in their reasons for wanting a date with Elvis. The best entries would win an opportunity to meet Elvis backstage. The *Toronto Star* offered its readers an eight-by-ten colored lithographic print for 50¢ each, including postage. An anti-Elvis club in Tennessee tried, unsuccessfully, to convince Toronto DJs to stop playing Presley records.

Meanwhile, the Toronto police prepared a large security force under the leadership of District Chief George Elliott. The plan called for ninety-five officers, the largest police contingent ever provided by the city, to be in the arena during the show. Some would be on regular duty, while others would be off-duty officers paid for by the show promoters. Six policewomen, some in uniform, some not, were included in the detail. Chief Elliott said maximum effort would be made to keep order during the Presley show. A number of special "flying squads" were organized to roam the arena and stop trouble before it began. "Anyone who gets out of his seat and starts to wander around will be ejected," Elliott vowed.[6] He anticipated that the most difficult task would be clearing the 6:00 PM audience quickly from the arena so that the 9:00 PM crowd could be seated.

As April 2 dawned in Toronto, the Elvis watch began in earnest. The *Star's* headline ran, "Where Is Presley? Can't Locate Him." The paper had been unable to learn how Elvis was coming to town and where he would stay. A survey of the city's big hotels turned up nothing. One manager explained, "It's possible we wouldn't know if he was here until someone recognized him." All the Maple Leaf Gardens press agent could say was, "He's supposed to be here by 6 p.m. Where he'll be up to that time we can't say." The secrecy was understandable, concluded the *Daily Star*. "Whether he rides in on a horse, drives, comes by plane or rambles into the city in a Sherman tank, he's bound to be mobbed and that's the reason his arrival is being kept hush-hush."[7]

When the *Star* hit the street that morning, however, Elvis was already fast asleep in a room on the fifth floor of the King Edward Hotel. Once word of the famous guest began to spread around the hotel, a handful of secretaries got together and headed up to his room. There a couple of bodyguards politely turned them away, but eighteen-year-old Irene Symsyk, a Board of Trustees secretary, refused to leave quietly. She pounded on Elvis' door and yelled his name. "Gosh, if I could just get my hands on that man," she said, as hotel guards led her away.[8]

As the afternoon hours wore away, the first wave of fans advanced on Maple Leaf Gardens two hours before show time. Entrances to the arena became clogged as traffic slowed on Carlton and Church streets. By the time the opening acts began, the crowd numbered 9,350, over 5,000 short of capacity. The four individual acts in the show's first half had come to expect a mild reception at best from crowds at previous stops on the tour, but some Elvis fans were openly hostile in Toronto. Frankie Trent, who led off The Elvis Presley Show, said there was much more heckling there than he had heard in other towns. Tenor Frankie Connors was booed, Rex Marlowe drew few laughs during his comedy routine, and Pat Kelly was described in the press as "a blonde lady singer of no distinction whatever."[9] The only opening act to draw a positive response from the audience was the Jordanaires.

As usual, while the opening acts were irritating the masses, Elvis met the press elsewhere in the building. His entrance and appearance didn't impress Angela Burke of the *Star*.

> The trouble with Elvis, from this observer's view, is young Mr. Presley's complete lack of naiveté. Even the way he handles himself in a press conference, parrying questions sometimes with humor, and sometimes with remarkable innuendo, is a shocker when one considers his age.
>
> Definitely, Elvis is an old pro when it comes to meeting the press. Last night as he slithered into the bare cement-walled conference room dressed in a silver metallic shirt (open at the throat), a red suede jacket and gold shoes (scuffed), he still managed, despite the improbable attire, to look a bit like a Greek god.

With a quick leap he was atop the table at the front of the room, sinking with cat-like grace to sit cross-legged to face the assembled press. In that get-up and in that position, one could only expect the worst.[10]

As the questioning began, though, Burke's attitude started to change. "Actually, Elvis proved himself interesting, forthright and undeniably attractive," she noted. "He was willing to talk on any subject and though his knowledge is strictly limited, he shows no lack of brains." Presley quickly answered reporters' questions.

Reporter: Do you have any plans to get married?

Presley: (Smiling broadly and turning both thumbs down) I haven't even thought about it. I was engaged twice, but I don't remember that far back. My first romance occurred when I was nine. I fell in love with a woman of 20 and I thought that was it. Now I like all girls.

Reporter: What's it like traveling from place to place doing one-night stands?

Presley: It's a hectic life, but I'd rather be on tour than making movies or appearing on television.

Reporter: Do you have any plans to quit show business?

Presley: Not for some time yet. It'll probably quit me first.

Reporter: Do you ever get stage fright?

Presley: Always. It's the waiting part that gets me. It's not so bad once I've done the first couple of numbers. But I'm never completely at ease.

Reporter: Does the affection teenagers have for you affect your private life?

Presley: It certainly does. I haven't been shopping since Christmas. Then I took a girl from Las Vegas along with me, and I got caught by so many people that she got completely lost and had to take a cab home. I've been scared a few times during shows, too, though I can only remember twice when the audience was actually out of hand.

Reporter: Have you ever thought about becoming a doctor, lawyer or psychiatrist?

Presley: I hadn't thought about becoming a psychiatrist, but I thought about going to a few of them.

Reporter: Have you ever considered wearing a disguise?

Presley: My sideburns would give me away. Besides, a disguise makes you look more of an oddball than you really are.

Reporter: Who chooses your songs?

Presley: My contract with RCA allows me to choose all my own material. That's a mistake a lot of artists make. Nobody knows what you can do better than you.

Reporter: How come you aren't wearing blue suede shoes?

Presley: I have five pair of blue suede shoes at home, but I never wear them. That kind of thing gets worn out after awhile.

Reporter: Do you have any advice for teenagers?

Presley: Stay in school if you can. I didn't realize how important it was until I got out.

Reporter: Do you write home to your mother while touring?

Presley: Honey, I haven't written a letter since I left the sixth grade.

By the time the questions ended, Elvis left Angela Burke with a favorable impression—temporarily. "No two ways about it," she wrote the next day. "Elvis has charm—and this reporter was a victim of it along with any number of colleagues. Even young Mr. Presley's answers regarding his remarkable success with ladies-at-large were models of propriety and modesty ... If this reporter had left the Gardens at this juncture, she would probably still be saying that Elvis was a poor maligned lad. But his show changed all that."

When the reporters were done with him, Elvis was turned over to the admiring teenage fans in the room for embraces, kisses, autographs, and photos. Among them were the six winners of CHUM's "Why I'd Like a Date with Elvis" contest. They were Valerie Stewart, 18; Beverly Ross, 19; Gail Cameron, 17; Katharine Schneider, 18; Toyoko Sameshima, 16; and Edna Manitowabi, 16.

Also on hand to meet Elvis and pose for pictures with him was renowned ballerina Mia Slavenska, a star performer at New York's Metropolitan Opera. She had brought her dance company to Toronto for a two-week run of performances at the Royal York Hotel's Imperial Room. Elvis admitted he had never heard of the famous ballerina, but she had heard of him. "Mr. Presley has a very definite form of dance rhythm," she said. "This may well be what creates the hysteria."[11]

Then it was time for Elvis' first stage show outside the United States. After local disc jockey Josh King came on stage to introduce Elvis, the crowd roared for thirty seconds straight. "Elvis isn't coming yet," he announced. "Elvis doesn't think you're making enough noise." That brought on a full two minutes of even louder screeching. The lights dimmed as Elvis came on stage, but a flood of camera flashes lit the scene brighter than the house lights could.

The crowd had been told they could take as many photos as they wanted, and they needed no second invitation. About a third of them had cameras and kept firing away throughout the performance. Between the two shows the clean-up crew carried off several boxes full of spent flashbulbs.

When all that film was processed, it revealed Elvis in his gold jacket, black pants, and a black shirt, with a gold locket hanging from his neck. At the evening's second show, Presley wore his full gold lamé tuxedo for the last time in public. In later live performances that year he usually wore the gold jacket, and sometimes other elements of the suit, but after that evening in Toronto, he never again wore the gold slacks.

The 6:00 PM show drew a smaller, younger crowd. The crowd for the second show filled the Gardens to its standing-room capacity of 15,000. It would be the second largest crowd to attend a Presley show in 1957. Among the eighteen cities that hosted Presley concerts that year, only Vancouver, B.C., attracted a bigger turnstile count than did the second show in Toronto. The throng ranged from socialites in their furs and fancy dresses to teens in jeans and black-leather jackets. Many of the youngsters had "Elvis Presley" sewn into their clothing or were wearing "I Like Elvis" buttons. Colonel Parker told the press that the evening audience was the largest Presley had ever faced on stage. (He must have temporarily forgotten the crowd of more than 26,000 that saw Elvis perform at the Cotton Bowl in Dallas on October 11, 1956.) In Toronto Elvis drew 24,350 for his two performances. The next day local promoters estimated that Presley's take for the night's work would be between $25,000 and $30,000, including proceeds from souvenir pictures and programs.

During each of the two Toronto shows, Elvis worked forty-five minutes, performing sixteen songs, including the opener "Heartbreak Hotel," followed by "Long Tall Sally," "Don't Be Cruel," "Love Me," "That's When Your Heartaches Begin," "Blueberry Hill," "Too Much," "Butterfly," and the finale, "Hound Dog." The *Telegram's* Colin Murray likened the loud and continual crowd noise to a "wavering scream that sank and rose like an air raid siren."[12] Several times Presley himself covered his ears with his hands. ("When I can't hear myself, I forget the tune," he later explained.)

Of course, Elvis controlled the noise level with his antics on stage. In the first show the screams increased when he accidentally conked himself on the head with the microphone. The reaction was the same in the second show when he stood still, held his thumb up and wiggled it. Dr. Charles Peaker, organist at St. Paul's Anglican Church and head of the organ department at the Royal Conservatory of Music, provided the best description of Elvis on stage in Toronto.

> He clutches the mike and begins to sing, twitching all over. Pandemonium—flashbulbs exploding so continuously I could see to write, an earthshaking din and through it all the band and the drums.
>
> Up and down the stage he goes, dragging the mike like a captive, undulating, shouting feverishly. He freezes, the orchestra stops—he glares at the audience like one in a hypnotic trance, then he leaps, gives tongue, and starts to dislocate his golden legs again.
>
> Apparently the audience doesn't want to hear him, and little he cares. Abruptly he stops, and says perfectly clearly, "Thank you very much."

Then his face sets, his lips curl back and seizing the mike by the scruff of the neck he prowls like a panther up and down the platform, snarling and driving his worshippers crazy.

Across the stage, a pitiful group, his quartet, surrounds another mike supplying harmony I suppose, but no one hears them, no one sees them; all eyes are on the sick Aztec god reeling up and down in his dreadful finery.[13]

The screaming aside, the crowds in Toronto were among the best-behaved Elvis faced in 1957. Dancer Frankie Trent noted that "the kids didn't screech and run around as much as they did in other places." Only when Elvis reached his arm out and pointed to a section of the crowd did any number of fans rise out of their seats, then to reach their arms back to him as their wailing intensified.

Much of the credit for keeping the crowd in its seats went to the Chief Elliott's special constable force. Joe Scanlon of the *Star* noted, "Whenever a youngster bounced up in his seat a policeman would reach over and plunk him down again. This sometimes gave the Gardens the appearance of a large jack-in-the-box, but it seemed to have the desired effect."[14] Three teenage girls who, one after the other, ran down an aisle toward the stage, were intercepted by police and returned to their seats with Colonel Parker's help. During the second show, two female fans who tried to break through police lines and reach the stage were escorted out of the building.

Chief Elliott positioned himself at the back of the stage where he could keep the entire audience in view. As he stood there, his foot could be seen tapping to the rhythm of the music. "I'm a bit of a Presley fan myself," he told reporters. "The kids all seemed to have a good time. And they were well behaved. The master of ceremonies told them to stay in their seats, stand up if they wanted to take pictures, but not leave their seats. And they obeyed almost to the letter. They were a good bunch."[15]

Between the two evening shows Elvis stayed in his arena dressing room. After finishing his second show at about 11:10, he rushed off the stage to a waiting cab that took him directly to Union Station to catch the night train to Ottawa. One police officer said, "I'll bet that guitar hadn't hit the stage from his hand by the time he was shooting through the door. His fast disappearance made it a lot easier for us."[16]

As soon as Elvis vanished, some teenagers leaped to the stage and started collecting the dirt Presley's feet had touched. Others, a crowd of nearly four hundred, rushed outside and around the north side of the building looking for the singer's car. Not finding it there, they moved quickly to the service entrance, but by then Presley was long gone. Within a half hour of Elvis' departure, only a few stragglers remained inside Maple Leaf Gardens. One of them was sixteen-year-old Marianne

Dunn, who kicked her shoes off during the show and was still trying to find them after most of the crowd had left.

Over the next couple of weeks, Toronto citizens of all ages and walks of life weighed in on the merits and effects of Presley's appearance in their town.

It's the most mysterious thing I've ever seen ... to see thousands of teenagers worked up to such a high pitch of frenzy. I can't understand it. It is a most remarkable case of mass hysteria. But it doesn't seem to do any harm.[17]—Fred Gardiner, Toronto Metro chairman

I didn't see him. If I had a daughter, she wouldn't have got inside the Gardens door. I'm a real Presley fan. I'd like to fan him with a brick.[18]—Joe Schulman, taxi driver

Your excessive Elvis Presley coverage is sickening. When will you awake to the fact that Toronto is becoming a city, not a small town where corny hill-billy singers rate the licked feet treatment? A brief mention surely but hardly the stomach-turning articles of recent days. After all who are you selling papers to, 13-year-olds? Who else could possibly be interested in such a hick?[19]—letter to the *Telegram*

It goes without saying he has all the appeal of one-part dynamite and one part chain-lightning to the adolescent girls, but to one like myself who is neither a girl nor adolescent, I could only feel he was strikingly devoid of talent. One rock'n'roll ballad sounded just like the other, and the basic theme and appeal were sex, which Elvis lays on with the subtlety of a bulldozer in mating season, you might say. He is Mr. Overstatement himself. He has to knock himself and his audience out at every beat.[20]—Hugh Thomson, *Toronto Daily Star* music reviewer

Elvis belongs strictly to the world of youth, and that is why teen-agers are so possessive about him. With his gold jacket and gold shoes with silver tassels, he represents a golden age that soon gives way to the sturdier metal of adulthood. The teen-agers instinctively sense that Elvis will not last. Lines will soon grow on that smooth face. The spring in his step that enables him to bounce onto the stage ... will vanish soon enough.

This may explain why teen-agers reach out to him. They really want to hold on to the golden hours of youth. Elvis' quality, like the green years, is ephemeral, but while it lasts it needs to be savored and relished.

The antics that go with admiration of Mr. Presley are the ritualistic accompaniment to youth's worship of itself. Is it Elvis they think of when the young and impressionable close their eyes in trance-like oblivion? May it not rather be youth's inward embrace of the powers that eventually have to be surrendered?[21]—*Toronto Telegram* editorial

It would be foolish, of course, to suggest that it is the failure of society to impose on young people the responsibilities of adulthood which alone accounts for the Elvis Presley rages of our time. The techniques employed by Presley were much like the techniques employed by the high-powered evangelist and the results were much the same.

As a general phenomenon, certainly, there is nothing peculiarly new or different about the Elvis Presley show. Society long has witnessed shows such as this even if, in an earlier age, the stage-lighting and flash-bulb cameras were lacking.[22]—Dr. S. D. Clark, professor of sociology, University of Toronto

Rock'n'roll will die in the near future, and Elvis will speed it along ... What a horrible experience. I came to find out what all the noise about Presley is about; and that's just what it all amounted to—a lot of noise.[23]—Dave Caplan, president of the Toronto Town Jazz club

Elvis Presley is a vulgar, tasteless amateur ... I find this no laughing matter. It is a desperate state of affairs when you consider millions of youngsters being brought up on horror comics and Presley ... Crosby does what he does with taste and voice. He is a professional in his field. Presley, on the other hand, is a cheap amateur in the extreme.[24]—Rudolf Bing, general manager, Metropolitan Opera Company

Elvis isn't a raving maniac. He's a boy just out of his teens, a fellow who has made good. He's put us teen-agers on the map, and we're grateful.

I stamped my feet and hollered like the rest of them at his show last night. I didn't see anything wrong with what he was doing up there on the stage. In fact, what he was doing was good. He was pleasing the crowd.

I'd like to tell my parents and the parents of all those screaming children there last night: Don't worry, there's nothing wrong with us. I'm 19, and for some of us there who were 14 or 15, Elvis might be a bad influence. But we older teen-agers know better, I think. What we saw and applauded was a good, clean show.[25]—Barbara Bromley, Toronto Presley fan club president

Ottawa, April 3, 1957. (City of Ottawa Archives, Andrews Newton Collection, AN 49378 #118)

Chapter 8

Ottawa

Ottawa, Ontario
Memorial Auditorium
Wednesday, April 3, 1957, 4:30 pm and 8:00 pm

While the citizens of Toronto seemed to welcome Elvis, if not with open arms, at least with open minds, 270 miles to the northeast in Canada's capital city of Ottawa, forces gathered in opposition to his appearance in that city. The most vocal resistance came from the leaders of Ottawa's private schools. On the evening of Wednesday, March 27, a week before Elvis' scheduled performance, the Ottawa Separate School Board held its regular monthly meeting. Trustee Leo Henri spoke out against Presley's show at the auditorium on April 3. "We don't want the good reputation of our students spoiled by attendance at this thing. Our teachers should discourage our students from attending the show."[1] When asked if there was any special reason for the proposed boycott, Henri said, "We all know the reason why. His actions are too vulgar." When trustee Matt McGrath then asked, "Is that a motion?" Henri responded, "It certainly is."

The board members briefly discussed the motion before voting on it. "I'm very serious about this thing," Henri warned. "And if I hear of anyone coming around to our schools to sell tickets to that show, it'll be just too bad for them." Board president F. M. Peters admitted, "I like his latest song." At one point the board's secretary treasurer displayed an Elvis Presley pencil, which had been sent to the board "as a sample." Henri declared, "We don't want any. We can't stop the students from using them, but we will most certainly not sell them ourselves in our schools." After the discussion, trustee Romeo Lachaine seconded the motion and it passed unanimously. The board directed that a special letter be sent to all principals requesting that they advise teachers to discourage their students from attending Presley's show.

Some individual voices in the community spoke out against the school board's action. *Ottawa Journal* columnists "Wayne and Shuster" advised the city's teenagers to stand up for their right to be and act young. "If you're a teen-age, dyed-in-the-wool Elvis Presley fan, don't let the old-timers look down their noses at you," they urged in their March 30 column. "The Elvis Presley of 25 years ago was Rudy Vallee, a singer who made millions out of a megaphone and a sinus condition. And your mother was down in the front row whooping it up for Rudy as you do today for Elvis."[2] Several letters decrying the board's actions appeared in the city's newspapers. In the *Ottawa Citizen* Helen Denny explained, "I think this is proof that the separate schools dominate their students in or out of school. Parents allow teachers and school boards to tell their children what they are to do—they are not allowed to choose or feel free to go on their own. If the teachers and the board did not think evil of Elvis, the students would not be afraid of committing a sin by going to see him. The students' fathers, and some of their brothers, fought for freedom to do what they think is best."[3]

While announcements discouraging students from going to see Elvis were made over the public address systems in some schools, the students at Ottawa's Notre Dame Convent received an even sterner message. The day before Presley's show, the students were asked to make a vow concerning the singer. The promise was written on a blackboard, and students were asked to copy it down and write their names on the bottom. The pledge read, "I promise that I shall not take part in the reception accorded Elvis Presley and I shall not be present at the program presented by him at the Auditorium on Wednesday, April 3, 1957."[4] How strictly Notre Dame's Mother Superior would hold the girls to their signed promises was unclear at the time.

In an interview with Ottawa DJ Mac Lipson, Elvis responded to the efforts of city educators to label him vulgar and keep their students away from his show. "I've run across 'em before," he said. "I just wish the people would stop judging a tree by its bark—something they've heard or something they've read or something. They should come out to the show and judge it for themselves. And then if they still think it, well just let 'em think it because that's all I can do. I certainly don't mean to be vulgar or suggestive and I don't think I am."[5] At his press conference that day, Elvis added, "They'd find there's nothing wrong with the rock. Jumpin', shakin' and dancin' ain't indecent. It don't incite the kids to rob banks or buy a gun."

Shaking off the discouragement of school administrators, the Ottawa's Presley fan club continued its plans to welcome Elvis to the city. With 1,935 members, the Ottawa club was said to be the biggest Elvis fan group in Canada. Under the direction of its president, twenty-year-old Peter Mercer, the club put up welcome banners and planned two big demonstrations, one to welcome Elvis and the other to receive the special train with fans from Montreal. Working with the incorrect information that Presley would enter Ottawa in a half-dozen pastel-colored Cadillacs caravanning up Highway 15 from Toronto, fan club members planned to line both sides of the road from the city limits to downtown. Club officers had been unable to identify the hotel where Presley would be staying, but they kept trying to do so. The club also commissioned Ottawa artist Sidney Ledson to do a charcoal rendering of Presley to be presented to the singer at the auditorium.

Meanwhile, the release of Elvis' latest single, "All Shook Up," was putting an end to reports that Presley's ability to sell records had run its course. As in Toronto, the song quickly rose to the top of the charts in Ottawa. Half-page ads placed in the city newspapers by RCA advertised the new record at 89¢ for a 45 r.p.m. single and 98¢ for the 78 r.p.m. format version. The song also was drawing favorable attention to Presley's singing voice. A *Journal* article noted that the song "promises to outstrip anything he has previously recorded. An avowed hater of Presley records said, upon first hearing it, 'Maybe I've been wrong about this boy.'"[6] CKOY disc jockey Keith Sterling gave the new record a positive review. "The new record is very typically Elvis," he wrote in the *Journal*. "The 'Shook' side is a first class rocker, and 'Heartaches' moody, with a touch of recreation thrown in for good measure. Despite anything you may have heard to the contrary (and I've said some things myself), this boy is going to be around for quite some time."[7]

When Elvis performed his newest song on stage in Ottawa, the screaming that kept everyone in the auditorium from hearing it disappointed Harold Lewis, the *Journal* high school reporter. "I found this particularly disturbing," Lewis wrote of the crowd noise, "in that I have become rather fond of the fellow's singing. When Elvis merely sings and does not gyrate, he indeed has a fine voice. This is easily illustrated by listening to one of his records."[8] According to Keith Sterling, the new song's popularity was to blame for the din at Presley concerts. In his "Sterling's Hot Pops" column in the *Journal,* he wrote of "All Shook Up," "This disc is already well over the one million mark in sales and has been heard by almost every living, breathing Elvis fan on the continent. The fact that all his records are heard so often by so many people I think explains why you couldn't hear him in person last Wednesday. Most of the crowd knew what he was singing, they've heard the records time and again, so they were able to devote their time to cheering his actions on stage."

After the cancellation of Presley's April 4 booking in Montreal, a travel agency and the Canadian Pacific Railway got together to make it possible for Montreal Elvis fans to see their idol in Ottawa on April 3. Round trip train passage to Ottawa and a $3.50 ticket to Presley's 8:30 show were included in a package deal. The eight-coach CPR train, dubbed the "Presley Special" and the "Rock'n'Roll Cannonball," left Montreal with around five hundred passengers late that afternoon. At 8:05 PM it pulled into Ottawa's Union Station, where the Montrealers loaded on eight special buses that took them to the auditorium. They were back on board the train when it pulled out of the station at 11:10 PM for the run back to Montreal.

Citizen staff writer Eng Hardy, a passenger on the train, called the experience a "weird and wonderful adventure."[9] His initial fears diminished when it became apparent that not all of the passengers were "bug-eyed Bobby-soxers throbbing with passion at the thought that they'd soon be seeing their idol in the flesh." He spotted a gray-haired grandmother among the passengers, as well as fourteen-year-old Billy Luomala, who had grown to love music and Presley's style after contracting polio. The boy was traveling with his thirteen-year-old friend Fred Torak, whose mother had overruled his father's objection to his making the trip. Then there was Father Lord of Montreal's Archbishop's Palace. Trained to work with adolescents, he made the journey "to see if I can discover why young people are so strangely fascinated by this Mr. Presley." Five women in their twenties told Hardy that their boss at the Montreal office of the Royal Bank was "a doll" to let them off early that day so they could catch the train.

Even the teenage Elvis fans comprising most of the train's load surprised Hardy. "I found no obnoxious adolescents with little pointed heads, no drooly dolls or yammering yokels engaged in gooey goings on. They were just kids—well-dressed and polite, for the most part—out for a good time." As the train pulled out of Montreal, Conductor Dan Gaw felt optimistic. "These are just a bunch of healthy school kids, and I don't expect any trouble," he said. When the train arrived in Ottawa, his prophecy had been realized. "Not a single untoward incident," he reported. "Maybe some of these kids are goofy to go for Elvis, but they've got manners." That's not to say that they all kept to their seats. The train promoters provided an onboard five-piece band, and Hardy noted that kids "jitter-bugged and snake-danced in the aisles" to Elvis tunes like "Love Me," "Love Me Tender," "Blue Suede Shoes," "All Shook Up," and "Heartbreak Hotel."

Among the train's passengers were four girls, all lucky winners of free tickets in a Montreal radio station's "Why I Want to Go to Ottawa to See Elvis" contest. One of them, seventeen-year-old Micheline St. Roch, explained through an interpreter that Elvis' inability to speak French didn't bother her. "He says so much when he just looks at you," she explained, and then added in broken English, "When I hear him sing I'm all shake up—crazy as a broomstick!"

Even after arriving at the auditorium, the Montreal gang continued to impress their hosts. "They couldn't have been better," an arena staffer said. "They got pretty pushy at times, but there was nothing at all which could have been called signs of juvenile delinquency. And, believe me, that's what we expected."[10] One young man explained that he and his friends weren't there to make trouble. "We just came to hear the man sing and maybe scream and have a ball," he said. "That's what we did. We had a great time."

Back at the station after the show, kids sang and danced a bit while waiting to board the train for the trip home. The shared experience was just as memorable as seeing Elvis. "I didn't really think much of the show," one teenager told *Journal* writer Robert Stewart. "I couldn't hear Elvis sing. Of course, I liked the way he performed and smiled and all that, but it was mostly being out on a trip with all the other kids that I got my kicks from."

However, the trip from Montreal to see Elvis was most memorable, even frightening at times, to two Westhill High School students who left their homes for school on Wednesday morning and then decided to walk to Ottawa instead. Joyce Sirkett, 17, and Diane Heaybird, 15, later said they knew it was wrong to skip school but just felt they had to try to get to Ottawa for Presley's 8:30 show that night. Just outside Montreal, a passing businessman wondered if the "two little girls" he saw walking by the side of the road were in trouble. He offered them a ride and dropped them off at Union Station in Ottawa at about noon. They had made the journey with plenty of time to spare, but still faced several obstacles. They had virtually no money, and that meant no tickets to see Elvis and no way of getting back home. Their friends on the special train from Montreal were not due in until 8:00 PM. For lunch they pooled their money and asked a cigar store owner on Sparks street what they could get for four cents. After listening to their story, he gave them each a 25¢ bag of peanuts. Then Joyce and Diane went in search of Elvis. Told he was at the Beacon Arms Hotel, they asked a policeman for directions. "We almost got to see him," Diane said. "We were right at the door when a man caught us. He threw us out." That night at the auditorium the girls couldn't find their friends from Montreal, but got inside when a kindly reporter took them in on his press card. During the show they met a man who lent them $10 to get a meal and tickets home. As they boarded the train, Joyce told a *Journal* reporter, "We really love Ottawa. I've never seen such kind people. This is the best city I've ever been in."[11] The comments of the girls' parents when their daughters arrived home went unreported.

Most Ottawa citizens learned that Elvis was coming to their city when Colonel Parker's newspaper ads appeared on March 19, two weeks before the performance in the city's Memorial Auditorium on Wednesday, April 3. Since the Montreal booking had been cancelled, two shows were scheduled in Ottawa to accommodate the expected flow of fans from the Quebec city located just a two-hour drive or train ride to the northeast. Tickets for the 4:30 matinee show were priced at $2.00, $2.50, and $3.00. Seats at the 8:30 evening show were at bit higher at $2.50, $3.00, and $3.50. Mail orders were processed by the auditorium box office, which also sold tickets over the counter, as did Lindsay's Record Rendezvous.

Local promoter and record store owner Alex Sherman worked out the details with Oscar Davis, Parker's lead man in the Canadian capital. The two chose station CFRA disc jockey Gord Atkinson to introduce Elvis on stage. Hoping to learn some last-minute lessons he could apply in Ottawa, Sherman traveled to Toronto to watch Elvis perform there the night before he was due in Ottawa. After watching the show, Sherman caught the night train back to Ottawa along with Elvis and his entourage.

When the train arrived in Ottawa at 8:00 AM, a sleepy-eyed Elvis stepped off wearing a brown topcoat, velvet shirt, white shoes, and what *Citizen* reporter Bob Blackburn described as "the happy smile of a man who is internally riffling through a stack of thousand-dollar bills." Accompanied by three policemen, Presley and his personal buddies, one of whom carried his guitar and another a brown and yellow teddy bear, walked quickly down the platform. Initially, only about a half-dozen teenagers awaited his arrival, but soon the commotion attracted the attention of passers-by, including a small group of middle-aged women who began jumping up and down when Elvis walked by. He said hello to a young snack-bar employee who reached out to touch him. Cut off by a band of photographers as he tried to exit the depot by a side door, Presley wiggled through the human roadblock and climbed into the back seat of the first taxi waiting in line. As the driver gently angled around an autograph seeker, Elvis obliged the photographers by smiling through the side window of the cab.

As word of his arrival spread, fan club members abandoned their plans to line Highway 15 and went looking for Elvis instead. Teenagers trying to find Presley's hiding place besieged hotels all around town. At the Alexandra Hotel on Bank Street, about sixty teenage girls, some of them displaying their signed pledges not to participate in Elvis activities, crowded the lobby when it was rumored some musicians involved in the Presley show were staying there. But Elvis was not there, nor was he at the Lord Elgin or Chateau Laurier, where other groups of fans congregated. Two Cadillacs parked in the garage of the Beacon Arms Hotel indicated that Elvis was resting in a room upstairs, although employees there insisted they had never heard of anyone named Presley.

While Elvis slept through the morning hours, about three hundred fans arrived in town from across the border on special buses from New York, Vermont, and Maine. Other buses came from Canadian towns in all directions from Ottawa. The crowd for the late afternoon show began lining up outside Memorial Auditorium, the city's thirty-four-year-old arena located downtown at the corner of O'Connor and Argyle Streets. The *Citizen* reported, "Some of the longest sideburns seen since Gone With The Wind was filmed were on display in front of the Auditorium as the first contingent of youngsters queued up an hour before the show was scheduled to start."[12]

Meanwhile, the Canadian House of Commons met that evening in Ottawa. On the floor, John B. Hamilton, a Conservative from West York, complained that the finance minister's tax concessions included only trial items, such as removing the ten percent sales tax on things like bubble gum. "It's a zoot-suit or Elvis Presley budget," Hamilton declared. Hearing Presley's name mentioned, CCF Whip Stanley Knowles asked, "By the way, where is everybody tonight?"[13] Of the 259-member house, only 37 were present, including 2 Cabinet ministers.

Just how many members of Parliament were at the Presley show is unknown. Also hard to determine was the total attendance at Presley's two shows in Ottawa. The *Journal* reported that over 16,000 paid to see Elvis, while the *Citizen* claimed the figure was closer to 12,000, with only 3,000 in attendance for the afternoon show and a near-capacity 9,000 there in the evening. The gross box office take of $45,000 supports the *Journal's* higher estimate. At his press conference later that day, Elvis claimed that the U.S. government took 85¢ out of every dollar he made for income tax. That created the bizarre illusion that his $20,000 guaranteed fee in Ottawa would net him only $3,000, and considerably less than that after Colonel Parker took his generous share.

At showtime, groans greeted the announcement that a series of variety acts would precede Elvis on stage. There was one change in the opening act lineup in Ottawa. Comic Rex Marlowe, dancer Frankie Trent, banjo-playing comic Jimmy James, and the Jordanaires reprised their performances, but singer June Bay took the spot Pat Kelly had filled in Toronto the night before. Of the show's opening, *Journal* teenage reporter Robert Stewart noted, "The first part of the show was highly entertaining—which is the polite way of saying that we tolerated it."

At the auditorium, Elvis held his seventh press conference of the tour. Bob Burgess of the *Journal* noted that some of the questions were designed to needle Presley. "More than one person wanted to have him knock a chip off their shoulders," wrote Burgess, "but even though some of them changed the chip for a two-by-six plank when Elvis ignored the shaving, the afternoon press conference passed without an angry word from Elvis."[14]

Again Presley conceded that his popularity with teenagers might be nearing an end. "It's a very uncertain business," he said. "The end may come in a lot less than a few years. I know I gotta accept it when they stop asking for autographs, but I'll keep singing as long as they like it." He did have a fallback plan, though, in case rock 'n' roll died. "I won't cry over spilled milk," he vowed. "If I could become as good an actor as Frank Sinatra, I'd go into films seriously." Elvis was honest about how far he was from that goal. Of his movie *Love Me Tender* he admitted, "Certainly it wasn't a great movie—just average. It would've done as well without me. I didn't do a top-notch job. I was just glad of the chance to be in it."

He explained being a teenage idol had its ups and downs. "Not having any privacy gets on your nerves all right," he admitted, "but it's part of the business. That's what made me. I haven't got a beef." He was equally balanced on his opinion of Ottawa. "I haven't had a chance to see it. I slept all day. The people are real friendly, but it's a little cool outside."

As at his earlier press conferences, Elvis impressed reporters more with his demeanor than with any information he gave them. Bob Blackburn was one of those reporters. "Presley handles a press conference like a veteran statesman," he concluded. "He answers readily and intelligently, doesn't try to weasel out of questions, doesn't get huffy, and remains honest, even if it is to his disadvantage. And he tops it off with a sharp sense of humor and quick wit."[15]

As usual, Elvis gave personal but brief attention to fan club officers and contest winners at the end of the press conference. One of latter was forty-three-year-old Patricia Thomas, a winner of DJ Gord Atkinson's contest. She cried when Elvis autographed her arm, and she was still sobbing, "I met him! I met him!" later during the show in the arena.

With his two shows scheduled at 4:30 and 8:30, Elvis had plenty of time to kill in his arena dressing room between shows. He used part of that time to do something he rarely did during 1957—give personal interviews. Atkinson, whose CFRA studios were located in the "Aud," entered a hockey dressing room, where he found Elvis eating a cheese sandwich and drinking from a carton of milk. "He was a very pleasant, very polite country boy," Atkinson recalled years later. "He called me 'sir' all through the interview, and I wasn't much older than him."[16] After recording a brief interview for his radio program *Campus Corner,* Atkinson presented Elvis with a scroll proclaiming Presley "The Top Man on the Campus Corner Popularity Poll" over the past year and a half.

Mac Lipson of CKOY radio also interviewed Elvis that day. Presley seemed at ease with the one-on-one interview format. He answered Lipson's questions with long, thoughtful answers, in contrast to the short, choppy comments common in his press conferences. When Lipson suggested that many girls were after Elvis' money, the singer responded, "I have no plans for getting married. Besides, if the girl is on the chase for that, well she's on a wild-goose chase, because I can usually sense whether or not that's what they're after or not."

Another Lipson question about the controversy surrounding Presley's act drew a rambling, philosophical answer in which Presley compared his situation to that of Jesus.

> Well, there are people that like you, there are people that don't like you regardless of what field you're in. And regardless of what you do, there're gonna be people that don't like you. I mean, even if you're perfect. I mean I'm not saying, you know, that I'm perfect, because no man is perfect. But there was only one perfect man and that was Jesus Christ ... and people didn't like him. You know they killed him. And

he couldn't understand why. I mean, if everybody liked the same thing, we'd all be drivin' the same car and married to the same woman and it wouldn't work out.[17]

When Gord Atkinson walked on stage to introduce Elvis, the noise was deafening. "I'll never get an ovation like that again," confessed Atkinson. "When I introduced him, the most incredible roar went off. It lifted the roof right off." For both performances Presley wore the jacket, belt, and shoes from his gold lamé suit, dark blue slacks, and a black shirt slashed open to the breastbone. Around his neck on a silver chain hung a large gold medallion that he later said had been given him by a fan in Ottawa. He probably received the gift at his afternoon press conference and decided to wear it on stage that same day. (During the year he wore the medallion on stage three more times—in Philadelphia, Spokane, and Tupelo.)

The *Citizen* reported that when Elvis first appeared, "Girls burst into tears. Girls covered their faces, overcome with emotion. Girls and boys shrieked, exulting in this tremendous experience. One girl screamed, 'He looked right at me.' Then she started crying."[18] As Richard Jackson of the *Journal* noticed, "Most of the mob were teenagers. Girls in their thick, white bobby sox and flat-heeled white bucks, full skirts and loose, white sweaters. And boys in their jeans, jackets and jack-boots. Great conformists, the teenagers all dress so alike they might as well be wearing uniforms."[19] One of those teens was a girl named Jackie Holzman, who thirty years later became mayor of Ottawa.

Another was Monique Cadieux, who had flown in from New York with her mother just to see the show. Monique's mother was among a contingent of adults whose presence scattered throughout the arena was clearly evident. "It was no uncommon sight," noticed *Journal* teen reporter Harold Lewis, "to see 'adults' wearing gigantic 'I love Elvis' buttons, and making themselves heard above the youngsters." The *Citizen* reported, "Well-dressed matrons and dignified gents mingled with the kids to see this atomic age sensation. Some stared in awe, others in amusement."[20] One foreign diplomat, choosing to remain anonymous, claimed he was there only to study Canadian culture.

On stage, Presley sang "Love Me Tender," which Richard Jackson described as Presley's "travesty of that old Civil War love song, 'Aura Lee.'" Jackson's *Journal* review was cynical throughout.

> While Elvis is only a few years out of stove pipe pants, he has become the knowing master of the leer and lurch.
> He makes it personal.
> He puts it on an individual basis.

With what might look like, but definitely isn't, a shyly downcast glance of embarrassed modesty, he leans lovingly into his hoochy-cooch.

He even bats his big, brown, long-lashed eyes before he goes all aquiver and the girls start screaming so loud they can't hear him sing.

Not hearing him perhaps really doesn't matter so much. For he's that kind of artist to be seen rather than heard. As a singer, he's an interesting contortionist.[21]

Concerning the passionate reaction of the teenage crowd, Jackson counseled Presley not to take it any more seriously than the excitement generated at a company picnic. Jackson noted, "Elvis should hear the girls from the department shriek when Johnnie, the cute little red-headed office boy from Central Registry, and that handsome Mr. Jones, the young executive assistant to the Deputy Minister, come humping along, neck and neck, in the potato sack race at the annual August outing at Lac Philippe. The two are comparable, potato sack racing and Elvis Presley's swivel-hipped singing, for both are athletic endeavors of a sort."

The *Journal* assigned Helen Parmelee to provide a "woman's eye view" of the proceedings in the auditorium, but she came away as befuddled as Jackson. "Some wept," she observed, "some moaned; some clutched their heads in ecstasy; everybody screamed, stamped, clapped hands, flailed arms; one person got down on all fours and pounded the floor. Elvis 'sent' them. Elvis 'sent' me too—home with a bursting headache. I'm still bewildered. Last night's contortionist exhibition at the Auditorium was the closest to the jungle I'll ever get."[22]

City Police Chief Duncan MacDonell had thirty city-paid, on-duty officers in the arena for the afternoon show. The auditorium guards and off-duty police officers paid by promoters brought the total security force to a hundred. The larger evening show crowd was controlled by fifty uniformed men, along with thirty off-duty officers and a force of detectives and morality officers. Before each show began the crowd received a stern warning against standing in the aisles, jumping up and down, and running toward the stage. Several times the crowd began pressing forward, but the police kept the situation under control. One group of adults kept crowding the stage until a constable warned them, "Do that one more time and I'll throw you out of the place." Police arrested two teenage boys and charged them with disorderly conduct following two separate crowd disturbances during the evening show. Conspicuous in front of the stage was Colonel Parker, who scampered back and forth making sure nobody got near his client.

The police officers faced their greatest challenge when Presley ratcheted up the crowd during his closing number. As the singer shimmied while performing "Hound Dog," his knees got progressively closer to the stage, until they finally rested on the floor, drawing a thunderous reaction from the crowd. Three police-men and Elvis' personal security men rushed down the center aisle and pushed kids back into their seats. With a final shudder, Elvis bolted from the stage, threw his guitar into a waiting car, and was gone.

The excitement drained from the crowd as many rushed for the exits, especially those needing to catch the 11:10 train back to Montreal. As usual, some teenag-ers hung around looking for Elvis. A group doomed to disappointment gath-ered around the outside back entrance. Some boys in black jackets tried to break through the barriers and reach Presley's dressing room, but the police quickly fought off the assault, although one officer injured his arm in the struggle.

A student at Notre Dame Convent, fifteen-year-old Louise Bowie, along with most of her classmates, had signed the pledge not to attend the Presley show. She went anyway. The next day she paid the price. "I went to school," she recalled. "The nun who was my teacher asked who went and I said I went. So she called me out into the hall and she told me I was no longer welcomed at the school and that my soul was condemned to hell. I was devastated."[23] She was one of eight girls expelled for the remainder of the school year.

Although no mention of expulsion had accompanied the pledge the girls signed, the Mother Superior stated that the girls had been informed of the conse-quences if they broke it. "Parents of the students were contacted," she announced on April 8, "and asked to withdraw their daughters because by attending the Elvis Presley performance, they deliberately defied the authority of the convent."[24] She indicated that some among the punished girls were not fully to blame, since their fathers had taken them to the Presley show in open defiance of the ruling. The eight girls were not being punished specifically for attending the Presley concert, said the Mother Superior, but rather for defying school authority. She left open the possibility of the girls' being readmitted to the school in the fall.

The school's action generated some criticism in the community. One parent declared, "This is a free country and they should not be allowed to dictate to par-ents that way. I was at the Presley show myself and saw nothing wrong with it." In a letter printed in the *Citizen*, W. L. Farmer questioned the wisdom of requir-ing the pledge in the first place. "There is a real shame attached to the Ottawa school that ousted a few Presley-goers," he wrote. "Such intolerance bespeaks less maturity than the Presley fans show themselves. Teenagers must have an outlet for pent-up emotions and oft-restrained expressions in the home, the school, the church and even in the streets ... This 'let-go' of self is what Elvis is giving the teenagers—the break we have failed to create for our youngsters."[25] Another Ottawa citizen questioned the Mother Superior's right to ask for such an oath in a secular matter. "Is it a sin to see Presley?" George Phoenix asked in his letter to the *Citizen*. "Is he the possessor of some evil powers? How sadly mixed up and confused those poor nuns are! They seem to think … that the teacher's authority is not only over the children at home, but over the parents as well."[26]

Another writer, however, approved of the convent's action. Wilfrid Lefebvre wrote, "The rightful decision taken by the authority of the Convent proves that the nuns wanted to protect their students from immorality or at least not permitting them to approve by their presence the public exhibition of un-Christian and impure contortions."[27]

Meanwhile, the man at the center of the controversy was on his way to Philadelphia to close his spring tour with four more exhibitions of his "impure contortions."

Being interviewed by high school journalists in Philadelphia, April 6, 1957.
(Temple University Libraries, Urban Archives, Philadelphia PA)

Chapter 9

Philadelphia

Prelude

In the 1950s Philadelphia was, as it is today, a university town. When Elvis Presley burst on the national entertainment scene in 1956, the college crowd didn't flock to his banner. In fact, many undergraduates were downright hostile to his gyrating style. Although he was their age, Presley was not one of them. For the most part, the college students of that day had already bought into the conformity of the mid-1950s. Elvis drew his devotees primarily from the junior and senior high school population. Much like their parents, the majority of the burgeoning young adults in the nation's colleges viewed Presley as a threat to their chosen way of life.

While parents and community leaders used censorship and stinging criticism in the press to lessen Presley's influence on the nation's youth, college students lacked the political and mass media power to broadcast their disapproval of Elvis. Some fell back on the long-practiced prerogative of college kids—the prank. And so it was that soon after the March 24, 1957, announcement that Presley would perform in Philadelphia, two plots—one simple, one complex—began to form against him on two of the city's college campuses.

The straightforward conspiracy—and therefore the one most likely to succeed—was hatched by four Villanova University students. They planned to carefully stuff their pockets with raw eggs and then, at a strategic time, rise from their seats in the Sports Arena and pelt the King of Rock 'n' Roll with their gooey ammo. The key unknown factor in the plan was the distance from the stage. Could they get close enough to insure direct hits on the constantly moving target?

The more ambitious plot was the work of fifteen freshman students, ten boys and five girls, who were attending the University of Pennsylvania. The guys were all in the same fraternity and the girls shared the same sorority. The plot's objective was no less than to physically nab Presley and shave off his hair, sideburns and all.

The initial plan, discarded as too risky, called for all fifteen conspirators to rush the stage while Elvis was performing, shear off as much hair as they could, and then disappear back into the crowd. Instead, a more involved scheme to corner Presley at his hotel after the concert was adopted. Four boys were to rent a room on the same floor where the victim was staying. Meanwhile, the five girls would be sharing a room on another, nearby floor. With two of the guys, the girls would stage a phony riot designed to draw security officials away from Elvis. That would be the signal for the four boys on Presley's floor, joined by four more who would come up the back steps, to converge on Elvis' room. The eight then planned to enter the room by either picking the lock or knocking the door down. Four of the huskier boys would then hold the singer down and keep him silent, while others with shears and clippers went to work. After the phone jack was ripped out, the plotters judged they would have five minutes to shave "Mr. Sideburns" bald. To discourage pursuit, Presley's clothes would be taken away, as would a bag of hair clippings, which the perpetrators planned to sell piecemeal on campus.

When Elvis Presley arrived in Philadelphia by train from Ottawa on the morning of Friday, April 5, he had no idea of the adolescent plots focused on him. Colonel Parker's extensive security measures designed to protect his boy from such evildoers were about to be tested.

Philadelphia, Pennsylvania
Sports Arena
Friday, April 5, 1957, 7:00 pm and 9:00 pm
Saturday, April 6, 1957, 2:30 pm and 8:00 pm

Having caught a head cold in Canada's chilly weather, Elvis spent his only open date on the tour resting his voice. When Montreal officials cancelled Presley's performance, it gave the ailing singer a much-needed day off before winding up the tour with four shows in Philadelphia.

Very few in the highly populated northeast section of the country had seen Elvis Presley perform live on stage. Other than his TV performances in small New York City theaters, his only other appearance in the area had been in March 1956 aboard the *Mt. Vernon Riverboat* in Washington, D.C. Expecting to draw heavily from Philadelphia and the other untapped nearby cities of New York, Baltimore, and maybe even Boston, Parker booked his boy for four shows in Philadelphia's Sports Arena, which had a seating capacity of 6,500. A mail-order form in the town's newspapers on March 24 announced the Philadelphia shows. Over-the-counter ticket sales started at ten o'clock the next morning at Gimbels and the arena box office at Forty-fifth and Market. Tickets were priced at $2:00, $2.75, and $3.50. By Presley standards, advance sales were sluggish for the April 5 and 6 performances, and an ad in the April 6 morning issue of the *Philadelphia Inquirer* announced, "Plenty of good seats still available up to show time."

The city's newspaper columnists had little to say leading up to Presley's appearances. One civic group that did offer its view about the rock 'n' roll singer prior to his arrival was the Germantown Boys' Club. During its Boys' Club Week festivities in early April, four hundred of the group's nine-to fourteen-year-old members were asked to give their opinions of Presley. Predictably, nearly three-fourths had a decidedly negative opinion of the singer, while only about one in five gave him a positive rating. "He's just a big boy who's never grown up," responded one fourteen-year-old. An eleven-year-old added, "I think he wiggles too much and the girls are nuts to like him." Some of the positive comments by those in the minority included, "He's just a young star trying to put on a show," and "He hasn't done anything to me, and it's not wrong to make money."[1]

Of course, Elvis fan club members in the area were ecstatic at the thought of seeing their idol live on stage. Linda Deutsch, who years later became a legal correspondent for the Associated Press, recalled those exciting days during a 2002 interview on *The Early Show*. She was only twelve years old and living in Asbury Park, New Jersey, when she first heard Elvis sing "Heartbreak Hotel" on the radio in 1956. The song "stopped me dead in my tracks," remembered Linda, who with two friends later started the Official Elvis Presley Fan Club of Asbury Park. She was one of the thousands who saw Elvis perform in the Sports Arena in April 1957.

Linda and her fellow fan club members were the target of one young entrepreneur who called the arena and offered to buy the dust swept off the stage after each Presley performance. He planned to sell it later in small amounts to Elvis fan clubs. Apparently arena officials considered the man's offer frivolous and denied it.

As at other tour stops, Colonel Parker arranged with local police officials for heavy security during Elvis' shows at the arena. A force of fifty policemen and fifteen female officers, under the direction of Captain Harry Fox, were assigned to keep order inside, while Inspector Maurice Pilner's force of sixty-five highway patrolmen and foot traffic officers would watch the subways and the streets surrounding the arena.

In addition to monitoring the early arriving patrons for Presley's 7:00 PM show on Friday, the security squad closely screened the photographers, cameramen, reporters, DJs, and fan club officers who showed up an hour earlier for Presley's press conference in an arena side room. The press first assembled in the publicity room, where they received identifying ribbons allowing them to pass through the security gauntlet leading to the interview room. Jerry Gaghan of the *Daily News* estimated that about sixty people were crammed into the stuffy room awaiting Presley's arrival. Looking around, Gaghan judged that the President Eisenhower couldn't have drawn as big a crowd for a press conference.[2]

Adding to the room's already high temperature were bright Klieg lights aimed at an empty chair prepared for Elvis. When he finally entered the room, he was accompanied by what a *Philadelphia Inquirer* reporter called "four outside city detectives," who were actually Presley's Memphis traveling companions.[3] Ignoring the chair and spotlight set aside for him, Elvis instead sat on the edge of a nearby table, pulling one leg up and grabbing it with both hands.

The raised leg accentuated the contrast between his white shoes and socks and the black silk suit he was wearing. His black velvet shirt was open halfway down his chest, exposing a chain supporting a gold medallion. With a dozen microphones suddenly shoved in his face, Presley started the press conference with a disclaimer. "I haven't got to the point where I'm completely at ease with this sort of thing." Still, he disarmed those reporters expecting to face a rebellious and arrogant young man. Gaghan later described Elvis' manner as "modest and winning."

The questions probed both his professional and personal lives. Asked how long he could stay atop the music world, Presley responded, "I don't know whether I am going to last. My future is uncertain, but I simply take one day at a time and take whatever comes with each." Another reporter asked Elvis if he thought people would come to see him five years from now. "I won't predict the future," was the modest response. "They may not. People get tired of you. You don't stay hot forever." He didn't believe his, or any kind of music, for that matter, could cause juvenile delinquency. "The kids might dance and yell a bit," he allowed, "but they aren't robbing anybody." Asked whether there was a special girl in his life, he answered truthfully, "There is none—period." He went on to say he wouldn't object to getting married, even to one of his fans. "I would just have to fall in love with somebody," he explained, sheepishly adding that the quality he looked for most in a woman was that she be "female."

Once, while leaning forward, the large medallion dangling from his neck fell out of his open shirt. "That?" he said. "It was given to me last Thursday night in Ottawa. What its significance is I wouldn't know." (His memory was a day off. Presley had first worn the medallion two days before during his Wednesday night performance in Ottawa.)

After he mentioned that a girl had given him the medallion, the interview temporarily stopped while fourteen-year-old Jeanne Mount of Philadelphia came forward to present Elvis with a small brown and white teddy bear. "Thank you," said Elvis, who went on to explain that he now had a collection of over two hundred stuffed animals.

During the rest of the press conference, Presley revealed that he always got nervous on stage; he didn't mind the yelling because it covered up his mistakes; he watched a lot of TV on the road; and while at home he enjoyed "shooting pool with my pappy."

As the press conference wound down, so did the opening acts on the arena stage. Only 2,300 were on hand for the first of Presley's four-show run, but, according to Gaghan, "What this audience may have lacked in size and maturity it more than made up in noise and sustained frenzy." Anticipating Elvis' arrival, the crowd rose and cheered wildly with each introduction in the series of opening acts. Meanwhile, vendor sales were disappointing. Elvis scarves and picture books moved slowly, as did the various buttons announcing "I Like Elvis," "I Hate Elvis," and "Elvis Is a Jerk."

When Presley finally came on stage, he was still in the black silk suit he had worn at the press conference. It was one of the few times during his 1957 tours that he didn't wear the jacket from his gold lamé suit. James Smart, reviewing the show for the *Evening Bulletin,* described the bedlam that ensued as the performance commenced.

> Elvis hung a guitar over his neck. Then there followed a half-hour of rubberlegged gyrations as he poured rock'n'roll lyrics into a microphone, thrusting arms and knees at the audience.
>
> Every new gesture and wiggle brought a variance in pitch from the howl of the audience, mostly young girls. It was rare that a word could be discerned even by those standing only a few feet from the stage.
>
> There were a few breaks when Elvis sang something more sentimental, clutching the microphone close to his lips and staggering around the stage. Even when he recited tenderly a few lines of "That's When Your Heartaches Begin," he was drowned out by the crowd.
>
> As he sang "Love Me," girls throughout the Arena stood up and stretched out their arms toward the stage. Elvis grinned and kept singing …
>
> Some held their hands to the sides of their heads as though the ecstasy of seeing Elvis was sweetly painful. One girl stopped screaming, sat down and wept quietly as Elvis concluded his concert with "You Ain't Nothing but a Hound Dog."[4]

Beyond the screaming, there was little commotion to trouble the security contingent. From time to time police officers blocked the path of girls running down the aisles toward the stage. One girl wearing a black leather motorcycle jacket and a red sweater would not be discouraged by the police blockade and had to be led to the rear of the arena. The only time the crowd challenged the security force came during Presley's final number. "When he went into an arm-flailing, hip-wiggling, floor-crawling finale with 'Hound Dog,'" observed Jerry Gaghan in his *Daily News* article, "the hysterical mob broke out of its seats. Fortunately, there were enough cops and plainclothesmen guarding every aisle to get them all back again."

Saturday's afternoon and evening shows were more of the same. Presley was back wearing his gold jacket and shoes, along with a white satin shirt and black pants. According to Joseph P. Barrett of the *Bulletin,* the final Saturday evening performance drew a seemingly older crowd than had Elvis' three previous shows. "There were more couples on dates, and more parents with children," observed Barrett, who nevertheless added, "There was hundreds of teen-age girls, too, and they accompanied Presley with their customary ear-piercing shrieks."[5]

A series of photographs circulated by United Press chronicled the emotions of Philadelphia teen Penny Taylor as she witnessed the show from her front-row seat. At the start of Presley's show, Penny constrained her passion by chewing on her Elvis fan club hat. Later she could be seen crying into the hat, and as her idol finished his act and made his getaway, she slipped off her chair to the floor in a state of exhaustion.

Linda Deutsch and her friends experienced it all from their seats far up in the back of the Sports Arena. From there Elvis was only a "teeny-weeny wiggling speck" on the stage to Linda, who nevertheless felt the incredible energy. She described it as the "closest I'd ever felt to an earthquake." One of Deutsch's friends was crying. "He looked at me!" she explained. For Linda that was the "magic" of Elvis Presley. "Everyone thought he looked at them," she said.

Although Elvis made his usual quick exit after the show, it nearly wasn't fast enough. Twenty police officers escorted Presley out to Forty-fifth Street, where an automobile waited at the curb. A group of fifty girls nearby saw Elvis exit the building and battled the police to get near their idol. Their yelling attracted other groups of girls, who rushed to the scene. As Presley's car drove away, the horde of girls pursued it down the street for more than a block before giving up the chase.

Ticket sales for Presley's four-show run in Philadelphia were a letdown. The Sports Arena had a capacity of 6,500, meaning the four shows had the potential of drawing a total of 26,000 Presley fans. Instead, there were no sellouts and a couple of disappointingly small crowds. According to reporters, the arena was less than half full for both Friday shows, with the afternoon show being estimated at about 2,300, or one-third capacity. At 5,329, Saturday night's performance drew the largest crowd in the two-day, four-show run. Even so, it was not enough to keep the promoters from losing money in Philadelphia. The crowds from the two days might have totaled enough to fill up the Sports Arena twice, but not four times. The gross take of $41,000 at the box office barely covered Presley's $10,000 per show guarantee, leaving local organizers to pay the venue and security costs out of their own pockets.

The hopes of Colonel Parker and the local promoters of drawing Presley fans to Philadelphia from all along the Northeast corridor from Washington to New York did not materialize. The case of Marion Shanhart of Rochester, New York, partially explains the reason. Without her parents' knowledge, the fourteen-year-old left her home at 4:00 AM Saturday morning and boarded a bus for the thirteen-hour trip to Philadelphia. Her $14 was just enough to pay for the bus ride and a ticket to see Elvis that evening. Those who arranged for Presley to do so many shows in Philadelphia should have realized that most of the singer's out-of-town fans, while as young as Marion, were not as resourceful and as determined as she. In nearby cities there were surely thousands of teenagers who wanted to go to Philadelphia to see Elvis. To get there, however, they needed their parents' permission and transportation assistance, and for most, once the first was denied, the second was no longer an issue. As for Marion Shanhart, her plan included a way of getting back home to Rochester, even though she was out of money. After Elvis' show ended at about 10:15 Saturday night, she turned herself in to the police. Her parents were called, and they arranged to pick her up the next morning. She spent the night in a girls' shelter in Philadelphia.

Marion's defiance of her parents would not have surprised Rev. W. Carter Merbreier, the pastor of St. Matthew's Lutheran Church in Philadelphia. As a delegate of the Police Juvenile Aid Bureau, he attended two of Presley's shows in the city. Viewing the spectacle through Biblical eyes, the pastor had harsh words for the young girls he saw there. In a *Daily News* article, he described how he was surrounded in the arena by "nervous, giggling girls who went so far as to even kiss the hand that shook the hand ... Screaming, falling to their knees as if in prayer, flopping limply over seats, stretching rigidly, wriggling in a supreme effort of ecstasy."[6]

Merbreier likened it to Moses descending from Sinai to find the children of Israel worshipping the Golden Calf. "A mere flick of this boy's thumb increased a shattering sound which seemed unincreasable," he explained. "By leaning his body to the right or to the left, he brought forth a new burst of frenzy. Every act and gesture of the girls in the arena were, without question, forms of actual worship."

The most abrasive part of Merbreier's sermon, however, was aimed at the girls' parents.

To condemn these teen-agers is to more strongly condemn those idiotic parents who would permit their children to participate in such an emotional orgy.

Indeed, any parent that would allow a daughter to leave the house dressed without regard for dignity and even morality, as were some of these youngsters, should have their heads examined.

As for the college pranks that had been planned before Elvis came to town, both were flops. The first was exposed before Presley even arrived in the city. A banner headline in the *Daily News* blared, "Dear Elvis: We Foiled a Hair Raid." In what read like a tabloid story, the writer told Elvis, "You're safe now. Thanks to the *Daily News*. Our reporters unearthed a dark and devious plot that, if successful, would have made Yul and Zsa Zsa (no mean baldies themselves) more than envious."[7] An unnamed source, it seems, called a *Daily News* reporter to a meeting on the Penn campus behind Houston Hall near Thirty-sixth Street. There, from behind a bush, a "mystery man" revealed the details of the plot to deprive Elvis of his hair sometime during the weekend. Names of the conspirators were not revealed, making it seem the schemers' goal may not have been actually to clip Presley's hair but rather just to get some publicity for the frat house.

When asked about it that evening at his press conference, Elvis seemed to think the plot was genuine. "I read that and I don't see no point in it at all," Presley responded. "They're college men—supposed to be tomorrow's leaders. What are they trying to prove?"

He might have asked the same of the four Villanova University students who walked into his Saturday night show with their pockets full of raw eggs. Elvis was just ten minutes into his performance when, at about 9:40 PM, a salvo of a half-dozen eggs flew toward the stage. Gordon Stoker remembers that Elvis and the Jordanaires saw the incoming eggs. "Elvis dodged and we dodged, but one egg hit the neck of Scotty's guitar. Boy, it made Elvis mad, real mad. He said, 'One more egg and we leave the stage immediately.' "[8]

The egging dominated the press coverage of Presley's second day in Philadelphia. The *Inquirer's* headline read, "Elvis Egged at Arena—'Gittar' Gets the Yolk." Newspaper accounts certainly indicate that Presley was angry but do not mention a threat to leave the stage. The Sunday *Bulletin* reported that Elvis' "face darkened into a frown, but he managed to finish his song, 'All Shook Up.'" Then, with his eyes flashing, he pointed to Scotty Moore and addressed the crowd. "He got egg on his guitar," he announced. "Whoever threw that will never make the Yankees." After a moment's pause, which did not cool his ire, the singer again faced the crowd. "Most of you people came here to enjoy the show. The guy who threw the egg will never make it. I mean it, Jack. We're just trying to put on a nice show."[9] The *Inquirer* claimed Presley called the egg-thrower an "idiot" and said, "I'm ready for him any time."[10]

Meanwhile, in the audience Presley loyalists quickly identified the perpetrators. When police got to the balcony, fingers from all directions pointed at four young men. Broken eggs were found at their feet, suggesting an attempt to destroy evidence. Police confiscated one intact egg found in the pocket of one of the boys. The four were immediately taken from the arena to the police station at Fifty-fifth and Pine Streets. There they were jailed on disorderly conduct charges.

The four were identified as William Quinn, 20, of New York City; William B. Oates, 21, of Brooklyn; James Stark, 20, of Greenport, NewYork; and John Eidt, 20, of New York City. After Presley's concert ended, *Bulletin* reporter Joseph Barrett made his way to the police station to interview the accused. Quinn admitted that he had an egg in his pocket, but he and the other three all denied that they had thrown eggs at the stage. "We don't like Elvis," Quinn said. "But we went to see what he is like. He is repulsive. He's all right for the teen-agers. The egg was thrown from behind us. I think it came from some Penn students."[11]

The four spent the night in jail, but landed sunnyside up the next morning when they were released with a warning after a hearing before Magistrate William A. Cibotti. An unidentified policeman at the station was disappointed in the four, however. "The only thing I'm mad about," he said, "is that they missed Elvis."[12]

That same morning, Elvis was preparing to leave Philadelphia. His ten-day, fifteen-show tour over, he was soon on a southbound train. He had another movie to make, and that would be followed by a long, leisurely summer vacation in Memphis. He wouldn't take his act on the road again until the fall.

Arriving at Great Northern depot, Spokane, Washington, August 29, 1957.

Chapter 10

Car 312

When Elvis Presley prepared to leave Memphis on August 27 for his Pacific Northwest tour, he had 5,617 miles of travel ahead of him before he would return to his hometown fifteen days later. The first leg was the longest—nearly 2,100 miles up the heartland of the country and across the northern plains states to Spokane, Washington. A commercial airline could have taken Elvis to Spokane in half a day. Yet he chose to make the trip by train, which stretched out the journey to more than two full days.

It wasn't that Presley enjoyed the leisurely nature of train travel; in fact, he found it both tiring and boring. But it was the next best alternative for him after he decided to stop flying. Over long distances, the train offered a greater degree of safety than traveling by car. (That summer Elvis had been shaken by the death of his *Jailhouse Rock* co-star Judy Tyler and her husband in an automobile collision on a Wyoming highway on July 3, just eight weeks before Elvis left for his Pacific Northwest tour.) In addition, Elvis found train travel offered more privacy and was less confining than traveling by car. Gone were the days when Elvis, Scotty, and Bill would cram themselves and their gear into a car and drive night and day across the South from one small venue to another. Now Elvis could afford to occupy an entire Pullman car to shield him and his entourage from the other passengers on the train and from the crowds that tended to gather at stations along the way. By 1957, whether he was on tour or traveling back and forth between Hollywood and Memphis, Elvis preferred rail travel.

Elvis had no instinctive fear of flying. In fact, in 1956, as his career first blossomed and then exploded, Elvis flew often. To meet his frequent personal appearance obligations, he traveled by car when he could, as he had done almost exclusively in 1954 and 1955. However, by 1956 the complexity of his commitments often made car transportation impossible. Booked into a North Carolina town one night, he had to be in New York for the Dorsey show the next night. The night after that he was due in Tampa to start a new tour of Florida. As the weekend neared, he had to get to Shreveport to fulfill his contract with *The Louisiana Hayride*. Back to New York. Off to Hollywood for a screen test. Home to Memphis. Back on the road. Hollywood again to film *Love Me Tender*. Taking to the air was the only way to make his 1956 schedule work.

During that year he flew over forty times. He flew into Shreveport, New York, Norfolk, Tampa, Nashville, Charleston, Minneapolis, San Antonio, Waco, Tulsa, Kansas City, and Houston. Out west he flew into Los Angeles, San Diego, Las Vegas, Denver, and Oakland. When he had a few days off, Elvis flew back to Memphis to be with his parents.

By the dawn of 1957, though, Presley had developed a full-blown fear of flying. In November of that year, he traveled by ship from Los Angeles to Hawaii for his last three concerts of the 1950s. During a shipboard press conference held upon his arrival, he was asked why he had come by ship while his band and the Jordanaires had flown over. "I don't like airplanes," Presley explained. "I'm scared stiff of them." That fear could be traced to two incidents that occurred in 1956.

The singer's faith in flight was first shaken on April 13, 1956. In a much-recounted incident, Elvis and his musicians boarded a chartered plane in Amarillo for a flight to Nashville, where they had a recording session scheduled the next morning. First, the pilot made an unplanned landing at an airstrip near El Dorado, Arkansas. Shortly after taking off at dawn, the plane's engine sputtered and died. One of the plane's fuel tanks had not been filled; but as soon as the pilot switched over to the alternate tank, the engine restarted and the flight was completed without further incident. Presley biographer Peter Guralnick reports that when Elvis got off of the plane in Nashville, he told Scotty and Bill, "Man, I don't know if I'll ever fly again."

Of course, Presley did fly again, many more times during the year, since his far-flung contractual obligations could only be met in that way. However, a couple of months later, another incident caused Elvis to immediately cut back on flying.

On June 30, 1956, the day before Presley appeared on Steve Allen's network TV show, two passenger airliners collided over the Grand Canyon. Both planes, a United Airlines DC-7 and a TWA Constellation, were flying from Los Angeles to Chicago. All seventy passengers on the TWA plane and the fifty-eight passengers on the United plane died.

The next morning, after Elvis arrived at Penn Station in New York City, photographer Alfred Wertheimer snapped a picture of Presley looking at the morning edition of the *Sunday Mirror*. A huge banner headline filled half of the front page.

2 Airlines
Missing
127 Aboard

Coming so soon after the troubling flight to Nashville, the Grand Canyon tragedy furthered Elvis' growing apprehension about flying. Instead of flying out of New York, as he had done after his Dorsey Brothers show bookings earlier in the year, he rode a train out of the city on July 3, two days after his appearance on *The Steve Allen Show.* At twenty-seven hours, the ride home to Memphis was his first long-haul train ride.

By the fall of 1957, Elvis had developed an intense aversion to traveling by air. During an interview in September before his appearance at the *Mississippi-Alabama Fair and Dairy Show,* a reporter from the *London Daily Express* asked Elvis about the chances of his crossing the Atlantic. "I'd like to go to England—if I could go on a ship," he responded hesitantly. "If something were to go wrong on a plane, there's no land under you. That's a long swim."

Certainly, Elvis' mother Gladys, who always worried about her son's safety, would have been more concerned about the dangers of her son flying than would Elvis himself. Lamar Fike, taken into Presley's entourage in 1957, claims that Elvis promised his mother that he would not fly again unless it was absolutely necessary. And it would be necessary several more times during 1956. During the making of the film *Love Me Tender,* Elvis took commercial flights to Los Angeles twice, and on October 25 he flew into New York for his appearance on *The Ed Sullivan Show.* That latter flight would be Elvis Presley's last for three and a half years. During that span, he traveled all across the U.S. by train, crossed the Pacific Ocean to Hawaii and the Atlantic Ocean to Europe by ship, and drove around Germany and France. But he did not fly again until March 2, 1960, when he flew from Germany via Scotland to Fort Dix, New Jersey, near the end of his two-year stint in the army.

Except for his sea voyages to and from Hawaii in November, Elvis used the train as his main intercity mode of travel while touring during 1957. Since his stage schedule was tight, usually requiring him to perform nightly in cities hundreds of miles apart, Presley spent much of his touring time aboard trains. Rail travel posed challenges for Elvis, the biggest being the difficulty of dealing with fans clogging the station when he arrived in a city. Even the way he chose to interact with his fellow passengers and the crowds that gathered on the platforms of small towns along the way, while not a big security concern, had public relations implications for Elvis. A close look at the singer's rail journey from Memphis to

Spokane to open his Labor Day weekend tour shows what train travel was like for Presley in 1957.

The evening of August 27, 1957, Elvis, with girlfriend Anita Wood on his arm, walked briskly into Central Station in Memphis. He had come to embark on what would be his next-to-last concert tour of the decade. Elvis and Anita arrived at the station in a black Cadillac, along with his parents and his traveling companions, George Klein, Cliff Gleaves, and Lamar Fike. Elvis' uncle Travis Smith and his wife followed in a separate car. Also on hand for the unannounced departure were about twenty-five young fans and a few reporters and photographers.

A reporter asked Elvis about Anita, a Memphis television personality and a winner of the *MidSouth Star Hunt* the previous week. "Anita is number one with me—strictly tops," Elvis announced, before kissing the nineteen-year-old blonde in a scene that was captured by cameramen and sent around the country as an AP wire photo. Elvis kissed his girl twice for the photographers and "about five times for himself," according to a *Press-Scimitar* article.[1]

After Elvis embraced his parents several times, he boarded the train. "Be good, son," admonished his mother, and his father added, "Take care of yourself, boy." Elvis waved as the train pitched forward. Three young girls in the front of the crowd began crying. "Three whole weeks," moaned one. "I can't stand it—I'll just die!" As Anita too began to cry, Gladys Presley put an arm around her and they turned to walk back to the waiting Cadillac. Even Uncle Travis was moist-eyed.

Elvis' first tour stop would not be in one of the small backwater southern towns he often played when first starting out with Sun Records in 1954, nor would it be in one of the great cities of the Midwest, whose concert halls he had sold out since making it big with RCA Records in 1956. Instead, Elvis and his entourage changed trains in Chicago and headed west across the northern tier of the country. His destination was a part of the country that Elvis had never toured—the Pacific Northwest. The first stop on the tour would be Spokane, Washington.

Elvis left Memphis at 11:25 PM on the *Panama Limited,* an Illinois Central Railroad all-sleeper train that stopped in Memphis on its way from New Orleans to Chicago. At nine o'clock the next morning, the train pulled into Chicago's Central Station. During a five-hour holdover, the Presley group moved over to a car reserved for them on the Great Northern Railroad's *Empire Builder,* which operated daily between Chicago and Seattle. At 2:00 PM the train pulled out of Chicago heading northwest. Crossing into Minnesota in the early evening, the train made its scheduled stops in St. Paul at 8:45 PM and Minneapolis at 9:35.

As the *Empire Builder* rolled across the state of North Dakota, there were stops in the darkness at small towns to drop off and pick up passengers. Just after dawn, the train pulled into the station in Williston, North Dakota, where it passed out of the Central Time Zone into the Mountain Time Zone. Passengers were reminded to turn their watches back one hour, from 7:30 AM to 6:30.

At Williston, a retired gentleman boarded the westbound train. When Elvis got off in Spokane, the man continued on to Seattle, where he made connections for his final destination of Vancouver, B.C. Presley caught up to him in the Canadian city a day later. There the press criticized Elvis roundly after a breakdown in security caused him to end his Vancouver concert early. It's doubtful that the Williston passenger attended the concert, but he nevertheless felt compelled to defend the boy from Memphis. His letter, signed only "Retired," appeared in the *Vancouver Sun.*

> I had the pleasure of traveling from Williston, N.D., on the same train as Elvis and his troupe, and found him to be a down-to-earth young chap, with fine associates. Nothing high-hat about him.
>
> Any hoodlumism shown here should be laid at the feet of the parents, and I am not a teenager. I am over 60 and like to look back on my own youth when I enjoyed Rudy Vallee, Valentino, Warren Kerrigan, etc. True, we did not have sound movies then, but on Saturdays in the theatre we must have sent many a theatre manager prematurely grey with our wild antics. And I don't think I am depraved. Have just retired from government service, and think the younger generation is tops.[2]

Since Elvis told a reporter in Spokane that he ate his meals on the train just like the rest of the passengers, there is a good chance the rock 'n' roller and the retiree crossed paths in the dining car. Wherever it happened, Presley did something on the *Empire Builder* to impress the senior citizen from North Dakota.

As the train rolled on westward, news of its famous passenger preceded it, and crowds began to form at the stations in the Montana towns where the train made brief scheduled stops. A large group waited at the Great Northern Railway station in Havre, a town of about ten thousand inhabitants. By the time the *Empire Builder* pulled into Havre on time at 12:30 PM, a crowd the length of the platform and thirty deep filled the boarding area. B. A. Swisher of Whitefish, Montana, a conductor with forty-two years of service on the line, was there waiting to board the train and go on duty. "It's the biggest I've ever seen in the Havre station," he said of the crowd. Reporter L. A. Bach of the *Havre Daily News* estimated that about 50 percent of the crowd consisted of teenagers, 40 percent were younger kids, and the rest were adults.[3]

Three Havre police officers—Leon Davidson, Ed Divish, and Woodrow McLain—were at the depot to keep the crowd under control during the train's scheduled twenty-minute stop. They were completely swallowed up, however, when the crowd learned that Elvis was in car number 312. The mass shifted and compacted in front of the designated car as everyone hoped to see the singer make an appearance.

The only Havre resident to see Elvis that day, however, was Hill County Sheriff Deputy Al Halladay, whose aggressiveness earned him two autographs and a short conversation with Presley. While the crowd pressed toward the windows of car 312, Halladay boarded the train one car closer to the front. "I told the conductor that I wanted Presley's autograph for a kid, and then he took me to the compartment," Halladay told a *Havre Daily News* reporter later that day. "I was taken through the car to 312 to Presley's compartment. What looked like strongmen were posted outside the compartment."

Allowed inside, Halladay found Elvis dressed in dark robe over light-colored pajamas and bedroom slippers. Presley was drinking a glass of orange juice from a breakfast tray when Halladay approached him. Although the deputy explained that he wanted an autograph for a child, at first Elvis resisted the request. "I'm pretty tired," he told Halladay. But then he agreed. Taking the fountain pen that Halladay offered, Elvis picked up a Great Northern coaster off his breakfast tray and wrote "Elvis Presley" on it. That satisfied Halladay, but not the singer. Deciding his first signature was too light, Elvis took back the coaster and signed his name again, darker this time.

Meanwhile, out on the platform, the crowd grew restless as the end of the twenty-two-minute stopover time neared and Presley had yet to appear. One passenger appeared on the steps leading up to car 312 and announced that Elvis was asleep in his compartment. Naturally, the crowd took that as their cue to wake up the celebrity, and so the chant "We want Elvis!" began. As the *Empire Builder* pulled slowly out of the station, the chant began to die down, finally being replaced by a low rumble of disappointment. One of those who then turned and walked away was Havre Mayor James Davey, who had patiently stood on the station pavement in front of car 312 to officially greet the pop idol should he come out to acknowledge his assembled fans.

Before leaving Presley's compartment, Deputy Halladay asked Elvis why he didn't acknowledge the Havre crowd waiting outside. Elvis responded that he was too exhausted from the riotous greeting he had received when the train passed through Minneapolis. It was a flimsy excuse, considering that the train had left that city fifteen hours earlier, more than enough time for Elvis to recover from any fatigue caused by his fans in Minnesota. No excuse was needed anyway, since the truth would have served just as well. Having just gotten out of bed, Elvis understandably didn't want to appear before the Havre crowd in his PJs. A professional photographer was there taking pictures for the *Havre Daily News,* and a good shot of the rock 'n' roll star in his nightwear would have been on the AP newswire within the hour. Still, in Havre that day the usually accommodating Presley certainly lost some fans who couldn't understand why he couldn't have shown his face through the window of his compartment at the very least.

The scenario was repeated later that afternoon when the *Empire Builder* made a brief stop at Shelby, Montana. There most schools excused their students for the afternoon so that they could fill the station platform and line the tracks to see their idol as he passed through. When Presley remained hidden again, an angry Shelby resident sent a blistering letter to the *Spokesman-Review* in Spokane.

> What a let-down! Mr. Presley wasn't even gentleman enough to appear. He had the shades pulled!
>
> I hope Elvis remembers—it was the people who brought him fame, and they can take it away just as quickly. No one is so big that he can't be broken.
>
> I have bought and worn out every record he has ever made. I waited an hour and a half, just to see him. He's definitely lost me and many more fans today. Serves him right! When he's too good for the people, they are too good for him.
>
> Was it too much effort for Elvis, after all the gyrations he goes through while singing, to walk to the door, so we could at least say we had seen the great Elvis?
>
> When Floyd Patterson came through, he even gave autographs. Do prize fighters have better manners than singers? Apparently some people appreciate their fans.[4]

With car 312 in tow, the *Empire Builder* crawled westward, making numerous stops at small western Montana communities during the afternoon of Thursday, August 29. It passed along the southern edge of Glacier National Park, making its final Montana stops at Whitefish and Libby before crossing into Idaho close to the Canadian border as the sun dropped low in the western sky ahead. Turning southwest now, the train made its only stop in the Idaho panhandle at Sandpoint. At about 11:00 PM, car 312 crossed out of Idaho and into Washington State. The station in Spokane was only twenty minutes away.

As the end of the long journey neared, Presley's security men prepared for the difficulties that arriving in a city always presented for their boss. There seemed to be no way for Elvis to avoid the assembled multitude waiting for him in Spokane, as he had at the Montana stops. After all, an article in the *Spokesman-Review* that morning had tipped off his fans. "Wanna know a big secret?" the writer asked. "Rock'n'Roll star Elvis Presley is due in Spokane at 11:20 tonight aboard the Empire Builder."

When the train reached the Great Northern depot on time, first onto the platform were Presley's bodyguards, charged with checking out the situation and devising a strategy for getting Elvis around the crowd and out of the station. They must have been surprised to find only fifteen to twenty fans on hand to greet Presley. The small turnout certainly made it easier for Elvis to exit the station, but he probably was a little disappointed. As he told a TV reporter in Portland a few days later, "If you come into a place and there's nobody there to meet you, you start wondering, you know."[5]

Two factors contributed to the small turnout in Spokane. First, there was no guarantee that Presley would disembark the train at the station. The same *Review* article that gave away the train's arrival time contained a disclaimer offered by Jack Engerman of Northwest Releasing Corporation, which had the booking for the Northwest tour. "What happens when information like that leaks out," said Engerman of Elvis' arrival details, "is that a lot of people turn out to meet Presley. But for security reasons his train is usually stopped outside of town and he finishes his trip in a car."[6] Believing that smoke screen, then, many Spokane Presley fans may have decided that waiting at the downtown station would be a waste of time.

The other cause of the low station turnout was the city's conservative disposition. Although school would not open until the following week, it was Thursday, a work night, and no doubt many parents were unwilling to transport their young daughters downtown for a late-night wild-goose chase, especially for the likes of Elvis Presley.

A *Spokesman-Review* reporter at the station asked Presley a few questions about the long train ride from Memphis. The singer responded that the trip had been "very enjoyable," and that he had taken his meals "just like regular folks" in the dining car. "We had some nice crowds along the way," Presley volunteered rather disingenuously, considering how he had disappointed the gatherings in Montana.

When Elvis stepped onto the platform at the Great Northern depot in Spokane, almost exactly 50 hours and 2,095 miles had passed since he had started his rail journey in Memphis two nights before. In terms of time and distance, it would be the longest single point-to-point land trip in Elvis Presley's lifetime.

At Spokane press conference with KNEW disc jockeys Bob Hough, Bob
Salter, Bob Adkins, and Bob Fleming on August 30, 1957. (Courtesy Bob
Hough)

Chapter 11

Spokane

Prelude

Colonel Parker was taking a big chance booking his boy into the far north-west corner of the U.S. During the 1950s, the Pacific Northwest was among the most culturally and politically conservative sections of the country. As was true everywhere else, rock 'n' roll was making inroads with the teenage segment of the population, but parents still controlled the money and their children's actions. Fourteen-year-old girls were the largest demographic group that attended Elvis' 1957 concerts, and they couldn't attend Presley shows without their parents' consent and ticket-buying power.

In the late 1950s there was only a trace of the cultural liberalism that a decade later would dominate the Pacific corridor from Vancouver, B.C., south through Seattle to Portland. Jimi Hendrix and Pat O'Day, two men who would transform Seattle into a center of the country's rock music and concert scene within a decade, were unknowns in 1957. The banner of rock 'n' roll music in the Northwest then was being held up by the sheer will of a few disc jockeys, like Red Robinson in Vancouver, B.C., and Dick Novak in Portland. That summer it seemed that Colonel Parker, known more as a money-maximizer than a visionary, had mis-calculated in sending Elvis thousands of miles diagonally across the country into culturally hostile territory.

The decision to tour the Pacific Northwest was questionable not only for cultural reasons but also for financial ones. Given the limited time for personal appearances in 1957, Parker could have toured his mega-star in several other regions that offered a greater potential for acceptance, as well as for the higher financial reward that was so dear to the Colonel's heart. Texas and Florida were two states that had brought out huge Presley crowds in 1956 and surely could have done so again in 1957. Then there was the Northeast corridor. It contained some large cities, including Baltimore, New York, and Boston, in which Elvis had never appeared in concert. The potential there for huge crowds far outstripped anything Parker could hope to draw in the Northwest.

Still, it was to distant cities in Washington, Oregon, and British Columbia that Colonel Parker sent the The Elvis Presley Show over the Labor Day weekend of 1957. Never one to act without deliberation, Parker had his reasons for the Northwest tour. For one thing, he knew that his twenty-two-year-old client could not hope to avoid being drafted into the army much longer, and that touring would not be possible for at least two years after that. There were potential advantages in booking Elvis into the Northwest in 1957. In exposing the entertainer for the first time to that growing section of the country, Parker may have been forsaking some immediate income in hopes of solidifying Presley's popularity there after the army years. The emotional fix of seeing the rocker live might keep the Presley fire alive in the hearts of his teenage fans as they began crossing over into adulthood while their idol was away in the army. Judging from the testimony of many Northwest Elvis fans fifty years later, that is exactly what happened.

Parker had reason to believe a solid foundation for future Presley fans already existed in the Pacific Northwest in 1957. All he had to do was check the membership roles of Elvis Presley fan clubs in the region. Such clubs in the Pacific Northwest were particularly well organized by the summer of 1957. In the Puget Sound area alone there were fan clubs in Everett, Anacortes, Bremerton, Tacoma, Port Orchard, and Renton, as well as three in Seattle. With the help of Seattle DJ Bob Salter, RCA's Seattle representative Wally Tolles arranged for all the local clubs to be brought together under an umbrella organization called the Elvis Presley Fan Clubs of Western Washington. No added dues were required, and anyone could join, although local clubs were cautioned to be wary of fifth columnists. In addition, Tolles encouraged fan clubs to have representatives in all local high schools to facilitate the recruitment of new members. The combined membership of the Puget Sound clubs numbered over 15,000 seventh-through twelfth-graders. About a third of the members were boys. Colonel Parker could count on a high percentage of these fan-clubbers buying tickets for a Presley appearance in Seattle.

Meanwhile, 175 miles to the south along Interstate 5, Presley fans in Portland also were organized. Fifteen-year-old Carol Fraser headed one club with 1,400 members, including 400 college students, many of them attending Portland's ultra-conservative Reed College on the city's southeast side. Mitzi La Chapel led another fan club with 900 members. Both clubs had branches all over the state of Oregon.

Colonel Parker needed the support of all the fan clubs and more to fill the venues lined up for the five stops on Presley's Pacific Northwest tour. All five appearances were booked into outdoor facilities, four of them high-capacity football and baseball stadiums. Elvis had played stadiums before, most notably the Cotton Bowl in Dallas, but such outdoor Presley stage shows were rare in 1956-1957.

After making the big time, Presley performed in the open air only about a dozen times, and most of those were in amphitheaters, small ballparks, and fairgrounds arenas. The rest of Presley's more than 150 personal appearances in those two years took place indoors in low-to medium-capacity theaters, arenas, auditoriums, and coliseums.

In the Northwest, Elvis faced the difficulties of performing outdoors for potentially large crowds at every stop. Using outdoor stadiums was risky for two reasons. Rain, just as common in the Northwest then as it is now, could dampen attendance, as well as the excitement the Presley stage act was designed to create. Even if the weather cooperated, there was the challenge of filling the large number of seats in the huge stadiums. Could Elvis sell out four stadiums, all of which had a seating capacity of more than 20,000, in four days? If he could, security would become an enormous problem. If he couldn't, public relations would become a problem. "Sold out" was the box office term Colonel Parker wanted associated with an Elvis Presley appearance. Many critics had long been predicting that Presley was a fad that would soon pass, and empty seats in the Pacific Northwest might be used to support their theory. As it turned out, in the Northwest Colonel Parker was more prepared for the public relations problem than he was for the security problem.

No doubt Parker would have preferred indoor venues for Presley's Northwest tour, but indirectly he forced local promoters to go outdoors. There were appropriate indoor facilities in all five cities. However, the limited seating capacity in those arenas, even if sold out, would not have allowed Northwest Releasing Corporation of Seattle to meet Presley's high cash guarantee under Lee Gordon's agreement with the Colonel, let alone make additional money. Therefore, the local promoter's only hope of making a profit was to go with the large outdoor stadiums in each of the five communities.

Spokane, Washington
Memorial Stadium
Friday, August 30, 1957, 8:30 pm

Located in central eastern Washington State, Spokane is 20 miles from the Idaho border to the east, 280 miles from Seattle to the west, and 2,400 miles from Elvis Presley's hometown of Memphis. In 1957 Spokane's population was estimated at 189,000, making it the second-largest city in the state. Spokane was a conservative city in every sense, including in its taste in entertainment. The city's favorite son was Bing Crosby, who grew up immersed in the area's conservative values from age three until leaving for Hollywood in 1925 at age twenty-two. America's most popular singer from the 1930s into the 1950s, Crosby rose to stardom with a personality that was as gentle and smooth as his singing voice. Spokane's elders were still comfortable with that in 1957.

But by the mid-1950s, rock 'n' roll music had begun rocking the boat in this all-American city. KNEW was the first Spokane radio station to start playing the new music, and soon seemingly every teenager in town tuned in to it. At age twenty-seven, Bob Hough came to Spokane in 1955 to play records on KNEW. "Everyone took to rock 'n' roll music like it was manna from heaven," he remembers. "Oh man, we thought it was great. I mean, we could do no wrong."[1] In the ratings race, the station soon overtook KREM, which had been the city's leading station for years. Bob Temple, KREM's manager, resisted airing rock 'n' roll records, seeing the musical style as a fad that would fade away in a few months. In 1957, Bob Salter left KJR, KNEW's sister station in Seattle, to run the Spokane station. It was Salter who handled the promotion for Elvis Presley's appearance in the city later that year.

Spokane's teenagers were not just listening to rock 'n' roll in 1957; some of them were playing it. Dick Baker graduated from North Central High School that year and played the drums in Spokane's first rock 'n' roll band, The Blue Jeans. "After rock 'n' roll first got started in Spokane," Dick recalls, "the girls screamed at us, like you'd see on TV. We signed autographs. It was kinda fun."[2] The Blue Jeans musicians were among the thousands in the stands when Elvis appeared at Memorial Stadium on the evening of August 30.

The citizens of Spokane, especially the teenagers, reacted with disbelief when they learned on August 9 that Elvis Presley was coming to the Inland Empire. Presley was then, after all, the most famous entertainer in the world. His latest single, "Teddy Bear," was at the top of the charts, and having just finished filming his third movie, *Jailhouse Rock*, Elvis was a top box office draw in theaters. And yet, he really was coming to Spokane. Local teenage girls bubbled in anticipation while their parents braced for the fallout.

When the performance date of August 29 was announced, a group of city businessmen was particularly disappointed. The Spokane Valley Chamber of Commerce had an event of their own scheduled for that date, and they didn't appreciate Presley's interfering with it. Rather than trying to reschedule the event, chamber president Delbert M. Stelljes decided instead to send Elvis a letter.

Dear Sir:
It was recently brought to our attention that your scheduled appearance in Spokane will be in direct conflict with our annual "All-Valley Night" promotion.

"All-Valley," which is a 100 per cent jaycee-sponsored project, is an attempt on our part to raise funds which will be used exclusively to light a baseball field for our Little League baseball players. The success of our project depends entirely upon the attendance which we can draw at the "All-Valley" baseball game.

We realize our attendance at this game will be seriously cut by your own personal appearance that evening at Spokane Memorial stadium. Our board of directors has taken up this matter and arrived at a solution which we feel would be equitable to your interests as well as ours.

In return for considerable publicity to you, we are asking that you assist us in our project of lighting a field for the boys by sending us a check made out to the Little League baseball fund.[3]

Mr. Stelljes closed by welcoming Elvis to Spokane. Then he waited for a response to his letter.

Although less than two dozen fans waited at the train station late on the evening of August 29, still Elvis' companions, more through habit than necessity, surrounded him, and shoulder-to-shoulder the whole group moved through the station. Having stepped off the train at the east end of the station, Elvis and his guards had to walk one block west to reach a waiting car on Washington Street. On the move, a *Spokesman-Review* reporter got Elvis to respond briefly to a few questions about his train trip. The last question the reporter asked was, "Are you ready for the big show at the stadium?" Wearing the "smirk" that the reporter said never left his face from the time he stepped off the train until he got into his limousine, Elvis responded, "Yeah, ready. Ready teddy."[4]

Most of the fans couldn't get close enough to get an autograph, but they seemed satisfied just to get a look at the star. One fan, thirteen-year-old Marge Street, told the *Review* reporter she was a little disappointed. "He doesn't look anything like he does on television," she said. "Only his hair. Guess they make him up to look different."

When the cordon of guards parted briefly to let Elvis step into the waiting limousine, three young girls slipped through the opening and asked for his autograph, which he gave willingly but quickly. The limo then took Elvis directly to the Ridpath Hotel, where he was seen in the hotel garage before he got on an elevator and headed up to his room.

Despite the eyewitness, a rumor persists that Elvis had been booked into the Ridpath as a diversionary tactic, and that he really spent the night a couple of blocks down the street at the Davenport Hotel. Several employees of the Davenport claimed they saw him there. One of them was Betsey Briggs, who, then fifty-five, worked at the hotel flower shop in 1957. In 2002, on the occasion of her hundredth birthday, Mrs. Briggs remembered selling flowers to Elvis, who she said was staying at the Davenport while in Spokane for his concert at the stadium. At the centennial birthday party forty-five years later, Belinda Montgomery said of her grandmother, "She took a group of young people from her hiking club to see Elvis, and I think she was disappointed."[5]

The city newspapers, however, were consistent in placing Elvis at the Ridpath Hotel, where during the morning of Friday, August 30, while Presley reportedly slept peacefully in his room, the hotel lobby filled up with teenagers hoping for an autograph, or at least a peek at their idol. These fans were soon shooed away by hotel officials and Elvis' guards, prompting the *Daily Chronicle* to observe that Presley obviously didn't like crowds, "unless, of course, they pay at the box office."[6]

As for the box office, tickets priced at $1.50, $2.50, and $3.50 were available at two downtown locations, the Desert Hotel and Jacoy's fountain and newsstand, and Smith's at the Northtown mall. A mail-order form also appeared in the Spokane newspapers.

Two girls who decided to use the mail-order option were Patsy Sturdevant and her chum Kathy Miller. Two weeks before the Elvis show, the girls had put seven one-dollar bills for two $3.50 seats in an envelope and dropped it in the mailbox at Eleventh and Monroe. When their tickets hadn't arrived by the day of the concert, the two girls went to the Desert Inn box office to find out why. When told their money had never arrived there, Patsy and Kathy, with no tickets and no more money, were the saddest girls in town.[7]

Still, advance ticket sales were "brisk," according to Jack J. Engerman, president of Seattle's Northwest Releasing Corporation, which had booked Presley's show in Spokane's Memorial Stadium. Engerman, whose company hoped for a total gate of from 15,000 to 18,000 people, told reporters that not all advance ticket buyers were teenagers. "Quite a few people in the 18-to 38-year age bracket" had also bought tickets, he said.[8]

One of those older customers was Spokane resident Eloise Moeller, who stood in line to buy a $1.50 ticket for her daughter, twelve-year-old Marlene. Then a student at Hutton Elementary School, Marlene recalls what made her want to attend the Elvis concert. "I wasn't a teenager yet, but I was attracted to his cool looks. And his music was different from what I had heard in the past."[9]

Out of place among the mass of teenage fans were Ken and Lavette Carpenter, then a married couple in their mid-twenties. Lavette remembers, "My husband and I both had our birthdays in August, and having small children at the time, we didn't have much money. So going to see Elvis was kind of a special way of celebrating our birthdays. We weren't real Elvis fans. We were more curious than anything."[10]

An odd advertisement appeared in the *Spokesman-Review* the morning of the concert. It announced, "6743 Choice Seats go on Sale Today!" Listing the exact number in the ad was unusual, but the message was clear. With so many tickets still available on the day of the show, the Presley concert was not going to be a sellout. One press report the following day put the crowd at over 12,000, while another said that there were 12,500 attendees. The crowd, then, seemingly reached only about two-thirds the size the promoters had predicted.

In the days before the concert, the Spokane police dealt with some overzealous teens who went to extremes in their efforts to see Elvis perform. Traffic Officer Warren Sullivan stopped a carload of teenage boys who said they had come from Montana to see Presley. After a search of their car turned up several bottles of beer and a billy club, the boys, charged with disorderly conduct, got to see the city detention home instead of the concert. In another case, policemen found two boys, aged thirteen and fourteen, sleeping in a car in the Sandifur Motors lot on west Second Street. It turned out the boys, determined to see the Presley concert, had hopped a freight train in Wenatchee (150 miles to the west of Spokane). Never mind that they had no tickets or money to buy them. Since the boys hadn't eaten in a couple of days, police officers gave them some candy bars before taking them to juvenile home to await the arrival of their parents.

More serious, though, was the case of a fourteen-year-old southside boy whose passion for Presley put him in the hospital. Police Officer John Blass found the boy bleeding on the corner of Boone and Howard. The boy told the officer he had slashed his wrists about twelve times with a knife, "because his buddy did not loan him money to see Elvis."[11]

There are varying reports of Elvis' activities during the day on August 30 prior to that evening's concert. One newspaper account claimed, "Presley never moved from the seclusion of his hotel room until time for his evening show at Memorial Stadium." However, in denying another reporter's request for an interview, Tom Diskin, an assistant to Colonel Parker, said, "Presley is tired from his long train trip and has to get some rest before rehearsals this afternoon."[12]

However, Hugh Jarrett of the Jordanaires doubts there were rehearsals in Spokane, or anywhere else Elvis toured in 1957. According to Jarrett, there was no need for rehearsals. "I don't ever remember just rehearsing with Elvis ... on the road," he said. "We created the session sounds, and then we used the sounds on the tour."[13]

Presley himself confirmed that while on the road he rarely went out for rehearsals or any other reason. "I never go out during the day," he said. "If I tried it, I would be a gone goose. I stay cooped up in the hotel room until it's time to do that night's show. They smuggle me out and away we go to work."[14]

DJ Bob Hough vividly remembers the events of August 30. "During the day, we played some rhythm and blues record, and someone called the station wanting to know the title of the record and who was singing it and the label," recalls Hough. "Finally the DJ said, 'Who is this?' And the guy says, 'This is Elvis Presley.'" The caller got the information he wanted. Others called KNEW with rumors of Elvis sightings. Hough remembers someone calling and saying Elvis was driving around Spokane, sitting in the back of a convertible. "It was late in the afternoon. Some people said it was an imposter. We didn't know; that's just what we heard was going on."

In fact, it was an imposter, a teenager with sideburns riding around in a convertible waving a guitar. One Spokane mother saw the phony Elvis, and it cost her some money. "It was all right. I had all four kids talked out of seeing Elvis Presley," the mother explained. "And then went to the grocery store—and they saw him riding around in a convertible ... Then I HAD to take them."[15]

While the imposter was being driven around town that afternoon, the real thing was back in his hotel room trying to get in touch with his girlfriend. The morning following Elvis' departure from Memphis, Anita Wood had left for New Orleans to compete in the *Hollywood Star Hunt* finals being held the same night Elvis performed in Spokane. After repeated calls went unanswered, Presley left a message for Anita at the Hotel Roosevelt in New Orleans. Then he left for the stadium in Spokane.

Motorcycle officers arrived at the Ridpath in the late afternoon to escort the singer's car to Memorial Stadium. One of those policemen was John Latta, then a six-year veteran of the force. He did not seek the job but was assigned with others as part of their regular shift to pick up Presley at his hotel and lead him out to the stadium and back again after the show. Years later Latta admitted that he had not been particularly impressed by the King of Rock 'n' Roll in 1957. "I really didn't know much about him," explained Latta. "I was busy with my own life and it didn't take in rock 'n' roll. So I really didn't have an opinion about him one way or the other. I got the assignment and I just did it and that was it." According to Latta, Elvis was indeed riding in a convertible, a late-model pink one. Latta doesn't recall any people lining the five-mile route out of downtown and along Northwest Boulevard to Memorial Stadium in the city's northwest corner. During the concert, Latta stood close to the bandstand, watching the crowd. "It kind of amazed me," he recalled, "the screamin' and yellin', but then I found out later that's what he did to the crowd."

It was not a big moment in the law enforcement career of John Latta, but he realized later that it could have been. "I read in the paper that he bought some police officers new cars at the great big functions they had. I thought, 'I missed out on that.' I should have played it up more."

At about eight o'clock Latta delivered Presley to the stadium dressing room building at the north end of the stadium. On the stadium floor the opening acts started The Elvis Presley Show. Chicago's Al Dvorin again put together the opening variety show for the Northwest tour. It featured fourteen performers in eight acts. First up was the comedy and juggling act of Howard Hardin, who also doubled as the show's master of ceremonies. Comedian Rex Marlowe, whose act included an imitation of a lady putting on a girdle, was also on the bill. Additional acts were dancer and vibraphonist Jodi Gray, Irish tenor Frankie Connors, tap dancers The Burns Twins and Evelyn, comedic singer Joe Termini, pantomime Paul Desmond, and (Billy) Wells and the Four Fays.

(The latter act—part contortionist, part acrobat, part comedy—won the distinction of both opening for Elvis and closing for The Beatles. When the "Fab Four" first appeared on *The Ed Sullivan Show* in 1964, they were the next to last act on the program. Then, just so The Beatles could leave the studio before the show ended, Sullivan brought on Wells and the Four Fays to finish the hour. Despite the difficult spot they were given, the group got a round of applause and a "Bravo!" from Sullivan.)

Most reporters missed the first part of the Spokane show. While it was going on, they met with Presley in the football dressing room. At the press conference, according to a newspaper account the following morning, "Presley confronted a room filled with hostile reporters and radio men and with doe-eyed young women representing high school papers and the like."[16] Seated behind Elvis were four men (Gleaves, Klein, Fike, and Smith) he called "high school buddies." Asked their purpose, Elvis responded, "to keep me from getting homesick."

Bob Hough was at the press conference. "The place was just jammed with media people," he recalls. "We were there standing right next to him. Of course, you've gotta remember we were beginners in that business. We didn't know what we were doing. It was powerful, the reaction he got." The newspapers sent their young investigative reporters, but according to Hough they were out of their element and out of touch with rock 'n' roll. "It was like a freak show. Everyone's still wearing sidewalls for haircuts and the butch. But this guy comes in and he's got the black greasy hair, and he's got this medallion hanging down on his bare chest. The reporters were going, 'Wait a minute. Where are we? He's a space case.' He answered most all the questions, but I mean, they were dumb. They had no relevance. This guy's a rock star. They tried to put the heat on him, get something controversial going, but Elvis had his head screwed on right. He just sloughed it off."

Also at the press conference was Ilah Black, a seventeen-year-old senior at Spokane's Lewis and Clark High School. As a writer for her school's newspaper, Ilah didn't fit the *Spokesman-Review's* description of a "doe-eyed young woman," as she had come to the news conference prepared to dislike Elvis. But her article in the *Lewis and Clark Journal* indicates that he changed her mind. "Although lacking the ease of a polished performer, Elvis answered all questions with genuine sincerity, without dodging or being evasive," wrote Black. "Afterward I decided he doesn't deserve all the unfavorable comments he receives." She described Elvis as wearing a black coat and shirt, blue slacks with a yellow cummerbund, and a large gold medallion he said was given to him by one of his fans in Ohio. (Either Elvis misspoke or Ilah wrote it down wrong. He had actually received the medallion a few months earlier from a fan in Ottawa). She asked Elvis his opinion of the millions of teenage fans who screamed when he appeared. "What other audience would have gotten me to the top as fast?" he responded. "Besides when they scream it covers up my mistakes." Ilah also noted Elvis' claim that he wore no make-up at all, but instead used a sun lamp that gave him a deep southern tan. And Elvis' favorite singers? Dean Martin, the Four Aces, the Four Lads, Pat Boone, and Tommy Sands, although he thought Sands could act much better than he could sing.[17]

Miss Black was not the only one won over by Elvis. According to the *Spokesman-Review* reporter, by the time the press conference was over, the journalists attending were "immeasurably impressed with the way [Presley] handled himself under their sharp fire." The press conference over, Elvis prepared to take the stage.

That morning, stadium officials and representatives of Northwest Releasing Corporation had decided to change the location of the stage. Originally, it was to be set up at the far northern end of the stadium, with seating open in both the east and west stands. Instead, due to ticket sales that were much lower than had been anticipated, officials decided to close the east stands and concentrate the crowd on the west side. The stage was then set in the center of the football field facing west. This provided a good view for all spectators and allowed security personnel to concentrate in half the area. Still, the last-minute setup change resulted in a number of disgruntled patrons. Ushers escorted hundreds who had purchased reserved seats in the east grandstand to the west side. The next day the *Spokesman-Review* described the resulting confusion. "The crowd jammed the west side, sitting in the aisles and on rails with complete disregard for order—many of the standees ruefully displayed stubs for $3.50 seats to helpless ushers. The seats had long since been filled and the crowd was so jammed in it was impossible to sort out individual rights."

Things worked out well for one couple, though. After seeking out and complaining directly to stadium manager Benjamin C. Moore, they got to sit on a stadium floor bench just thirty feet away from the stage.

The team dressing rooms, where Elvis had conducted his pre-concert press conference, were located in a street-level building at the north end of Memorial

Stadium. Leaving the building, Presley jumped into the back of an open Cadillac convertible that drove him down a ramp to the stadium floor. Passing through a double line of police officers, the car pulled up next to the stage. (This process of delivering Elvis to the stage via automobile for outdoor performances was not new. Elvis began the practice back in 1955, when he was known only on a regional basis. In August 1955, he delivered himself to the stage at Spudder Baseball Field in Wichita Falls, Texas, by driving his pink Cadillac onto the field and leaping onto the platform. There were only 2,000 spectators in the stands that night, and most of them were there to see country singer Johnny Horton.)

Much had changed for Elvis in the previous two years, but arriving at an open-air stage via Cadillac was still his style. In addition to creating the emotional impact of delivering Presley to his throne by chariot, having the car nearby had a practical purpose. When a performance ended, Presley could jump back into the vehicle and be driven out of the stadium within seconds.

When Elvis leaped from the back of the convertible and took the stage at 9:37 PM, he faced a live crowd for the first time in nearly five months. The last time he had been on stage had been on April 6 in the Philadelphia Sports Arena. The five-month stretch between live performances was by far Elvis' longest absence from the stage since he had first taken his act on the road in 1954.

From all accounts, despite the lay-off, Presley quickly got his body into high gear. The thousands who had come to see him and had politely sat through ninety minutes of opening acts were ready as well. With his sequined gold jacket accentuated by the pink footlights, Elvis quickly worked the crowd into a frenzy with his opening number, "Heartbreak Hotel." In constant movement, he swiveled, jerked, and yelled his way through eighteen songs in fifty minutes.

According to Jim Spoerhase's article in the *Spokane Daily Chronicle* the next afternoon, it didn't take Presley long to turn the crowd into a "screaming, squealing mass."

> Standing stiff and still he wiggled one thumb—and that did it—the crowd screamed and moaned. A wiggle of Presley's knee or the droop of an eyelid set off the same kind of reaction. Those who went out to hear the popular rock'n'roller didn't stand a chance; you simply couldn't hear, the screaming was so loud.[18]

Marlene Moeller, who had one of the cheapest tickets, remembers what she saw and heard. "I had a fairly good view but it was quite a ways from the stage. It was sort of like watching a miniature Elvis. The audience screamed and hollered all through the performance. Although I didn't scream, I was overwhelmed. I'd never seen anything like it."

Throughout the concert, "flash bulbs bloomed like sunflowers in Kansas," according to the *Spokesman-Review* reporter. "And all through it, twisting, bouncing, vibrating and at times sliding back and forth behind a guitar, was Presley. Often his face wore the sneer that his critics find so abhorrent, but mostly he looked like a 10-year-old who was having the time of his life—but a 10-year-old with the showmanship of a P.T. Barnum."

Spokane resident Gary Pinkley was there, but not entirely by choice. His sixteen-year-old cousin, Linda Evans, was visiting from her home in Wallowa, Oregon. "She wanted to go to the Elvis concert, but my dad wouldn't let her go alone," recalls Gary, who was then thirteen. They had good seats, in the second or third row from the field, only about twenty-five yards from the stage. Gary was impressed by all that was going on around him. "There was lots of excitement. I'd say about 80 percent of the crowd were girls, and these women were all screaming."[19]

The screaming began when Elvis' car first started down the ramp into the stadium. "I couldn't even breathe," Linda remembers. "I grabbed Gary around the neck and all of us were just screaming." That she was one of the screamers caught Linda by surprise. "I didn't know I was going to yell and scream," she says. "I'd never done that in my whole life. It was spontaneous. When he wiggled and got that leg going, all of us just started screaming." It wasn't until a few years later that Linda understood the emotions that made her scream that night. "He could excite you with his music so much," she explains. "There was that feeling there. When I matured, it was almost like that feeling. It went through your body kind of like that."[20]

Gary remembers another girl who was standing close by. "She was yelling over and over, 'Do it, Elvis, do it!' I thought to myself, 'What's he supposed to do?'" At one point Gary wanted to go to the restroom, but he stayed because he didn't want to miss "it," whatever "it" was.

Lavette Carpenter and her husband sat toward the front, somewhat to the right of the stage. "Elvis gave a wonderful performance," she recollects. "We were well entertained for the money we spent. I thought the girls who were screaming were nuts, but we could still hear the music over them."

Spokane authorities were ready with heavy security. A ring of about fifty off-duty policemen stood between Elvis and the crowd. For most of the concert, all they had to do was stand in position with their hands over their ears. Occasionally, a couple of officers moved quickly to save swooning girls from falling over the front rail of the stands. Sitting in the infield, city juvenile officer Robert Brumblay worried about the crowd reaction during Elvis' final number. Presley pulled the microphone off the stage and crawled toward the stands on his knees. The crowd noise became deafening, but there was no movement toward Elvis, who jumped in the waiting car that sped him from the stadium.

Although the Spokane newspaper writers judged Elvis' performance as something between exciting and harmless, one out-of-town journalist was not so judicious. The *Vancouver Sun* sent reporter Mac Reynolds to critique the Presley concert in Spokane so it could give its readers an idea of what to expect when Elvis performed in Vancouver. Reynolds' review appeared in the *Sun* the morning of August 31, prior to the concert in Empire Stadium that evening. In a thorough condemnation of Presley's performance, Reynolds offered his interpretation of what had happened at the Spokane concert.

> On his Friday night show, he didn't say a dirty word. He didn't sing a dirty song. His bumps and grinds, although odious coming from a man, were in themselves no more erotic than half-witted scribblings on a fence. Yet from his tawdry green stage on the 50-yard line of Spokane's Memorial Stadium, an obscenity penetrated the crowd like an electric spark jumping a gap.
>
> When he shook one pant leg, they screamed like jets, these fresh-faced girls of this pleasant wheatland city. When he shook both pant legs, they screamed, and quivered, and shut their eyes. And when he did the most grotesque and imbecilic things with his body, they screamed, and quivered, and shut their eyes, and reached out their hands to him as for salvation. It is a frightening thing for a man to watch his women debase themselves ... Yes, they screamed. And when he staggered across the stage, twitching, mouth open, spastic, he was one with his audience.[21]

In the end, though, about the only thing officials could complain about was the loss of some stadium soil. After Elvis departed, about fifty teenagers descended from the stands and scooped up handfuls of dirt where Elvis had knelt during his final number. Gary Pinkley remembers the dirt-diggers well because his cousin was one of them. "She went down on the field with a bunch of other girls and started digging," he said. "I lost her in the crowd and couldn't find her until a half hour later." Linda Evans had gone over the wall looking for something, anything, she could take home as a souvenir. She grabbed some small rocks from the tire tracks Elvis' car left behind and put them in her pocket. The treasure was later transferred to a sack, which she kept until her mother threw it out about three years later.

No doubt most of the dirt gathered in the heat of passion that Spokane summer evening in 1957 returned to the earth from which it came after the gatherer's passion waned. But not all of it. "Bubblehead Bob" Hough remembers how some of that dirt resurfaced ten years later.

> In 1967 I was reminiscing on the radio one day. I was talking about the great time we had at the stadium when Elvis was there. And I said, "You know, one of the neatest things I saw then was when he got off stage, went over to the track, got on his knees and sang, 'You ain't nothing but a Hound Dog.'" And then I said the thing that was exciting about that was seeing these high school girls vaulting this six-foot wall, coming down and scooping up dirt and putting it in their purses. After telling the story, I got a call that day from a lady who said, "I have my purse up in the closet in the back of the house with the dirt in it." When I got that telephone call, I about fell off my chair.

After the concert, Elvis was driven back to the Ridpath Hotel to grab a few items before heading for the train station. While in his room, he received a phone call from Anita, who had finally gotten his message after celebrating in New Orleans. "Guess what?" she asked. "You won," Elvis guessed. "I told you so all along. I'm so glad Honey. It's wonderful. My little girl's gonna be a movie star," predicted Elvis, referring to the Hollywood contract she had won.[22]

Then it was quickly on to the Great Northern depot, where he boarded a Pullman car on the *Empire Builder* that came through Spokane that night. He stood in the vestibule signing autographs until the train departed at 11:57 PM. According to Conductor C. E. Hertzog, a Pullman porter was injured when a group of teenagers surged against the car steps. Hertzog talked with Presley and Colonel Parker and found Elvis to be a "very sensible and polite young man when not endangered by a mob of screaming youngsters."[23] Presley got to bed at 1:00 PM, but was up by 5:30 to eat breakfast in the dining car before the train arrived in Seattle. The ever-vigilant Conductor Hertzog reported that Elvis "signed his name for nearly everyone on the train while having breakfast." In Seattle, Elvis and his entourage made a quick transfer to a northbound train heading for the Canadian border.

With Presley gone, the debate over his impact on the city's young people began in the Spokane newspapers. It started in the *Spokesman-Review* with a letter from William Weitzman, who saw Elvis as a positive outlet for pent-up teenage emotions. "If they yelled like that at home their parents would want to pin their ears back," argued Weitzman, "but Elvis gives them a chance to let out steam by wiggling and banging heck out of an instrument he can't even play. I'm still glad the kids like him. As long as we have youth with zip and enthusiasm we will have the drive and energy to create progress ... Clean them up and the parents along with them—and just watch what the schools, churches and the kids themselves can do."24

An editorial in the *Chronicle,* however, focused on the vulgarity that so many adults associated with Presley.

> The issue is not whether Presley has talent, because obviously he has a talent to suit certain tastes. The issue is not whether he is a good showman; of his kind he is a great one, abetted by the calculating aides around him. The proposition, rather, is precisely this: Is it right or necessary for Spokane or any community to condone an entertainment spectacle based on vulgarity? Even the kindliest of mature critics at Spokane Memorial stadium agreed that Presley's physical exercises were of a fundamentally base nature ... He drew a big crowd here. But the size and frenzy of an audience is not the right yardstick by which to evaluate standards of entertainment. A strip-teaser would pack'em into Spokane Memorial stadium too.25

The editorial board of the *Review,* however, opted for a more philosophical assessment in trying to help Spokane's citizens understand the whirlwind that had passed through their community.

> Many mature persons have been amazed—and frequently disgusted—over the apparent popularity of Elvis Presley among young teenagers, especially girls. The exhibition staged in Spokane the other evening by this jerky, guitar-strumming vocalist was something that many adults have difficulty in comprehending. The adoration on the part of his fans is all the more mystifying. But doesn't the temporary popularity of Elvis represent the innate admiration that most young people have for an individualist? Of course, his popularity won't last, but he has given the youngsters an occasion for a release from conformity.
>
> The "success" of Elvis ... does demonstrate that the day of the individualist is not yet gone, and that thousands of youngsters may be expressing their own revolt against a planned society in their enthusiasm for this smirking exponent of crude individuality in the field of entertainment.26

Some Presley critics, though, weren't buying the "individualist" assessment of the rock 'n' roller. In a letter Gottfried S. Ehrenberg took the newspaper to task.

And now—according to your editorial—Elvis Presley is supposed to be an individualist! That is about as far from the truth as you possibly can get. Mr. Presley appears as a most outstanding example of everything that is not individualism.

I would rather define him as an excellent salesman, who, better than the next guy, peddles some stuff that the teen-age masses are craving for. He exists on mass appeal in a society that glorifies mass-satisfaction. He is a phenomenon of our age together with cheap movies, cheap TV, cheap comic books, cheap entertainment, cheap chewing gum and cheap mass-education.

If there is anything to deplore we should blame neither Presley nor his teen-age fans. They both were born into a society made by us, the generation that grew up during the twenties with too much Freud and Dewey and too little religion and discipline. "Children should express themselves." They are expressing themselves right now all right, both entertainer and entertained, to the point of mass-hysteria where riot squads are needed.

Has all that anything to do with individualism? One thing the individualist does not need or seek is popularity and mass appeal.[27]

Those in the stands that evening were probably too wrapped up in their passion for or against Presley to understand the significance of what they were experiencing. In the young and energetic singer they saw the burgeoning embodiment of a pop culture phenomenon that changed not only music, but also the values of America's youth for decades to come. The *Spokesman-Review* editorial writer had a rare sense of the long-term influence of Elvis Presley.

And as for Delbert Stelljes, he never did get a response from his letter asking Elvis to help the Spokane Valley Chamber of Commerce pay for lights for a little league baseball field. On the evening of August 30, the Presley appearance at Memorial Stadium brought in $21,708. The chamber's "All-Valley" fundraiser event cleared $15.

Empire Stadium, Vancouver, B.C., August 31, 1957. (Courtesy Red Robinson)

Chapter 12

Vancouver, B.C.

Prelude

In 1957, the nearly 400,000 residents of Vancouver, B.C., were experiencing many of the same cultural changes as in U.S. urban centers. The 1950s brought Vancouver an international airport, highways, malls, and bomb shelters. A legalized six-day shopping week, the city's first cocktail bars, and the emergence of rock 'n' roll heralded a weakening of accepted moral standards.

The shift in teen music toward rock 'n' roll in the city began harmlessly in 1953 when Al Jordan began hosting *Theme for Teens*, an hour-long show on radio station CJOR. Rock 'n' roll music had not fully developed by then, and rhythm and blues records were being played only on stations for black audiences. Still, Jordan got teens involved by inviting them to the studio to take part in the show and by accepting phone calls on the air.

One of the callers invited to come down to the studio was sixteen-year-old Robert "Red" Robinson. Soon, every day after school Robinson was dropping by CJOR and learning the ropes of the radio business from Jordan. Late in 1954, Jordan left the show and Robinson took over the *Theme for Teens* program. His career as a DJ had begun. It was high school during the day for Robinson, but from afternoon until midnight he immersed himself in radio. Given freedom over the content of his program, he began playing the records he knew his high school mates wanted to hear—rhythm and blues records by black artists, such as Lloyd Price, Ruth Brown, Wynonie Harris, and LaVern Baker. The rock 'n' roll sound was catching on in the U.S., and Robinson was determined to bring it to his Canadian audience. While other stations in town stuck with the mellow pop tunes of the day, Red began mixing in rhythm tunes like "Sh-Boom" by The Crew Cuts, "Shake, Rattle and Roll" by Joe Turner, and "Honey Love" by The Drifters.

For Robinson, it all came together a month after he graduated from high school in June 1955 when Bill Haley and the Comets' recording of "Rock Around the Clock" hit the airwaves. The record launched rock 'n' roll, changed radio forever, and sent Robinson's career soaring. He started taking the records out on "remotes" to high school "sock hops." Soon he stepped up to larger venues, like theaters and ballparks, where local and imported American bands played. As automobile and transistor radios allowed teens to take their music wherever they went, the ratings of rock 'n' roll stations went through the roof. Survival forced other Vancouver stations to switch over to the new music, but no DJ was as in tune with his teen audience and their music as Red Robinson, who presided over British Columbia radio's transition to rock 'n' roll. In 1957 he moved over to CKWX, Western Canada's first 50,000-watt station, which could be heard all the way into northern California.

Starting in 1956 with Bill Haley and the Comets, all the big rock 'n' roll touring shows began appearing in Vancouver. Fats Domino came and so did Little Richard. Right in the middle of it all was Red Robinson, and when he heard in early August 1957 that Elvis Presley was coming to town, he made plans to be right in the middle of that spectacle as well.

Vancouver, British Columbia
Empire Stadium
Saturday, August 31, 1957, 8:00 pm

On the morning of August 31, Vancouver teenagers and their parents awoke to see the following headline in the *Vancouver Sun*: "Daughter Wants to See Elvis? 'Kick Her in the Teeth!'" Staff reporter Mac Reynolds, who had attended Presley's concert in Spokane the night before, wrote the article. Reynolds started his review with, "It's hardly original, but if any daughter of mine broke out of the woodshed tonight to see Elvis Presley in Empire Stadium, I'd kick her teeth in." No doubt he felt his decidedly negative assessment of Presley was validated that evening after bedlam occurred at the most controversial and confusing concert of Elvis' career. The controversy centered on the crowd's movement toward the stage, the way security forces dealt with it, and the resulting episodes of hooliganism. Confusion still exists today over the conflicting accounts of the concert and its aftermath, making it difficult to determine exactly what happened.

After his Spokane concert on Friday night, Elvis and his entourage left the city just before midnight on the Great Northern *Empire Builder* bound for Seattle. In the Emerald City, Elvis switched trains at 8:00 the next morning and headed north toward the Canadian border. The train was scheduled to arrive at noon at Vancouver's Great Northern station at the corner of Station Street and National Avenue.

There is some question, though, about whether Elvis was still on the train when it got to the station. At a press conference later that evening, a reporter asked Presley whether he had gotten off the train two miles outside of town to avoid the crowd waiting for him at the station. Elvis' response seemed to verify that he had done just that. "Well, usually that's right," explained Elvis. "I can't get in. You see, I have to prepare for a show that night, and ... I have to rest and we have rehearsals in the afternoon, so I don't have too much time. I'm actually pressed for time. It's not that I'm trying to avoid them, because that's certainly not it. It's just that I'm rushed for time and I have to make every moment count when I'm on the road." Red Robinson was there, however, and he remembers seeing Elvis get off the train at the far end of the station passenger platform and get into a waiting Cadillac on the south side of the station. That was Presley's usual pattern when arriving in other cities, and it's undoubtedly what happened in Vancouver. Most of the fans and press representatives waited in the terminal building, and when they didn't see Elvis come through the depot, many mistakenly jumped to the conclusion that he got off before the train reached the station.

Robinson, Hugh Pickett, and Zollie Volchok formed a trio of personalities closely associated with Elvis Presley's Vancouver appearance in 1957. Robinson, then only twenty and host of the highly popular *Teen Canteen* program on CKWX radio, was chosen to introduce Elvis for his appearance at Empire Stadium. In that capacity he was given unprecedented access to Elvis during the day leading up to the concert. Much of what is known about Presley's actions during that day comes from the subsequent writings and interviews of Red Robinson. That, and Robinson's foresight in recording Elvis' entire pre-concert news conference, have linked Red's name forever with the Presley legend. His association with Elvis has grown through the years, despite his having spent just five and a half hours with Presley on August 31, 1957, after which he never again talked with Elvis.

Robinson's name is so linked with Elvis' 1957 appearance in Vancouver that he is often given credit for booking Presley's appearance there. However, that was the work of Hugh Pickett. Through his company, Famous Artists, Ltd., Pickett worked out the details with Seattle entrepreneur Zollie Volchok, whose Northwest Releasing Corporation had organized Elvis' entire five-city Pacific Northwest tour. Though initially he had some reservations about Presley's act, Pickett said booking him into Vancouver was easy. "Our company, Famous Artists, brought in many entertainers from all over the world, and booking Elvis was nothing out of the ordinary," according to Pickett. "I wasn't sure if it was such a good idea to have him here because of the controversy surrounding his stage act. But when I met him, all of the hesitancy went out the window. He was very charming and nice—a real gentleman. He endeared himself to me."[1]

Looking after his company's interests, Volchok closely monitored events in Vancouver. He was there at the train station with a rented Cadillac to pick up the singer and whisk him off to the Georgia Hotel, where he was ensconced on the top floor in room 1226.

The air of anticipation for Presley's appearance in Vancouver was "electric," according to Red Robinson. Tickets, priced as they were in Spokane at $1.50, $2.50, and $3.50, were available via mail order or in person at Kelly's Music Store at the corner of Georgia and Seymour Streets.

One acrobatic thief got some tickets for free, however. Three days before the concert, Miss Mary Kaufman reported to police that a prowler had entered her apartment at 1622 Vine by climbing over a retaining wall to reach her balcony and then squeezing through an open window. Taken were $25 in cash and four tickets to the Presley concert. The tickets were for seats 15-18 in Row 3 of Section R. If Miss Kaufman or the police thought they could catch the thief by staking out those seats, they were mistaken. In the frenzy to get as close to Elvis as possible, many in the crowd simply occupied whatever seats were empty, and besides, that evening the police would find themselves occupied by much more pressing duties than trying to catch a ticket thief.

While there might have been a growing level of excitement among Vancouver's youth as Elvis' appearance grew closer, there were also a few voices warning of a catastrophe on the horizon. On August 14, just five days after the Presley appearance in Vancouver was announced, the following letter was published in the *Vancouver Sun.*

> The citizens of Vancouver have paid for the most beautiful stadium in Canada. It would be a shame to let a rollicking group of teenagers demolish Empire Stadium because of Elvis Presley. Rock and roll concerts (bashes) such as the one he intends to put on have ruined public gathering places in the past. It is impossible to imagine the damage that could result out at Empire Stadium if his concert is allowed. This concert featuring Mr. Presley should not be held here in Vancouver, especially not in Empire Stadium. If through folly Elvis and his 22,000 fans are allowed in our stadium, I sincerely hope that it rains.[2]

However, a *Vancouver Province* column on August 30, the day before Elvis' appearance, pointed out that even the Vancouver concerts of Harry Belafonte and other singers had been rowdy in the past and warned that the appearance of the volatile Presley carried the possibility of much worse. In his "A Teenager's Views" column, Ian Smith offered a foreboding message.

Movies, rock'n'roll dances, and other assorted teenage entertainments in and around the city of Vancouver will have an air of death and disaster about them as they are deserted in favor of the raucous confines of Empire Stadium.

Said Empire Stadium, on the other hand, used to the cheering crowds, will shake and rumble deep in its concrete foundations as the palpitating Mr. Presley lets loose with his characteristic brand of Elvistics.

Approximately 22,000 screaming females will go deliriously out of their minds as the man from Memphis lays hand to guitar and opens his mouth to sing.

Moments later, as that famous pelvis begins to twitch, such females will scream the Tennessee Twister into the background as they give voice to their emotions in sobs designed to render the hearts of anyone within fallout distance.

Whatever happens, you can bet that in Vancouver it never happened before. As we said, Little Richard and Domino both came. They were entertainment. Belafonte? He was a little higher.

But Elvis—he's almost a god. He's an idol, at any rate. Some people would crawl just to lick his white bucks.

So what'll happen Saturday at Empire Stadium is anybody's guess. One thing is sure, though. It'll be interesting.[3]

Such was the mood of mixed electric anticipation and foreboding in Vancouver when Elvis arrived in the city on the morning of Saturday, August 31.

As that night's master of ceremonies, Red Robinson set out early in the day to take full advantage of the access to Presley he had been granted. Soon after Elvis had settled in his room at the Georgia Hotel, Red met Zollie Volchok and Ernie Henn and Knox Coupland of RCA records in the hotel lobby. They rode the elevator to the twelfth floor, where Elvis' bodyguards confronted them in the hallway. After Volchok explained who they were, they were allowed to continue down to room 1226. Tom Diskin, Colonel Parker's assistant, answered the knock on the door, invited them in, and introduced them to Elvis.

"At first, everything seemed a bit strained," remembers Robinson. "But once Elvis heard that I was an enthusiastic fan, he relaxed and became most cordial. When people ask me what I thought of Elvis, I have to answer that I found him polite, shy and charming. He was very soft-spoken and there was nothing pretentious about the man. I guess one of the main reasons I have always been a Presley fan is that when I met him he was down-to-earth and seemingly unaffected by his incredible success."[4]

Robinson describes Elvis as seeming "quite energetic" in his room, despite having gotten little sleep since his previous night's concert in Spokane. He alternated between lounging on the bed and walking up and down in his room while he talked with the four visitors. According to Robinson, he and Elvis conversed about their mutual dislike for school and other basic, non-musical topics. "He was bored, young, single, and what did we talk about? Cars. Girls. Football. He loved football. I loved football. We talked about guy things." The interview left Robinson a life-long admirer and defender of Elvis Presley. "Of all the people who knew him that I've met in my career, I have yet to meet someone who didn't like him," explained Red. "What happened later, who knows? I think he didn't know who he was later."

Robinson, Henn, Coupland, and Volchok were not the only ones who came to the Georgia Hotel that afternoon hoping to see Elvis. Hugh Jarrett of the Jordanaires remembers that, despite hotel security's efforts to keep them out, kids already were walking the halls by the time the singing group got to their rooms after the overnight drive from Spokane. According to Jarrett, the kids were streaming up the back fire escape.

Robinson was in Presley's hotel room for about an hour and a half, his cue to leave coming when, he says, "an attractive, young brunette—similar in appearance to Priscilla Presley—entered the room." Robinson later learned that she was a paid companion. "The truth is that she was a call girl," Red asserts. "Hugh Pickett remembers this vividly. The reason was that Parker didn't want his boy getting into trouble, thinking about the Charlie Chaplin and the Errol Flynn stuff, I guess. My understanding was that she was a very highly paid professional."[5] The young woman accompanied Presley to Seattle, as well, according to Robinson, who concluded, "Since nothing more has ever been heard about her, it also appears that she was very discreet." Jack Wasserman was not so discreet, however. About two weeks after Elvis left town, he briefly mentioned the story in his *Vancouver Sun* column. "Elvis Presley has a local flame," he revealed. "She's older and wiser than him. The date was arranged after the show in Vancouver. She later followed him south."[6]

How long Elvis spent with the "young brunette" in his Vancouver hotel room is unknown. All that is known of the remaining afternoon and early evening hours is that sometime during that period the singer called his parents in Memphis and that he went to Empire Stadium. Hugh Pickett recalled, "We had a rehearsal before the show began at Empire Stadium, with Elvis being driven around the track, and we thought it was a great idea."

After the rehearsal, which was actually a logistical run-through and not a performance rehearsal, the next reported sighting of Elvis was at about 8:30 PM, when a black Cadillac pulled up in front of the dressing room at Empire Stadium for the pre-concert press conference. Since most of the fans were already inside the stadium, only a small crowd caught a glimpse of Elvis as he quickly stepped from the car and vanished inside. The room set aside for the press conference was jammed with newspaper reporters, radio people, photographers, and young female fans. Elvis climbed onto a table and began taking questions.

Sandra Sheppard of the *Vancouver Sun* reported that "Elvis, bending over five microphones, winking at the girls present and toying with the rings on his fingers, had all the answers."[7] Another *Sun* reporter wrote that as Elvis sat "cross-legged on a table in a football team's dressing room, he tried valiantly to answer reporters' questions, [while keeping] blinking flash bulb explosions out of his eyes and nervously twiddling a spool of film with his fingers."[8] As Elvis knelt on the table, the more assertive reporters, including Robinson, closed in on him. The questions began.

Red came prepared to preserve the encounter. "I had a microphone and a reel-to-reel 601 Ampex Tape Recorder," he recalls. "It was wrapped in leather—beautiful—and weighed about sixty pounds. That's why the quality is so good. People remark on that all the time. They say, my God, it's like he's in the studio. But take a look at that equipment and you'll know why. I mean, the quality was just fantastic. No speed variation, nothing."[9] The recording has been available to the public in various formats through the years, so that instead of relying only on press perceptions, listeners can hear Elvis' voice and judge for themselves his demeanor and the significance of his answers.

The tape reveals a relaxed Elvis Presley, courteously and calmly answering most of the questions fired at him. He is serious and seemingly thoughtful in his responses, making it easy to understand how he disarmed so many of the assembled reporters who expected to be confronted by a wild-eyed, rock 'n' roll hooligan.

Several other reporters echoed Robinson's assessment of Presley as a "down-to-earth guy." One *Sun* reporter noted, "He appeared a quiet, personable youth proud of his millions and his fame but some times yearning for the quiet sanity that went with driving a truck in Memphis, Tenn."[10] Thirteen-year-old Judy Root, sent to the press conference by the *Province* to get a teenager's impression, also judged Elvis a regular guy. "I met Elvis Saturday night," she started her story in the *Province*. "I didn't faint, and I didn't scream, but I was pretty scared—until I actually saw him. Now I can think of him as just an ordinary person. If he weren't at the top like he is, he wouldn't stand out. He would just be another man in Memphis, Tenn."[11]

The questions asked ranged from ridiculous to insightful, with the vast majority in the former category. Many of the questions clearly indicated that, although the world was nearly two years into the Presley phenomenon, some reporters had no idea of its cultural significance. That lack of understanding resulted in such pointless questions as, "How's the weather down in Memphis?" "Would you like to go for a holiday somewhere?" "What do you say about permanent retirement?" "You like driving a truck?" "What's your favorite sport?" "If you went into the army, how would you feel about getting your hair cut?"

Some questions did touch on meaningful topics. Elvis was asked about the lifespan of rock 'n' roll, the reason for his success, his movements on stage, his feeling about being drafted, his acting career, and his plans for the future. For the most part, his answers were short, superficial, and no more revealing than his responses when he had been asked the same questions numerous times before.

Some reporters accused Presley of being evasive on the tough questions. Les Wedman of the *Province* noticed, "When it came to pertinent queries he hemmed and hawed, said once 'you're trying to trap me' and then 'next question.'"[12] Red Robinson recalls one reporter at the press conference who tried to corner Presley but failed. "Mark Raines, later a member of Canada's Parliament, fired questions about Elvis' likes and dislikes as reported in the gossip magazines. Elvis obviously didn't appreciate Mark's line of questioning and became a bit annoyed. But the press was always looking for a sensational story."

Wedman obviously felt Presley had trapped himself with brief and insincere answers to the questions asked. In his *Province* story of September 3, Wedman used sarcasm in describing Presley's press conference performance.

> Poor boy, said a couple of theatrical intruders to Presley's dressing room press conference.
>
> Poor boy! Elvis echoed the remark in his answers to eager-beavers radio disk jockeys who did everything but jam a microphone down his precious throat.
>
> Ah cain't go out for a cuppa' coffee. I hafta eat in my hotel.
>
> Ah have no personal life.
>
> If ah wanta go to the fair, I hafta rent the fair grounds after it closes up.
>
> Ah got five cars—four Cadillacs and a Lincoln but haven't got time to drive them. They just sit around and the tires go flat.
>
> Poor boy and lonely too out there on the stage, frightened of crowds—he confided to reporters.[13]

In the end, though, the long press conference, with its dozens of questions and answers, revealed little new information about Elvis Presley. The assembled press heard nothing to help them judge Elvis, the rock 'n' roll star. That judgment would have to wait until they saw him on stage within the hour. What the press conference did, though, was to alter or confirm the listener's perception of Elvis the man. And the fact is that, unlike Les Wedman, most came away with a more positive view of the personal Elvis. For instance, Duncan Holmes, then a correspondent for *Canadian Press,* pronounced Elvis a gentleman. He was both impressed and amused that Presley called him "sir," considering that the two were about the same age at the time. "I didn't ever detect, at the time that I was with him, any kind of an attitude," Holmes asserted. "He was incredibly civil to all of us, and it was a very pleasant experience." Norm Pringle, then a Vancouver disc jockey, had a similar reaction. "He was a real gentleman, a real nice guy," recalled Pringle. "At that time he didn't smoke, or drink, and he was just a nice, clean-cut kid. He kissed my wife's hand and I had to do the dishes for a week."[14]

One topic apparently interested nearly all who attended the press conference, since comments on it appeared in almost all subsequent press reports. That was Elvis' appearance. An unidentified *Sun* reporter noted that Presley wore "a black suit, black shirt, black loafers, silver socks. A star sapphire glittered on his left hand." The *Province* reporters added further details—the black shirt was half buttoned up with white buttons, a white belt held up the black pants, a gold watch was worn mostly up on the fingers, and the socks were white, not silver.

Several accounts had Elvis wearing thick makeup, even though the night before in Spokane, he had claimed that he wore no makeup. Teenager Judy Root later wrote, "Elvis looked exactly like I thought he would up close except that he was wearing so much stage makeup I could barely see his face." Wedman offered, "He's handsome, is Elvis, almost pretty. His pancake makeup blanched his hairless face so it made it appear as if he dyed his hair and sideburns black and touched up eyebrows and lashes." Another report had Elvis wearing mascara. Oddly, among all the banal questions, no one asked about the makeup. He was asked about the ring, however. "That's a star sapphire," Elvis explained. "There was a girl gave that to me in California."

Despite the alleged makeup, Presley's presence startled most who saw him close up at the press conference. Looking back over forty-five years later, Red Robinson confessed, "He was a very impressive guy and probably—I know this probably sounds strange, but I'm going to say it anyway—probably the handsomest man I ever saw in my life. I'd never seen anybody this handsome. It was unbelievable."[15]

After the press conference ended, Elvis spent a few minutes posing for pictures with reporters and signing autographs for their children. Judy Root got an autograph. When Elvis handed back the signed paper, she thanked him, and, smiling down at her, he said, "OK." Then, as she watched Elvis accommodate others in the room, in one respect she felt she understood the man. "I realized that he was just an ordinary guy capable of laughing and joking with people he hardly knew and treating them as if they were old friends."

There was another Elvis Presley, though, and as the reporters filed from the room, this one listened to the screaming, foot-stomping crowd outside and grimaced in anticipation. One reporter said he looked like a gladiator about to face the lions. "Man," said Elvis. "I'm all shook up."

In the stadium the opening acts were winding down. Hawkers in the stands sold field glasses and souvenir programs for $1 each, single color pictures for 50¢, and three different buttons. In his dressing room, Elvis took off his black coat and white belt and put on the jacket and belt from his gold lamé suit. Because he was to introduce Elvis on stage, Red Robinson remained with the singer after the reporters departed. According to Red, Elvis moved about "like a caged animal, never stopping, never sitting, a man in constant motion, looking for distractions that hopefully would take his mind away from his upcoming stage show."

Constantly twisting and turning his gold watchband, Elvis engaged the DJ in small talk to pass the anxious minutes. Red recalls, "Our topics of conversation included comparison of our boyhoods (we each grew up poor), the changing world, our families, the normal things that two young men would talk about anywhere. Elvis also said that he hoped the whole rock'n'roll scene would not lose its fire. He said he wanted to continue to perform as long as it was possible. In addition, he asked me all kinds of questions about my CKWX radio show, the kids who listened and how they reacted to his TV appearances, and his records. I answered as honestly and as clearly as I could—remember, I too was a fan and terribly in awe of the man."[16] There were moments of silence mixed in, as both men stared at the stark dressing room walls and listened to the faint sounds of the opening acts in the stadium.

As showtime drew near, Red got caught up the playfulness Elvis sometimes used to cut the tension before a performance. The singer borrowed a nearby policeman's handcuffs, and before Red knew what was happening, Presley had handcuffed him to a shower rod. Elvis laughed while Red grew nervous, fearing Presley would actually leave him there and start the show without him. But when Colonel Parker appeared at the door and signaled that it was showtime, a smiling Elvis unlocked the cuffs.

After exchanging a few final words with Presley, Robinson, accompanied by Tom Diskin and two police officers, headed down the tunnel that emptied onto the stadium floor. As the Jordanaires concluded their set, Red walked to the back of the stage. "Imagine 25,000 voices screaming, 'We want Elvis!' in unison," he reflected. "Every fiber in my body was caught up in the excitement of the evening ... The warm summer air added a special glow to the amphitheatre and the adrenaline within my system was running wild. I was just twenty years old and had never stood on a stage in front of a gathering this large."[17] With shaking hands and a dry mouth, Red approached the microphone. "Ladies and gentlemen, on behalf of Canada's largest teen show, it's my pleasure to present the man you've all been waiting for, the King of Rock'n'Roll, Elvis Presley."

The emcee pointed to his right, and Elvis came running out of the tunnel on the west side of the stadium. He jumped into the back of a black Cadillac convertible, which began a slow, counterclockwise circuit of the stadium's dirt track. A slow human sound wave reached its pinnacle as the car passed each section of the grandstand. Unfortunately, it was the only close look most the spectators would get of Elvis that evening. Its circuit of the track complete, the Cadillac pulled up close to the stage. Elvis jumped out and ran up the back steps. Walking casually to the front of the stage, Presley shook hands with Robinson, who then retreated to a small cubicle at the side of the stage to watch the show. Elvis then took the mike in his hand and began singing "Heartbreak Hotel."

Much of what happened during the next hour in Empire Stadium is clouded in the conflicting accounts of eyewitnesses. Sometimes descriptions of historical events become confusing due to third-party accounts written by people hindered by personal bias who did not witness the events they recount. That is not what prevents a clear understanding of what happened in Empire Stadium the evening of August 31, 1957. Contrary accounts exist from those who were on the ground that night and witnessed the same series of events. The high level of excitement, colored by unyielding expectations, resulted in people who shared the same experience seeing and interpreting it differently.

If there is one thing on which all who were present agree, it is that early on there was a loss of crowd control in the stadium. There is disagreement, though, about why it happened. All of the concert reviewers in the Vancouver newspapers concentrated on assessing blame for the inability of officials to manage the crowd. Some blamed Elvis, some blamed rowdy fans, and others blamed the police. All of the crowd problems during the concert, however, can be traced to one fundamental mistake in pre-concert planning—stage placement. In Vancouver the flatbed stage was set at the north end of the stadium on the goal line of the football field. Since at least 16,000 tickets were sold for the 22,000-seat capacity Empire Stadium, the option of putting all spectators on one side and moving the stage to midfield, as had been done the previous night in Spokane, was not possible. Both the east and west grandstands had to be used to accommodate the crowd, and it seemed the only possible location for the stage so that all could see it was at one end of the stadium.

"We must have looked like ants to them back there where they were sitting," said Scotty Moore of the crowd.[18] Since the spectators had bought tickets in anticipation of seeing Elvis, when they couldn't, it shouldn't have surprised the concert planners when many in the stands sought a closer view.

Just before Elvis appeared, a warning was issued over the public address system. The show would be stopped if anyone came down on the field. That warning, along with the departure of the ushers to join the security forces on the field, was the signal for the more aggressive fans to improve their view of the stage. Many with lower-priced tickets moved in to take any empty seats they could find in the more expensive sections closer to the stage.

Even those who were sitting closest to the stage were not close to their idol by any means, as Les Wedman observed. "While on stage he was at least 200 feet from the highest-priced seats and those in the south bleachers had about the same sight of Mr. Presley as if they'd put their TV set at the bottom of the garden and watched from the back porch." After the crowd had squeezed northward in the stands as far as it could, only one other avenue was left open for those farthest away to improve their view. They longingly eyed the vast open space of the stadium floor, and soon they would occupy it and challenge the security forces there entrusted with the hopeless task of keeping the fans in their seats.

Colonel Parker certainly anticipated the need for security in holding a Presley concert in a large, open stadium. Fifty-six off-duty police officers had been lined up to work the Presley show. Four sergeants, four policewomen, and forty-eight constables signed up through the Police Union, the sergeants to receive $12 pay and the rest $10 each. Also on hand were forty teenage air cadets, who were brought in primarily as ushers but also had backup security responsibilities.

Such security forces had been more than adequate in a similar-sized stadium in Spokane the night before, but the unfortunate placement of the stage in Vancouver effectively stretched the police officers and ushers into a thin gray line that was insufficient to deal with a determined crowd on the move.

The crowd remained at their seats as Elvis sang his first song, but during his second number the dam burst. Fans poured out of the stands on both sides toward the stadium's south end, and, like a tidal wave, surged toward the stage nearly a hundred yards away. From his position on the stage, Scotty Moore was not surprised. To him, what happened was logical. "All they wanted to do was to get closer," Scotty explained. "They didn't care whether they had seats or not."

The crowd, mostly teenagers from the cheap seats, swallowed up the cops who roamed the field. "This is it. We'll never stop them now," yelled one officer. In front of the flimsy four-foot metal fence surrounding the stage, the police and air cadets turned their backs on the advancing mass and hastily locked arms to block the crowd's movement toward the stage. Like Scotty Moore, drummer D.J. Fontana saw no hostility in the crowd advance. "The funny part is that the stage crew had some little security fences up that were about three or four feet high that you could push down with your hands," Fontana recalled. "They (the crowd) got right to the fences, stopped and sat down."[19] Still, the floodlights came on, shining into the faces of the crowd, and the fans were ordered to return to their seats or the show would end.

It is at this point that conflicting accounts start making the sequence of events difficult to pin down with certainty. The *Province's* Ben Metcalfe reported that, as the crowd first approached the stage, Colonel Parker himself came on stage and issued the initial threat to stop the show. George Klein agrees that the Colonel came on stage but claims it was later on. Klein gives the following account of Parker's actions.

> The Colonel came out and pulled Elvis offstage, and the MC said, "You are going to have to get back in your seats, or we can't go on with the show." Meanwhile, the Colonel told Elvis, "Elvis, don't tease this crowd. These people are crazy." Well, if you tell Elvis not to do something, that's the surest way you're going to get him to do it, so he goes back onstage and the first thing he does is, "Welllllll ..." And here come fifty thousand more people! So the Colonel runs out again—this is the first time I ever saw Colonel Parker go out onstage—he got mad, and he went onstage because he was protecting his property. And he said, "Okay, you can stay on the field if you act right and don't tear the stage up. Otherwise, Mr. Presley's not going to be performing."[20]

Red Robinson, however, who stood at the side of the stage the whole time Elvis was on, adamantly claims that Colonel Parker never came on stage. "I was standing right there," he recalls. "No, Colonel Parker never came on stage. There could have been a warning over the PA, but no one came on stage except Elvis and myself." Gordon Johnson, who later became a Vancouver disc jockey, was in Empire Stadium that night and supports Robinson's contention. "The Colonel did not come on the stage and warn anybody," Johnson declares. "The crowd was moving too fast for this kind of reaction." Columnist Jack Wasserman even reported that Colonel Parker approved of the crowd sitting down in front of the stage. "They'll form a human wall," Wasserman heard Parker say.[21]

Fontana says Elvis himself stopped the show "two or three" times to pass on management's warning that the show would end if everyone didn't go back to their seats. Despite the warnings, however, some reporters blamed Elvis for enticing the horde on the field, one even contending that Elvis urged his fans on in their battle with the security forces. The *Sun's* John Kirkwood wrote that Presley "staggered across the stage ... like a drunk picking his way home on New Year's morning. He glazed his eyes, twisted his youthful face in a sullen sneer, swiveled his hips, dropped drunkenly to his knees and threw himself into more bumps and grinds than the PNE [Pacific National Exhibition] girly show has seen for years. He made love to the microphone and the teen-age girls in the crowd reached out to him."22

Of course, not all of the spectators left their seats that night, so the size of the crowd that took to the stadium floor can only be estimated. Gordon Johnson sat way in the back and had a good view of the entire field. To him it seemed that a large portion of the crowd spilled onto the field. However, a letter in the *Province* two weeks later claimed, "Out of all the thousands in the stadium a very small percentage ran on the grass." Another letter was more specific, stating that three-quarters of the crowd remained in their seats. If the latter estimate is close to accurate, then at least 4,000 people were on the field. *Sun* columnist Jack Wasserman reported that "less than 3,000 of this mob behaved like morons." In the end, the odds of up to four hundred to one made the job of the fifty-six police officers and forty air cadets extremely difficult, if not impossible.

Still, it is clear that the security forces did not abandon their duty and did the best they could under the circumstances. Kirkwood observed, "Girls crawled through policemen's legs, then were dragged screaming off the field on all fours; several fainted in the crush; the backs of angry policemen's hands rattled smartly across the pouting faces of hysterical hoods." Ben Metcalfe of the *Province* added, "Girls were punched, lifted bodily back into the heaving mass. Their escorts, teenagers like themselves, threatened the police and cadets. One bulky youth, his nose spurting blood, was hurt till he screamed." One officer used to riding crop to keep a man in a wheel chair from being trampled by the crowd.

Meanwhile, Colonel Parker watched the confrontation from near the stage. "This ever happen before?" a reporter asked him. "Yeah, yeah," answered the Colonel. "Happens all the time. They don't mean no harm." Then he ducked as a bottle flew past his ear, according to the reporter.

There are varying descriptions of the crowd's dynamics, of how it moved on the stadium floor. Kirkwood described the crowd's movement in military terms. To him the grassy sward was a battlefield over which a teenage army fought the law for its possession. The opening sentence of Kirkwood's report in the *Sun* reads, "It was like watching a demented army swarm down the hillside to do battle in the plain when those frenzied teen-agers stormed the field." Kirkwood went on to describe how the teenaged forces were repeatedly repelled, but, like a Confederate Civil War army, kept attacking the Union line. "They left," he observed. "But slowly, slowly, ever so slowly and cunningly, they crept pugnaciously back as Elvis … sang? Three times more the demented children charged the sweating police who linked arms to push them back." Les Wedman of the *Province* also described an almost organized back-and-forth movement of the crowd. "All they could do was push, crush, draw back and rush again," stated Wedman.

Kirkwood and Wedman saw the mass on the field from the side. From his position near the stage, Red Robinson watched the front of the crowd up close. He disagrees with the suggestion that there was any kind of attack mentality or that the crowd acted or moved in unison. "I think what happened is that some kids came up to take a look, then went back while others came up," Red explained. "The crowd changed all the time. There wasn't one major thrust, like a big flood wave coming in, ever. The first four or five rows, the ones who were standing right in front of the stage, never moved."[23] Fontana, who also had a front-on view from the stage, agrees with Red that the crowd, the front of it at least, never retreated. "They tried and they tried, and they wouldn't move," D.J. recalls of efforts to disperse the determined mass. "The people that were sitting never did move. They just sat right there in front of us. All they really wanted was to see and hear. You can't blame them for that."

Meanwhile, once it became obvious that the crowd was not going to return to the stands, Elvis continued to sing numbers in quick succession, each accompanied by his unique style of body language. Everyone on stage could see the battle in front of them, though, and apprehension began building among the performers. "We were all scared," said Neal Matthews of the Jordanaires. "They kept closing in, moving in. They were wild-eyed."[24] Fellow Jordanaire Gordon Stoker could read the fear in Elvis' face too. "Elvis was really scared," remembers Stoker. "When you talk about thousands screaming, pushing the guards, and running towards us, we were all scared. That was the reason he stayed as close to us as possible. Being there, and thinking back, it's amazing someone didn't get hurt or killed."[25]

Finally, Colonel Parker decided to end the show early, and Elvis cut right to "Hound Dog." For the finale, of course, Elvis increased the arm and hip movement on stage, and seeing it, the crowd on the field pressed forward again. The police saw Presley's intensified actions and, taking them as an open attempt to encourage the crowd, they gave up trying to hold the fans back. The frustrated, sweating officers were reduced to yelling, many of them demanding that the fans get out of the stadium and Elvis himself get out of town.

Having completed the finale, Elvis abruptly left the stage. Just how he left, though, is another matter of debate, as several varying stories of his departure have been told. Kirkwood of the *Sun* wrote, "Then, as though he might suddenly have thought nobody was looking, Elvis disappeared. Quick as a flash of gold-spangled lightning, he zipped down stairs at the rear of the stage and still bawling 'You Ain't Nothin' But a Hound Dog,' flung himself into a black Cadillac. It shot away through a rear exit like a bank bandit's getaway car." Albert Goldman in his biography contends that two guys, presumably Elvis' bodyguards, grabbed him under the armpits, carried him off the stage, and threw him in the back of the Cadillac.[26] Jordanaire Neal Matthews claimed Elvis stopped singing in mid-song, announced, "I'm cuttin' out, man," and took off, leaving his backup men stranded on stage.[27] Scotty Moore confirms that at least the band was left behind by Presley's sudden and unexpected departure, but another person on stage recalls those hectic moments differently. Gordon Stoker of the Jordanaires asserts, "There was never a time when Elvis ran and we didn't. I can assure you that we were right behind him."[28]

The common thread in all these versions of Elvis' departure is that Presley got into a car that was immediately driven out of the stadium. Years later Gordon Johnson interviewed a police officer who claimed he literally sat on Elvis as his car drove out of the stadium.

Red Robinson's story of Elvis leaving the stage is quite different from the other accounts. He claims that Elvis did not leave the stage after his last number; instead, he went under it. In his 1984 book *Rockbound*, Robinson explained how Elvis rushed backstage, took off his gold lamé jacket, and handed it to one of his attendants. The impersonator, then, not Elvis, jumped into the Cadillac behind the stage. Meanwhile, Presley, along with Robinson, went through a trap door to an area beneath the stage and waited there until the crowd dispersed. Meanwhile, the fake Elvis was not driven out of the stadium, but instead to the dressing-room entrance from which Elvis had first appeared at the start of the concert. Robinson says the man wearing the gold jacket jumped out of the car and ran up the tunnel, with the crowd in hot pursuit.

Gordon Stoker couldn't confirm Robinson's version, but he couldn't discount it either. "Trap door? Seems I remember something like that," Stoker says. "Elvis was always game for anything, and I mean anything, so I wouldn't be surprised if this is true."[29] Colonel Parker had a history of using sleight-of-hand to protect his boy. Jordanaire Neal Matthews recalled how deception was used to get Elvis past adoring fans in 1956. "They'd use decoys a lot," explained Matthews. "Send a big, black limousine up to the stage door, have somebody that sort of looked like him and dressed like him. All the kids would come over there and Elvis'd slip in the side door."[30]

After the PA announcer yelled, "For your information, Elvis has left the stadium. Please go home," many seated on the grass immediately rose, pushed down the metal fence, and advanced upon the stage. The crowd on the field behind them began chanting, "We want Elvis!" and when they realized he was not coming back, those who felt they had been cheated by the short show began to vent their frustration. The *Sun's* John Kirkwood described what happened next.

For 15 minutes after the show's end the hoodlum patrol engaged in open warfare with the police near the stage. One sergeant was attacked by six youths. Another youth, knocked semi-conscious by a well-aimed police blow, was dragged bodily from the turf. A seaman—Daniel Pichtigen, 26—was arrested by four policemen and charged with obstruction and assaulting a police constable.

"What do you do?" gasped one sweating policeman. "They are just animals—punks."

"Move," yelled another, shoving a sideburned lout off the infield. "You're not moving fast enough for me—get out of my sight."[31]

For Jeannine Pepin, one of the young air cadets working with the police that evening, the real action didn't begin until after Elvis left. "I wasn't scared about the teenagers rushing onto the field," she said. "But I was scared after the concert ended. It turned ugly. I remember there was one drunk who was causing trouble near the stage and around eight people were trying to control him."[32] One long-time police officer likened the spectacle in the stadium that evening to the Canadian Post Office riots he had seen in the 1930s.

On stage, the musicians, who had their instruments to protect, didn't get away fast enough, and they soon found themselves surrounded by some of the angry, shortchanged fans, some looking for Elvis, others looking for revenge. What exactly they did at and to the stage is, again, difficult to determine, as the accounts of the eyewitnesses differ widely. Neal Matthews claimed the stage was turned over, along with everything on it. George Klein supports Matthews' version. "When we left that stage the last thing we saw was the stage being turned over—sheet music flying up in the air, they grabbed music stands, instruments, drumsticks, everything they could get. That was a pretty scary sight," said Klein.[33]

Drummer D.J. Fontana, however, dismisses the notion that the stage was completely turned over. "The kids all ran up there and the platform kind of tilted to one side," he recalls. Fontana and Scotty Moore both deny that instruments were lost. Scotty remembers how they kept the fans occupied while they packed their instruments. "They'd ask us where he was and we'd point over that way and they'd take off running. Then they'd come back and we'd point off in another way, and they'd take off screaming again."[34] Finally the three musicians got their instruments loaded into their car, but in his 2002 book, Fontana explained that, while getting into the car was easy, driving away was a lot more difficult.

> We had gotten our equipment off the stage okay, and we all jumped in the car. It was Scotty, Bill, George Klein, and I. Scotty was driving, and boy, was George nervous. He said, "Scotty, put this car on race!

They're gonna kill us!" (Because the fans were shaking the car.) "We're going to get killed in here!" And Scotty said, "Well, we can't run over these people, George." I thought we were going to have to stay there all night long until they decided to leave. We were there for about thirty minutes to an hour, then security came and got rid of all the kids. They meant well, they just got excited, I guess.[35]

So was the stage in Empire Stadium turned over? Well, yes and no. Certainly it would have taken a concerted effort by a large number of people to turn over the heavy double-flatbed trailer stage. Much more credible is Fontana's claim that it was only the much smaller bandstand that got flipped over. "We had a little bandstand maybe a foot high," he explains, "that was set up there for us, but there wasn't much to it. A bunch of kids got on one side of the bandstand. So, of course, the bandstand turned over." D.J.'s version is supported by the comments of Hugh Pickett, who remained at the stadium until 1:00 AM trying to deal with the mess. He mentions damage to the stage but nothing about its having been turned over. "I remember the stage, which was made out of pieces of lumber, was just destroyed—sheet music, musical instruments flying everywhere. It was chaos! I have no idea what these people were trying to accomplish," recalled Pickett.[36]

"It was a good old-fashioned ass-kicking rock'n'roll riot." That was how author Albert Goldman labeled what happened at Elvis' Vancouver concert. But did the mayhem that evening really rise to the level of a "riot"? To read the city's newspaper accounts, you'd think so—thousands repeatedly charging the police, fainting girls hauled off, fistfights between fans and cops, the stage turned over. However, Scotty Moore, ever a calming voice in the Presley saga, has another interpretation of the events that evening. Scotty believes the vast majority of the spectators who spilled onto the field acted reasonably and peacefully. "The media called it a riot, but it wasn't really," contends Scotty. He says the kids moved forward and sat down in front of the stage in an unthreatening manner. It was then that officials came on stage and threatened to end the show if everyone didn't return to their seats. Some in the crowd then turned defiant as the police cordon tried to force them back. In the minds of those who accept Scotty Moore's viewpoint, there would have been few problems had officials simply let the teenagers sit on the grass and watch the show. From their perspective the aggressive behavior of the police escalated tensions, resulting in the riotous behavior of some frustrated fans.

Red Robinson had seen this kind of fan behavior before, though not on this level. For him, there was only one word to describe it. "There was pandemonium," he says. "Pandemonium occurred because this was all so new ... When Bill Haley came to Vancouver in '56, it was the first rock 'n' roll concert in this town. It was wild, pandemonium, euphoric—but a riot? No. To me a riot means that every-thing's under control, the people are under control, and then all of a sudden, out come the water hoses, out come the guns. Nothing like that happened here. With Elvis that night it was troublesome, it was pandemonium, but it wasn't a riot. I'd say … the gathering in front of the stage was where the problem was. That's where the fear was. That's where some people passed out and had to be carried out because they couldn't breathe. The rest of the people were well behaved."

Of course, there had been real rock 'n' roll riots in 1957. In Pittsburgh on the evening of April 7, two hundred and fifty teenagers rioted in a parking lot after a rock 'n' roll dance ended. According to police, the youths "went wild," screaming, fighting, and smashing car windows. Two parked cars were shoved into a creek. The rioters ignored police when they fired fifteen pistol shots into the air and didn't quiet down until officers threatened to turn fire hoses on them. No such extreme action was needed to calm the thousands at Presley's Vancouver concert.

Finally, all the players had drifted away from Empire Stadium, and the drama that was Elvis Presley's 1957 Vancouver, B.C., concert passed into the history and mythology of rock 'n' roll. In moods ranging from excitement to disappointment, the crowd of over sixteen thousand went home. Zollie Volchok, wearing both "I Hate Elvis" and "I Love Elvis" buttons, went to the post-concert party in the penthouse of the Georgia Hotel. Red Robinson went back to the CKWX radio studio for his 10:00 PM show and played nothing but Elvis records until six the next morning. Presley returned to his hotel room to rest. He had slept for only two hours the night before and he had a big day coming up. An early train from Vancouver would take him back into Washington State, where he had afternoon and evening performances scheduled. Still, he did not sleep through the night. At 2:30 AM he called Red Robinson on the DJ's private line to thank him for playing his records all night. Robinson never spoke to Elvis again.

On the morning of Sunday, September 1, Elvis arrived at the Canadian National station to catch the eight o'clock train for Seattle. One of the few people there to see him off at that early hour was thirteen-year-old Alice Peters, who had been tipped off about Presley's departure time by her two brothers-in-law, both Great Northern Railway employees.

"When I saw Elvis," Alice recalled years later, "my brothers-in-law quickly told me to go say something to him. So, I called his name and he turned to me and he put his arm around me and he was incredibly beautiful. And my brothers-in-law said that too, that he was just so well-groomed, and so good-looking, that every-thing about him—his face, his hair, his clothes—he just looked fabulous. And he was also very gentle in the way he spoke; he was very polite."[37]

When Elvis asked Alice whether she had been hurt at the concert the night before, she was too embarrassed to admit she hadn't been there. Before boarding the train, Elvis autographed a piece of paper for her and her hand, too, although her mother made her wash that one off. Alice kept several photos taken at the station that morning to remember what she calls one of the highlights of her childhood.

When Elvis left Vancouver, never to return, controversy and confusion lay in his wake. For nearly two weeks, the blame for what happened in Empire Stadium was debated in the pages of the city's two newspapers. The *Sun's* John Kirkwood and the *Province's* Les Wedman, Ben Metcalfe, and Dr. Ida Halpern all wrote lengthy articles disparaging Elvis' show. As far as they were concerned the real story was not Presley's performance, which they all dismissed outright, but rather the rowdiness of the crowd and determining who was to blame for it.

Metcalfe placed all the blame on Presley and his "gang," implying that the entire show was purposely designed to create the havoc that occurred. "A gang moved into OUR town," Metcalfe wrote, "to exploit 22,000 pre-conditioned adolescents, hired OUR policemen to stop anybody who wanted to get too close, then left with the loot and let the police and the kids fight it our for what was left—nothing ... For that's what happened in Vancouver Saturday night as sure as I'm writing it. And it was a set-up from the word GO." From his stage-front vantage point, Metcalfe at first was surprised to see the crowd take over the field, but soon became convinced that the confrontation between the kids and the police had unfolded just as both Elvis and Colonel Parker wanted.

Metcalfe outlined the plot. "The kids moved back. A girl, her dress torn, was carried screaming in very real hysteria, off the field. Presley came forward, winking gleefully at his cronies, and started it again. This time the kids met the full force of the law and the ushers, while Presley urged them on from the stage." And Colonel Parker's threat to stop the show if the crowd didn't behave? It was delivered "cheek full of tongue," according to Metcalfe, who concluded, "The irony of it all was that the kids went away still loving Elvis, but hating Vancouver policemen. And it should have been the other way round."

Certainly there was the feeling among some patrons, particularly teenagers, that the police caused problems instead of solving them. In a letter printed in the *Sun*, one teenager commented, "Of our policemen I have only this to say. If they would treat teen-agers like human beings instead of shoving them around like cattle they would get better results."[38] A few days later, another letter added, "From what I heard from the kids talking around me they did not hate the police but laughed at them because they mostly stood and watched Elvis instead of keeping everyone back."[39] Looking back years later, Grace Darney, only twelve when she attended the concert, also felt the police should have done their jobs and forced the fans off the field and back into their seats so that Elvis could finish his show.

As for the police, they put the blame on hooliganism and the shortness of Elvis' appearance. Detective Inspector Ian MacGregor said that most of the trouble was caused by "booze and disappointment." He added, "The actual hoodlum element was small. Those who police had trouble with had been drinking. Most of the patrons were just excited kids, who were disappointed Presley wasn't on the stage for more than a half-hour." Years later Grace Darney remained disappointed at Elvis' quick departure. She explained, "He was only on stage for such a short period of time. I think we all got gypped really ... I felt we all should've gotten our money back." For then sixteen-year-old Joe Lee, who took his girlfriend to see Elvis, the disappointment softened over the years. "I didn't think we got our money's worth at the time. But in retrospect, we did see a legend in the making, so I can't complain."

How short did Presley cut his stage performance that evening? Estimates in the Vancouver press had his time on stage ranging from fifteen minutes to just under an hour. Had Colonel Parker not shut him down early, Presley no doubt would have given the Vancouver crowd his full forty-five-minute show. Red Robinson has always contended that Elvis was on the Empire Stadium stage for just twenty-two minutes, and if that is accurate, then the members of the Vancouver crowd got less than half the show they paid for.

Thirteen-year-old Judy Root apparently was one of the few members of the press who actually listened to Elvis that night. In her *Province* article she listed the songs he performed. In order, they were "Heartbreak Hotel," "All Shook Up," "I Was the One," "I Got a Woman," "That's When Your Heartaches Begin," "Fool's Hall of Fame," "Don't Be Cruel," "Love Me," "Mean Woman Blues," and "Hound Dog." The ten songs were eight short of what the Spokane audience had gotten the night before. And, in fact, Presley told the *Sun's* Jack Wasserman that he had planned to do eight more songs in Vancouver. Still, considering the delay for several mid-show crowd warnings, Presley evidently packed a lot of songs into those twenty-two minutes in Vancouver.

The quality of Elvis' performance that night was a mere sidebar to the city's press corps, which viewed the crowd chaos as the main story. As expected, Red Robinson gave Presley a rave review. "Elvis was the consummate showman and his show was magnificent," he concluded. Red, however, could be accused of having the bias of a self-proclaimed Presley fan.

Dr. Ida Halpern, music critic for the *Province,* had no such predisposition as she watched Elvis on stage. Neither did she have the perspective to review the likes of Elvis, since her main role for her paper was to cover the city's symphony performances. Elvis' concert, she attested, "had not even the quality of true obscenity; merely an artificial and unhealthy expression exploitation of the enthusiasm of youth's body and mind. One could call it subsidized sex." Of course, being one more accustomed to the graceful movements of the opera, Dr. Halpern saw no meaning in Presley's gyrations. "Anyone who has seen the convulsions of a frog injected with strychnine, with its legs shivering and jittering, will have already received an impression of Elvis Presley's distorted dangling legs," she wrote. "With the frog the cause is science, but what is the motivation for the cause of Elvis?"[40] She couldn't come up with a good answer.

And what did Presley himself think of the doings in Empire Stadium that late summer evening? In his "The Early Bird" column in the September 3 edition of the *Province*, Hugh Watson, without explaining its context, claimed Elvis said, "Without doubt this was the worst audience I ever played to. Only my first time in Chicago would compare with it. I'd heard that Canadians were a little more rational. Still, they seemed to like it."[41]

As might be expected, the letter columns of the *Sun* and the *Province* were filled with commentary on the concert from both adults and teenagers. Some adults provided negative feedback, while some were positive. Most of the teenagers defended Elvis from what they saw as unfair newspaper reviews, police actions, and adult lack of understanding.

> I am not a teen-ager, but, out of curiosity I attended, with my niece, the performance of Elvis Presley at the Stadium ... He is an egotist and a clown and the songs he murdered made me envy the deaf. I think and hope that Presley did himself more harm than good in Vancouver. Our youngsters have the brains, let's hope they will use them.—Jean Stuart[42]

> As for his jigging his feet while singing, I would say that the sexy interpretation to this habit of his is one of the adult mind; the old duffers who have nothing but sex on their minds. Presley is just a boy, and if our boys and girls want to idolize him, let them.—M. Morrison[43]

> We're Elvis Presley fans and fighting mad. We have some respect for your music. We don't always say it sounds like a bunch of cats on the back fence. Well, it does. You should show us a little respect too. When you criticize Elvis you are criticizing us. Picture yourself doing the Charleston, then try to criticize Elvis.—Fifteen Fans[44]

> I like Elvis. His actions are not grotesque, demented or suggestive. These movements are rhythmic, the same steps teenagers around the world are dancing today, similar to jitterbug of the war years ... I am a teenager, 17 years old, who firmly believes that for all the delinquents

we read about in the papers, there are thousands of clean, decent boys and girls we never hear of. And many of these good teenagers are ardent fans of Elvis Presley.—Ann Archibald[45]

Recently a person of little virtue visited our elite city of the west looking for "suckers." He found $20,000 worth of them. Our girls, who swooned and grinned and guffawed at his salacious "art," are mothers of tomorrow. What may be expected of this future generation? Our city fathers would do well to use some of their profound wisdom to protect our youth and to censor unwanted immorality.—Archibald Beavan[46]

I am sure that if there is a God, he must prefer Elvis, with his naturalness and humanity, to these physically grown creatures who are supposed to be human. These bleating Shylocks who would rob a young boy of all decency and good, merely to satisfy their lust for turning the innocent and harmless into something immoral and obscene.—P. Rowley[47]

A few fans had to answer in court for their behavior at Empire Stadium. One was Daniel Picktigen, who stood before magistrate Alexander McDonald on September 10. Constable J. H. Herriott testified that Picktigen kicked him twice in the leg and punched him in the chest. Picktigen said he "did not remember" what happened. While sentencing the twenty-six-year-old seaman, the magistrate lashed out at rock 'n' roll shows. "These shows are a disgrace," said McDonald. "They should not be allowed here."[48]

In his "Red's Record Rack" column in the September 6 edition of the *Sun*, Red Robinson wrote, in a bit of understatement, "'Mr. Sideburns' has come and gone and there seems to be a mixed reaction to the show." Obviously willing to let the controversy fade, Red continued, "In this column I don't wish to tread over the line of controversy. If you liked the show that's fine … If you didn't like the show that's fine."[49]

There were others, though, who sensed that the fallout from Presley's appearance had dealt a fatal blow to Vancouver's rock 'n' roll scene. Just a few days after the concert, local promoter Jack Cullen proclaimed, "It looks as if Elvis Presley's appearance has finished rock and roll shows in Vancouver. For the past two years I have been instrumental in booking into town such stars as Bill Haley, Little Richard, Fats Domino, Al Hibbler, Ivory Joe Hunter, Earl Bostic and many others. I won't argue that it hasn't always been an uphill fight to find a location to hold these dances or concerts. Arena managers are genuinely cautious of anything that sounds like rock and roll music … As far as Vancouver goes unless there's a change in thinking with the arena owners the kids will get their rock and roll from records or movies but not from personal appearances."

Cullen's dirge for rock 'n' roll shows in Vancouver was premature. In August 1964 a concert by The Beatles in the same Empire Stadium ended early after just twenty-seven minutes due to riotous fan behavior. And there have been other opportunities for Vancouver teenagers of successive generations to uphold their city's reputation as a home to rowdy rock music fans, a reputation born on the night of August 31, 1957, when Elvis Presley played their town.

On stage in Seattle with the Jordanaires (Gordon Stoker, Neal Matthews, Hugh Jarrett, and Hoyt Hawkins), September 1, 1957. (Seattle Post-Intelligencer Collection, Museum of History & Industry, Seattle)

Chapter 13

Seattle–Tacoma

Prelude

Seattle had a population of 865,000 in 1957. Add to that the 157,000 who lived in Tacoma just thirty-two miles to the south, and the two cities nestled up against Puget Sound in western Washington State were home to over a million people the year Elvis Presley came calling.

Of the five Northwest cities Elvis Presley visited that year, Seattle had by far the most dynamic homegrown music scene. The jazz sound down on Jackson Street dated all the way back to the 1920s. During its boom years around World War II, more than thirty nightclubs lined the street. While white musicians worked in the uptown ballrooms, black musicians, including young jazz stars like Quincy Jones and Ray Charles, played the small after-hours clubs up and down Jackson.

In the mid-1950s the new, upbeat, danceable sound of rhythm and blues started taking hold in Seattle. Some jazz spots began to have R&B nights. The most popular was Birdland, which featured national and local acts, as well as David Lewis' house band. The jam sessions at Birdland drew in all the top local musicians. The club soon became the hub of the horn and keyboard R&B sound that eventually became the focus of Northwest rock music.

Unlike in Vancouver to the north and Portland to the south, when true rock 'n' roll came to Seattle, it was not dominated by one radio station or one disc jockey. Teenagers could find the new music up and down the AM dial, as various stations tried to tap into the economic potential of the new style. In 1954, KRJ took a shot at it, but when management pronounced it a passing fad, the station switched back to its old middle-of-the-road sound. (It wasn't until after DJ Pat O'Day arrived on the scene in 1958 that KJR became the rock giant of the Northwest.)

There were no significant Seattle rock 'n' roll bands in the mid-1950s. High school dances, or sock hops, featured disc jockeys playing the latest records by Bill Haley and Elvis Presley. The opening of Seattle's first Dick's Drive-in on January 28, 1954, provided teenagers a venue at which to merge their devotion to cars and rock 'n' roll. Dick Spady and his two partners opened the first Dick's on Forty-fifth Street NE in Seattle's Wallingford neighborhood. The second of many more opened the following year on Capitol Hill. A trip to Dick's was the classic 1950s experience. It was a place to eat cheap hamburgers, hang out with friends, and listen to rock 'n' roll music blasting from the car radio.

Such was the rock 'n' roll music scene in Seattle at summer's end in 1957 when Elvis came to town. Presley's appearance there would inspire the likes of Jimi Hendrix and Pat O'Day to reinvent the city's live music scene. Then, however, it would not be jazz, but vibrant rock sounds that would make Seattle a music haven again.

Tacoma, Washington
Lincoln Bowl
Sunday, September 1, 1957, 2:00 pm

When Elvis Presley awoke on the first day of September, he faced a busy and tight schedule that day. A four-hour train ride, two press conferences, and two concerts were ahead of him. After the morning ride from Vancouver, Elvis stepped on the platform at Seattle's King Street Station a little after noon. A short twelve-block drive took him to the Olympic Hotel, where he had a little time to relax before going to work. About an hour after arriving in Seattle, he climbed into a rented Cadillac for a forty-minute ride south of downtown Seattle to Tacoma.

Bonnie Meier and Judith Yerbich were up early that day. Wearing the matching gray, shiny shirts they had purchased just for the occasion, the two thirteen-year-old Tacoma girls were psyched for their encounter with Elvis Presley that afternoon. Judith's mother got up early with her daughter that Saturday morning to transport the two friends to the Lincoln Bowl. Judith's father thought Presley was a bit corrupt and a poor influence on kids, but her mother was more understanding and tolerant of her daughter's desire to see Elvis. So Judith and Bonnie bought their tickets on the first day they were available and counted down the days to September 1.

Judith's mother dropped them off at the Lincoln Bowl at 7:00 AM, seven hours before the scheduled 2:00 PM show time. Their plan included seeing Elvis if he arrived in Tacoma early and getting the best seats possible. The gates weren't scheduled to open for hours, so the girls decided to do some reconnaissance. They tried to sneak inside the trailer placed on the grounds as Elvis' dressing room, but they were spotted and chased off by security officers. When the gates finally did open, Bonnie was the first one through, with Judith right behind her. They claimed seats in the second row of the folding chairs right in front of the stage. As the hours passed, they guarded their seats and talked with other kids seated around them.

A small crowd of less than six thousand awaited Elvis in Tacoma for what would be the most intimate of the five concerts he performed in the Pacific Northwest. Like those in Spokane and Vancouver, B.C., Tacoma citizens first learned that Presley was coming to their town on August 9. Tickets, at the standard tour prices of $1.50, $2.50, and $3.50, went on sale a week later exclusively at the Bon Marche ticket office.

The venue was the Lincoln Bowl, a small stadium (capacity 14,000) owned by the Tacoma School District and used primarily for high school football games. Some Tacoma citizens viewed the use of a public school facility for an appearance by the likes of Elvis Presley as grossly inappropriate. In a letter to the *Tacoma News Tribune,* Richard F. Perkins complained, "We can use schools for such vulgar acts as Elvis Presley, and our Council of Churches and so-called citizens sit back and allow Elvis Presley to capitalize and put on a show of vulgarism without lifting a hand to try and put a stop to such as this. Yet our school board allows these people to use our school grounds to enable them to put such an act over."[1] Despite the complaints of Perkins and others, plans for Presley's appearance moved forward quickly and inexorably.

A few days before the Presley tour began in Spokane, Colonel Parker visited the Tacoma site. He called for a local security force of sixty officers, most of whom would be off-duty city police officers augmented by a half-dozen Pierce County Sheriffs. The security bill for these officers came to $2,300, which was paid out of the gate receipts.

A week before the Tacoma concert it became apparent that ticket sales were going to fall far short of expectations. As a result, the intended arrangement of the stage and crowd was changed, as had been done in Spokane. The stands on the west side were closed so that the crowd could be concentrated on the east, or G Street, side of the bowl. The stage was placed in the center of the football field facing east, and folding chairs were placed on the grass between the stage and the grandstand. Wood barricades separated the front row of chairs from the stage, but there was only about a dozen yards' worth of open space between them. The setup provided good views of the stage for all. In fact, those seated farthest away in Tacoma were still nearer to Elvis than those seated closest to the stage in Vancouver had been the night before.

Elvis' taking the stage at about 3:30 in the afternoon was another bonus for Tacoma's teenagers. With the sun still high in the sky and the crowd being comparatively close to the stage, fans with cameras had a realistic opportunity to get good images of Elvis in action. The same could not be said for the Brownie-toting fans in Spokane, Vancouver, Seattle, and Portland, where Elvis did not arrive on stage until around 9:30 PM. It was impossible for camera flash bulbs to illuminate Elvis from a distance in the darkness. Forty years later, Cherie Peterson still prizes the photos she took that afternoon in the Lincoln Bowl. "I took pictures with my Brownie camera—one of Elvis' Cadillac, one of the Jordanaires and one of the King," she recalled. "All are far away and somewhat shaky, but to me, they are true treasures."[2]

That afternoon Elvis held his pre-concert press conference in the low, drafty, concrete dressing room of the Lincoln High School football team. Colonel Parker introduced his boy to newsmen and officials of Tacoma and Seattle fan clubs. According to the *Tribune's* Don Duncan, Parker pointed at Elvis and said, "This fine Christian young man, Suh, a model of rectitude and a pride to his mother, will someday be the greatest star the movies have ever known. Comedy, even Shakespearean drama, are within his range."[3] As Elvis, wearing a straw hat and a blue and white sweater, sat through his manager's introduction, *Tribune* photographer Wayne Zimmerman set up his bulky 4 X 5 Speed Graphic and studied camera angles.

Then Elvis, described by Duncan as "shy, polite and almost boyish in appearance," answered questions. He denied that he was engaged to the girl (Anita Wood) he had left crying in the Memphis train station a week ago, "although you all can say she's more than just a friend," he added. "I'll know when the right girl comes along." He was saving his money, he told those assembled, and then listed for them the vehicles he owned—four Cadillacs (one pink, one blue, and two white), a Messerschmitt, a Lincoln, a Mark II, and two motorcycles. As in Vancouver, he denied having any affinity for teddy bears. "Sure I have about seventy all over the house," he said. "But they were all sent to me by fans after a reporter saw me carrying home a teddy bear I'd won at the fair. Besides, little kids who visit my home go nuts when they see all the bears." He denied seeing a threat in any of the newcomers in the rock 'n' roll field. "There's plenty of room for all of us," Elvis assured his listeners, and named Ricky Nelson and Tommy Sands as his favorite young singers. At the other end of the pop spectrum, Elvis also allowed that there would always be people who preferred the likes of Bing Crosby (who had been born in Tacoma) and Perry Como. "After all, they've been around for years, and me, I've just been on top for a year and a half," he said.

As usual, there were many inquires about his personal musical style. Elvis admitted that he was a different man when on stage. "I lose myself in my singing," he explained. "Maybe it's my early training singing gospel hymns. I'm limp as a rag, worn out, when a show is over. Why I had a couple of nervous breakdowns a while back when I was making too many of these one-night stands." No sir, he didn't mean to be vulgar when wiggling his hips during a song. "It's just my way of expressing my inner emotions," he explained yet again.

After the questions stopped, Elvis taped a get-well message to Caroline Jardeen, a bedridden Tacoma girl who couldn't attend the concert. Then Presley mingled informally with those fans lucky enough to be present. He signed autographs for fan club members and policemen who gathered around. The most unusual autograph went to Tacoma's Diane Steinke, who asked Elvis to sign his name on her forehead. "I'll never wash again as long as I live," the star-struck teenager vowed in the glow of the moment.

Another teenager who had an unforgettable encounter with Elvis that day was Sharon O'Malley. "My dad, Pat O'Malley Sr., was a Tacoma policeman who was helping cover security," Sharon explained years later. "He asked me if I wanted to meet Elvis before the show in the football dressing room. Well, I walked in the door and there he stood! I started crying, so he came over and put his arms around me and said, 'Don't cry darlin' or I'll start crying, too.' And then he kissed me on my left cheek! I was 14 and thought I'd died and gone to heaven!"[4]

At the show's advertised starting time of 2:00 PM, the parade of opening acts began. Elvis went on stage at about 3:30.

Judith Yerbich and Bonnie Meier had a great view of the stage. Since they were so close, they could actually hear Elvis sing over the continual screaming behind them. Of course, from time to time they also contributed to the din. For Judith, the concert ranked as one of her first experiences as a teenager. "I really was so excited about the group gathering and the crowd mentality," she recalls.[5] Bonnie kept busy cranking her camera. She had her picture taken with Colonel Parker and snapped six black-and-whites of Elvis on stage.

Tacoma was a one-newspaper town in those days, so only one account and review of Elvis' performance that afternoon appeared in the press. Reporter Don Duncan's testimony, along with Wayne Zimmerman's photos, dominated the *News Tribune's* September 2 edition. On September 7, the paper printed a letter condemning Duncan's article.

> After reading your write up on the performance Elvis Presley gave at the Lincoln Bowl Sept. 1, I do not wonder at the many adults who disapprove of Elvis so strongly. I attended the performance and found your article so grossly exaggerated it was sickening. You made Elvis sound so utterly vulgar and the audience so like a screaming mob of

idiots that it was hard for me to believe that you were referring to the same performance I attended.

I do not feel, either, that such over-dramatization of the facts (many of which were exaggerated to the point that they were untrue) was entirely necessary.

Though I am a teenager, I am not an ardent Elvis fan, so this letter is not based on prejudice.

All shook up.[6]

Immediately following Lexi Arick's letter was the following response from the *Tribune.*

Editor's Note: After the appearance of TNT staffer Don Duncan's article, Elvis Presley called Mr. Duncan and said that it was "the best article ever written about me."

Allowing for the young Presley's well-known tendency at times to embellish and overstate his appreciation for writers, disc jockeys, and other media types who treated him fairly, his phone call made clear that the singer very much liked Duncan's account of his afternoon appearance in Tacoma. Indeed, Duncan seemed to capture the sensual presence of Elvis on stage better than most journalists who covered the singer's concerts in 1957. "He wiggled his hips in tight-fitting black pants and several thousand girls gasped and screamed in unison," Duncan wrote. "He spread his arms and they shrieked again. 'I'll take care of you in a minute,' Elvis Presley said husky-voiced to the loudest of his fans. And 6,000 people in Lincoln Bowl yesterday erupted in shouts, screams and hand-clapping." Then, as the band cranked up the beat, Elvis pulled the microphone to his mouth. Duncan described what happened next.

As he sang be began a slow, rhythmic movement of his pelvic region, his legs vibrated, his upper torso caught up the movement and alternately swayed and shimmied. Each new movement was greeted by fresh screams.

He fell to his knees and socked out the rock'n'roll beat with his body. He waved at the crowd and sang always in that pulsating, almost native beat—"I lu-u-u-v yew-ew-ew-ew."

Often the great roar of the crowd snuffed out the words. But no stranger in the crowd could doubt 'twas Elvis at the mike.[7]

Duncan described Presley's interaction with his audience. "Elvis was here to make them cast inhibitions aside," the writer explained, "to blend his personality into theirs so each would think he was singing just for them. He succeeded." And while other reporters labeled Elvis' stage gyrations as mere cheap tricks, Duncan saw them as purposeful elements in a choreographed performance. "Each squirm was as carefully calculated as a Shakespeare soliloquy to heighten the dramatic effect," he noted. Duncan's description of Presley's closing number makes the scene easy to visualize. "He strutted like a duck," Duncan wrote, "his hands dangling loosely in front of him. He went to his knees in an attitude of prayer, taking the slender microphone with him. And he finished with a burst of shimmying that left him limp, his thick black hair hanging over his eyes and perspiration pouring down his pancake makeup."

At one point during the show, Duncan noticed a "chunky, effeminate-looking man with long hair" standing near the stage. The man seemed in a trance as he snapped his fingers, wiggled his body, and repeatedly shouted, "yeah man" at Elvis. Although Lamar Fike probably resented Duncan's description of him as "effeminate-looking," in retrospect it is difficult to understand how Miss Lexi Arick could have gotten so all shook up over the reporter's account of Elvis' performance in Tacoma. Certainly, compared to the caustic attacks on Presley by numerous Canadian journalists in the wake of the Vancouver debacle the night before, Duncan's article seems almost an affirmation of Presley and thus downright treasonous to the adult race, whose media seemed almost unified in its condemnation of Presley's onstage behavior. It is evident from his writing that Duncan went to see Presley with an open mind. He described what he saw that September afternoon in the Lincoln Bowl and left it for his readers to do the judging. That's probably all Elvis Presley ever asked of the press, and that's probably why he took the time to call Don Duncan and praise his article.

Compared to the controversy and confusion surrounding the concert in Vancouver, the Presley performance in Tacoma was trouble-free. About the only controversy resulting from the Tacoma event concerns what happened to some of the dirt in front of the stage after Elvis departed. Don Duncan noted that some girls "kissed" handfuls of dirt before dumping it in their pockets or purses. However, in a 1997 article in the *News Tribune,* writer Bart Ripp asserted, "Some girls ate the dirt." Ripp probably got that notion from Ernie Misner of Tacoma, who was only eleven years old when he saw Elvis in the Lincoln Bowl in 1957. Forty years later, Ripp quoted Misner as saying, "Whenever I recall that wonderful event, I think of those darn girls eating the dirt that he walked on after the show." Certainly, it would please many of Elvis' most rabid supporters today to think he actually had the power to make young girls eat dirt. However, it is doubtful that any of those Tacoma girls, who stayed in their seats throughout the concert, became hysterical enough when it was over to consume dirt just because Elvis Presley's footprint was on it. No doubt, as Duncan observed, some girls raised the dirt to their mouths and kissed it, and young Ernie Misner, seeing that action, mistook the kiss for consumption.

Duncan's *News Tribune* article and a letter from Carole Rae Norman, published in the paper forty years later, provide the following partial list of songs Elvis performed in Tacoma: "Don't Be Cruel," "I Want You, I Need You, I Love You," "Blueberry Hill," "Heartbreak Hotel," "That's All Right," "Too Much," "Ready Teddy," and "Hound Dog."

In 1997 the *News Tribune* printed a retrospective look at the Presley concert in Tacoma forty years before. Bart Ripp wrote a short introduction for the article. He had previously asked readers who had been in the Lincoln Bowl that day in 1957 to send in their remembrances, and the 1997 article is filled with their recollections.[8]

> I was 11 and it was the thrill of my young life … When Elvis came onto the stage, all the girls went crazy. An announcer had warned the crowd to stay in their seats or Elvis would leave. Everyone was screaming and jumping up and down … Elvis did not disappoint the excited crowd. His swivel hips and shimmering gold jacket ignited the flame in all of us.—Helen West, Puyallup

> I was 13. My heart pounded in anticipation of my first real glimpse of my idol, Elvis Presley. My 45 rpm records were nearly worn out as I played my favorites over and over, and dreamed of him as I kissed his picture before going to bed each night. He was the first of many teenage crushes, but certainly the most powerful. My father thought I was on my way to becoming a juvenile delinquent by following this "degenerate," but luckily my mother prevailed and I was allowed to go to the concert … We were just mesmerized. I was hoarse for three days afterward from all the screaming.—Rose C. Faulk, Gig Harbor

> My friend Anna and I walked from the old Rhodes department store downtown to Lincoln Bowl. Anna had new shoes and had blisters on her heels by the time we got there. It was quite a hot day. We had seats about halfway back from the stage. Some of the girls were just going crazy. They screamed most of the time the show was going on. One girl who had a seat up front on the aisle actually rolled in the dust. Anna and I were quite conservative and thought that this girl was slightly odd.

The performance was great. Elvis put his all into the event. I couldn't believe I was there to see this great performer.—Gwen Adams, Milton

I took my 10-year-old daughter Candace, her friend Kathy and a friend visiting from Portland. I almost felt ancient since I was 27. What a thrill to see and hear Elvis!!! What a great show that very young boy in the gold jacket put on!!! My friend and I screamed, yelled and stamped our feet while our two pre-teens sat and just stared and tried to pretend they were not really with us.—Beverly Ahnert, University Place

I was 17 and just graduated from Lincoln High ... There was a group of 14-15-year-old girls seated behind us that was screaming, shouting and crying. One completely tore a handkerchief to shreds. Elvis acknowledged their screams by saying, 'Hang on honey, I'll be right there.' This drove them wild.—Dick Flom, Anderson Island

I was there, second row right in front of the stage, all by myself. My husband purchased one ticket and baby-sat while I attended. Believe me, it was a thrill and then some! Elvis was a *very* handsome man and I can still conjure up his dynamic presence in my mind whenever I hear his music.—Jan Wells, Puyallup

Yes, I was one of those electrified fans ... My mother, bless her heart, sat there with me. She had no idea how much that day meant to me.—Bev Rarey, Spanaway

After the concert ended, Bonnie Meier and Judith Yerbich went home, but they kept plotting to get a souvenir from the concert. The next day the two girls went to the Betz Trailers lot, just blocks from where they lived in South Tacoma. They found the trailer Elvis had used the day before and snuck inside to look for something connected to him. As it turned out, they found very little and settled for a stack of coat hangers, which they stealthily took away with them.

At fewer than six thousand, the crowd at the Lincoln Bowl in Tacoma the afternoon of September 1 was by far the smallest Elvis Presley faced during his five-city tour of the Pacific Northwest. No doubt the local promoter lost a good amount of money by bringing Elvis to town, but for Elvis fans, Tacoma provided a much better backdrop for experiencing the Presley phenomenon than did Spokane, Vancouver, B.C., Seattle, or Portland. When it became obvious that ticket sales were going to be low, venue and tour officials had the foresight and wisdom to create an intimate setting that brought Elvis and his audience close together. The afternoon daylight enhanced viewing, as did the majority of the spectators, who paid heed to the pre-concert warning to stay in their seats. They screamed and yelled as much as the fans in the other cities, but photos taken in the Lincoln Bowl that day show that most did so from a seated position. The Elvis experiences in Vancouver, B.C., and in Tacoma could not have been more different, although they occurred only eighteen hours apart. The nonsensical arrangement of stage and crowd in Vancouver produced a disappointing experience for most spectators, while the cozy arrangement in Tacoma allowed for a personal, interactive rock 'n' roll experience, leaving many who were there with vivid and cherished memories of seeing a young and vibrant Elvis Presley.

At Presley's Tacoma press conference, Don Duncan asked for and received the singer's autograph. When Elvis neglected to use capital letters in that autograph, Duncan decided to do the same in a follow-up article in the *Tribune* a week after the concert. Since Elvis was in a Hollywood recording studio that day, and since Duncan's article was buried at the bottom of an inside page of the newspaper, it's doubtful Presley ever read it. Still, it's likely "old sideburns" would have enjoyed it. Duncan fashioned the article in a humorous, folksy style, in contrast to his sensual morning-after review.

> memo to the boss:
> since a lot of folks have sidled up to me in the past few days and asked for the plain, unvarnished truth about old sideburns hisself, i figured i'd let you in on all the secrets i learned.
> first off, this elvis has all his own hair and don't let anybody tell you it's a wig or those sideburns are painted on, and wen those locks fell down on his forehead and he had to peek through them like veronica lake did before she went out of style, that was the real elvis …
> he's quick on the uptake, too. i asked him if it was true that he flunked his army physical and wasn't going to be called into the service and have his hair cut off gi-style, and all that, and he answered, "well hardly, sir. shucks, i passed it all right" …
> well, the music was really the thing out there at lincoln bowl, and make no mistake about it this boy elvis could have taught dr. goebbels a thing or two about mass psychology.
> this rock'n'roll business has a real slugging beat that twists your insides all around and sets up some sort of chemical action that comes out in foot-tapping and screams. since i am too old to be screaming at 22-year-old singers, especially when they aren't girls, i just fixed a silly grin on my face and it served the purpose.[9]

Duncan was undecided about what to do with the autograph Presley had given him. He had it down to two options. He asked himself, "should i send it to the smithsonian institute or to poor old cousin harry who married a hula dancer?"

Seattle, Washington
Sicks' Seattle Stadium
Sunday, September 1, 1957, 8:30 pm

In the summer of 1956, sixteen-year-old Kathy Mansfield thought Harry Belafonte was "absolutely dreamy." About to start her senior year at Highline High School, Kathy couldn't understand why many other girls swooned over Elvis Presley. While working in a record store, however, she became annoyed by criticism of Elvis voiced by older customers and decided to listen closely to his music. Then she took a close look at his picture and suddenly she was swept into the Presley whirlwind.

Along with Vicki, her eleven-year-old sister, Kathy played Elvis records repeatedly for the rest of the summer, and before long, she too screamed whenever she heard Elvis sing. She was sure she was in love with him.

A lot can happen to a girl between the ages of sixteen and seventeen, however, and so by the summer of 1957, Kathy knew she really wasn't in love with Elvis. She remained convinced, though, that Presley was definitely "neat," talented, and here to stay. So when the president of the Elvis Presley Fan Clubs of Western Washington left Seattle, Kathy stepped in to keep things from falling apart. Although president in name, she was more like a coordinator, a disseminator of information, and an organizer for the various state Elvis fan clubs west of the Cascade Mountains. Members didn't pay dues and anyone could join. Recruited representatives spread the gospel of Elvis in their schools, and Kathy spearheaded a drive to come up with a slogan to put on the group's pink and black membership cards.

On learning in early August that Elvis would appear in Seattle on September 1, Kathy began spreading the news among the membership. Predictably, the president herself grew quite excited about seeing Presley in person. Even though she had passed her obsessive state concerning Elvis, she knew she'd probably do some screaming when the time came. "It just happens," she explained to John Voorhees of the *Seattle Post-Intelligencer* a week before the concert. "You can't explain it. He does funny things—the way he looks at you, kind of mean-like, or he lifts an eyebrow. And you find yourself screaming."[10]

Speaking for her 15,000-strong membership, Kathy answered Voorhees' questions. No, there won't be a riot. There will be a lot of screaming, but that hardly constitutes a riot. That fear is just a figment of adult imaginations. No, the weather doesn't matter. "What if it should rain?" she asked. "Why, we've been waiting a year to hear him in Seattle. All his fans will go anyway."

It was after 10:00 PM when Elvis Presley climbed the stairs to the stage in Sicks' Seattle Stadium to face a crowd of over sixteen thousand for his second concert of the day. The setting for this performance differed from those in Spokane, Vancouver, B.C., and Tacoma. In those cities, Elvis performed in football stadiums, which presented difficult viewing angles and resulting security problems. In Seattle, and the next night in Portland, Presley performed in cozier and spectator-friendly baseball fields. At Sicks' Stadium, home of the minor league Seattle Rainiers, the forty-by-sixteen-foot makeshift stage sat directly over second base facing home plate. A semi-circle of low wooden barriers separated the stage from rows of folding chairs that filled the infield. The majority of the crowd sat in the baseball grandstands, which curved inward toward the stage as they extended down the left and right field sides. Still others watched for free from "tightwad hill" overlooking the stadium beyond the left field fence.

Presley came to the stage in his standard dress for the tour, his shimmering gold lamé jacket with a matching sequined, gold belt on his black pants. The shirt was black as well. Nothing like the crowd insurgence of the night before occurred in Seattle, but how Elvis chose to both start and end the Seattle concert created mild dispute and controversy.

After finishing up his afternoon concert in Tacoma at about 4:15, Elvis jumped into the Cadillac that brought him there and was driven from the floor of the Lincoln Bowl directly back to Seattle. It was a Sunday, so traffic on the freeway was light. Presley and his men were back at the Olympic Hotel by about 5:00 PM. With the Seattle show that evening scheduled to start at 8:30, Elvis had several hours to rest up and have dinner.

Although everyone seemed to know Elvis was staying at the Olympic, two days before he arrived in Seattle, the local promoter tried to set up a smoke screen by telling the press that Elvis had been registered in at least three hotels under names that even he didn't know. One hotel manager who got caught up in the search for Elvis was Haruo Fujino of the Presley Hotel at Sixth and Weller. According to Fujino, he got so many calls asking if Presley was staying at the Presley that the hotel's phone number had to be changed.

Tickets had gone on sale for the Seattle appearance on August 16. They could be purchased downtown at Sherman and Clay, which handled the mail orders as well. Tickets also were available in person at several Seattle suburb locations, including Johnson Brothers Record Shop in Ballard, the Treasure Chest in Burien, Rouse TV in Renton, the Northgate Music Box, and the Music Bazaar in Bellevue. Zollie Volchok later announced that the first mail order for tickets came from Mrs. Carolyn Taylor, who stated that she wasn't wild about Presley but did have two sons who were.

As the newspaper's music critic, John Voorhees led the *Post-Intelligencer's* coverage of Presley's appearance in town. In the paper's August 18 issue, he pondered what might happen at the rocker's show, then still two weeks off. In his "Look and Listen" column, Voorhees predicted that the real Elvis Presley, stripped of the hype, would reveal himself the night of September 1. "At any rate," wrote Voorhees, "it will be an experience to see the controversial Presley in person and be able to see whether he's the exciting personage that teen-agers find him to be or whether he's the noisy, no-talent, annoying individual that so many adults have labeled him."[11]

As advertised, The Elvis Presley Show got underway promptly at 8:30. The second game of a scheduled doubleheader between the Seattle Rainiers and the Los Angeles Angels had been cancelled so that the stadium could be configured into a fortress for the show. Five thousand seats were placed on the field in front of the stage. The rest of the expected 17,000 spectators would sit in the stadium grandstand and bleachers. Between the field seats and the stage, fifty construction sawhorses were linked together to create a flimsy four-foot-high barricade, which one promoter termed merely a "psychological barrier." Just in case emotion overrode psychology, a human wall of sixty-five policemen and a hundred ushers had been hired to provide a secondary line of defense for the night's headliner. Twenty-one reserve policemen, all serving without pay, were assigned to control traffic around the stadium.

As in other cities, the crowd tolerated, at best, the string of opening acts. Voorhees trivialized them in his review the next morning. "Before Elvis came on we were treated to a whole group of singers, dancers, comedians, jugglers, marimba players and orchestral numbers—all performed by those whom the management assured us were 'personal friends of Elvis.' (Do you suppose a Major Bowes unit ever got stranded in Tennessee?)"[12]

Between each act, the announcer urged spectators to buy Elvis hats, Elvis buttons, Elvis souvenir albums, Elvis photos, even Elvis ice cream bars. Sales were brisk, although Voorhees explained that many teenagers feared leaving their seats for the concession area. "One of the evening's pastimes had been for some joker to announce loudly, 'There he is!' And the whole audience would jump to its feet, search the baseball field frantically, then sink back foolishly, realizing they'd been taken."

Of course, during those false alarms, their idol, after motorcycle policemen had escorted him the three miles from the Olympic Hotel to Sicks' Stadium, sat in the Seattle Rainiers' locker room giving his second press conference of the day. Kneeling, sometimes sitting, on a wooden training table, Presley faced about two dozen reporters and young female fans, all of whom sat calmly in two rows of wooden folding chairs in front of him. Behind Elvis stood two of his traveling companions, Lamar Fike and Gene Smith, along with Parker assistant Tom Diskin. Parker himself sat strategically in the far right seat of the back row. A couple of press photographers kept snapping pictures, but unlike in Vancouver, no radio men pushed their microphones into Presley's face. A single microphone sat unattended at one end of the table on which Elvis perched.

Out of place among the group of journalists at the press conference was Royal Brougham, the eminent sports writer for the *Post-Intelligencer.* Just why Brougham would be covering an entertainer like Presley is a mystery, but in keeping with his job description, he asked Elvis some sports questions.[13]

"What's your favorite sport?"

"I love football most of all, but I haven't any time for it. I haven't any time for anything I like. On the move every minute. Why, I've only averaged three hours sleep a night the last week. Can't go to a football game or a baseball game or a movie or even the county fair in my own home town. It's the girls … they tear a guy to pieces."

"Are you following the exciting big league baseball races?"

"Same thing—too busy to even read the sports pages. Don't know who's in first place."

"But the girls love you. Is that bad?"

"It's pandemonium. They don't mean no harm, but I've been clawed and scratched, mauled, shoved and kicked. I've even been bitten. Football was never like this."

A photo of Elvis appeared on page eighteen of the *Post-Intelligencer* on September 3, possibly the only time his image ever appeared in a newspaper sports section. Under the headline "Elvis Unhappy; Misses Sports," Brougham wrote, "Elvis Presley is just a frustrated football player. He's a boy who couldn't make his high school team, so he picked on a $12 guitar instead. He's the lonesomest man in the world."

A little after ten o'clock, Elvis, surrounded by a cordon of police officers, issued from the visitors' dugout and jogged across the infield to the stage, where Scotty, Bill, and D.J. awaited him. Security was extensive from the start. After the fiasco in Vancouver the previous night, Colonel Parker had hurried down to Seattle and demanded that local promoters hire more off-duty police officers than had originally been planned. The estimate by Marjorie Jones of the *Times* that a hundred officers were on the field was probably an exaggeration, but there is no doubt that Parker was determined that his client would not be put in danger again. Before Elvis appeared, repeated announcements came over the public address system warning that the show would be stopped if anyone crossed the wooden barriers. As Elvis took to the stage, a phalanx of policemen encircled the platform.

The added security was unneeded. Despite the large crowd, the stage's position and the tight U-shaped grandstand provided good views for all spectators. The mass screaming was as earsplitting as elsewhere, but beyond that, the throng behaved reasonably. Voorhees saw no rowdiness in the crowd. "High-spirited, yes," he observed. "But no more so than a pep rally or at a revival meeting."

When Elvis first approached the microphone, the crowd quieted somewhat, awaiting his first utterance. And that first sound—a burp, according to John Voorhees—produced the night's first sustained mass scream from the crowd. But was it a burp? Not according to Patrick MacDonald, who was there and heard the sound. In 2002, MacDonald, then the *Times* music critic, wrote an article looking back at the event forty-five years before. In his retrospect, MacDonald wrote, "The screams were deafening as he mounted the stage, and he just stood there grinning for a few minutes. When it quieted down a little, he grabbed the microphone and slowly purred 'Well,' in a Southern accent (the morning paper said the next day that 'he belched,' which taught me to never trust newspapers)."14 However, in the same article, MacDonald asked his readers who had attended the 1957 concert to send him their own remembrances of the event, and one of them disagreed with him about the nature of Presley's initial sound that night. In her recollections, subsequently printed in the *Times,* Laurie Warshal Cohen noted, "All of the people I can contact from that night swear that the King came out on the stage, walked to the microphone, held it in his hand close to his mouth, and burped. None of us remember (him saying) 'Well.' I would like to know from others who were there what they think—but I have five able-bodied votes for the burp."15

MacDonald's assertion that Presley voiced a drawn-out "Well" stands alone against Voorhees and Cohen's group, who all heard a burp. History throws its weight behind the ears of the majority in this controversy. Elvis had belched on stage before, many times. As his popularity began to increase after his TV appearances in early 1956, Elvis soon realized that any kind of nonsensical action or stunt on stage, such as burping, produced equally nonsensical screaming from the girl-dominated crowd. It pleased Presley's sense of humor and met his need to make his performances fun for both himself and his audiences to sprinkle such non-musical antics throughout his stage show. Even at age twenty-two, Elvis Presley still was a bit of a little boy unwilling to grow up. So his fans in Seattle may have been surprised to hear him belch on stage in 1957, but had they known him better, they would have realized it was completely in character.

Following the initial burp, the remainder of Elvis' Seattle concert followed the pattern of the earlier shows in Spokane and Tacoma. Reporting the event for the *Times,* Marjorie Jones took her assignment as an opportunity to practice her obvious fondness for alliteration. The opening paragraph of her article in the next morning's paper read, "A shrieking, screaming mass of 'tingling' teen-age worshipers squealed their devotion last night to their idol, the writhing, wiggling country-singer, Elvis Presley, at Sicks' Seattle Stadium." Later she referred to Elvis as a "sexy, side-burned, sullen-eyed Southerner," and observed that he "shook, shivered, slumped, slouched and staggered through all his hit record songs." Jones neatly packed her honest evaluation of Presley into one sentence tucked in the middle of an otherwise superficial review. "Vulgar is the kindest way to describe Presley's pulsating gyrations," she concluded.[16]

Those gyrations, which posed a moral problem to some observers, also posed a practical problem on stage. The makeshift stage was small, especially considering that seven other performers shared it with Elvis. The Jordanaires stood behind Elvis, and according to the group's Gordon Stoker, it made Presley feel safer to perform close to them. This caused a special concern for bass singer Hugh Jarrett, whose position in the group often placed him closest to center stage. "I worried sometimes," Jarrett recalls. "I was on the side of Elvis. He was in the middle of the stage, and we were on the left side facing the audience. When he'd jump across, stomping his feet, I was scared he was going to stomp on my foot. You know, he never did. It was just something that occurred to me and I watched out for."[17]

In his review for the *Post-Intelligencer,* John Voorhees had the same problem experienced by most other journalists seeing a Presley concert for the first time— figuring out how to review a singer whose singing couldn't be heard. "Elvis began singing some of his recorded hits in his own inimitable fashion," wrote Voorhees. "His now famous (or notorious) bumps and grinds accompanied each of the numbers and each and every one elicited great screams of joy from the audience. Actually Elvis' movements seemed to delight the onlookers much more than the singing—which could mean burlesque is on the way back."

Reporters of the day often resorted to some kind of comparison to describe the reaction of the crowd to Presley's stage behavior. Voorhees came up with one of the better ones when referring to Elvis' closing number. "He sang 'Hound Dog' … and the roof came down with a scream that sounded like 12,000 girls all having their heads shaved at once."

Press reports confirm that in addition to "Hound Dog," Presley numbers at the Seattle concert included "Heartbreak Hotel," "Fool's Hall of Fame," "Teddy Bear," "Loving You," and "All Shook Up." In addition, Patrick MacDonald recalls that Elvis sang "maybe a dozen more songs," which would bring the total to about eighteen, the same amount he is known to have performed in Spokane.

In his 2002 *Times* article, MacDonald mentioned an unusual song that Elvis included in his Seattle show. "Elvis historians cite the (Seattle) concert as the only one at which he sang 'Fool's Hall of Fame,' which he introduced as 'my next single.' ... As it turned out, Elvis never recorded the song, and he never sang it again. (If anyone recorded the concert, including that song, the tape would be worth millions.)" The Elvis historians MacDonald consulted misled him, as Presley definitely also sang "Fool's Hall of Fame" during the shortened Vancouver concert the night before. Before going on stage in Vancouver, Elvis told Red Robinson that his version of the song would be coming out on RCA records. Red was familiar with the song, which he referred to as a "southern rhythm rocker," since it had already been recorded by little-known Sun recording artist Rudy Richardson. In Red's "Record Rack" column in the *Vancouver Sun* a few days after Elvis left town in 1957, Robinson wrote, "Elvis' Fools Hall of Fame is a song to watch because if he is on the wane, as some people claim, the sales of the new record will indicate it."

As MacDonald noted, however, Presley never released the song, although Elvis' claims in both Vancouver and Seattle that the song by him would be released indicates that he tried to record it. Since he had done the song live on stage, an arrangement with his band and the Jordanaires obviously had already been worked up. Recording the song should have been easy and quick, but for some unknown reason, it didn't work out that way. Drummer D.J. Fontana recalls that the song worked better on stage than it did in the studio. "We tried that tune, I guess a half a dozen times," Fontana said in a 1998 interview. "I don't remember if we ever got a good cut ... On stage it was great ... but there was something about it. It was just one of those songs that you can't get a feel on. I think they finally cut it, but it was a throwaway song."[18]

When Patrick MacDonald wrote, "If anyone recorded the concert, including that song, the tape would be worth millions," he may have been exaggerating the dollar amount, but he was correct that such a tape would be valuable. No viable audiotapes of a Presley stage show in 1957 are known to exist. In a 2005 interview on Sirius Radio, Ernst Jorgensen, the keeper of Elvis' musical legacy for Sony BMG and the RCA label, said, "We're desperately looking for anything from '57." There was one particular concert song Jorgensen wanted to find. "There is a rumor," he told the interviewer, "that Elvis in '57, at one of his shows, played a song that he never recorded, called 'Fools Hall of Fame.' Obviously that's a main target."[19]

As usual, Elvis ended his concert in Seattle by singing "Hound Dog." However, due to the omission of a telling detail by one of the newspaper reviewers, the closing number caused Presley's patriotism to be questioned. Marjorie Jones of the *Times* correctly reported that Elvis introduced "Hound Dog" as "the Elvis Presley national anthem." However, Voorhees of the *PI* apparently did not hear the complete introduction, and his account the next day read, "Toward evening's end, Elvis gave everyone a turn by feigning a serious look, standing relaxed and quiet and announcing that the next number would be the National Anthem. Wham! He sang 'Hound Dog' instead." Of course, Presley's seeming disrespect for the national anthem drew a letter of protest that both the *PI* and the *Times* published several days later.

> After the Elvis Presley exhibition I am sick. Until now I have never really said much about Elvis, but after the show and his comparison to the national anthem with "Hound Dog" I feel somebody should say something.
>
> I am 19 and in the Naval Reserve. For the last three months I have been a color guard for the Sand Point Naval Air Station and have marched in a majority of the Seafair celebrations. In this position you see what respect the flag commands. For this reason I feel any person who would make fun of the flag in this way should be condemned to the highest degree.
>
> Also Elvis is not to be blamed completely as any person who would act the way the 10,000 people did when Elvis started singing "Hound Dog" should also be condemned.
>
> I've always considered the majority of the youth of the nation to have fairly high morals. I can see now why we are not considered mature until we are 21.
>
> I also feel that if Elvis would use his perfectly-toned voice for good music and would drop the emphasis that he puts on body motions, he would do our youth a lot more good.—Charles S. Hadley Jr., Seattle[20]

Singing the redundant "Hound Dog" lyrics, Presley fell to his back on stage, and then came to his knees to finish the final chorus. While Scotty played eight more bars, Elvis jumped off the stage without a wave or a bow and hurtled into the back of a waiting Cadillac. Leaving tire tracks on the outfield grass, the car disappeared through a gate in the right field fence before most spectators realized the show was over.

When they realized their prey was escaping, a throng of girls, intent on pursuit, rushed the wooden barrier around the stage. Security forces held most of them back, but a few crossed "no woman's land" to the stage. Their leader implored a stagehand, "We just want to touch the microphone," and it was obligingly lowered to them. As they caressed it, one voice was heard coming through the stage speaker system. "He touched it! He touched it!" it said. "Ohmygawd! Ohmygawd!" Others scooped up dirt around the stage and dumped it into purses and pockets. There was nothing, though, like the battle with police that had taken place the night before in Canada. The theft of a taillight from a convertible mistaken for Presley's was the only damage reported to police.

After the show, Elvis and his entourage returned to the Olympic Hotel to get some rest before catching the morning train to Portland. Scotty, Bill, and D.J. retreated to their hotel rooms, as did the Jordanaires. All of the backup musicians and singers would be driving the 175 miles to Portland in the morning. According to Hugh Jarrett of the Jordanaires, by 1957 there was not much contact between Elvis and his stagemates after a performance. "Whatever his plans called for the rest of the night, he would do, and we would do our thing," explained Jarrett. "Sometimes we hadn't had dinner yet, or we'd go into a bar and have a beer or something. We just had our time. We had to make sure we knew what the schedule was and where we were to be, and we did that."[21]

Ten days after Presley left town, letters to the editor began to appear defending him against Hadley's charge that the singer lacked the proper respect for the national anthem. Leonard Butcher wrote to the *PI*, "Certainly Presley and his fans had no intentions of supplanting the national anthem with "Hound Dog," catchy as the tune may be. As for disrespect for the flag, that is ridiculous. Being past 50 I am no Presley or Rock and Roll addict, but I do believe that any time a youngster can get the attention of the world or draw that many spectators in Seattle, he must have something."[22]

In another letter, Grace O'Dell scolded Hadley for criticizing what he should be protecting. "People either like [Presley] or dislike him," explained O'Dell. "Thus we have personal opinions, something which everyone has the right to—a right which is granted to all Americans and one which Charles Jr. is supposed to be standing for now as a member of the Naval Reserve—lest he forget. I fully appreciate Junior's right to dislike him but must admit that I can not see where he has the right to criticize other people for their likes ... Elvis, I am quite sure, meant no disrespect to the flag of our country, or to our National Anthem. It had the same meaning as if he had said 'theme song' but Junior was too busy looking for the flaws to give heed to meanings."[23]

That spring Kathy Mansfield graduated from Highline High School. Since she would be heading east to college in the fall, she gave up her office as president of the Elvis Presley Fan Clubs of Western Washington. She had no intention of giving up on Elvis Presley, though. She made sure she chose a college where he and rock 'n' roll music were still "very popular."

Perhaps the most important story surrounding Elvis Presley's Seattle appearance went completely unnoticed at the time. Fourteen-year-old Jimi Hendrix couldn't afford to buy a ticket, so with others he watched Elvis perform from "tightwad hill" overlooking Sicks' Stadium's left field fence. Though he could barely see Elvis, Hendrix felt the excitement as the sixteen thousand in the stadium reacted to Presley on stage. He heard Elvis sing his hit songs, and as the singer launched into his "Hound Dog" finale, Hendrix clapped his hands and stomped his feet with the others on the hillside. As Presley exited the stadium in the backseat of a Cadillac, Jimi got his closest look at the rock 'n' roll star as the car drove by on the street below him. Two months after the concert, Hendrix acknowledged the effect the event had on him by drawing a picture of Elvis in his notebook. Around the image of the guitar-playing Presley, Jimi wrote the titles of a dozen of the singer's hit records.[24]

In 1970 Jimi Hendrix, by then arguably the world's most famous rock guitar player, performed in concert at Sicks' Seattle Stadium, just as Elvis had done thirteen years earlier. By the time he died of a drug overdose later that year, however, Sicks' Stadium had been torn down. Still, the two-hundred-car funeral procession that accompanied Hendrix's body to Greenwood Memorial Cemetery in Renton drove by the former stadium site where both he and Presley had performed. It was a sad but vivid reminder of the fluidity of American rock music as it passed through giants from one generation to the next.

With Bob Blackburn and Nancy Welty after Portland press conference, September 2, 1957. (Courtesy Bob Blackburn)

Chapter 14

Portland

Prelude

Located in northeastern Oregon, Portland sits astride the Willamette River, close to its confluence with the Columbia River to the north. With a population of 412,100 in 1957, Portland was then about half of size of Seattle. Historically, however, Portland had been a more conservative city than her bustling urban neighbor to the north. The conservative temperament of its citizens began to soften in the 1950s, however. The 1950 census revealed more avowed Democrats than Republicans in Oregon for the first time, and in 1956 Portland elected forty-four-year-old Terry Schrunk, the city's first liberal Democrat mayor since 1905.

Disc jockey Dick Novak helped expose Portland teenagers early on to the effects of rock 'n' roll music. As early as 1954, Novak was buying rhythm and blues records at local record stores and playing them on KGON, a low power radio station in the Portland area. In 1955 he was the first DJ in the city to play Elvis records. High ratings allowed him to step up to the more powerful station KPOJ, where he took over the coveted night slot. Playing rock 'n' roll records, he quickly shot to the top of the ratings.

In the mid-1950s Novak did his radio program live from Scotty's Drive-in restaurant at the corner of Sandy Boulevard and Burnside. From 7:00 PM until 2:00 AM, six nights a week, Novak played requests and dedications, which he tabulated along with mail-in votes to create his Top 50 Hits playlist. During this time some credit Dick Novak, and not Philadelphia's Allan Freed, with first using the phrase "rock 'n' roll." Teenagers flocked to Scotty's nightly to watch and listen to Novak do his live show. (On an average weeknight, Scotty's sold about two thousand hamburgers.) By 1957 the city of Portland was getting uncomfortable with the activity surrounding Novak's live show. Teenagers milling around Sandy and Burnside were becoming a nuisance, causing the city to consider revoking Scotty's business license.

Dick Novak then moved his radio show downtown to Amato's Supper Club, an adult establishment on SW Broadway. From an annex on the side of the club,

Novak broadcast his *Rhythm Room* program. A large picture window allowed Portland teenagers to stand outside and watch Novak broadcast his show. There he continued to play requests and dedications in a kind of musical give-and-take relationship with the city's youth.

Thanks to Dick Novak, Portland teenagers were well schooled in the sound and mannerisms of rock 'n' roll when Elvis Presley came to town on Labor Day of 1957.

Portland, Oregon
Multnomah Stadium
Monday, September 2, 1957, 8:30 pm

In the summer of 1957, Nancy Welty and Bob Blackburn lived in two different but intersecting worlds—Nancy a typical thirteen-year-old traversing the perils of adolescence in her hometown of Salem, Oregon, and Bob a thirty-three-year-old sportscaster and disc jockey on KEX radio in Portland. They were a generation apart, especially when it came to musical tastes. That summer, though, Elvis Presley, then generally considered a divisive force between generations, brought them together for a moment they both would remember for the rest of their lives.

From the first time Elvis appeared on TV in early 1956, Nancy followed his career and bought all his records. "His music was so much different from anything that was popular in the Northwest," she recalled of what first drew her to him. "His music was compelling, easy to remember, and the feeling that he was singing just to me always set him apart from other singers of his era. He was good looking, and also the 'bad boy,' a James Dean of the music world, the kind of guy your mother would never, ever let you date. It all added up to his charismatic personality and his blatant sexual attraction. Then he would smile and look like an innocent boy. It was as if he was saying, 'I caused that?'"[1]

Bob Blackburn was not so taken with Elvis, but necessity brought the controversial singer into his world. "To be honest, a lot of the early rock songs got a little too raucous to be my favorite songs," Bob admits. "But I played them because I knew they were the favorites of the young people listening to the show. Every afternoon I would play all of the top songs, and quite often, if Elvis had a hot one, I'd play that every day."[2]

Early in August, both Nancy and Bob learned Elvis would be coming to Portland in less than a month. As part of promoting his appearance, RCA Victor's representative in Portland suggested to Blackburn that he run an on-the-air contest. "The basic idea of the contest," Bob explained, "was to write, I think it was in fifty words, why you want to meet Elvis. We got hundreds of pieces of mail, probably four or five hundred. At that time, when you got so much mail, you knew the guy was a pretty hot item." When Nancy heard about the contest, she jumped at the chance to actually meet Elvis. She wrote her fifty words and sent in her entry. To increase her chances, she entered again. And again. And again. And again. Then she crossed her fingers and waited.

Frank Breall had been on the run for weeks. Through his relationship with Northwest Releasing, Breall was the local promoter for Elvis Presley's appearance in the Rose City on Labor Day. From the August 9 announcement of the Presley booking, the local impresario had just three weeks to do the promotional work and all of the on-the-ground preparations for the biggest entertainment event the city had ever seen.

Lining up the venue came first. Multnomah Stadium was the only site in the area capable of accommodating the huge crowd expected. A problem arose with using the stadium, however. It was the home field of the minor league Portland Beavers baseball team, and they had a doubleheader scheduled to start in the late afternoon of September 2. Breall had to insure the Presley show for one million dollars with Lloyd's of London in case it had to be cancelled by a weather delay or in case extra innings extended baseball play past 8:30 at night.

Breall then turned his attention to ticket sales. Mail-order sales began Monday, August 12, with public ticket offices scheduled to begin sales four days later. On the fifteenth, Breall announced that advance mail-order sales had been so heavy that staff had been added to handle the load. The next morning more than two hundred people lined up in front of J.K. Gill's at SW Fifth and Stark downtown for public sales beginning at 9:30. Several teenagers at the front of the line told reporters that they had been waiting since 4:30 AM because Elvis was "the most." Tickets were also available at Stevens & Son in Salem, at Melvin's Men's Store in Vancouver, and at the Beaverton Music Center.

"It's easily understandable why Elvis and his shows don't play in theatres nor auditoriums," Breall told Dorothy Lois Smith of the *Oregon Journal*. "In Portland, with only six days of sales, we'd already sold tickets to sufficient Presley fans to fill the Paramount theatre three times over." The promoter said that mail reservations had come in from all over Oregon and even from as far away as Yreka, California, and Lewiston, Idaho. When the Salem ticket outlet reported that Presley tickets were "selling like mad," Breall began chartering private buses to, as he said, "bring in that Valley gang" from the state capital sixty miles to the south.[3]

While ticket sales chugged along through late August, Breall kept busy attending to details, including arranging for stadium help, stage workers, soundmen, electricians, and concessionaires. The magnitude of the show, the crowd, and the money involved understandably put the heat on the promoter to have everything ready on time. As if that weren't enough, however, added pressure came from a predictable source, as William Moyes reported in his *Journal* column on August 29.

> Mr. Breall, by the way, who expects to hear at least the thanks of art-appreciating teenagers, not to mention his promoter's cut of the take, has been receiving thousands of instructions from Colonel Parker as to details that must be just so for Presley's appearance. The prize winner is this instruction: "No power shortage!" That means Mr. B. will have to get Hell's Canyon bill passed and the dam built and operating by next Monday.[4]

Of course, the Colonel was not about to let any local promoter use his judgment when it came to security. Following the problems in Vancouver, B.C., two nights before, an edgy Parker insisted that the number of officers on hand in Portland be twice what the original contract required. In the end, Breall arranged for 30 on-duty and 103 off-duty and auxiliary Portland police officers to be at Multnomah Stadium the night of the concert.

Another Portlander whose name was often in front of the public during the lead-up to Elvis' appearance was journalist Dorothy Lois Smith. Timing helped Smith play a prominent role in Presley's visit to her city in 1957. During August she sat in for the absent *Oregon Journal* drama editor Arnold Marks, whose "Stage and Screen" column focused on the local entertainment scene. Using that forum, Smith got the honor on August 9 of announcing Presley's upcoming performance in Portland. During the ensuing three weeks, Smith served as a conduit through which Colonel Parker and Frank Breall funneled promotional information to Portland's citizens. The two men couldn't have been any more pleased with her copy if they had written it themselves. Her revelation of Elvis' arrival in the August 9 column included the most Presley-positive pitch from the press on the entire tour.

> The lad who started his career with a $3 guitar today requires a staff of 50 persons to handle fan mail, merchandise, public appearances and recordings. His unique style is said to have sold more than 20,000,000 records during the past year, also said to be a figure no other recording artist has approached in history. At the moment, the No. 1 national hit is his "Teddy Bear." Often, Presley has had as many as four out of 10

top selling hits and currently has four in the popular list in the Portland area.[5]

Smith later tried to encourage adults to check out Presley. "Many adult acquaintances are just as hopped up about seeing Elvis as are the teenagers; say they wouldn't miss it for anything. In fact, many are cutting Labor day weekend jaunts short to be here for the big show."[6]

Later Smith reported, "It's been claimed that Elvis fans are so eager to get near to and/or touch their idol that the young singer needs more police protection than the president of the United States." She also informed Portlanders that the time and manner of Presley's arrival in town that coming Monday would not be revealed for security reasons (although she would feed that very information to the Portland press herself on Monday morning). In the same column, Smith again helped Frank Breall pitch tickets to area adults by including the following anecdote from the promoter.

> All Presley fans are not teenagers, and to prove this, here's an experience the Portland promoter tells. He has a huge, full-colored picture of the star in his famous gold suit and gold shoes. He was taking it to a cohort at a hotel this week, got into the elevator and told the middle-aged woman operator he wanted the second floor. "Isn't that Elvis?" She gasped. "It's a lovely picture. I'm crazy about the fellow. Already have my two tickets for the show. He's the greatest!" When the elevator stopped, Breall found himself on the sixth floor.[7]

The morning of the Presley concert, Smith devoted most of her column to that evening's performance, and she sounded perfect giddy in anticipation. "This reviewer and Journal Photog Eddie Lee have been in training with spinach, vitamins and other strength-building items to be in top condition to cover the event," she claimed. "To tell the truth, wouldn't miss the spectacle, the mobs and seeing this Presley guy in person for anything. (What condition we'll be in Tuesday is a different story; might as well sound mad and gay while in good health.)"[8]

The editorial staff of the *Journal's* rival paper, the *Oregonian,* was less willing to promote the Presley appearance. In the final few days running up to the concert, readers conducted a spirited debate in the paper's entertainment page letter column, "Behind the Mike by B. Mike," edited and commentary added by William Moyes. After Oscar Bond of Delake contributed some not-so-flattering comments about Presley, a thirteen-year-old Portland girl took issue and fired off her own letter to B. Mike.

Trying to prove you can write, Oscar? I'm referring to that stupid letter you so foolishly wrote to B. Mike's column. Get this through your big fat head. We millions of teen-age girls are NOT fond of Elvis because he reminds us of our mothers. For your information, "Bright Boy," we love El because he's so handsome, talented, romantic, dreamy, super colossal and very tender and sweet. And don't you dare call Elvis plump, because he's not (he has a marvelous physique). El's hair is not long like you stated. Just because he has sideburns (wow!) and nice wavy hair is no reason to call it long. And he doesn't squirm! You're just jealous because you can't sing or act and you're not handsome and masculine like Elvis ... If you call yourself a he-man, then I'm Jayne Mansfield! ... So wise up and drop dead. Elvis is so darling and terrific. Your childish mind just can't take it.[9]

In his August 28 column, Moyes, in an apparent attempt at humor, observed, "Presley fans are obviously tone-deaf." That drew the ire of Mrs. R. Holden, who roasted Moyes in a letter printed two days later.

Do people like you make nasty cracks like the one in Wednesday's Oregonian concerning Elvis Presley to help poor misguided souls, or is it from sheer meanness? What you people hope to gain by saying mean things about Elvis eludes me ... Perhaps poor Elvis never read in the Good Book, "A good name is rather to be chosen than great riches," for I hear he is still hauling that money to the bank. I suppose that makes you happy. To say nasty things about Elvis Presley is one thing, but to say mean things about his listeners is another. I'll have you know that I like to hear him sing. (I suppose you could do better?) And I'll have you know I am not a "silly tone-deaf teen-ager." I have a teen-age daughter and son. They also enjoy hearing him sing. Any objections? Everyone to his own taste is a nice little thing to remember in case you never heard it before. Thanks for nothing.[10]

B. Mike responded tersely to Mrs. Holden's letter, "Well, Wednesday's remarks apparently didn't help ALL poor misguided souls." He added, "Frank Breall should be awarded a medal, says one reader. Look at all the juvenile delinquent hotrodders he's keeping off the road by bringing Elvis here Labor day."

The editorial staff of the *Oregonian* apparently was apprehensive about the arrival of "E-Day," as its opinion column labeled September 2. An *Oregonian* editorial suggested that it would take a long time to analyze the effect of Presley's show on the community.

Someday, maybe, a panel of psychologists will put their heads together and figure out how what is about to happen in Portland could possibly happen. On Labor Day that entertainment phenomenon, Elvis Presley, is to appear at Multnomah stadium to whomp the daylights out of his guitar, wiggle his mid-section and utter the strange cries which trigger remarkable reflexes in very young females.[11]

Nancy Welty never found out which of her multiple entries won radio station KEX's "Why I Want to Meet Elvis Presley" contest. She asked, but no one seemed to know. Bob Blackburn didn't know either, because he hadn't read the entries or picked the winner. Bob thinks the RCA guy who suggested the contest in the first place may have picked the winner. No matter. Nancy was just amazed that she won. Her prize included two free tickets to the concert and the opportunity to meet Elvis beforehand.

On Monday, September 2, Nancy's parents, Raleigh and Alice Welty, drove her to Portland in the family's 1956 Ford Victoria. As Nancy had won only two tickets, her father planned to visit friends in the city while Nancy and her mother attended Elvis' news conference and concert. At Multnomah Stadium they met up with Bob Blackburn, who took them to a room in the Multnomah Athletic Club for the press conference. Together the three of them sat with the assembled reporters and other contest winners to await Presley's arrival.

As the morning of "E-Day" dawned bright and beautiful, one of Frank Breall's fears was eased. However, his financial worry was still there. Multnomah Stadium was far from sold out. As Elvis got dressed in his Seattle hotel room, Breall announced that good seats were still available and that two ticket wagons at Multnomah Stadium would be open all day up until showtime.

While Breall dealt with the final details in Portland, in Seattle Elvis and his associates prepared to leave the Olympic Hotel and catch the early afternoon train for Portland. Waiting for Elvis at Seattle's King Street Station that morning was Frank's wife, Annette Breall, who had gone to Seattle to escort Presley to the Rose City. There was no danger that Elvis might get lost along the way, but it was a nice touch by an experienced promoter trying to make Elvis feel at ease in Portland.

As the Northern Pacific Railroad train pulled out of Seattle at 12:30 PM for the four-hour run to Portland, Mrs. Breall settled into a compartment with Elvis and the guys. "He was the nicest, nicest young man you'd ever want to meet," she recalled. "He had these four big, burly guys with him—I guess they were there to protect him, but they looked like they belonged under a bridge—and he told one of them to sit in the other seat so that I could sit next to him. We talked about my daughter being a Rose Princess and all this other stuff, and he was just so delightful."[12]

In Portland the Colonel booked Elvis into the stylish Multnomah Hotel, known for hosting celebrities who passed through town. (It previously had put up Charles Lindbergh, Bob Hope, Bing Crosby, Jimmy Stewart, Lana Turner, and Dwight Eisenhower.) That morning the hotel staff was tense. They knew Presley was coming, but they were kept in the dark concerning how and when. Normally the hotel arranged to have the luggage of such high-profile guests transported from the airport or train station to the hotel, but Colonel Parker declined their help. The Multnomah had just two days' advance notice of Presley's coming, and during that forty-eight hours, hotel assistant manager Bill Williams labored to complete Colonel Parker's advance list of requirements. Since the list didn't include how many rooms would be needed, Williams prepared several suites that could be opened up to make a multi-room lounging area. Attendants stocked the pantries with food and soft drinks, and the hotel cooks were put on call to prepare whatever Elvis might order, day or night. Clean linens and towels were laid out. Bosses warned housekeepers, who might have been tempted to smuggle Presley's sheets out of the hotel and sell them, of the Multnomah's reputation for "discreet service and protective care of all guests, famous or not."[13]

At eight o'clock Monday morning, everything was ready at the hotel. The extra security men manned their positions, leaving them only to occasionally escort fans out of the lobby. Fearing they would miss the big arrival, bellmen rushed to complete any job that took them out of the lobby area for even a moment. The staff mistakenly believed, thanks to Parker, that Elvis and his party would arrive in town late Monday morning by private plane.

When the train carrying Elvis arrived at Union Station in downtown Portland at 4:30 PM, word of its precious cargo had preceded it. That covert information had been revealed by none other than the *Journal's* Dorothy Lois Smith. A self-described "frequent train rider," Smith just happened to be riding on Presley's train from Seattle. Sensing some excitement on the train, she persuaded a porter to reveal that Elvis was aboard. When the train stopped in Centralia, Washington, Smith jumped off for a minute and quickly wired her paper that Presley was coming.

The word spread among the city's press corps, and they, along with about five hundred fans, were waiting when the train neared the station. The screaming in the depot began as soon as the teenagers heard the approaching train engine. As usual, Elvis escaped most of the crowd by making his way to the last car on the train and stepping off at the far north end of the platform, where a rented convertible awaited him. A small crowd of fans quickly surrounded him, and while he tried to keep moving toward the car, Presley accommodated as many of them as he could. He knelt to sign autographs for some teenage girls. He stopped to pluck the strings of a miniature guitar held by a four-year-old girl. He shook hands with and gave an autograph to Charles Halbrook, an elderly man who told Elvis that he, too, was from Memphis.

Ivan Smith, a reporter for KGA-TV in Portland, collared Presley at the train station for about a ninety-second recorded interview. The short exchange went as follows.

Smith: Your concert tonight, how long in duration will it be?

Presley: The entire show is about two-and-a-half hours. I think I'm on for about 40 minutes.

Smith: What songs are you going to hit?

Presley: Well, I'll do practically all of my songs.

Smith: Which song do you think is the biggest right now?

Presley: "Don't Be Cruel" is the biggest.

Smith: How about "Teddy Bear"? How is it doing?

Presley: It's about two million now.

Smith: We have a bunch of teenagers up the other side of the studio awaiting to see you. And, as you can see, in spite of all the secrecy in this little devious plan, that a lot of it's leaked out ...

Presley: Yes, it always does. It always does. I don't mind it. In fact, if you come into a place and there's nobody there to meet you, you start wondering, you know.

Smith: Surely. Are you going to allow film at your press conference tonight during the show?

Presley: Oh, yes.

Tom Diskin: No, not movie film.

Smith: Not movie film?

Diskin: I'll explain it at the press conference.

Smith: That won't do us a great deal of good, you know.

Presley: Excuse me. I said yes. He says no. I don't know what's gonna happen.

Diskin: Well, I'll explain tonight.

Presley: Very nice talking to you, sir. We're gonna have to run here.

Smith: Elvis Presley leaves in his official car with motorcycle escort, and heads now for his hotel. All these youngsters and people who came down to see him and no one even knew where his car was going to be, but in spite of all the secrecy, there they are. Now you can imagine the pandemonium going on right now in Union Station.

Ironically, as Tom Diskin told Smith of Colonel Parker's ban on movie film, a KGA-TV cameraman was recording the scene. In fact, the singer's arrival at Union Station in Portland the afternoon of September 2 is one of the very few events captured on film during Presley's entire 1957 tour schedule.

From Union Station, Portland motorcycle police officers escorted Presley's car ten blocks south along Fifth Avenue to the Multnomah Hotel. There they found hundreds of people blocking the front entrance. That problem had been foreseen, however, and Elvis quietly entered through a side entrance. Once inside the hotel, the much-anticipated guest impressed manager Bill Williams with his quiet manner, kindness toward employees, and apparent lack of ego. Presley reportedly went out of his way to shake hands, sign autographs, and talk with hotel staff, as well as with other guests who approached him.

Elvis retired to the Governor's Suite with his cohorts to rest up for two hours before the press conference and performance that evening. Portland police blocked off the street in front of the hotel, Presley's floor was made off-limits, and added hotel security was on duty. Still, teenage girls swarmed in and around the building like bees around a hive. Hotel detectives caught one daring girl trying to scale the Pine Street façade to a second-story window. A couple more somehow reached the forbidden seventh floor, but were quickly surrounded by a squad of policemen, Presley bodyguards, and cleaning women.

One of those daring girls was Jo Ann Waldo. "I was 17," she recalled years later. "My girlfriend and me got there in the morning and stayed around the whole day, riding up and down in the elevators and trying to get to where he was. Once we got up to the floor where he was and saw him, but my girlfriend screamed and the cops chased us out of there and said if they caught us one more time they would kick us out."[14] The two girls retreated to the hotel coffee shop, where sympathetic waitresses asked if they wanted Presley's autograph. Of course they did, and during a room service delivery it was obtained for them.

During the evening newscast on KPTV, just a few hours before show time, John Salisbury commented on Presley and his chances for longevity in the music business. Amidst the sea of hysteria on both sides, Salisbury's analysis was not only uncommonly balanced, but also quite prophetic.

> Of course, he's a downright nuisance, this kid. He's caused riots, he's accused of leading teen-agers astray, he purveys a kind of excitement in music which causes youngsters to bop and parents to boil. Yessir, he's a doggone nuisance. Of course, there's never been anybody like him. There was never anyone like Sinatra, either—or Johnnie Ray, or Bing Crosby, or, reaching way back, Rudy Vallee ... Whether this southern boy is a product of the times or reflects the moods of a generation is not

of particular moment actually. What matters in the long run is—how good is he?

A season of oblivion might be the best thing for him, for out of it he could grow something less synthetic, less meteoric, something more solid and lasting. Now don't mistake me, he's good. You don't appeal to hundreds of thousands of people without being good, without having something on the ball. There's no such thing as mass hypnotism, just forms of mass hero worship, and that's an ephemeral thing ... Like all entertainers who eventually prove their staying power, he'll have to go through a touch of neither here nor there—a form of Presley, who's he? Oh yeah, I remember, back in the '50s, wasn't it? If he has it, if he really has it, he'll survive to become not a passing fancy, but a full-fledged artist.[15]

At that moment, in his suite in the Multnomah Hotel, Elvis was relaxing and watching TV—tuned to KPTV. As he listened to Salisbury's perspective, did he recognize the truth in it? And, if so, did the prospect frighten or encourage him? Who knows? His public statements in those days seem to indicate that he thought very little about the future. He was riding a wave for all it was worth, with no idea where or how it would all end. That afternoon he just knew he had another concert to give in a couple of hours.

The baseball doubleheader at Multnomah Stadium ended early, allowing Frank Breall to straighten out the two fingers that had been crossed for weeks. "We were lucky they didn't go overtime," he recalled. "We hauled two huge Fruehauf flat-top trailers onto the field following the game and within an hour the stagehands had a stage complete with backdrop and bunting."[16] The turnstiles turned, the crowd found its seats, and the lengthy opening portion of the The Elvis Presley Show began promptly at 8:30 PM.

About that same time Elvis left the Multnomah Hotel for the one-mile drive west along Burnside Street to the stadium. Some fans still lingered around the hotel, hoping to get an autograph or just to see the rock 'n' roll icon. One fan fated for disappointment that evening was thirteen-year-old Sandra Johannessen, who, with her sister Susan and mother, decided to wait at the hotel's rear entrance. It wasn't a bad choice, since Elvis rarely came or left by the front door of any hotel in those days. But that was exactly what he did when he left the Multnomah that Monday night in Portland. The following morning, the *Journal* printed a picture of Sandra—in her wheelchair—waiting at the back door. Her sister and mother stood behind her.

Meanwhile, Elvis arrived at the Multnomah Athletic Club, adjacent to the stadium, for a half-hour press conference held in club's shower room. For some reason, perhaps in deference to the city's conservative tradition, Presley dressed more conventionally for the press in Portland than he had in the previous four cities on the tour. The usual black shirt, open to the breastbone, gave way to a white shirt with a black and silver tie and stickpin. Black slacks, black shoes and socks, and a light blue dinner jacket completed his fashionable ensemble. Except for replacing the blue jacket with a gold one, it would be the combination he later wore on stage.

As at previous press conferences, Elvis answered all questions directly and politely. On marriage rumors, he explained at uncharacteristic length, "Often, when I'm supposed to be marrying one girl a certain night, I'm out with another girl on a date. This is confusing to me, and I may be surprised and wake up and hear I'm married sometime. I don't want to get married now, and don't know anyone I want to marry. But if I do meet her, I'll marry her. I won't pass love by. All these fans of mine will be getting married and having families. I do think that marriage would hurt my career now, though."

On how he created a special mood before recording a song, Elvis explained, "I don't have the best voice in the world, so I must feel it. When you're singing ballads, I guess you always do think of some girl." As examples of his "many" favorite recording artists, Elvis named The Four Aces, Nat King Cole, Dean Martin, and Pat Boone.

At one point, Presley spotted John Salisbury in the crowd of reporters. "Weren't you just on TV?" he asked. Salisbury nodded. "Thanks," said the singer. "You didn't say whether I was good or bad." In return for the reporter's balanced comments, Elvis later suspended the ban on TV filming and allowed Salisbury's cameraman to get a few shots of him.

As the shotgun questioning continued, numerous other personal tidbits came out. He did not wear makeup. That pasty skin was natural. He wore sideburns because the truck drivers he had admired as a kid wore them. Yes, he got lonely sometimes. No, he didn't do everything Colonel Parker told him to do. He was independent. He respected his mother and father, and didn't smoke or drink. He liked to "send you" with the fast songs, but he also enjoyed singing gospel songs. The wiggling came naturally to him, and there was nothing wrong with it. If people couldn't understand the words on his records, that was their fault.

That last response applied to a question asked by KPOJ radio DJ Mark Allen, who came with a list of questions gathered from listeners. One on his list was, "In the song, 'Got a Lot of Lovin' to Do,' what do you say in the last few sentences? I've never been able to understand them."

Then came the usual autograph and photo session, which ran longer than in most other cites. In addition to the expected DJs, journalists, and TV reporters, a couple of fan club presidents and the winners of five or six radio station contests were present, all of whom met Elvis personally and individually had their pictures taken with him and their DJs.

"I was by far the youngest of the contest winners," recalls Nancy Welty. When her turn came, the long-awaited encounter was quick, but memorable. "I wasn't scared," she says. "It was more awe than anything else. He just said hello and what's your name and that sort of thing. Then they posed us for a picture, he gave me a kiss, and then we were on our way. What really impressed me was how respectful and polite he was with anyone who talked with him. He treated me the same as the better-looking, older girls that were there. He was just an extremely handsome man who seemed to be very sure of himself while in public."

Bob Blackburn was not so star-struck at the time. "As a disc jockey, I had no problems meeting famous people," he explained. "Elvis was a showman, and these show people are always 'on' when they're meeting people. It was a nice moment, a very pleasant thing. He was very friendly and very affable. He didn't act like, 'What the hell am I doing here with these two people.' He tried to make her feel at home, asking her what she liked in school, and about music, and which one of his songs was her favorite. During the whole time, I recall Elvis as being extremely friendly, making this young lady feel at ease." Then the rock 'n' roll singer, the DJ, and the young lady had their moment together recorded on film.

At the other end of the female spectrum, Rose Shevach, Annette Breall's mother, got a hug from the rock 'n' roll king before the show. "I love mothers," he told her.

Donning his gold jacket, Elvis climbed on the back of a white convertible, which also carried Portland Mayor Terry Schrunk and Ken Moore, Presley's chief of security. The stadium lights faded temporarily while the car started down the ramp into the stadium. When the lights came back on, a waving Presley was driven slowly around the dirt warning track along the first and third baselines. Crescendoing applause and screaming, along with the blossoming of count-less flash bulbs, greeted his passing by each section of the grandstand. Unlike in Seattle, there were no rows of folding chairs on the infield grass.

After the convertible pulled up close to the stage, Elvis got out and walked up the stairs. Before stepping to the microphone, he shook hands with George Arnold, the director of the local band that was backing him. Presley just stood quietly for a moment at stage front, allowing the crowd to waste another thousand flash bulbs. Then he burst forth with the first note of "Heartbreak Hotel," the remainder of which was drowned out by screaming. Such things depend on perspective, however. Fourteen-year-old Holly Johnson claimed that "Heartbreak Hotel" sounded "louder and clearer than ever."[17]

In their September 3 editions, both the *Journal* and the *Oregonian* gave extensive coverage to Presley's show. The *Oregonian's* front-page article had no byline. Whoever wrote it was impressed with the behavior of both the man on stage and the fans in the stands. "Elvis himself wasn't on stage very long, but he worked like a hound dog when he was," the writer concluded. "He clowned and he hammed it up, and he seemed to be having as good a time as his audience obviously was." Of that audience, the reporter observed, "It was bedlam, noise-wise, but physically it was in the true Portland conservative tradition. Maybe they would have liked to, but no one swarmed out of the stands and onto the stadium ground as has happened in other cities and as is feared and guarded against by the Presley entourage."[18]

On an inside page, staff writer Phyllis Lauritz gave her impressions of what she had experienced the night before. Lauritz was on the bad-adult list of many Portland teenagers after her recent negative review of the current Presley movie, *Loving You.* (In a letter to the *Oregonian,* one teenager referred to her as "Mrs. Fathead.") In her concert review, she tried to regain some of her lost esteem among teenagers. "All right, kids, I give in," she began her review. "He really isn't horrible. It just seems that way to us grown-ups. But anybody, and I do mean Elvis Presley, who can do what he did to you in Tacoma, and Seattle, and Vancouver, and Portland, must have something. What is it? I don't know. How could I? You whooped and hollered so, I couldn't hear him."[19]

In an adjoining column, teenager Holly Johnson gave her views, which were predictably positive. "I think these teen-agers were quite well-behaved considering the large crowd," she said of her peers. "They were bustling with excitement and remarks as follows were overheard: 'Oh, I can't wait to see Elvis,' and, 'Oh, I'm so nervous.'" When he did appear, Elvis didn't disappoint Holly. "You know, I think all of the songs he sang sounded as good as his recordings, even better," she concluded. She closed her analysis with an optimistic prediction. "Anyway almost everybody loved him and his show was a success. It goes to show that somebody who became successful overnight and has been so popular in the past two years has a talent that cannot be ignored as long as teen-agers love Elvis!"[20]

Meanwhile, over at the *Journal,* staff writer Don Horine found something positive in the symbiotic relationship between teenagers and their idol. "How they loved it!" Horine observed of the hysterical teenagers he saw in Multnomah Stadium. "They thrilled to every word, every breath of the famed entertainer. Here was heaven, a haven in otherwise conservative life of studies, dishes and mowing the lawn. Here was a miracle wrapped handsomely in a single package—a miracle wearing the exciting name of Elvis Presley." Horine also praised the restraint of his city's youth. "The mass eruption from the stands of berserk teenagers, such as greeted Elvis in Chicago and recently in Vancouver, B.C., did not materialize.

Instead, the woozy fans, many of them members of two Presley fan clubs here, were content to stay at their seats, to shake and wiggle hands, hips and feet, and to convince the singer that Portland, like all other U.S. cities, is 'real gone.'"[21]

Finally, there was the review by Dorothy Lois Smith, whose *Journal* columns in the preceding weeks helped build anticipation for the Labor Day show. When the event finally came, Smith learned that watching Presley perform was a multi-sensory experience. "It was sometimes almost impossible to know which of his rock'n'roll hits he was singing, burping and wiggling for his fans," Smith observed. "The blare of the music whistled through the right ear and the screaming of the audience pierced the left ear conking out my equilibrium. But my eyesight was perfect, and there's no doubt that it's the bumps and grinds, the wiggles and the sinuous writhings that the fans love the most. Each wiggle brought forth another in the succession of ecstatic screams." Those screams reached their height, according to Smith, when Presley grabbed a guitar and sang "I Got a Woman." She described the rhythmic back-and-forth movement of the guitar as being more like a cheek-to-cheek dance than playing an instrument.[22]

Although Nancy Welty and Bob Blackburn had front-row seats, they were not close enough for the girl from Salem. "He set up his stage there inside the dog track, so I'd say he was thirty or forty feet away from the audience." With most of the screaming behind her, though, Nancy could hear Elvis singing clearly.

Bob Blackburn was both amused and amazed by the event. He explained, "It was the first time that I ever saw musicians up on the stage going through all the gymnastics and gyrations that he used to do. In my era of the big bands, the great vocalists of the time sang, but they didn't prance out on the stage. Their personality came out through their voice. Of course, Elvis was the first one who did that, and now everyone who sings rock music feels they have to sing that way."

During his final number, Elvis sat down on the edge of the stage and swung his legs back and forth. Then he dropped down to the infield turf, where he sang most of the rest of the song squirming on his knees with one hand on the ground. Finally, he arose, apparently exhausted, and laboriously made his way behind the stage. There he jumped into the convertible and vanished in a heartbeat. From the loudspeaker came the open-air version of that famous refrain in Presley lore. "Ladies and gentlemen. Elvis Presley has left the stadium."

"The silence was as deafening as the performance," observed Dorothy Lois Smith. Don Horine added the lament, "They had lost him, the lead actor in so many teenage dreams, and he was not to return. But for seven hours, give or take a few precious minutes, he belonged to Portland."

Many of the teens present that night have their own stories. They've retold them through the years, and even passed them down to their children and grand-children. Two of them who told their stories to the *Oregonian's* Jeff Baker for a retrospective article in 1999 were Sharon Ury and Vera McGrew. Ury remembers sitting in her seat, screaming like everyone else around her, when another girl came running up the aisle. "I touched him," the newcomer screamed. Impressed, Ury asked for the girl's autograph. The signature read, "girl who touched Elvis." On a roll, Ury then approached the girl's mother, who signed, "mother of the girl who touched Elvis." The other girl's real name turned out to be Jeanne Allen. Later, Sharon and Jeanne became best friends and together started a local chapter of the Elvis International Fan Club.[23]

Vera McGrew's story testifies to Presley's powerful magnetism in 1957. She risked her marriage to see him. Vera was an Elvis fan and wanted to see his show, but her husband Leroy was against it. "Elvis was kind of new back then," recalled Vera in 1999, "and you know in the old days the husband wanted his wife to stay at home. My husband was of the old school." Vera was determined, though. She bought a new dress, arranged for a babysitter, and with her husband gone to a business meeting, she headed to Multnomah Stadium to see Elvis. By the time Leroy walked in the door, Vera was back home in her bathrobe.

Vera thought she had gotten away with it—until she saw the front page of the *Oregonian* the next morning. There she was in a photograph taken at the Elvis show. "My friends were calling all day," Vera remembers. "I thought 'I'm divorced. I am hung out to dry.'" But Leroy, who saw the picture while eating breakfast in a coffee shop, didn't say a word about it when he got home that day. And he hasn't said a word about it through five decades of marriage. When she tells the story today, Vera says her husband "just smiles and never says a thing."[24]

Another Portland story in 1957 is about a man who stepped forward to bask in the glory of Elvis Presley's persona in 1957. He was Mayor Terry D. Schrunk. In conservative cities like Portland, most mayors, afraid of alienating voters, would have distanced themselves from the youth-corrupting influence of Elvis Presley. Schrunk, though, seemingly wanted to be as visible as Presley himself in Multnomah Stadium that Labor Day evening. First, he rode in the convertible that brought Presley into the stadium and drove around the grandstand. Then, when Elvis took to the stage, the mayor took to the stands, drifting around, observing the bedlam, and assessing crowd behavior, he claimed. The next day Mayor Schrunk issued a statement, which both the *Journal* and the *Oregonian* printed. He complimented teenagers for their orderly conduct at Elvis Presley's appearance at Multnomah stadium Monday night. The statement continued, "They were noisy, but they were orderly. I look forward to the same type of actions when we have the high school football jamboree later this month." Why was the mayor so visible on "E-Day" in Portland? Perhaps he was trying to earn the future votes of the city's teenagers. After all, the political career of the young mayor was unsteady. Just two months earlier, in June, he had stood trial for perjury relating to an accusation of taking a bribe. He was acquitted and apparently retained enough political capital to get a ride in Elvis Presley's convertible.

By 11:00 PM Elvis was back in his suite in the Multnomah Hotel. Reports circulated that Presley and his entourage would leave Portland at midnight on a chartered bus bound for parts unknown. However, that turned out to be another Colonel Parker smokescreen. Instead, Elvis spent the night in the hotel, visiting with friends and members of his traveling group until 5:00 AM. Nothing was then heard from him until 2:30 in the afternoon, when the hotel's executive chef, Clovis Soubrand, received a breakfast order from, as Soubrand told a *Journal* reporter, "Mr. Elvis." The order called for fresh orange juice, twelve slices of very crisp bacon, two eggs with yokes broken and cooked hard, four cups of coffee, and two orders of toast and milk. Soubrand later told the *Journal* that Presley was "very pleased with the breakfast, especially the burnt bacon."25

When Elvis emerged from an elevator into the lobby at about 4:00 PM, between seventy-five and a hundred teenagers were there to greet him. Bob Dupar, resident manager of the hotel, said a courteous Elvis signed autographs, posed for pictures, and kissed one girl, who fainted on the spot.

A taxi then carried him the ten blocks back to Union Station, where another crowd awaited him. As on his arrival, Presley disappointed most of the assembled teenagers by having the cab driver drop him off at the far north end of the boarding area, where he and his followers got on the train. At 4:45 PM, Tuesday, September 3, 1957, the Northern Pacific *Cascade* pulled out of Portland bound for California, where a studio recording session in Hollywood awaited Presley two days later. His whirlwind tour of the Pacific Northwest was over.

Sometime later Bob Blackburn had two eight-by-ten, black-and-white copies made of the picture he and Nancy Welty had had taken with Elvis. He sent one copy to Nancy and kept the other for himself. Fifty years later, they both still treasure those original photographs. Nancy's copy was autographed by Blackburn, who also included an apology for not being able to get Elvis to sign it too. The picture is a lasting reminder of the idol of her youth. "I just think there was always a fondness," Nancy says of her connection with Elvis through the years. "When I heard him sing, I would always remember that I had met him. I had the privilege to have met him, and when you're thirteen years old, that was a big deal."

Bob Blackburn, whose DJ career ended in 1967, has a picture gallery in the basement of his home. "They're pictures I've had taken with a lot of famous people," he explains. "The minute anybody sees that one, they obviously recognize

Elvis and say, 'Boy, you have to really prize that one.' Of course, my kids have argued through their lifetimes who is going to get it when I'm gone." And Bob's early feeling about those "raucous" Elvis songs has evolved. "When you go back to his songs, you realize he was a great artist," he now admits. "He was a great leader in rock 'n' roll music, obviously."

Nancy Welty Ramsden still lives in Salem, Oregon. Bob Blackburn, who gained fame as the voice of the Seattle Supersonics basketball team from 1967 to 1992, lives in Bellevue, Washington. They never met again after sharing that moment with Elvis Presley in 1957.

Elvis with Scotty and Bill, Ottawa, April 3, 1957. (City of Ottawa Archives, Andrews Newton Collection, AN 49378 #117)

Chapter 15

Changes

When Elvis Presley stepped on the stage in Spokane to open his Pacific Northwest tour on the evening of August 30, 1957, he must have felt that he was back where he belonged. A childhood dream already had moved his career more in the direction of Hollywood and away from the stage, but he still craved the thrill and excitement of performing before a live audience. Behind him on the Spokane stage were the same seven backup musicians he had come to depend on since his career had exploded in early 1956. With Scotty, Bill, D.J., and the Jordanaires forming a sort of security blanket around him, Presley felt the confidence that underscored his wild stage show. He was in his element again, one that he alone controlled.

However, Elvis' comfort level, both on and off the stage, would soon be shaken by two events beyond his control, even beyond his understanding. Within a week, the two musicians who had been with him from the beginning would resign. Even worse, in the coming months the peacetime draft would slowly but inexorably draw him in until the King of Rock 'n' Roll was forced into the army like any other young man walking the streets of Memphis. At its height, his entertainment career would come to a sudden stop, with no guarantee that it could ever be revived. For the past two years, with his manager's guidance, Elvis Presley had controlled the world around him. After one last fling of supremacy in the Pacific Northwest, that world would begin to control him.

The Blue Moon Boys

The defection of Scotty Moore and Bill Black was the first bit of unwelcome reality that invaded Presley's magical world. While in Los Angeles for a recording session just days after the end of the Pacific Northwest tour, Elvis got wind of the coming resignations. In his 1995 book, Presley road companion Lamar Fike recalled what his boss did next.

> I remember this because the scene was really terrific. We were at the Beverly Wilshire Hotel in Los Angeles. I was sitting in the living room,

191

and Elvis walked in and said, "I think Scotty and Bill are fixin' to quit." I said, "Well, you better call Colonel."

Elvis got on the phone, and he said, "Colonel, Scotty and Bill are quitting. What am I going to do?" And Colonel said, "You're going to get another band. That's what you're going to do."

Elvis hung up and said, "What am I going to do without them?" I said, "You're going to do a show. They're just musicians." Elvis thought it was the end of the world.[1]

To Lamar Fike, Scotty and Bill may have been "just musicians," but to Elvis Presley they had been much more. The three of them had been together from the beginning in 1954. Elvis and The Blue Moon Boys had recorded all the legendary Sun Records sides together. In 1954 and 1955 they had loaded all their instruments and gear into Scotty's wife's '54 Bel Air Chevy and driven thousands of miles along the back roads of the rural South, sharing motel rooms and playing to small crowds in any backwater community that would have them. When the explosion came, they rode it up together—the TV appearances, the RCA recording sessions, the wild stage shows. By the fall of 1957, the three men had made over four hundred stage appearances together. Under such conditions, a close bond between Elvis, Scotty, and Bill inevitably developed.

That bond was more than just friendship; it had an artistic element as well. In Jerry Hopkins' 1971 Presley biography, Sam Phillips of Sun Records is recorded as claiming that Scotty Moore contributed as much to Elvis Presley's musical style as anyone. And, according to Hopkins, "Bill Black's clowning, his riding that battered standup bass around the stage as if it were a horse, had been a large part of the show Elvis had to offer an audience."[2] Scotty Moore had even been Presley's first manager.

In those early days, the trio divided the income by a simple formula. As the star of the show, Elvis received 50 percent of whatever they brought in. Scotty and Bill each got 25 percent. Under that arrangement, Scotty and Bill did well for themselves. For instance, in January of 1955 the act grossed $2,083 from its personal appearances. Scotty's and Bill's take of $521 that month wasn't bad, especially as bookings and income promised to increase throughout the year.

Within a few months, though, Bob Neal, who had taken over management duties from Scotty, decided that since Elvis' voice and stage presentation were largely responsible for the group's increased income, he should get a larger share of the money. After talking it over with Elvis, Neal told Scotty and Bill the percentage deal was over and they both were going on salary at $100 per month. "The eventual basic decision to change from a percentage to a salary was Elvis'," Neal told Jerry Hopkins in 1971. "We talked about it, he and I, and we talked about it with his parents, and decided it had to be done. It was my job to carry the word. I remember there was quite a bit of unhappiness about this at the time. That they would quit and so on. But they stayed on."[3]

One of the reasons Scotty and Bill stayed was that, at the time, Elvis seemed concerned about their financial situation. In the Hopkins biography, Scotty recalled Elvis' willingness to supplement Scotty's and Bill's income in another way.

> One day we were sitting on the front steps talkin' about it all, and he wanted to draw up contracts saying we'd always get twenty-five per cent and he'd take fifty, and I told him it wouldn't work out, because if it keeps goin' like it is, you got records and a lot of other things that possibly we wouldn't be involved in. It wouldn't be right. So we ended up he was gonna give us—only off the records, which was at my suggestion—Bill and I were gonna take one-fourth of one per cent each, outa record royalties. I believe this was right about the time we were talkin' about goin' on salary, getting' so much per week whether we played or not. Anyway, the percentage deal never did get put on paper and I doubt very seriously if he'd ever remember it.[4]

Late in 1955 things changed quickly for Presley. Those changes weakened the bond between Elvis, Scotty, and Bill, and led to the split between the singer and the musicians two years later. First, when Bob Neal's contract ran out, Presley signed with Colonel Parker and gave his new manager total control over his finances. From the time of his arrival on the scene, Parker believed Scotty and Bill were not strong enough musicians to back Presley at the elevated level he had reached in the music business. Scotty saw it as a power thing for the Colonel, who seemingly was out to consolidate his control over Elvis by getting rid of people who had had any influence over the singer before Parker came along. Over the next two years, Colonel Parker turned a deaf ear to the financial concerns Scotty and Bill brought to him. The only raise the boys got during that time period was an increase to $200 per week when they were on the road with Elvis. When Presley wasn't working, Scotty and Bill still received $100 per week. Furthermore, Parker shot down any proposal the two men came up with to enhance their income, like a car dealership's offer to give Scotty and Bill a new Chrysler each year just for Elvis' saying, "My band members drive Chryslers."

Meanwhile, the disparity in income began physically separating Elvis from Scotty and Bill. In early 1956, Elvis flew to and from some personal engagements. Since Scotty and Bill had to pay all their own travel expenses from their $200 a week road salary, they continued to travel by car, no matter how distant the booking. For the week-long Pacific Northwest tour, for example, Scotty and Bill, along with D.J., drove about four thousand miles from Memphis to Spokane, then to Vancouver, B.C., then to Seattle, then to Portland, and finally to Los Angeles for a recording session—all at their own expense. At every stop, the band members now stayed in a different hotel from Elvis. When in Los Angeles, for instance, Presley always stayed at the posh Beverly Wilshire Hotel, while the band took $7-a-night rooms at the Knickerbocker. Since there were no rehearsals on the road, about the only times Scotty, Bill, and D.J. saw Elvis were during their forty-minute stints on stage each night.

Off stage, the formerly close-knit trio went their separate ways. By 1957 Elvis had surrounded himself on the road with a group of companions. They were all free, footloose single men, who, like Elvis, couldn't relate to the financial concerns of family men like Scotty and Bill.

In his 1994 book, *Good Rockin' Tonight,* Joe Esposito explained that even after Elvis got out of the army, he still remained oblivious to his employees' financial needs. "Elvis never thought about money. He just assumed everyone was fine. If you needed money, you asked, or he just gave you something, like a car. Elvis simply lacked a concept of what it took to live. He had grown up poor, so the minimal salaries he paid the guys seemed substantial to him."[5]

When the police came to Scotty Moore's door in July 1956, the inadequacy of the salary he received from Elvis was revealed. While Elvis appeared on a series of national TV programs and skyrocketed to the top of the entertainment world, his guitar player was arrested in Memphis for being $240 delinquent on child support payments to his former wife.

Still, Scotty Moore and Bill Black drove to the Pacific Northwest to back Presley for his Labor Day weekend tour in 1957 with high hopes. According to Scotty, Elvis had promised them some studio time at the end of his recording session in Los Angeles after the tour ended. At least recording an instrumental album would allow the band members to make some extra money beyond their meager salaries. So sure were they that Elvis would come through for them, Scotty, Bill, and D.J. had held a press conference in Memphis to announce their forthcoming album. So when Tom Diskin, Colonel Parker's assistant, squashed their plan at the last minute, they looked to Elvis for support. When he offered none, it was the final straw. Scotty and Bill drove home to Memphis, and, after discussing the situation with their wives, sent special delivery letters of resignation to Elvis in Hollywood.

Initially unwilling to take his manager's advice to get a new band, Elvis returned to Memphis and called Scotty to ask what it would take to keep him on. Scotty proposed a $50 a week raise, plus a $10,000 payment to pay off some bills that had piled up during the past couple of years. Elvis said he needed some time to think about it. Obviously, whatever he gave to Scotty would have to go to Bill as well. What Elvis would have done will never be known, as the *Commercial Appeal* in Memphis interfered by running a story in which Scotty and Bill aired their grievances. "I don't believe Scotty and I could raise more than fifty bucks between us," Bill Black was quoted as saying. Scotty explained in print, "He promised us that the more he made the more we would make, but it hasn't worked out that way."[6]

Feeling betrayed, Elvis stopped thinking about Scotty's proposal and fired back with an open message to Scotty and Bill. "Scotty, I hope you fellows have good luck," it started out. "I will give you fellows good recommendations. If you had come to me, we would have worked things out. I would have always taken care of you. But you went to the papers and tried to make me look bad, instead of coming to me so we could work things out. All I can say to you is 'good luck.' "[7] Vernon Presley's letter to Scotty accepting his resignation, effective the same day as the article, was dated three days earlier.

Scotty blamed Parker for the split, and while the Colonel certainly wasn't heart-broken about it, there were other anti-Scotty and Bill voices whispering in Elvis' ear. Lamar Fike, like the rest of Presley's entourage, had no history with the band and thus no sympathy for Scotty and Bill. "I don't blame Scotty, Bill, and D.J. for trying, but they could be replaced," Fike explained in his 1995 book. "You could have put them in the Seattle Fair and they wouldn't have drawn twenty people. Musicians have a tendency to forget that." And when Steve Sholes, RCA Victor's lead man for Elvis, heard of the resignations, he wrote a letter to Colonel Parker, stating in part, "From a practical standpoint as far as recordings are concerned, I do hope Elvis doesn't take Scotty and Bill back. As I have told you and Tom Diskin, these two musicians certainly hold up the Presley recording sessions a good deal. I am confident that we can move faster and make better records if we don't have to use these two musicians."

Scotty and Bill also have had their supporters, both then and through the years. Elvis himself would have to be counted as one. By all accounts, the resigna-tions saddened him, and he might have come through for them in the end, had the newspaper article not embarrassed him. The other member of Elvis' band, drummer D.J. Fontana, declined to resign along with the other two, explaining to Scotty that since he had come on later as a salaried employee, he had no right to expect more from Elvis. "I don't blame them one bit," Fontana explained. "They should have left before that. It was Scotty and Bill and Elvis who started out. They had a legitimate reason to complain. I told them, 'If I had started like you guys, I'd be right with you.'"[8]

Two members of the Jordanaires who shared the stage with Scotty and Bill dur-ing Elvis' heyday also defend the two band members. Gordon Stoker lamented,

"Sorry to say, Bill, Scotty, and D.J. were not paid for what they were to Elvis. He could not have appeared without them. Elvis knew they were unhappy and could have done something about it, but he would not buck the Colonel."[9] Bass singer Hugh Jarrett added, "Scotty Moore was good for what Elvis did. He was the kind of guitar player that Elvis needed. I would have quit if I was making what Scotty and Bill made. We were certainly making a lot more than that."[10]

Jarrett's comment underscores how differently Colonel Parker treated the Jordanaires compared to the band members. "I do not know the exact dollars we were paid," explained Stoker. "We were an established group, appearing on the Grand Ole Opry every Saturday night we were in town. For that the Colonel respected us, and we were paid whatever the going rate was for quartets. I know we were pleased with it, or we would not have appeared." In addition to the higher salary, the four Jordanaires got the same $1,000 Christmas bonus from the Colonel that Scotty, Bill, and D.J. received. And like the band, they were responsible for their transportation on tour, but Parker always made hotel reservations for them. Not so for Scotty, Bill, and D.J., whose first chore when they pulled into a tour town was to find a hotel for the night.

Stoker continued, "We had worked with the Colonel long before Elvis—with Eddy Arnold and others—and he always seemed to like me, which really helped. He always came through with whatever we agreed on. Whatever he said he would do, he did."

The Jordanaires' manager as well as their first tenor, Stoker says Scotty and Bill made a big mistake by being too passive and too trusting. "The main problem was the guys did not work out the deal before the dates," he explained. For the early RCA recording sessions, for instance, Stoker negotiated having the Jordanaires name below Elvis' name on the record label. As a result of that, the Jordanaires today continue to get royalties for reissues of some Presley records. The same holds true for reissues of movies and TV shows. "I have never asked Scotty if they were [still getting paid]," says Stoker, "for fear of opening another can of worms." Scotty admits he and Bill should have pressed harder to retain The Blue Moon Boys on record labels when Elvis first signed with RCA records. As it was, they were always listed on the session worksheets as musicians and received the going one-time fee as such.

Their resignations did not mark an end to Scotty and Bill's relationship with Elvis, although they were never again salaried employees. After the Pacific Northwest tour, Elvis next appeared on stage in Tupelo, Mississippi, on September 27. D.J. Fontana was the drummer, but guitarist Hank Garland and bass player Chuck Wiginton replaced Scotty and Bill. According to Lamar Fike, the new band "blew everybody away," and Elvis had a big grin on his face after the show. Fike claims Elvis said, "Shit, I didn't need Scotty and Bill anyway."[11] If he really felt that at the time, he changed very quickly. Just a few days later, Elvis had Tom Diskin call Scotty to ask him if he and Bill would return to play on the upcoming West Coast tour. They agreed, and for the five shows in San Francisco, Oakland, and Los Angeles, Scotty and Bill each received $1,250, over six times what they would have received under the agreement before their resignations. In addition, the Colonel provided the band transportation by limousine from Memphis to the West Coast.

According to Scotty, when he and Bill Black rejoined Elvis' troupe in California, things were as they had been before. Elvis joked and laughed with them as if nothing had happened between them. But the professional and personal bond that had formed between the three men through the hardships of the early years of anonymity and on into the brilliant years had been severed forever. Each of the three men soon went their separate ways. And although their personal and professional lives caused their paths to cross occasionally after Elvis got out of the army, Bill Black's death in 1965 assured that there would never be a reunion of Elvis Presley and The Blue Moon Boys. Those who saw Elvis, Scotty, and Bill perform on stage in 1957 got a final glimpse of the trio that helped give birth to rock 'n' roll.

When the masses screamed, "We want Elvis!" it was obvious to all three men who the teenagers really had come to see. However, in the stands there were still a few who understood the contribution of the band. In Spokane, members of the local band The Blue Jeans were on hand. They thought the whole spectacle of girls screaming as Elvis shimmied was "funny," according to drummer Dick Baker. He locked in on another musician, whose name he didn't know then. "I remember the lead guitar player was really good," he says.

Private Sideburns

"You are hereby ordered for induction into the Armed Forces of the United States and to report to Room 215, 198 South Main St., Memphis, Tennessee, at 7:45 a.m., on the 20th of January, 1958, for forwarding to an armed forces induction station."

After the Memphis Draft Board issued his draft notice on December 20, 1957, Elvis showed it to his friend George Klein. While Klein was shocked, his reaction was nothing compared to the devastation he knew Presley felt. While the threat of the military service had been hanging over Elvis for some time, like most young men in the affluent post-war 1950s, he hoped it wouldn't happen to him. At the height of his popularity and with Hollywood contracts for eight more movies, Presley naturally felt all of it might be lost if the army took him away for two years. "Elvis couldn't understand why Colonel Parker hadn't fixed things up," remembered Jordanaire Gordon Stoker.[12]

Elvis, along with all the other young men of his generation, fell under the provisions of the Universal Military Training and Service Act of 1951. Originally Congress passed the measure to supply the manpower needed to fight the Korean War, but it remained in effect after the war due to cold war fears in the U.S. It resulted in the only instance in American history of conscription during a lengthy peacetime period. Under the act, all men between the ages of eighteen and twenty-six were required to register. The minimum age for induction was eighteen and a half. For those drafted, the length of service was set at twenty-four months. When a man would be drafted depended on where he lived. Each local draft board had an annual quota of men to supply for military service. If volunteers did not meet the quota, the board was required to draft enough men to fill it. While far fewer eligible men were drafted during the late fifties than were during wartime, few exceptions were made once a man's name rose to the top of the board's list. It is doubtful that Colonel Parker had any legal recourse to keep Presley out of uniform once his number came up.

Early in 1957, however, Elvis and the country's other young men of draft age were given some hope that their numbers might never come up. Soon after President Dwight Eisenhower's second inauguration, the Department of Defense announced a 100,000-manpower cut in the U.S. Army. It looked as though fresh troops would not be needed for a long while. The draft remained in effect, however, for without the fear of conscription, the government felt too few young men would be motivated to enlist in the military.

For August 1957, the month Presley started his Pacific Northwest tour, the national draft call was set at 11,000 men. Then, however, the reduction program began to lower the monthly draft calls. The number was 8,000 in September, and it dropped to 7,000 in October, November, and December.

On January 8, 1957, Elvis' twenty-second birthday, the Memphis Draft Board held a press conference to announce that Presley had been classified 1A and likely would be drafted within six to eight months. Just when depended on the number of volunteers who enlisted and the several hundred 1As who were in line to be drafted ahead of him. But when the country's draft quotas began to fall dramatically toward the end of the year, Elvis received an indefinite reprieve. Despite his spring show swing through the Midwest and Canada being touted in some cities as a "going away" tour, by then Elvis felt it would be a long time before the Army claimed him. In early April he told the press in Toronto that authorities had advised him that the draft was "slowing up" and he didn't expect to be drafted for a year or more. The eight-month window he had been given in January closed just days after the Pacific Northwest Labor Day weekend tour ended. He still had heard nothing from his draft board, and there was hope he would never be called.

In November 1957, however, the Pentagon dashed Elvis' hopes by increasing draft calls for the first six months of 1958. January's call jumped up to 10,000, with even greater increases possible into the summer. The quotas went up, according to the Pentagon, because "Army losses will be greater than the reduction program calls for." Troop attrition was greater than originally expected because the Army refused to allow what it called "unfit" men to reenlist. The November announcement once again accelerated Presley's draft number toward the top of the list.

Of course, Elvis' legion of young fans didn't want to lose their idol and were unwaveringly against his being drafted. On March 1, White House officials revealed that President Eisenhower had received a threatening letter from an unnamed fourteen-year-old girl who "protested bitterly regarding the induction of young Presley." The nature of the threat was not made public, but Secret Service agents investigated and discovered that before writing the letter the girl already had been "under supervision of juvenile court authorities" in Minneapolis. A less volatile fan but one still distressed by the thought of Elvis entering the army was Toronto Elvis fan club president Barbara Bromley. After seeing her idol perform in Maple Leaf Gardens on Aril 2, she told the *Daily Star,* "Gosh, just thinking about what will happen to him when he joins the army makes me mad. I saw him last night in the flesh and he's as wonderful as the girls in my fan club think he is. But if the army gives him a crew cut, it'll ruin him. It would be just terrible."[13]

Presley and Colonel Parker found themselves in a quandary. Elvis' adult critics decried any special treatment for the obviously healthy rock 'n' roller and pointed to the passing months as evidence that he somehow was trying to avoid the draft. One option was for Elvis to go into the military as part of the Special Services. That way he could spend his hitch traveling around entertaining troops. But critics pounced on the possibility of Presley's getting special treatment in the military. An editorial in the *Ottawa Citizen* a few days before the singer appeared in the Canadian city spelled out the damage such soft duty could cause to Presley's reputation.

> The latest emanations from news sources reveal that Elvis ... will be assigned to special services when entering the service and will not be subjected to basic training, latrine digging ... or any of the other servile duties placed upon the youth of America as they are obligated to answer their country's call to war in time of peace.
>
> It must give the youth of America a fine idea and spirit of democracy at work to have such a thing rammed down their powerless throats by Pentagon procedure. It must salve their bitter feelings as they pay their

military obligation to their country under the pretense of preparedness for one youth who has absolutely contributed nothing to the material, spiritual or educational welfare of the nation to enjoy special privileges and exemptions while they are abruptly snatched out of college or career to pay a military obligation.

It must be a nice thought to a draftee to think about the ease with which Presley is paying his obligation while they are marching blisters on heels, lackying for brass, mess cleaning or any one of hundreds of other very distasteful things in the Army.[14]

By the end of March, Presley hadn't yet ruled out the Special Services option. Asked about that possibility at a press conference in Detroit, Elvis responded, "Well sir, I'll be honest. I'm not gonna ask for it. If they put me in Special Services, okay; if they don't want to it's still okay. In other words, just whatever they want me to do, I'll try to do the best I can."

However, as the promoter and protector of Presley's public reputation, Parker opposed the Special Services option for Elvis. He also resisted it for another reason. It would result in his losing control over Presley's public exposure, something he was desperately trying to limit in 1957. The best strategy for Elvis was to publicly claim readiness to serve in any capacity, while hoping the Colonel could somehow keep him out of the military altogether. For the rest of the year, Presley never again mentioned Special Services. When the subject came up, he merely responded that he wanted "no special treatment" from the military.

So when Presley toured in 1957 and reporters asked about his draft status, which they did during nearly every press conference, Elvis gave a standard answer that hid his true feelings. At Fort Wayne in March he said, "I'm not gonna ask for anything. I'll do what they want me to do." Three days later in Toronto, he told reporters, "Whenever the army wants me, I'll be ready to go. My career won't be able to continue, although the army may let me make records on my own time. Above all, I don't want any special favors." When asked in Spokane in August whether he'd heard from his draft board, he said, "I haven't heard anything from them since I took my physical. When I do go, I don't expect any favors from them. I'll just do what they tell me."

In Portland, the *Oregon Journal's* Dorothy Lois Smith revealed, "Elvis said he has taken his physical for entering the service and is 'waiting for them to let me know. I just take every day as it comes and don't look into the future,' he said." Phyllis Lauritz of the *Oregonian* added, "Where does he stand on the draft? He is ready and willing when they call him. Yes, he will part with his long locks and not reluctantly, because he wants to be one of the boys, and they wear crew-cuts."

On August 29, five days before Presley closed his Northwest tour in Portland, *Oregon Journal* columnist William Moyes offered a tongue-in-cheek theory about how Elvis Presley could be useful to the U.S. Army.

> About the 24-carat hillbilly that Jeweler Frank Breall is importing to exhibit here on Labor day—Elvis Presley, I mean—People have been asking for days, "How come this character is still on the loose? Isn't he supposed to be in the army?"
>
> It could be, of course, that Elvis is coming to Portland expressly to hide in a deep hole dug at 19th and Morrison, known as Multnomah stadium ...
>
> As near as can be judged from clippings, Presley's draft number did come up. However, he was not inducted into the army. It would seem his draft board has been able to fill its quota from volunteers and has no need for draftees.
>
> Another theory is this (and I am having it patented): To those who know Presley best it is obvious that the army could use him for only one thing—driving mules ... urging them on with his voice and brandishing a silent guitar and shouting at them "Yer Nothin But a Houn Dawg!" Any mule that doesn't get up and run like an antelope with Elvis putting on an act like that has only one other choice—he can stand where he is and have a complete nervous breakdown.
>
> To conclude the theory—before Elvis could be drafted, the army sold all its mules. That left this Spike Jones of song with nothing to do but traipse around the countryside with a guy named Col. Hadacol Parker, singing for money.[15]

By the time of Elvis' appearance in Portland, the Memphis Draft Board's pursuit of him was nearly a year old. On October 24, 1956, the board had sent the then twenty-one-year-old Presley a questionnaire, designed to "bring his status up to date." Then, on January 4, 1957, Elvis reported to Kennedy Veterans Hospital in Memphis for his pre-induction physical. Assigned the draft board's highest physical rating and having earned an "average" score on their aptitude test, Presley was classified 1A four days later.

Of course, any young man tagged as 1A had the option of not waiting to be drafted and enlisting in any branch of the service instead. The *Memphis Press-Scimitar* reported that, just in case Elvis took that option, each of the services had come forward with special deals to offer him. The Air Force would allow him to tour recruiting centers around the country. The Army offered him a two-year enlistment with a 120-day deferment to complete any entertainment commitments. The Navy proposed forming a special "Elvis Presley Company," comprised of Memphis enlistees who would train together. Of course, Elvis never seriously considered any of these offers, as he secretly hoped to escape military service altogether.

That was not to be. Elvis had time for one more personal appearance tour of California and Hawaii in October and November of 1957. Six days before Christmas that year, Milton Bowers, civic leader and chairman of the three-man Memphis Draft Board, informed Elvis that his induction notice was ready to be picked up, indicating that he would be sworn into the army within days. On Christmas Eve, Elvis formally requested a sixty-day deferment so that Paramount Pictures would not lose the financial investment it had already made in *King Creole*, Elvis' next movie. On December 26, 1957, the draft board granted the deferment.

As the new year dawned, Milton Bowers was getting fed up with it all. The letters and phone calls that had poured in to the board since Presley had been drafted only increased after the deferment was granted. To the continuing anger over Presley's being drafted were now added accusations of favoritism over the deferment. Bowers finally vented in a Memphis newspaper article.

> With all due respect to Elvis, who's a damn nice boy, we've drafted people who are far, far more important than he is. After all, when you take him out of the entertainment business what have you got left? A truck driver.
>
> One woman in a letter yesterday called us a bunch of damn southern goons. Well, she's the one who's a goon.
>
> I talk Elvis Presley more than I sleep. A crackpot called me out of bed last night and complained that we didn't put Beethoven in the army.
>
> Considering that Beethoven was not an American and has been dead for some time, I suppose he felt we were discriminating against rock and roll music.
>
> I told him we put Mr. Eisenhower in the army and that ought to count for something. Then I asked him how old he was and he told me he was 52. I asked him how he got so stupid in 52 years.[16]

Despite Milton Bowers' contention that the Memphis board had drafted more important people, in retrospect Elvis Presley was clearly the most famous person conscripted into the army during the peacetime period between the Korean and Vietnam Wars. That he went willingly, at least publicly, earned him a degree of respect that many adults had withheld during his short show business career.

With his work on *King Creole* complete, Elvis Presley reported to the Memphis Draft Board office at 198 South Main Street on March 24, 1958, to be sworn into the U.S. Army. Four and a half months had passed since his last personal appearance in Hawaii the previous November. The screaming was over, and his fans had only memories of seeing the reigning King of Rock 'n' Roll in his prime. Elvis never lost the loyalty of that generation. However, by the time an older, more sedate Presley came out of the army two years later, a band from Liverpool, England, was developing a style that would take rock music in a different direction.

Chapter 16

Tupelo

Prelude

Memphis was Elvis Presley's second hometown; Tupelo was his first. The story of his poor upbringing in that Mississippi town has often been told: How he was born in a two-room house that his father, grandfather, and uncle built with a $180 loan. How he grew up in Tupelo surrounded by an extended family of grandparents, aunts and uncles, and cousins. How he was first exposed to gospel music at the Assembly of God Church and then the blues in the town's Shake Rag community. How at the age of ten he sang "Old Shep" in a youth talent contest at the Mississippi-Alabama Fair and Dairy Show and won second prize. And how his father's search for work took the family to Memphis in 1948 when Elvis was thirteen.

As his fame as an entertainer surged, first regionally and then nationally, Elvis returned to Tupelo to perform annually from 1955 through 1957. The first time was on August 1, 1955, while he was still recording for Sun Studio in Memphis. Although known throughout the South by then, Elvis was just one of many acts that summer night on a jamboree headlined by Webb Pierce at the Mississippi-Alabama Fairgrounds.

A little more than a year later, on September 26, 1956, Elvis returned to Tupelo as the star of the show. A series of smash hit records and television appearances had made him the country's most popular and controversial young singing star. He headlined at the same Mississippi-Alabama State Fair and Dairy Show where he had sung "Old Shep" eleven years earlier.

"I've been looking forward to this homecoming very much," Elvis told reporters before the first of his two performances that Wednesday. There were several reasons for Elvis to feel good about returning to the town of his birth. Other than his current hometown of Memphis, Tupelo was the only place in the country where he could expect to be received with open arms and without criticism. A long parade down Main Street Wednesday morning welcomed him home, although Elvis did not participate. (The risk was too great, according to Colonel Parker.)

Tupelo businesses honored the success of the town's native son. The Rex Plaza Café's special menu for the day included "Love Me Tender" Steak (with gravy), "Ready Teddy" Pork Chops, "Hound Dogs" with Sauer Kraut, "Rock'n'Roll" Stew and "Heartbreak Hotel" Cobbler for dessert.

The chief executives of both the city and state were on hand to honor Presley. Tupelo Mayor James L. Ballard presented Elvis with the key to the city. Telling Elvis that the state was proud of him, Mississippi Governor J. P. Coleman presented Elvis with a scroll honoring him as "American's No. 1 entertainer in the field of popular music."

While pleased by the warm reception, Elvis also seemed to enjoy the opportunity to reminisce about his youth in Tupelo. "Why, I used to sneak into this fair," he recalled. "I got carried out once or twice, too." Taking note of the large crowd that awaited him, he added, "Hope I get escorted out today. Last time I was here, I didn't have a nickel to get in." When someone reminded him of how poorly he had been dressed in his sixth-grade class picture, a smiling Elvis replied, "I'd like to see that picture. I forgot how I looked in overalls; it's been so long since I wore them." A couple of relatives who still lived in Tupelo stopped by to say hello, including one he didn't remember. When a man named Joe Presley told Elvis he was his uncle, Elvis responded, "Oh, really?"

Many of the questions about his current wealth somehow reminded Elvis of his youth in Tupelo. In March he had purchased a midget racing car. "I guess really that I haven't got any business owning one," he admitted. "After all, I'm no racing driver or anything like that. It's just that a long time ago I watched a movie or something and there was this midget racing car and I wanted it real bad. So, when the man said, 'Elvis, you want one of those cars?' I said I sure did ... Maybe you'd understand me better if you'd been living with me and my folks ... in Tupelo, Mississippi, during the depression."[1]

Asked about what he learned in school in Tupelo and later in Memphis, Elvis responded self-patronizingly, "'Nuff to write my own name." Turning serious, he added, "I used to think that school was a waste of time—for the birds. After I got out of school and started to work for a living as a truck driver, I saw how important education is and I wished I'd been better at it."[2]

Presley was a bit sensitive, as well, about how Northern reporters at times made him appear uneducated in their translations of his slight Southern drawl. In 1957 he gave a Toronto reporter his favorite example. "They got everythin' cept mah pants. They even ripped the tayssels offen mah shoes and mah wrisswatch for souvenirs." Laughing, he said, "That's a classic," but after a moment's thought, conceded, "But I guess that's really the way I talk."[3]

Still, he told the Canadian writer he believed he'd been brought up right. "Down where I come from, nobody's got one of those inferiority complexes," he said. "People do what they want to do, and they don't worry about what people think. But they don't go around doing anything wrong. Why, in Tupelo, I got my Bible-learning same as everybody. And in Memphis, too. All these things I'm doing, all the money I'm making, is on account of my mother and my father. If it wasn't for them, I wouldn't care about being so famous. They aren't the kind of people who'd stand for me doing anything wrong."

Presley's 1956 Tupelo performances were the best recorded of all his 1950s stage shows. Fox Movietime News shot some classic film footage of the afternoon show, and the audio recordings of both shows are among the few that exist of Elvis on stage in the fifties. The newsreel footage shows hundreds of young girls pressed up against the stage, their arms outstretched in an effort to touch their idol.

It was a day to remember for the 15,000 who saw him and for Elvis himself. The genuinely warm reception and the chance to share this homecoming with his parents left Elvis with a desire to return to Tupelo again when his busy schedule allowed. That opportunity presented itself a year later, and Elvis eagerly made the pilgrimage back to his roots in northwestern Mississippi. By then, though, things had changed. When he came back to Tupelo for the third time, he came at the height of his popularity. By then he was a Hollywood movie actor, the star of two of the year's biggest motion pictures, with a third one opening soon. Tupelo's small stage again would host a native son whose wildest dreams had come true.

Tupelo, Mississippi
Mississippi-Alabama Fairgrounds
Friday, September 27, 1957, 8:00 pm

Elvis Presley's 1957 appearance in Tupelo differed in many ways from those in the other seventeen cities he visited that year. The return performance in the city of his birth was a day trip, not a stop on one of Presley's three city-to-city tours in 1957. It came three weeks after his Labor Day weekend tour of the Pacific Northwest and a month before his fall California tour. The engagement in Tupelo required no train ride, night travel, or hotel stay. In fact, Elvis didn't miss a night's sleep away from his Graceland home. With Tupelo located just a hundred miles southeast of Memphis, he was able to drive one of his cars to the Mississippi town Friday afternoon for the 8:00 PM show and be back home the same night.

Tupelo was a tiny community to be hosting the nation's most popular musical entertainer of the day. With a population of around fifteen thousand in 1957, Tupelo was dwarfed by St. Louis, Chicago, Detroit, Philadelphia, Seattle, Los Angeles, and the other large cities Presley played in 1957. Even the smaller cities he visited, like Fort Wayne, Spokane, and Tacoma, were each more than ten times the size of Tupelo. Of course, Tupelo's draw for Elvis was not its potential as a huge payday, but rather its nostalgic lure as the singer's birthplace.

The venue of the Mississippi-Alabama Fair and Dairy Show was unique for Presley's stage shows in 1957. For all of his other twenty-seven appearances that year, he played large indoor arenas and spacious outdoor sports stadiums. To say the least, for an entertainer of Elvis' status, the grandstand area of a rural fair was quaint by comparison. While Presley topped the list of attractions during the week, many other events and entertainers competed for the attention of fairgoers. Among the "entertaining features" listed in fair advertising were the "Horse and Mule Pulling Contest," the "Calf Scramble," and the "State Boys' Tractor Driving Contest." In addition, at 5:00 PM each day the public could watch a balloon ascension in front of the grandstands. Sitting on a trapeze, aeronaut Ralph Wiggins rose up with the balloon and then descended to the ground using a parachute. And Elvis wasn't the only big-name entertainer scheduled to perform at the fair. Gospel singing groups the Blackwood Brothers Quartet and the Statesmen Quartet headlined on opening night, the day before Elvis' Friday night show. Among those scheduled later in the week were Carl Perkins, Johnny Cash, and Eddy Arnold.

Another unique feature of Presley's Tupelo show that year was that it was his only live performance in the South. Elvis played the Midwest and Pacific Northwest states along with New York and California, and even three cities in Canada in 1957; but other than Tupelo, the southern-most city he visited was St. Louis. As was to be expected, Elvis' appearance brought a stream of visitors to Tupelo from surrounding states. Fair manager James Savery announced that advance ticket orders had come in from nine states. Although he didn't name the states, certainly many Elvis fans from the bordering states of Arkansas, Louisiana, Alabama, and Tennessee must have made the trek to Tupelo to take advantage of their only opportunity to see Elvis perform that year.

That he received no compensation was another unique aspect of Elvis' 1957 Tupelo appearance. While all other cities he passed through that year reported (sometimes lamented) record box-office takes by Elvis, Tupelo kept all proceeds from the singer's performance. When Colonel Parker announced on March 21 that Elvis would be returning to the Mississippi-Alabama Fair and Dairy Show, he stipulated, "We'll come to Tupelo, but all money over actual expenses will go to build a youth recreation center for boys in the East Tupelo section where Elvis grew up." Elvis had received $5,000 for his show in Tupelo the year before, and Parker predicted that his boy would raise $15,000 this year for the youth center project.

Finally, the makeup of the ensemble on stage with Elvis in Tupelo was truly unique. For the only time among the hundreds of personal appearances Presley made during the 1950s, The Blue Moon Boys were not among his backup musicians. Just three weeks earlier Scotty Moore and Bill Black had resigned. They rejoined Elvis for his California tour in late October, but in Tupelo Presley played with replacement musicians Hank Garland on the guitar and Chuck Wiginton on bass. Garland was an established studio musician at the time and D.J. Fontana knew Wiginton from when they both were on the staff band of *The Louisiana Hayride*. The new band and the Jordanaires gathered at Graceland for several days of rehearsals before the Tupelo show.

"Elvis has been thinking about returning to Tupelo ever since last year. He has spoken about it a number of times," Colonel Parker explained when he and Tupelo Fairboard chairman James Savery jointly announced on March 21, 1957, that Elvis Presley would return in the fall to perform at the Mississippi-Alabama Fair and Dairy Show. The big news, of course, was that all the proceeds would go toward a new youth center in East Tupelo. With the fair still six months away, however, there was some concern that Elvis might be drafted into the army before then. "We thought about that, of course," Savery explained. "The arrangement is that if he is not in service he will come. And if he is in service, perhaps some arrangements might be made to get him away for one day for a worthy cause such as this."[4]

The late September booking in Tupelo fit nicely into the middle of Elvis' six-week break between his late summer Pacific Northwest tour and his California appearances in October. After fair officials booked the rest of their entertainment, they scheduled Elvis for an 8:00 PM performance on Friday, September 27, the fair's second day. Savery had hoped for two shows from Presley, as he'd gotten the year before, but considering that Elvis was coming for free, he could hardly push the case. So one evening show it would be. As had been the case the year before, there were 10,000 seats in front of the grandstand. Tickets for all 10,000 seats were priced at $2.00, and there would be no reserved seats or refunds. The show would go on, rain or shine.

When the fair opened on September 26, officials were a little concerned about the Presley appearance. They had hoped that the show would be sold out, but twenty-four hours before showtime only about four thousand tickets had been sold, most of them to out-of-towners. In Friday's edition of the *Tupelo Daily Journal,* Savery reminded citizens that all proceeds would go toward a new youth center in their town and urged "Tupeloans to support tonight's show with a sell-out crowd."

Tupelo merchants positioned themselves to capitalize on Presley's ability to draw thousands of outsiders to their community. Moore and Pearce Motor

Company on East Main Street headlined its ad in the *Journal* with "Welcome Elvis! Come Out and Trade Us Your Newest Pink Cadillac." Its top offering was an almost new two-door '57 Ford Custom 300 with radio, heater, and white tires. Shainberg's Black and White Store had 600 Elvis knit shirts in blue or gold on hand for $1.99 each. In its *Journal* ad, Shainberg's claimed to be the "first in the whole United States" to have the shirts, which were "ideal for the fair, school and casual wear." In addition, the store had stocked 288 Elvis necklaces for $1 each.

Presley's reception in the town of his birth was just as cordial as it had been the year before. On the morning of his appearance, an editorial in the *Tupelo Daily Journal* entitled, "Let Our Welcome For Elvis Be Truly Warm," read in part as follows.

> The welcome sign, the red carpet, the latch string, and all the other emblems of appreciation for visiting dignitaries are out today for the return of Elvis Presley to the town in which he grew up.
>
> And seldom has a community had greater reason to make sure that its expressions of welcome are as warm as it is numerous.
>
> For in order to return to Tupelo, Elvis is breaking into a hectic schedule at the height of his national popularity to present without receipt one dime for himself a program which would cost any other town in America $25,000.
>
> It is not primarily, however, the fact that Elvis is sacrificing a sizeable sum of money to come here that our community should give him a really warm welcome.
>
> The real reason for our appreciation is that since attaining nationwide fame at the very top of the entertainment world he has never ceased to be the best ambassador any town could have, never getting too big for his former friends and relatives, and his old home town, and never by word or deed doing anything that would make our community anything but proud to claim him as a native son.
>
> There probably are several factors which contributed to Elvis' agreement to return to Tupelo tonight for a benefit performance to finance an East Tupelo recreation center.
>
> But our guess is that one of the biggest of them is that hanging around in a rock-speed world that is completely new to him, he needs to feel appreciated in at least one community in America for just being himself.
>
> And if the town in which he grew up cannot give him that feeling of warmth which is missing in much of the tumultuous applause he receives elsewhere, he has nowhere to turn in search of it.

It is particularly important, therefore, that residents of our community not only turn out in numbers to welcome Elvis tonight, but that we put a special note of warmth and appreciation into the reception we give him.[5]

Unlike in other communities, no religious or educational group opposed Elvis' appearance in Tupelo. The East Tupelo Parent-Teacher Association, for instance, sold Presley pictures and other souvenirs from their booth at the fair. Colonel Parker, who elsewhere always reserved for himself the right to profit from the sale of Elvis mementos at concerts, contributed the items sold at the PTA booth. As with ticket sales, all proceeds from souvenir sales were to go to the youth center fund.

That Friday the fair opened its second day with an early morning beef cattle show in the livestock arena. At 10:00 AM the annual 4-H Club style show began in front of the grandstand. About fifty girls modeled the clothes they had made. The midway featured forty amusement rides, including a giant roller coaster, the "helicopter," the "whip," and a triple Ferris wheel. The day's balloon ascension and parachute jump by Ralph Wiggins was moved up two hours to 3:00 PM to avoid the huge crowd expected for Elvis' evening show.

With none of the 10,000 seats reserved, the crowd lined up early, and as soon as the gates opened, they rushed for the seats closest to the stage. The worries of fair officials vanished as all seats sold quickly, along with about two thousand standing-room tickets. As soon as the crowd entered, the Elvis watch began. Every time a large car pulled into the grandstand area, someone shouted, "Here he comes," and the seated mass would rise to its feet before sitting again to await the next false alarm.

At about 5:00 PM Elvis left Graceland in a Cadillac for the two-hour drive to Tupelo. Accompanying him were his parents, girlfriend Anita Wood, and friends George Klein, Lamar Fike, Cliff Gleaves, Alan Fortas, and Louis Harris. The state patrol escorted the Presley group into the fairgrounds at about 7:15 PM. As the waiting crowd roared, Elvis ducked into a tent behind the stage for his pre-concert press conference. There Tupelo Mayor James Ballard welcomed him home. Then Elvis jumped up on a table to face about twenty reporters and photographers.

Most questions were brief and answered quickly. His favorite record? "'Don't Be Cruel'—I guess because it sold more." When would his Christmas album come out? "Around Christmas, I guess—that was smart, wasn't it?" How was his acting going? "I'm learning a little more about it. Director said I did real well." The name of his next movie? "That I don't know; haven't seen the script yet."

The questions then turned to his love life. "Elvis, are you engaged?" someone asked. "Not even close," he quickly responded. "I'm not ready for that. That's not saying I wouldn't if I wanted to. It's just that I haven't found any girl I want to marry." Standing behind his right shoulder, Anita lowered her head and blushed visibly. Taking advantage of the uneasy moment, a reporter decided to throw Elvis a little more rope. "Elvis, what do you think of Anita Wood?" Smiling, Presley said, "Well, she's female." When the interviewer continued, "Is there a possibility ..." Elvis stopped him short. "No sir. I know what you were going to ask. There's no possibility." After the press conference, a reporter asked Anita about her reaction to Elvis' answers about her and marriage. "I don't blame him for saying that," she answered. "I would have said it, too."

The questions seemed to fade away, and Presley's shortest and quietest press conference of the year came to an end. Elvis then met, embraced, posed for photos with, and signed autographs for the privileged teenage girls who had been admitted to the press conference. Two girls, one on crutches and the other in a wheelchair, were brought into the tent to meet Elvis. Twelve-year-old Ann Hill of Ashland had been born with a type of infantile paralysis, and Shirley Martin, 14, of Dorsey, had been crippled for three years. Elvis talked with each and hugged them both.

Meanwhile, the grandstand crowd sat through Colonel Parker's standard set of opening acts. Included were singer Joyce Paul, comedian Howard Hardin, comedic dancer Rex Marlowe, and tap dancer Chris Dahl. Bob Morris and his fourteen-piece orchestra provided the background music. As usual, several songs by the Jordanaires brought the show to intermission.

When Elvis finally took the stage, he wore the same combination he had worn on stage in Spokane a month before. A black shirt open to the breastbone revealed the gold medallion and silver chain given to him by a fan in Ottawa that spring. Navy blue pants, black shoes, and his shimmering gold jacket, buttoned at the waist, completed the ensemble.

The show's content repeated Presley's standard stage fare for that year. The performance ran about forty-five minutes and included "more than a dozen songs," according to *Journal* staff writer Arnold Collins. As usual, Elvis opened with "Heartbreak Hotel" and closed with "Hound Dog." There were no songs from *Jailhouse Rock,* since the movie and its soundtrack numbers had not been released. (Elvis would first sing the title song of his third movie on stage in San Francisco the following month.)

The performance featured the hip movements the crowd expected, but Elvis also threw in one of his theatrical belches to inflame the fans. James Page of the *Memphis Press-Scimitar* characterized the burp as "accidental," but Presley's history of such throat sounds on stage belies that judgment. The crowd reacted throughout with screaming, near hysterics, yelling Elvis' name and reaching out their hands toward the stage. "Take it easy," the singer yelled from the stage. "We'll have a party later."

"I hope these soldiers can hold the crowd back," said fair manager Savery, referring to the seventy National Guardsmen forming a barrier between the crowd and the stage. Only the heavy rope they supported kept the teenage mob from storming the stage, according to the *Journal's* Arnold Collins. One girl suffered a sprained ankle when another teenager picked her up and threw her out of the way. After the show, a guardsman said, "I've fought in the Golden Gloves for a long time but those girls gave me the worst beating I've ever taken."[6]

As Elvis delivered his high-energy version of "Hound Dog," the throng made its final surge toward the stage. While the guardsmen held the line, highway patrolmen and Tupelo police officers quickly escorted Elvis off the platform and onto the highway back toward Memphis. One girl fainted as the show ended but was revived by a guardsman.

Elvis was gone, never again to perform in Tupelo. When the Mississippi-Alabama Fair and Dairy Show opened the following year, Presley was on a troop ship bound for army service in Germany. Still, the proceeds from his 1957 concert promised to create a legacy for Elvis in Tupelo in the form of a new youth center on a plot of land on the east side of town. The project was much more than a tax write-off to Presley. "The youth center and park will be a deep personal interest to me," he declared during his 1957 visit to Tupelo. "I guess everyone has a deep personal interest in the communities where they were born."[7]

The 12,000 fans paid gross receipts of $24,000 that late September night. A couple of days later, James Savery announced that the tabulating of profits from the Presley show was ongoing, but unofficial estimates put the profit somewhere near $20,000. The plan then was for the money to go toward the construction of the center in East Tupelo. The city was to bear the responsibility of gaining title to the land. Governor J. P. Coleman would head a committee overseeing the construction. After the youth center and park were complete, the Tupelo Park and Recreation Department would take over administration of the project.

After passing a bond issue, the city of Tupelo purchased fifteen acres of land, including the house where Elvis was born. An architect drew up plans for the youth center and park, but for some reason the project then stalled. It wasn't until 1971 that improvements were made on the property, and even then not by the city, but as a project of the East Heights Garden Club. That same year the old Presley home opened to the public. During the next few years the club purchased furniture and other objects to restore the contents of the house to resemble what they had been when the Presleys lived there in the late 1930s.

Shortly after Elvis Presley's death in 1977, his Tupelo birthplace was designated a Mississippi Historical Site by the state Department of Archives and History.

That same year, the city of Tupelo created the Elvis Presley Memorial Foundation. The foundation added the Elvis Presley Museum and Memorial Chapel, developed Elvis Presley Park, and, along with the refurbished Presley home, christened the fifteen-acre property the Elvis Presley Center. On what would have been Elvis' sixty-seventh birthday in 2002, a life-sized bronze statue, entitled "Elvis at 13," was unveiled in the park. It memorializes a young Elvis wearing overalls and carrying a guitar. Fifty years after Presley's fundraising show at the fairgrounds, the attractions of the Elvis Presley Center draw about fifty thousand visitors to Tupelo each year.

However, the youth center so important to Elvis, and toward which the profits of his 1957 benefit show were intended, was never built in East Tupelo.

Colonel Parker stands guard as Elvis takes the stage in Seattle, September 1, 1957. (Seattle Post-Intelligencer Collection, Museum of History and Industry, Seattle)

Chapter 17

The Parker Propaganda Machine

When he traveled around the country in 1957 making arrangements for his client's personal appearances, Colonel Tom Parker was well known for his association with two products—Hadacol and Elvis Presley. The former was a patent medicine that the Colonel had ballyhooed for a few years before he caught a ride on a rocket ship named Elvis. Like most elixirs, a swallow or two of Hadacol made the patient feel better temporarily. And, like most elixirs, the secret of Hadacol's healing power was a substantial alcohol content. At one point, with Parker's considerable promotional ability behind it, millions of Americans consumed Hadacol at $1.25 a pint. When reality inevitably overtook promotion, Parker moved on in search of other products to test Barnum's maxim.

When asked about the elixir during Presley's 1957 tours, the Colonel commented briefly, but then shifted the focus to his current product. "Some folks still drink it," Parker told Don Duncan of the *Tacoma News Tribune*. "Elvis is a good kid, no trouble at all. I don't know which was easier to sell—him or Hadacol." Presley critics, however, couldn't resist making a comparison between the way Parker promoted his potion and the way he promoted Presley. Five days before Elvis' appearance in Portland, an editorial in the *Oregonian* spelled it out.

> It could be that Elvis Presley, like Hadacol, is just another example of what can be achieved by a promotional genius in making things appear to be more worthwhile and desirable than they really are. If so, when Colonel Parker gets tired of blowing the trumpet for Elvis, this young man speedily will find his way to his proper niche in the temple of the Arts. This we imagine would be as a pretty good hillbilly singer on some barn dance TV show.
>
> And what will all the swooners over Presley do then? Why, they will quickly forget and find new subjects for allegiance. Just as the ex-customers for Hadacol did.[1]

Of course, Tom Parker had no intention of letting Elvis fade away as Hadacol had. By the spring of 1957, his managerial strategy focused on dispelling the perception that Presley was no more than a shooting star in the night sky of show business. Knowing that sooner or later Elvis would be swallowed up by the military, Parker set about developing for Presley a positive image that would lay the groundwork for an enduring career after he returned to civilian life. By the time Elvis hit the road for his first tour of 1957, the Parker Propaganda Machine was running smoothly.

One of the Colonel's strategies involved the tireless promotion of Presley fan clubs, both local and national. He started the Elvis Presley National Fan Club, which Parker claimed had over 250,000 card-carrying members in the U.S. alone by early 1957. An additional 150,000 international members spread across the globe from Canada to Australia. According to the Colonel, by March 1957 the club headquarters was answering three to four thousand fan letters each day. Each member received an Elvis Presley membership button and could purchase an Elvis Presley souvenir package, including photos and booklets, which came in three sizes at varying prices. (In 1962, soon after he began managing The Beatles in England, Brian Epstein studied Colonel Parker's Presley fan club strategies and applied them himself in an effort to build a solid fan base for his new clients.)

Through the fan clubs, Parker pushed the sale of records and merchandise to Presley's teenage fan base. Indeed, such fan clubs ravenously consumed Presley merchandise. On the market then were Elvis scarves, pillows, statues, Capri pants, perfumes, cosmetics, and bubble-gum cards. Particularly hot sellers in the summer of 1957 were Teddy Bear Perfume and autographed tennis shoes. The most sought-after and cherished photograph of Presley that summer was the now classic image of the singer clothed in the complete gold lamé suit made for him earlier that year by Nudie of Hollywood. Naturally, fan club members could be counted on to buy all of Presley's records. *Oregonian* reporter Phyllis Lauritz, after interviewing a couple fan club officers in Portland, made the following condescending observation about how fan club members used Elvis records: "The really devout soften them over heat and form them into urns."[2]

As a reward for the efforts of fan club leaders who rallied the troops, Colonel Parker issued them credentials to attend Elvis' press conferences prior to his appearances in their communities. There they had an opportunity to meet their idol, get a kiss, and have their pictures taken with him. Even a couple of months later in California, when Parker denied the press free passes to Presley's show, he still embraced the fan club officers. Leaders of the King's Klan and the Sideburn Set dominated the San Francisco press conference on October 26.

While Parker solidified Presley's fan base, he maneuvered behind the scenes for over a year to get total control over Elvis Presley's public image. In his early days as Presley's manager, the Colonel sent his boy out on the road as part of a packaged tour with other name performers. But that practice began to change in March 1956, when Presley signed a contract naming Parker his "sole and exclusive Advisor, Personal Representative, and Manager in any and all fields of public and private entertainment."

Soon the Colonel developed a concept called The Elvis Presley Show, which he alone managed. The structure of the new touring format gave Parker the absolute control he needed. First, while there were other performers in the show, Elvis would be the sole headliner, thus eliminating competition. After all, the Colonel had seen how Presley himself had stolen the show from Hank Snow and other established stars when he toured with them as an "extra added attraction." So the Colonel packed the first half of the show with old-style pop singers, jugglers, and comedians of the sort normally seen as filler material on *The Ed Sullivan Show.* In a March interview, just before Elvis' first personal appearance tour of 1957, Colonel Parker explained the difference between Elvis and the other performers in The Elvis Presley Show. He told *Toronto Telegraph* writer Leon Kossar that the Presley program was not a rock 'n' roll show. "It'll be a sit and jump show," he explained. "They sit in their seats most of the program and they jump when Elvis sings."[3]

Also, Parker wanted to create some distance between Elvis and rock 'n' roll's bad reputation. In April 1956, for instance, after Elvis performed in Corpus Christi, Texas, the Colonel heard complaints that vulgar acts had been committed on stage. His assistant, Tom Diskin, called him from the road to assure him that it was not Elvis, but another performer who was to blame. Parker knew that Presley would always have to answer for his own actions on stage, but he wasn't about to have Elvis associated with the bad press of other rock 'n' roll acts. In the March 1957 interview with Kossar, Parker denied reality by claiming the Presley show did not provoke teenagers to "aisle dancing and rock'n'roll frenzy like 'another' touring rock'n'roll show." Despite the obvious contradiction, Parker sought to move Presley's image more toward the mainstream by purposely using a series of opening acts that were bland compared to Presley. "He'll have a good variety show with him," the Colonel said on arriving in Toronto. "The Jordanaires, a top-flight comedian, and a top band group."

In complete control, Parker micro-managed every facet of an Elvis Presley personal appearance, taking the opportunity to shape his client's image as he thought best. The Parker Propaganda Machine was born.

The Colonel's actions in the Pacific Northwest are a good example of how he controlled every aspect of a Presley tour. By mid-August, two weeks before the tour began, Parker and his staff were on the ground, inspecting and ordering changes in the planning done by Northwest Releasing. Traveling back and forth between the five cities on the tour, Parker coordinated advertising, inspected the venues, and gave detailed security instructions.

Given sole control over advertising by his contract with the local promoters, Parker placed similarly formatted ads in the newspapers of all five cities. They touted Elvis as "America's Only Atomic Powered Singer," a catchy slogan Parker had coined the year before when he booked Presley into Las Vegas, whose surrounding deserts were the scene of numerous atomic bomb tests in the mid-1950s. Although *Loving You,* Elvis' second movie, was just opening in Northwest theaters over the Labor Day weekend, Parker was thinking ahead and decided to use the tour to plug Presley's next movie, which would not be released for several months. At each of his appearances in the Pacific Northwest, Elvis performed in front of a huge banner that read, "Greater Than Ever—Elvis Presley in Jailhouse Rock." That movie opened nationwide on November 1 while Elvis was in the middle of his final tour in California.

Of course, Parker never missed an opportunity to feed positive information about Elvis to the press, often building up his client while downplaying his own role in Presley's success. "He's got so much talent," the Colonel assured John Voorhees of the *Seattle Times,* "he'd have become successful no matter who his manager was. Actually, I'm the lucky one because fate threw us together." Parker went on to portray his boy as being misunderstood. "You know, Elvis can't go out on the street like you or I. He's paying the price of that fame. Most people don't think about that when they say: 'Why, I've got just as much talent as he has and I'll bet I could be famous too.' They probably wouldn't even like to be that famous."[4]

Of course, to get the press to print the pro-Presley stuff, the Colonel threw in some of his down-home humor. He told Voorhees about harder times back in the 1930s, when he was touring tent shows throughout the South. "Why we had ten trucks," he said, "but only five sets of tires. We'd have to drive half the trucks to the next town, put them up on jacks, take the tires off and go back and put them on those trucks left behind."

When it came to advertising, Parker spent his money solely on newspaper ads, and then sparingly. Relatively small ads, one per day, began appearing in local newspapers two weeks before a Presley appearance. The ads were tied to ticket sales. If a sellout seemed certain, Parker saw no need to continue hyping Elvis in that community and would yank any further advertising. For Presley's show in Fort Wayne on March 31, the manager bragged that all it took was "one small ad in the paper about his Fort Wayne appearance, and the place was sold out the next day."

Of course, Parker didn't place the advertisements himself. He hired people to take care of that and other tour details. The top man on the Colonel's staff was long-time assistant Tom Diskin, who worked tirelessly behind the scenes to keep The Elvis Presley Show running smoothly. "Tom had more things to take care of than anyone should have had to," recalls Gordon Stoker. "He was a jewel, and Elvis liked him very much."[5]

The Colonel also took advantage of the free publicity local rock 'n' roll disc jockeys could provide. He allowed them to run contests on the air, giving readers a chance to win free tickets and even meet Elvis at the pre-show press conference. In each city Parker picked one prominent DJ to introduce Elvis on stage, such as Josh King in Toronto, Red Robinson in Vancouver, and Tom Moffatt in Honolulu. The Colonel knew that, in addition to stirring up a lot of excitement before the concert, treating the DJs well ensured increased Presley hype on the radio for months after he left town.

When Elvis finally arrived on the scene, Parker shadowed his star every step of the way through the tour. The pre-concert press conference held in each city was more than a time-saving strategy to reduce the number of press interviews Presley had given in the past. They were also an integral part of the Parker Propaganda Machine. First of all, by using credentials, the Colonel controlled who had access to Elvis at each press conference. Then, when the questioning began, Parker managed Presley's answers from his seat in the back row. When asked a question he considered controversial, Elvis would look over the heads of journalists at his manager. If Parker nodded his head, Presley answered the question. If he shook his head, Elvis either dodged the question or said something like, "Well, you'll have to ask Colonel Parker about that." The system worked well. In nearly every city, journalists indicated in their articles the next day that they left the press conferences with a favorable opinion of Presley's poise and courtesy. Of course, they got very little useful information from their encounters with Elvis, since under the Colonel's guidance the singer usually gave short, nondescript answers, even sometimes being downright evasive.

At the end of each press conference, while Elvis signed autographs and posed for photos with fan club presidents and contest winners, Colonel Parker held court for any reporters still looking for quotes. It gave the Colonel another opportunity to hype his client—and tell another story or two.

In Seattle, Emmett Watson of the *Post-Intelligencer* recalled an anecdote told by Parker. The Colonel claimed he had been waiting patiently to check into a hotel at an earlier stop on the Presley tour. In front of him, an arrogant woman addressed the desk clerk. "And be sure," the woman demanded, "to wake me at 6 AM. Not a minute later!" Not one to miss an opportunity, Parker furtively made note of the woman's room number. At the crack of dawn, the Colonel told Watson, he went down to a lobby phone and dialed up the woman's room. When she answered, Parker said in a polite voice, "Good morning, madam. It's six o'clock. Get your big fat carcass out of bed!"[6] The story was probably fallacious, but it was the kind of yarn that endeared Tom Parker to the press corps around the country in those early years of Presleymania.

Parker spread more of his homespun humor in Honolulu in November. Over lunch, he told columnist Cobey Black that he'd read in a local paper that he'd talked with Hal Lewis about Elvis over dinner. "I've never had dinner with Hal Lewis," the Colonel told Black. "I called him right away to ask who'd picked up the tab." He also told Black that he had another deal in the works if the Elvis thing didn't work out. "For my next promotion," he explained, "I'm going to try to get that little dog in Sputnik II. Seriously, honey, he'd be great on a personal appearance tour. And I could get a good deal on dog food."

Using numbers, big numbers, was one of the strategies Parker used in marketing and hyping Presley. The publicity value of the numbers he used was more important than their accuracy. For instance, at Elvis' press conference before his March 31 show in Detroit, the Colonel threw out some spurious numbers. "We get 25,000 to 30,000 fan letters a week," Parker boasted. "Why, he even got more than 270,000 Christmas cards, a lot of them from right here in Deeetroit."[7] Earlier the Colonel had told a Canadian reporter that Elvis received 45,000 of those Christmas cards from the Toronto area alone. If Parker's numbers were accurate, then nearly 17 percent of all the holiday cards sent Elvis came from that one Canadian city. By November, when Parker was in Hawaii for Presley's last concerts of the year, the total number of Christmas cards Elvis received the previous year had grown in the Colonel's mind. He told columnist Cobey Black that Elvis got 400,000 cards in 1956, 21,000 of them from his Hawaiian fans. Whatever the real numbers were, Parker assured reporters that none of this had gone to the boy's head.

A clear example of how Colonel Parker manipulated numbers occurred during Presley's 1957 tour of the Pacific Northwest when Parker inflated the crowd sizes and misled the press about gate receipts in the five cities. To understand just why and how he did it requires an examination of Colonel Parker's contract with the tour sponsor and an understanding of why the Northwest crowds were smaller than expected.

By 1957 the conditions of an Elvis Presley personal appearance contract were rather simple, although the contract itself was literally a yard long. Tour promoter Lee Gordon remembered the first time he saw one of Parker's contracts. At the top was a foot-long portrait of Presley, and there were other images of the singer in various poses around the sides and bottom. Between was a foot and a half of Parker legalese and conditions. An impressed Gordon told the Colonel, "I've never seen anything like it. Could I have an extra one for myself?" Parker paused for a moment before responding, "They cost money." Gordon paid a dollar for his unsigned document.[8]

The contract called for a basic up-front guaranteed fee per performance for Presley. For his 1957 tours that guarantee was usually $20,000, although that amount could be reduced when Elvis performed two shows on the same day at the same venue. After taxes and Presley's cut, the contract also called for the sponsor to use the remaining gate receipts (and his own money, if need be) to pay for all advertising, venue lease fee, and wages for stagehands, ticket-takers, and off-duty police for security. Colonel Parker reserved the exclusive right to sell Presley-related merchandise and keep all proceeds from such sales.

Presley's expenses, to be paid out of his fee, included wages for the opening acts, his three musicians, and the Jordanaires. In addition, transportation and hotel expenses for Elvis and his traveling companions had to be absorbed. (The opening acts, Scotty, Bill, D.J., and the Jordanaires were responsible for their own traveling expenses.) Of course, after expenses on the Presley side were paid, Colonel Parker received his sizeable percentage, as stipulated in his contract with Elvis.

With those conditions in place, the Pacific Northwest Tour of 1957 got underway. Elvis and the Colonel were guaranteed to make a pile of money, and Zollie Volchok and Jack Engerman, owners of Northwest Releasing, hoped to make a bundle as well. When tickets went on sale in Seattle on August 16, Volchok announced that a total of 118,400 tickets were available for the five shows on the tour, and he expressed confidence that they all would sell. Spokane's Memorial Stadium had the largest seating capacity at 25,000. In Vancouver, B.C., Empire Stadium had a capacity of 25,000 as well, but since the stadium had seating all around the oval, seats could not be sold behind the stage, and so only 22,000 tickets were printed. At 14,000 seats, Tacoma's Lincoln Bowl had the lowest capacity on the tour. Sicks' Seattle Stadium had 17,000 seats in the grandstand, and Multnomah Stadium in Portland had 20,000. The existing seating in all five venues, then, totaled 98,000. Volchok obviously planned on adding another 20,000 seats on the playing surfaces of the various stadiums to bring the total tour capacity up to the 118,400 total he stated on August 16.

The Colonel would have had these numbers in front of him before he drew up the contract with Northwest Releasing. Rival promoter and later a Parker employee, Oscar Davis explained the Colonel's basic contract strategy. "There was never a time when Tom sold Elvis ... when the promoter made more money than the act did," Davis explained. "The Colonel always adjusted the costs so that the promoter didn't get away with anything. It's uncanny. He'd figure the capacity of the audience and the popularity of his artist in that particular area, and he priced him, so that the artist made more money than the promoter. The promoter didn't lose any money, mind you, but he wouldn't make very much either."[9]

Unfortunately for Northwest Releasing, Parker overestimated Presley's draw-ing power in the Pacific Northwest, and the contract he presented Volchok and Engerman, with its steep guarantee for Elvis, resulted in a final loss for the two promoters. Probably trusting Parker's judgment more than their own, the two men signed on the dotted line. Though they had hoped for a complete sellout, less than half of the seats available for Presley's five-city tour sold. Of course, the crowd sizes still set records in each community, but they came nowhere near what the promoters expected or needed. The result was that, while Presley got his money, Volchok and Engerman, as well as their local sponsors, lost money on the deal.

In Elvis Presley they certainly had the biggest draw in the entertainment busi-ness in 1957, but if Volchok and Engerman had considered the nature of Pacific Northwest cities and the kind of audience Presley drew, they shouldn't have been surprised by the smaller than hoped for crowds and revenues Elvis drew in that area. The singer attracted mainly a teenage crowd, and a young one at that, most in the thirteen to fifteen age group. While teenagers would use the tickets, their parents would buy them. In the 1950s, the Pacific Northwest was one of the most politically and culturally conservative sections of the country. With no small assistance from rock 'n' roll music, the area was just becoming aware of the lib-eral ideas it would embrace a couple of decades later. When Elvis came there in 1957, a predominately white population that adhered to Christian principles still controlled the money and decision-making structure in the Northwest. Seeing in Elvis Presley a threat to the traditional values they wanted their children to embrace, many parents in the area denied those children the opportunity to see his "vulgarity" on stage.

"This was a church town," local rock 'n' roll musician Dick Baker says of Spokane in 1957. "There was a lot of controversy from church people when he came. He wasn't well received by the older people at the time. Maybe that's why the ticket sales were down."[10] Indeed, in 1957 over a quarter of the city's 35,000 schoolchildren attended parochial schools. As for high schools, where most of Presley's fans could be found, Spokane had four parochial secondary schools and only three public ones. Church attendance was high in Spokane, as well as in the other four cities on the tour. Seattle had 428 churches in 1957. All of that pointed toward lower attendance than might otherwise have been expected for Presley's show.

An overview of ticket sales for each of the tour stops shows how the promoters overestimated Presley's drawing power in the Pacific Northwest. In Spokane, city records show that 8,341 tickets, just a third of those available, were sold for Elvis' appearance in the 25,000-seat Memorial Stadium. As a result, officials closed one entire side of the stadium for the concert. In fact, the city's indoor facility, the

Spokane Coliseum, with its 9,000 seats, could have been used instead of the stadium.

Only in Spokane, where 8,341 tickets were sold, resulting in gate receipts of
$21,708, are exact figures known for Presley's Northwest tour in 1957. However,
using press reports and extrapolating using the Spokane numbers, a reasonably
clear picture of ticket sales and income in the other four cities comes into view.
For instance, in Vancouver, B.C., the reported crowd size varied widely in press
reports, but it is known that ticket sales brought in about $44,000. Assuming the
average ticket price was about $2.60, as it was in Spokane, places the Vancouver
crowd at just under 17,000. At 77 percent capacity, Canadian Presley fans came
closer to filling up Empire Stadium than any of the four American cities could
do in their stadiums. In Tacoma, about $11,000 in gross ticket sales indicated
that only about 4,250 tickets sold for the show in the 14,000-seat Lincoln Bowl,
meaning the facility was only at 30 percent capacity, a significant disappointment. Only thirty miles south of Seattle, where Elvis appeared the same day, the
Tacoma venue had no chance of drawing people from the larger population center
to the north. In fact, all of the 4,250 spectators in Tacoma on the afternoon of
September 1 could have fit into the empty seats in Seattle's Sicks' Stadium that
evening without filling up the place. As it was, slightly under 14,000 showed up in
Seattle that evening, about 8,000 short of a sellout. At 63 percent capacity, Seattle
beat out Portland, where the next night 12,004, or 60 percent, of the 20,000
seats in Multnomah Stadium sold. Overall for the five-city tour, Elvis sold about
55,500 tickets, under half of the 118,400 available. Total gate receipts totaled
about $147,000, out of which Elvis received his $100,000 guarantee. That left
Northwest Releasing about $47,000 to cover their expenses in all five cities, which
included paying state and local taxes, advertising costs, stadium rental fees, security forces, and wages for all stadium workers. For sponsoring Elvis Presley's swing
through the Pacific Northwest, Zollie Volchok and Jack Engerman made a pit-
tance, if anything, and most of their local sponsors, like Frank Breall in Portland,
didn't make a cent. Some even had to pay out of their own pockets to make ends
meet. Their main reward was the satisfaction and remembrance of bringing to the
Northwest the world's top entertainment personality, one who would become a
cultural icon. For most of them, that was enough. They made their fortunes in
other ways, but for the rest of their lives and beyond, they would forever be linked
with the legend of Elvis Presley.

Back on the ground in 1957, Colonel Parker had a public relations problem.
He knew from low advance ticket sales in the Northwest that there would be no
"sellouts" to crow about when the tour was over. It was all about image now for
the Colonel. Presley's critics eagerly watched for any indication that the singer
and the crude music he espoused were about to flame out. Parker realized that

diminished crowds at personal appearances and promoters losing money could be the evidence the critics sought. So the Parker Propaganda Machine went into high gear before Presley even stepped on stage for the tour's first stop in Spokane on August 30.

There had been a time, and not so long before, when the thought of local promoters losing money hadn't troubled Tom Parker. When Presley first hit the big time in early 1956, Parker managed his client with the single goal of maximizing income. In February that year, he explained his management strategy in a wire to RCA's Bill Bullock. "I'm using the old circus style promotion," Parker wrote, "and it's paying off. No gimmicks and giveaways. Just plain old advertising. It's coming, it's here, and now it's gone."[11] By 1957, though, with Presley sitting atop the entertainment world, the Colonel felt he could afford to resort to a few gimmicks and giveaways to keep him there.

First, now that Elvis appeared under guaranteed contracts, there was no reason that certain people should not be let in without buying tickets. Fan club officers, disc jockeys, winners of radio station contests, journalists, photographers—anyone who had the power to keep Presley's name before the public bypassed the turnstiles during his Northwest tour in 1957. In addition, they were invited to the pre-concert press conferences to meet the star and learn that he was a nice, respectful young man, not the immoral demon they saw on stage. Additionally, freebies padded the crowd numbers at personal appearances, making Elvis look better.

Padding crowd numbers—that was precisely Colonel Parker's strategy when he realized advance ticket sales were lagging for Presley's Northwest tour. And he didn't just inflate the numbers a few hundred here and there. When Tom Parker did anything, he did it big. If the press could be fooled into thinking a few hundred extra people had bought tickets, why not go for thousands more? There is evidence that Parker did just that at most stops on Presley's Northwest tour. In Spokane, for instance, city cashier records show that 8,341 tickets were sold for Presley's appearance in Memorial Stadium on August 30. However, the next day a different story was being told. The *Spokesman-Review* reported the crowd at "more than 12,000," while the afternoon *Spokane Daily Chronicle* had the crowd at 12,500. So who were the roughly 4,000 others who allegedly were there but didn't pay? First of all, it was Colonel Parker who fed the 12,000-plus number to the press. To come up with his crowd size, Parker started with the real ticket-buyers, to which he added everyone else in the stadium. That meant counting all the off-duty police officers and other security personnel, ticket-takers, ushers, concessionaires, technicians, even janitors. Then he included all the entertainers, including Elvis himself. "Give-or-take" allowed him to toss in another thousand or two, and just like that, a gate of 8,341 became a crowd of over 12,000. Since reporters couldn't wait for city financial records to be finalized, they went with the crowd size given them by "a Presley official."

More of the same happened in Vancouver, B.C., the next night, but this time the writers were not as easily fooled. A *Vancouver Province* reporter wrote that Elvis had drawn "Twenty-two thousand people in Empire Stadium, his backers proudly announced, but if they sold that many tickets about 7,000 Presley fans stayed home. PNE (stadium) officials said that 18,000—a generous guesstimate—were in place."[12] Dr. Ida Halpern, another *Province* writer, claimed the 25,000-seat stadium was "half-filled." Jack Wasserman had Parker's numbers game figured out and reported it in his "About Now" column in *Vancouver Sun*.

> Official figures given out by the platoon of flunkies surrounding Presley indicated that the attendance totaled 22,000. This figure was distributed in the hope that it would get in the newspapers so that it could be clipped out and used to sell Elvis to promoters in other towns. An estimate of 16,500 in the Stadium gives Elvis by far the best of it.[13]

Still, fifty years later, it is a much higher number that most Presley scholars cite as the crowd size at the infamous concert in Vancouver. In various articles and books over the years, Vancouver DJ Red Robinson has claimed 25,000 were there. Peter Guralnick repeated that number in his 1994 Elvis biography.

In Portland, the *Oregonian's* headline on September 3 blared, "14,600 Fans Squeal, Jump As Elvis Shakes, Gyrates." One *Oregon Journal* writer went along, numbering the crowd at "more than 14,000." Buried deep in the *Journal* article, however, was the following factual information.

> Turnstile attendance at Monday night's show was announced today by stadium officials as 12,004. Performers, policemen and ushers swelled the total to about 14,000. Frank Breall, Portland promoter who negotiated for the Presley appearance, estimated proceeds for the show at approximately $32,000. This would indicate Portland financiers lost money on the venture.[14]

The cumulative effect of Parker's manipulating the crowd numbers in the tour's five cities was substantial. As noted before, about 55,500 tickets were actually sold for the tour. However, adding together the Parker-generated crowd sizes (as printed in the newspapers of the five cities the day after Elvis appeared in each) gives a total tour attendance of 74,582. Overall, the Colonel inflated the tour attendance by over a third. Some 19,000 seats, empty on show night, became filled on paper due to Parker's machinations. While certainly not of great importance in the on-going legend of Elvis Presley, in augmenting Presley's ability to draw a crowd, Colonel Parker was effectively massaging history. Using newspaper reports as their primary sources through the years, most Elvis writers—biographers, music histo-rians, journalists, fan publishers—have taken as fact and repeated the exaggerated crowd sizes that Colonel Parker fed to the press in the Pacific Northwest.

In retrospect, there was no need to inflate the number of people who paid to see Elvis Presley perform in the Pacific Northwest in 1957. For a short four-day, five-city tour, drawing over 55,000 people and grossing $147,000 at the box office was a record no other entertainer of that era could hope to match. Still, Colonel Parker couldn't resist an opportunity to make the performer look even better than he was, even if it meant inflating Presley's already impressive ability to sell tickets. When the Parker Propaganda Machine started humming, the dividing line between fact and fantasy often got blurred.

When Elvis went on tour in 1957, Tom Parker's reputation preceded him and lingered after he had left. His charm and humor no doubt assuaged some of the ire evoked by promoters' red ink and the moral damage many adults were sure his boy caused in their communities. Still, to those who knew him best, his tactics on tour were business as usual. Hugh Jarrett of the Jordanaires succinctly described the 1950s Colonel Parker thus: "He was a strange duck but a very sharp operator as far as dealing with people and personalities."[15]

Girls waiting to buy tickets for Elvis show at Civic Auditorium, San Francisco, Oct. 26, 1957. (The Bancroft Library, University of California, Berkeley)

Chapter 18

The Bay Area

Prelude

When the people of the Bay Area learned that Elvis Presley was coming to Oakland and San Francisco for three shows in late October 1957, their reaction was less intense than in other communities Elvis visited that year. The Bay Area, after all, had seen Elvis' act before. During the first phase of his exploding popularity, Presley performed at the Oakland Auditorium on June 3, 1956, just two days before his infamous rendition of "Hound Dog" on *The Milton Berle Show* earned him the nickname "Elvis the Pelvis."

With Presley's first appearance on *The Ed Sullivan Show* still three months off, Bay Area civic leaders could judge the rock 'n' roller only on press reports of his wild shows in other communities. San Francisco officials gave in to their fears and refused permission for Presley to appear at the city's Civic Center. Across the Bay, however, Oakland's Auditorium Arena opened its doors to the controversial singer for two shows.

By that time Colonel Parker had already come up with The Elvis Presley Show format that would be used for the remainder of Presley's 1950s stage appearances. Elvis performed for only twenty minutes, but it was long enough to electrify the combined afternoon and evening crowds of 6,400. When he first appeared, clad in a Kelly green tweed jacket and black denim slacks, the crowd, according to *Oakland Tribune* writer Elinor Hayes, "blew its top. A noise meter would have thought it was recording the '06 earthquake." Another *Tribune* columnist described Presley as "the singer who shivers, shudders and twitches like a man wearing underwear four sizes too small." *The Daily Knave* column continued, "When Mr. Presley staggered about the stage like a man walking in mud, at the same time dragging behind him the microphone with which he engages in an occasional wrestling match, teen-age girls for some obscure reason could hardly contain themselves. They howled like banshees. They visibly trembled. They jumped up and down." One Oakland cop on security detail remarked, "If he did that same stuff on the streets, we'd lock him up."

A woefully inadequate force of twelve officers tried to keep Elvis and his fans apart. After the afternoon show ended, Elvis retreated from the arena stage to a dressing room to await the evening show. A single officer stood guard by a set of doors to protect the singer from post-concert autograph seekers. Suddenly, the doors flew open and hundreds of teenaged girls surged down the hallway toward the surprised cop. Later the dazed officer reported, "One doorway—and what must have been 3,000 girls come running through it, and they wedge tighter and tighter, and I am in the middle of them. It is a wonder somebody didn't get hurt. It was awful. I've never seen anything like that before in my life, and I never want to again." Meanwhile, inside the dressing room, a perspiring Presley sipped on a soft drink and listened to the cries of his fans in the hallway outside. "I'm gonna stay here," he wisely announced, "and get me some rest."[1]

When Elvis returned sixteen months later, lessons had been learned and were acted upon. Police presence increased considerably to prevent young-girl stampedes. Newspaper writers knew what to expect and had their quips prepared ahead of time. San Francisco decided to let down its guard and allow Presley to appear in its treasured Civic Center. The only unknown was how the Bay Area teenagers would react. Had they outgrown Elvis' antics, as so many pundits had predicted? The question would be answered at the box office when The Elvis Presley Show rolled back into town in the fall of 1957.

San Francisco Civic Center
Saturday, October 26, 3:00 pm and 8:15 pm
Oakland Auditorium
Sunday, October 27, 8:15 p.m.

On the morning of October 26, just hours before the first of his two shows at the Civic Center, Elvis and his entourage arrived in San Francisco by train and quickly checked into a five-room suite in the prestigious Mark Hopkins Hotel atop Nob Hill. (One columnist referred to the accommodations as the "Presleydential suite.") His top-of-the-line digs were a sign of the heights to which Elvis Presley had soared in the year since his last Bay Area visit. No longer just a Tennessee hick with a volatile stage act, he was a full-fledged Hollywood star, one of the film industry's top draws. His third movie, *Jailhouse Rock*, had premiered in Memphis the week before his arrival in San Francisco, and while most critics panned it, some, like *San Francisco Examiner* drama critic Hortense Morton, saw the star potential in Presley. "I liked the kid," she wrote in her film review. "He gives a better account of himself than did the scriptwriter ... It's a stupid plot. The little guy who becomes a national hero and a fat headed snob. But performances are rather good ... Frankly, I think Presley will turn into quite an actor. It isn't going to happen tomorrow or next year. But, it will happen."[2]

In addition to financial gain, Presley's success on stage and screen in the previous year had earned him not only the adoration of country's teenage girls, but also the admiration of a good percentage of its teenage boys. In a Gilbert poll released on October 10, teenagers across the country were asked, "Who would you like to be most like when you grow up?" Only President Eisenhower out-polled Elvis among the boys. One out of seven named Presley, making him a more popular role model than the likes of Vice President Richard Nixon, Mickey Mantle, and Albert Schweitzer. In giving their reasons for choosing Elvis, however, many of the boys revealed that they admired the fruits of Presley's success more than his musical talent. "Girls! Girls! Girls!" exclaimed a Texas teen. "Elvis has them by the hundred. Man, wouldn't I dig that! You bet I would." A sixteen-year old from Tennessee added, "This Presley lives it up. Cars, gals, money to burn. Any kid would like his share."[3]

Whatever it was that Elvis had, the Bay Area was about to get a triple dose of it. Within a week he would appear on stage in San Francisco and in Oakland, followed a few days later by the opening of his new movie in both cities. Ads in the San Francisco's *Call-Bulletin*, *Chronicle* and *Examiner* and the Oakland's *Tribune* on October 8 announced his coming concerts. Tickets for all performances were available in Oakland through Sherman and Clay at Broadway and Twenty-first, and in San Francisco at the Crane Box Office on Powell, the Music Box on Market, State Radio and Music on Mission, and Portals Music on Stonestown.

At $3.75 and $2.75, tickets in the Bay Area were priced somewhat higher than they had been for the singer's Northwest tour eight weeks before. Ticket sales started the morning of October 19, and the next day Sherman and Clay told the *Oakland Tribune* they had been "swamped" with ticket orders. "I wouldn't want to guess at the demand ... 10,000 would cover it," the head of the box office said.

As usual, some Bay Area businessmen, hoping to increase business, tried to take a ride on the Presley publicity with marketing gimmicks. Helnick's restaurant in Oakland temporarily put "Rooney's Wild 'All Shook Up' Rice" on the menu. The renowned rice came from Cass Lake, Minnesota. "I've instructed the chef to give the wild rice an extra shake for Elvis," announced Helnick's owner Marie Rooney.[4]

One young Oakland resident had hopes that Elvis would remember a promise he had made to her a year before. At age thirteen, Maurine Moore had suffered third-degree burns over 40 percent of her body when she tossed some trash into a fireplace and a can of hair spray exploded. Critically injured and in the hospital, Maurine begged (successfully) to be allowed to watch Elvis on *The Ed Sullivan*

Show. Somehow Presley (or Colonel Parker) heard her story, and the following Thursday a big package containing a picture, records, a charm bracelet, and clothing arrived at Maurine's bedside. Elvis included a letter wishing her well and expressing the hope that he might meet her the next time he came to Oakland. By the time he did come back in October 1957, Maurine, still facing more surgery, was a sophomore at Oakland High School. As Presley's return to town neared, a *Tribune* columnist said Maurine was "tremulously wondering—Will Elvis Presley remember?"[5]

Probably due to the relatively low seating capacity of the Bay Area auditoriums compared to the outdoor venues Presley had played in the Northwest, Colonel Parker adopted a "no free tickets" policy for the California concerts. The policy rankled an already hostile Bay Area press corps. "HARRRUMPH," Herb Caen sounded off in his *Examiner* column. "No free press tickets are being handed out for Elvis Presley's two shows Sat. at Civic Aud. because, to quote his mgr. Col. Parker, 'Elvis doesn't need the press.' Which is okay by me, but Mr. Presley's press agents (he doesn't need the press?) are spreading the news that the Pelvis will be available for a press conference Saturday. Because the press needs Elvis?"[6]

In the days leading up to the Presley appearances, Bay Area media pundits piled on the putdowns. In the *Call-Bulletin,* Paul Speegle referred to the "illusion" of Presley's guitar playing, "which is what he fondly, if erroneously calls it." In his "Baghdad by the Bay" column, the aforementioned Herb Caen wrote, "Elvis Presley, who entertains, if that's the proper word, at Civic Odditorium tomorrow ..." In what may have been one of the first references to Elvis impersonators, the "Daily Knave" column in the *Oakland Tribune* declared, "Nobody could be funnier than Presley doing Presley." *Chronicle* columnist Terrence O'Flaherty, however, proved the most critical of Elvis. In a string of columns both before and after Presley's appearances, O'Flaherty patronized the Elvis faithful, at one point declaring, "Anyone who hasn't seen this donkey appear in person cannot possibly get the complete picture."[7]

O'Flaherty promoted Pat Boone in the media-fostered competition between the two young male singers for the teenage record-buying market in 1957. When Elvis appeared in the Bay Area in late October, his rock 'n' roll number "Jailhouse Rock" sat atop the national record charts, while Boone's new ballad, "April Love," was rising quickly. Often Presley had expressed publicly his admiration for Boone's music, and the ballad singer in return saw no basis for a feud with Elvis. "I don't know how that story got started," Boone told O'Flaherty. "I don't think we have the same kind of audience at all. Gosh, maybe they ought to put us in Madison Square Garden and let us fight it out," he suggested jokingly. O'Flaherty took the bait. "If that should ever happen," he declared, "I know where MY money would be." The columnist saw Presley and Boone as offering two diverging moral roads for the country's teenagers. Addressing their parents, O'Flaherty suggested they steer their kids in the direction of Pat Boone's road.

> If your youngsters prefer him to Elvis Presley, you can put it down as a clean triumph of honest performance over phony showmanship. The fact that he is the new idol of teen-age America is evidence of the innate good taste of this country's young people—especially when everybody in show business has been trying to snare their affection with a shaking torso or a jelly-roll bust.[8]

In October 1957, while Presley toured in California, Boone debuted his weekly network television program. He promised to focus on talented newcomers rather than on big-name guest stars. O'Flaherty condescendingly announced that he knew of one performer who would not be appearing on Boone's show. "I learned from another source," wrote O'Flaherty, "that one of the 'big-name stars' he WON'T be having on his show is Elvis Presley. The sponsor, Chevrolet, insists on the final okay of guests and wants to keep it clean. Hence, no belly dancers."

As evidence that Boone held the high ground in the moral struggle with Elvis, O'Flaherty pointed out that Boone, the product of a deeply religious upbringing, was already a family man (married with two kids and another on the way), and even had taken a stand against kissing girls (even on the cheek) in his movies. Of course, San Francisco's Elvis faithful could not let O'Flaherty's criticism of their man go unchallenged. Teenagers Caren Hopkins and Gaylene Patterson fired back in a letter O'Flaherty printed in his column on October 21. "I think it's pretty hard-up of you to cut Elvis the way you did," their letter stated. "Elvis gives all he's got while Pat just stands there half dead and murmurs. As for Boone and his no-love-scenes, who would want to kiss a nut like that?"[9]

Many newspaper reporters' open antipathy to Presley resulted in poor press coverage of his Bay Area concerts. The journalists' dislike of Elvis probably intensified when Colonel Parker withheld press passes for the singer's shows. Only the *Chronicle* gave the star's appearance the depth of coverage normally seen in other communities. Carolyn Anspacher's article was accompanied by one photo of Elvis at his press conference and another of girls screaming while he was on stage. None of the other area newspapers printed photographs of the event. The *Call-Bulletin* failed to report on the Presley show at all, and the *Examiner's* only coverage came three days after the show in Dwight Newton's "Day and Night" column on page 23. Across the Bay, the *Oakland Tribune* ran a short news story the day after Presley's appearance there, but its headline—"Elvis Ducks Frenzied Teen Fans"—emphasized the negative.

The press' condescending attitude toward Elvis was evident at the press conference held in a Civic Center dressing room prior to his Saturday afternoon show. A few apathetic reporters stood in the background while for half an hour Presley played court to contest winners and fan club officers. The *Chronicle's* Carolyn Anspacher, at least, took notes. She described the scene as follows.

> Pasty faced and nervous, he wiped his sweat over the front of his tight trousers and grimaced at the group in front of him.
>
> In response to what they took for a smile, the young girls huddled close together. One burst into tears. Seven snapped pictures of him. Three sketched him. Then they began raising their hands, as if they were in class, asking recognition.[10]

In a husky drawl, Presley gave brief answers to their questions, most of which he had answered many times before.

"Do you wear a wig?"

"No."

"Who are you mad about now?"

"No one in particular."

"Did you say you didn't need the press anymore?" interjected a reporter in the back.

"No."

"What is your ultimate ambition?" asked another girl.

"My ultimate ambition is to become an actor."

"Are you studying drama?"

"I'm not studying anything. I figure it's experience that counts; not studying."

Elvis revealed some news, which Anspacher described as a "chilling." In December, he announced, his Christmas album would be released. "Silent Night," he told them, was the only song he hadn't "monkeyed" with when he recorded the seasonal songs six weeks ago. "It'll be a rock 'n' roll Christmas," he said.

When the questions stopped, the photographing and autographing began. As the young girls bunched around their idol, he signed everything handed him, including shoes, programs, scarves, and bits of paper. Inspired by his second movie, Elvis signed it all, "Loving you, Elvis." He called each of his admirers "honey" and rubbed the shoulders and necks of some.

While the lucky fan club officers and contest winners attended Presley's dressing room press conference, thousands of others were out in the arena sitting through what Anspacher termed "a mediocre variety show." Local bandleader Howard Frederic led off the string of opening acts. "Colonel Parker asked me to have an opening number ready with 'screaming brass," Frederic later told the

Examiner. "It sure was. My orchestra was 'brassy' all right."[11] Singer Paula Page received mild applause for her number. Comedian Paul Desmond (real name Paul Robrecht) got the best reaction. Desmond, 26, a local Oakland boy, had been a regular performer on The Elvis Presley Show since he'd caught Colonel Parker's eye the year before when Presley first played Oakland. Desmond, who featured an Elvis impersonation in his act, got better reviews from the Bay Area writers than did the headliner. "Where are all those show-business characters who are forever discovering talent?" asked the *Oakland Tribune.* "There's discovering to be done—of Paul Desmond ... who panicked 6,000 customers at the Elvis Presley show with his excruciatingly funny act. A clean show-stop."[12]

When he took the stage for Saturday afternoon's show in San Francisco, Presley wore a wine red suit and tie. Elvis had a new set of suits, and he wore a different one for each of his three shows in the Bay Area. After the afternoon show at the Civic Center, Elvis changed out of the wine-colored suit and into a light blue one for the evening show. The next day he wore a Kelly green jacket with black shirt and black slacks at the Oakland Auditorium.

Having learned from the near disaster caused by stampeding girls in Oakland the year before, Colonel Parker insisted on beefed-up security for the 1957 shows. He announced several days before the concerts that there would be no seats within twenty-eight feet of the stage. A cordon of thirty to forty uniformed policemen guarded the front of the platform. Forming the second line of defense were Presley's Memphis bodyguards, who roamed the open space shouting at the audience to stay back and waiting to pounce upon any girl who infiltrated the cops' front line. Colonel Parker was there, too, determined to prevent an audience assault on the stage. *Examiner* columnist Dwight Newton described the antics of Presley's manager in San Francisco. "During the entire show, hefty Colonel Parker, wearing a sort of Pinky Lee hat on his big noggin, patrolled this 'No Woman's Land' like a belligerent rhinoceros ready to take on the whole bloomin' auditorium. While Elvis exhorted the teen-agers to frenzy, Colonel Parker cowed them into remaining in their seats."[13]

The San Francisco shows were typical in that the crowd's screams drowned out most of the music. In her *Chronicle* review, Carolyn Anspacher observed, "Whether the preponderantly female audience came to hear Presley sing or to watch his caricature of sex could not be determined. They roared through every one of his 14 rock and roll offerings in such crescendo that three policemen and four firemen were forced to leave the building." Anspacher found the whole affair somewhat phony, however. She claimed that groups of young girls wearing official Elvis ribbons had been coached all morning to "give Elvis everything you've got." These preconditioned shills, the reviewer claimed, led the choruses of screams, swoons and tears that filled the arena.[14]

The Civic Center was half-filled at best for the afternoon show in San Francisco, and not even the wholehearted shrieking of the crowd, according to Anspacher, could disguise "what was painfully apparent to Presley's managers. The afternoon was skimpy." The turnout was much better across the Bay the following evening, when a near-capacity crowd of 7,000 filled the Oakland Municipal Auditorium. "The singer brought loud shrieks with virtually every smile, glance and body gyration," reported the *Oakland Tribune*. "While singing he dropped to his knees, flat on his stomach, and then on his back sprawled across a piano holding the microphone."[15] Some girls cried as he sang; others slid out of their seats and onto the floor. When Elvis sang "Treat Me Nice" from his new movie, a chorus of voices from the crowd cried back, "I will."

In his Bay Area appearances, Presley reprised his early Pacific Northwest performances, singing fourteen songs during forty minutes on stage. In California, he sang on stage for the first time both sides of his newest record, "Jailhouse Rock" and "Treat Me Nice." Although both songs had already been recorded before he toured the Northwest over Labor Day weekend, he omitted them from his repertoire there since the record had not yet been released. As in all his 1957 concerts, Elvis closed his Bay Area shows with his signature version of "Hound Dog."

As he sang the closing bars of his most notorious song, Elvis edged closer to the back of the stage, finally disappearing from sight by jumping down through a rear door into the Arena Theater. Exiting the building by the theater entrance, Presley jumped into a car and headed back to the Mark Hopkins. Colonel Parker had let it be known days before that, unlike his last appearance in the Bay Area, Elvis would not be hanging around his dressing room after the show. Columnist Herb Caen revealed it in the *Examiner* the day before Presley's first show. "Insidem for Presley addicts," he reported. "Yr boy has figured out a sneaky way to avoid his fans here tomorrow. At the end of his show, he'll pretend he's coming back for another encore—but instead he'll scoot out the back door and disappear in a getaway car. Outta me way, peasants!" Caen concluded cynically.[16] Still, many in the Oakland crowd refused to believe Elvis had left them so abruptly. They hung around the auditorium for another half hour before wandering away. As she finally left, one teenage girl was overheard telling her friend, "I'm absolutely weak. I've got Elvisitis something awful."

Presley's disappearing act was not the only way his '57 show differed from his Bay Area performance of the year before. For that first appearance, area teens paid $1.50 to $2.50 to see Elvis on stage for twenty minutes. Before his show the following year, the *Chronicle's* Terrence O'Flaherty ingenuously stated, "I hope he's learned to give more of a performance—especially at $2.75 and $3.75 a throw."[17] He had. In fact, with fourteen songs over forty minutes, Elvis gave the Bay Area crowds over twice the stage time that he had in 1956. And although most critics judged both years' performances as obscene, the lying down and rolling on the stage was an additional offensive-to-adults move that Presley had added to his act in 1957. His ability to draw bigger crowds the second time through the Bay Area also must have disappointed his critics. Drawing from the entire Bay Area in June 1956, Elvis attracted 6,400 fans combined for two shows in the Oakland Auditorium. The following year, 7,000 people filled the same venue for a single show. The two San Francisco shows the day before were not sellouts, but after combining the attendance at the three shows, it became apparent that well over twice as many Bay Area residents came out to see Elvis in 1957 as had in 1956.

After Presley left for Los Angeles, emotions still ran high in the *Tribune's* space for readers' opinions. First up was Oakland resident Dennis Lewis, who admitted Elvis was a king—just not of rock 'n' roll.

> Well, I see we have the doubtful honor of playing host to the "King of Trash" again. Of course I could be referring to none other than the one, the only, Elvis Presley.
>
> I should be very interested to learn where the demand for this reappearance originated ... Wherever the order came from it is obvious to me that someone plans to make a neat little pile of cash from the sexy gyrations of "Mr. E.P." and again, as always, the effect on our youngsters will be totally disregarded.
>
> If I had my way I would suggest that the city place a ban on any further appearance of Presley.[18]

Of course, a legion of Presley loyalists came to his defense with letters of their own. Pat Droke allowed Lewis the right to voice his opinion, but went on to defend Presley on moral grounds.

> I know we have freedom of press, but there's a lot of things far worse than a youth who sings grand and makes a few sexy wiggles. Just about anyone would do the same as Presley does if they could make the money he does.
>
> I read the article about Elvis, "God is my Refuge," and if any man thinks and does what Elvis does I would hardly call them trash. Is praying to God and doing good for people bad? I hope not cause I've been doing it for years and so have millions of other people. I think I better say so long before I say something I shouldn't.
>
> But to me Elvis is not Trash. He's a human being with a lot of good ideas and a wonderful personality. I think Elvis is the "King of Rock'n'Roll." And not the king of trash![19]

Marilyn C. Rushmer of Berkeley wrote in to answer Lewis' question, and then went on to praise Presley's kindness toward his parents.

> The demand for Elvis Presley's reappearance came from us, Mr. Lewis. His fans. The people who like and admire Elvis … Fans of Elvis know him for what he really is, not what the trash magazines say about him.
>
> When Elvis first became popular, one of the first things he did was buy a home for his parents. Then he retired his father. How many of us would think of our parents first when we get into a lot of money?[20]

One adult, Mrs. M. Lopez, encouraged parents to remember their own youth when judging Presley.

> I do not care for E.P.'s singing, but I do not see why he is to be condemned for what is called his sexy gyrations by parents of the teen-agers … I do not condemn the Rock'n'Roll. It is no more sexy than some of the dances done by parents in the 20's. So when parents start condemning E.P. let them look to their own children doing almost the same thing and remember their own gyrations in dances of their times.[21]

Across the Bay, two letters in the San Francisco papers produced a sort of reverse generation gap—an older writer unapologetic about her fondness for Elvis, and a teenager guilty about his.

> To The Examiner: … it was a walloping good clambake and a whale of a ball. When it ended I was deaf from screeching, blind from the flash "bulbs" and more smashed to pulp than by any other experience in all my 58 years. The kids weren't the only ones who had a day to remember.—Louise Bevitt, Monterey[22]

> Chronicle Editor—As I watched all the real old-timers who recently appeared on the Ed Sullivan show, I wondered about my own generation. I'm 15 years old and, in my lifetime, there are very few, if any, good records. When I am old and gray I won't be able to look at television and suddenly recognize an old tune like my parents and grandparents do now.

I don't suppose that Elvis Presley will ever sell 86 million records like Gene Austin. And he probably won't be half as spry as Joe Howard when he's 83 either.

Don't get me wrong. I like some of these records that become popular too fast, and then are outdated with yesterday's newspaper. The only thing I want is something I can remember from when I was young. Do you suppose any other kids feel this half-guilty, half-wondering feeling I feel?—Ronnie Kleinhammer, Albany[23]

Amidst all the debate between Presley critics and admirers in the Bay Area that October, one voice's moderate judgment and assessment of Presley's show has been validated by the passage of five decades. Dwight Newton of the *Examiner* attended Presley's afternoon show in San Francisco. Several days later in his "Day and Night" column, he recorded what he had seen in the Civic Center.

All I remember is thunder and lightning. The thunder of shrieking kids, the lightning of a thousand flash bulbs as they took pictures.

For 70 sustained minutes I never heard a word Elvis said or sang. Because of the shrieking. It was Lindbergh back from Paris, VJ Day on Market St., voodoo night in Haiti. It was pandemonium.

Elvis grunted, groaned, growled, shook, jigged, knocked his knees and rattled his bones. He didn't coast on his fame. He gave the kids all he had. He perspired, panted, ranted and raved. Girls jumped from their seats like schools of salmon rising to the bait. They waved both arms. They shrieked continuously.

When Elvis feigned passion, the kids gasped and sighed as they shrieked. When he laughed at his own crazy antics, they laughed and hooted as they shrieked.[24]

Then Newton demonstrated an understanding of the Presley phenomenon that very few adults achieved in those early days. He realized that the whole thing was really not about Elvis Presley. "Actually, it wasn't Presley's show at all," he noted insightfully. "It was the teen-agers' show, their day to howl and have fabulous fun. Elvis was just the excuse … Do I disapprove? Of course not! For the kids who saw him it was a day they'll never forget, a day to tell their grandchildren about as I've already told mine."

Then Newton saluted Presley and wished him well. "I've seen many spectacular performers," Newton noted, "but I've never witnessed a storm of excitement like the one generated by Elvis Presley. May he endure and mature with the kids who idolize him."

Chapter 19

Los Angeles

Prelude

By the fall of 1957, rock 'n' roll music was four years old and had dominated the nation's pop charts and sales for half that long. The prevailing opinion of veterans in the music business continued to be that the new music was a fad that soon would disappear under the weight of its obvious absurdity. But despite the continuing predictions of its impending death, rock 'n' roll continued to thrive under the leadership of Elvis Presley and others equally characterized in the media as unintelligible hooligans posing as singers to take advantage of the country's impressionable teenagers. Frustrated by the inexplicable staying power of rock 'n' roll, some critics began describing it as a racket. The "gold record" concept was a publicity stunt, some said, and the huge record sales numbers claimed by Presley manager Tom Parker and other rock 'n' roll promoters were but a fraction of their artists' actual sales. Then there was payola. Disc jockeys were accused of taking money under the table to play rock 'n' roll records, which pushed the "good songs" off the radio.

Another accusation, voiced by Bing Crosby and others, charged the music distribution company BMI (Broadcast Music, Inc.) with perpetuating an artificial rock 'n' roll boom. Radio stations created BMI in the late 1940s to combat the high fees being charged to play tunes owned by ASCAP (American Society of Composers, Authors and Publishers). Since most rock 'n' roll and rhythm and blues songs were in BMI's catalog, which was owned by the radio stations, critics asserted that artists felt pressure to record them if they wanted radio play. During a congressional investigation in 1956, composer-conductor Billy Rose testified, "With BMI publishing 74% of the top songs on the hit parade ... I do not see how it can escape the charge that BMI is responsible for rock'n'roll music and the other music monstrosities which are muddying up the airways."[1]

Other big names in the music industry bypassed the blame game and instead launched frontal, public assaults on rock 'n' roll. Foremost among them was Frank Sinatra. In a 1957 magazine published in France, Sinatra applauded American jazz and popular music for its positive influence around the world but added the following hostile disclaimer concerning rock 'n' roll.

> My only deep sorrow is the unrelenting insistence of recording and motion picture companies upon purveying the most brutal, ugly, degenerate, vicious form of expression it has been my displeasure to hear—Naturally I refer to the bulk of rock'n'roll.
>
> It fosters almost totally negative and destructive reactions in young people. It smells phony and false. It is sung, played and written for the most part by cretinous goons and by means of its almost imbecilic reiterations and sly, lewd—in plain fact, dirty—lyrics, and as I said before, it manages to be the martial music of every sideburned delinquent on the face of the earth ... This rancid-smelling aphrodisiac I deplore.[2]

The *Los Angeles Mirror-News* covered Sinatra's comments on the morning of October 28, 1957, the same day Elvis Presley was to perform before a full house in the city's Pan Pacific Auditorium. *Mirror-News* entertainment editor Dick Williams must have cheered Sinatra's denunciation of Presley's musical style. Long a critic of Presley, Williams three weeks earlier had refused to let Colonel Parker pin an "I Like Elvis" button on him at a movie premiere in Louisville. "I have made some rather pointed comments on Elvis' professional ability at various times in the past," Williams explained. "If it ever got out in Los Angeles that I wore an Elvis button, even momentarily, I'm afraid I would never live it down."[3] Now that Presley had brought his stage show to L.A., Williams saw his chance to save America's youth. He openly admitted in his daily column that "Presley was due for an airing" and that the time had come for him to get it. Hoping to gather ammo for his column the following morning, Williams joined the crowd the crammed into the Pan Pacific the evening of October 28 for what would become the most controversial performance of Elvis Presley's career.

Los Angeles, California
Pan Pacific Auditorium
Monday, October 28, 1957, 8:15 pm
Tuesday, October 29, 1957, 8:15 pm

Controversial Presley biographer Albert Goldman called the first of the singer's two performances at the Pan Pacific Auditorium "the pinnacle of his entire career." Indeed, Elvis came to Los Angeles on the top of his game. Seven months earlier he had taken the stage in Chicago amid reports that his popularity and record sales were slipping badly. Since then the huge crowds at his concerts had refuted the first charge and three chart-topping single records—"All Shook Up," "Teddy Bear," and "Jailhouse Rock"—had destroyed the second. His second movie, *Loving You*, had been a big commercial success, and his next movie, *Jailhouse Rock*, was due to open nationally in four days.

In addition, Elvis had come to a city where he felt somewhat at ease. He had played Los Angeles' Shrine Auditorium in 1956 and had three extended stays in the city while making movies during the previous eighteen months. The Beverly Wilshire Hotel had become a sort of home away from home for Elvis and his entourage. While working at the film studios, he had met and made friends with many Hollywood personalities; so in Los Angeles Presley felt a certain comfort level that he had not experienced in the other large cities he had played earlier in 1957.

To conclude his brief California tour, Presley was booked for two nights at the Pan Pacific, located at 7600 Beverly Boulevard in Los Angeles' Fairfax district. The auditorium was the city's main indoor venue until the opening of the Los Angeles Convention Center in 1972. Behind a modern, streamlined outer façade, the Pan Pacific resembled an oversized gymnasium on the inside. For entertainment shows, temporary creaky, wooden bleachers, seating up to 9,200, were erected on the main floor. When full, as it was for Presley's two shows, the auditorium was an uncomfortable place to view a concert. For Ruth Thomas the experience was decidedly unpleasant. "I was over-anxious to see the show at Pan-Pacific," she recalled. "That was until I walked into the auditorium. Believe me, that was the biggest rob of the public I have ever seen. The seats so expensive and so cheap in the setup. Just like a can of sardines. It is obvious they only crammed as many people in there as they could, and had no regard whether they could see or hear."[4] Mrs. D. Forest also complained about the "outrageous seating" in a letter to the *Mirror-News*. "There were thousands of us who were not even able to see the stage and at $3.75 yet," she protested.

Despite Ruth Thomas' feeling that the auditorium was crammed full, neither night's show was completely sold out. Tickets were available at the door for each performance, but by showtime only a few hundred seats were left of the 18,400 available. The $2.75 and $3.75 ticket prices produced a two-night gross of $56,000. Colonel Parker had refused again to provide passes for the press or city officials. Calling the two shows "sellouts" was a little deceptive, though, since the William Morris Agency purchased huge blocks of seats for its clients, and tour promoter Lee Gordon provided seats for reporters.

At his press conference prior to Monday night's show, Elvis responded to Frank Sinatra's critical comments on rock 'n' roll, which had appeared in the L.A. newspapers that morning. Sinatra had never been one of Presley's favorite singers. "I can take him or leave him," he had replied in April when a Canadian reporter asked his opinion of Frank.[5] So Elvis chose his words carefully in Los Angeles. "He is a great success and a fine actor," he started thoughtfully. "I admire the man. He has a right to his own opinions. He is a great success and a fine actor, but I don't think he should have said it. I don't think anyone has the right to take potshots at something that is definitely a trend. It's an American development, just like crooning was a few years back." Probing for more, a reporter asked, "That's all you have to say?" Elvis added only, "You can't knock success." A British reporter asked about rock 'n' roll causing juvenile delinquency, another of Sinatra's charges. "I haven't set any pattern for juvenile delinquency," Elvis maintained. "In my opinion, delinquency is such things as robbing, beatings or knife fights and the like. If these people mean by delinquency 'riots,' we've had those for years." In response to the suggestion that his style was on the way out, Presley merely gestured toward the door, then pulsing with the screams from the auditorium beyond.

(In fairness to Frank Sinatra, it should be noted that he had not mentioned Presley's name in his comments about rock 'n' roll, and, in fact, five months earlier, Sinatra had been neutral in his assessment of Elvis. In June on the set of *Pal Joey*, Sinatra said it was too early to label Presley a "freak" in the music business. "I was a freak when I first hit, but I'm still around," he reminded the interviewer. "Presley has no training at all," he added. "When he goes into something serious, a bigger kind of singing, we'll find out if he is a singer. He has a natural, animalistic talent."[6])

When Presley took the stage later that evening, he had no idea that his show, one of his last of the decade, would be the most controversial of his career. It started, as had all others that year with his first big record, "Heartbreak Hotel." His bright gold jacket contrasting with his black shirt, pants, shoes and hair, Elvis pressed on through his other hits, including "Don't Be Cruel," "All Shook Up," and "Teddy Bear." He sang "Jailhouse Rock" and "Treat Me Nice," two songs from his new movie and recently released soundtrack record. In all, he sang seventeen songs during fifty minutes on stage. He moved quickly from one number to another, stopping only once, to introduce his background men. As usual, the Jordanaires and Scotty, Bill, and D.J. were merely shadowy figures, lost in the din and the gyrating spectacle created by Elvis. In a rare gesture, George H. Jackson took the time to praise the trio briefly in his *Los Angeles Herald-Express* review. "He ... has a trio which provides excellent backing," Jackson noted. "The guitar work of Scotty Moore is exceptional."[7]

By this time, Colonel Parker had his security strategy down pat. Fifty police officers circled the crowd, rushing in pairs up and down aisles to deal with fans leaving their seats. Dozens of other officers surrounded the stage, their backs to it, ready to keep the aisles leading forward clear. No one got started toward the stage, much less reached that promised land. The efficient crowd control in the Pan Pacific that evening seemed a contradictory backdrop to the fury with which Elvis' actions on stage were condemned by some journalists the next day.

In addition to employing his trademark gyrations, Elvis worked his wardrobe in ways Dick Williams judged as "contrived sensual gestures." According to Williams, Elvis was "hitching up his pants, fooling with his belt buckle and yanking down his coat to elicit further wild screams from his audience."[8]

Certainly the crowd reacted predictably, screaming and shrieking with every Presley maneuver on stage. One girl fainted and was helped out by police, ushers, and a friend. Others in the crowd, ranging from junior high students to college students and on to some grandmothers, reacted with comments like, "He sends shivers up my spine," "He's a living doll," and "He's the most!"

Show business personalities mixed in with the crowd, but the one who drew the most attention was Ricky Nelson. Having grown up in front of the country's TV viewers on the *The Adventures of Ozzie and Harriet,* the seventeen-year-old recent high school graduate had just started a new career as a rock 'n' roll singer. His first single, "I'm Walkin'," sold a million copies, and his first album for Imperial Records was due out in a few days. Notified that Nelson would attend Elvis' show, Colonel Parker took precautions against the boy's being mobbed. During the intermission before Elvis came on stage, someone in the crowd recognized the new singing sensation, but the cordon of police Parker had placed around him held off the rush of young girls. A plan was ready to get Ricky out of the auditorium ahead of the crowd. As soon as Elvis started his final number, Nelson and his friends were to head toward a designated exit, where a squad of police officers waited to whisk them away.

As he had done in all his previous twenty-three stage shows in 1957, Elvis launched into an extended, vigorous version of "Hound Dog" as his performance's finale. With that final number, Presley intended to end this show as he had all the others, by cranking the crowd's passion up to a fever pitch and then leaving them hanging there while he made a quick departure. In other cities, that meant increasing the amount and intensity of his writhing on stage. Back and forth across the stage he would go, pointing to groups of young girls and beckoning to them to throw restraint aside and come to him, emotionally if not physically. At the height of excitement, he would drop to his knees on stage, screaming the song's inane lyrics. In outdoor stadiums he often jumped off the front of the makeshift stage and, going to his knees there, thrashed around on the ground. At the Pan Pacific that Monday night, however, Elvis added a prop to his final act. His interaction with that prop led to that show's becoming arguably the most controversial one in Elvis Presley's career.

Throughout Elvis' performance that night, a three-foot tall plaster replica of Nipper, RCA's trademark black and white terrier mutt, sat patiently to one side of the stage. Presley had decided he was going to work the dog into his "Hound Dog" number. When the moment came, Elvis grabbed Nipper around the neck with his left arm and lifted him from the floor while continuing to sing into the microphone in his right hand. What he did next is a matter of dispute. As often happened at Presley concerts in the fifties, eyewitnesses saw the same stage events differently as they were filtered through predetermined prejudices, both for and against Presley. No one disputes that Elvis went prone on the platform and rolled to the front of the stage, dragging the dog with him.

Some writers made no mention of the incident in their reviews, while some, like George H. Jackson of the *Los Angeles Herald-Express* and Hollywood columnist Hedda Hopper, made only passing reference to Elvis' "rolling" across the stage. To Dick Williams, though, Elvis by definition was obscene, and in that final number Williams spotted the vulgarity he had come to see. "The madness reached its peak at the finish with 'Hound Dog,'" Williams wrote in the *Mirror-News* the next day. "Elvis writhed in complete abandon, hair hanging over his face. He got down on the floor with a huge replica of the RCA singing dog and made love to it as if it were a girl. Slowly, he rolled over and over on the floor. The little brunette of maybe 15 sitting in front of me bent her head and covered her eyes, whether with embarrassment, fright, sickness or excitement, I know not."

Gordon Stoker of the Jordanaires saw nothing inappropriate in Elvis' actions that night. "Elvis did not do anything on stage with Nipper that was suggestive or off color," Stoker insists. "We were standing very close to him on stage as we always were. We would have seen him. He always looked our way while he was singing."9

For nearly fifty years mild controversy continued to surround Elvis' actions on stage in Los Angeles on October 28, 1957. Then an article in the November 2005 issue of *Playboy* magazine declared Presley guilty of obscene acts that night. The author was Byron Raphael, who was a twenty-three-year-old member of Colonel Parker's staff in 1957. Raphael claimed Parker had placed him on "Nipper patrol" the night of Presley's infamous show in Los Angeles. "Previously published accounts have only hinted at precisely what went on that evening," Raphael wrote in *Playboy*, "leaving out the explicit details that made this one of Elvis' most legendary appearances."10

The details that Raphael then revealed were explicit indeed. Raphael says Parker positioned him beneath the stage with the task of making sure Nipper didn't fall off the platform during the performance and then making sure the dog didn't tip over while Elvis was using it as a prop during his "Hound Dog" number. When the finale began, Raphael says he was stunned by Presley's actions. He asserts that

Elvis pulled down the zipper of his pants and began stroking his body against the plaster dog in an obviously sexual manner. "Then all of a sudden Elvis pulled the dog out of my grip and began rolling around on the floor with it in full simulation of bestial bliss," Raphael wrote. "It was one of the most shocking things I'd ever seen."

Gordon Stoker flatly denies Raphael's entire story. "I remember Nipper being on stage," he says. "Elvis sang to him, but anything other than that is a lie. He did not unzip his pants. He was taught from his mother such was wrong, and he would just not have done that. I don't know why people start stories like that."

After finishing his finale, Elvis jumped to his feet and bolted off stage. This time, though, he didn't immediately leave the building. When some excited teenagers went looking for him, they actually found him. "After the show, a bunch of us went backstage, looked up and there was Elvis, hanging out the window, tossing stuff out, like his socks, shirts," remembered Dina Angus years later. "It was unbelievable! We were all yelling back and forth. Elvis was just a kid himself and having a ball with the fans."[11]

Later that evening, Elvis, unaware of the storm of controversy over his show that would break in the L.A. papers the next morning, hosted a party in his private suite at the Beverly Wilshire Hotel. Many Hollywood celebrities were among the guests, but historically the most significant event at the gathering was the first meeting between Elvis and Ricky Nelson. Photoplay writer Marcia Borie was on the guest list and convinced the shy teenager to come along. The start of Ricky's singing career had had an Elvis connection. After a January 1957 episode of his family's TV show, in which Ricky impersonated Elvis and sang a few words of "Love Me Tender," fan mail poured in requesting that Ricky sing more on the show. From then on, songs for the youngster were worked into the plots of future episodes, and by April Ricky had his first hit record.

From the beginning, Nelson was clearly inspired by rockabilly singers like Elvis and Carl Perkins. Borie recalls that in the car on the way to the Presley's hotel, Ricky couldn't stop talking about the show he had just seen. "Gee, Elvis is fantastic," he said. "Did you hear those chords …? Did you see the way that he moved …? Man, that isn't sex, that's rhythm, he's … well, he's just something else." When they reached the Beverly Wilshire, however, Nelson decided he wasn't up to meeting Elvis. "Rick was just downright scared," recalled Borie, "just like the average fan who's dying to meet his favorite celebrity who then goes weak at the knees the closer the moment actually comes." After sitting in the hotel coffee shop for a while, Ricky decided to take the plunge and go up to Elvis' suite. "I don't know what I'm worrying about," he told Borie. "I'm sure he wouldn't even know who I am!"[12]

As they entered and stood in the crowded, large entry-hall foyer of Presley's quarters, across the room Borie saw Elvis towering above the crowd around him. She caught his eye and smiled, and he smiled back. In her *Photoplay* article, Borie described what happened next.

> Then I saw his eyes shift and, before anyone knew what had happened, he was literally running through the entryway, saying, "Excuse me, excuse me." People stood aside. When he got to the door he calmly grabbed Rick in a bear-hug that lifted the skinny six-footer off the ground.
>
> "Ricky, hey it's Rick Nelson," he shouted. Then still holding on to him, Elvis continued, "Why I never miss one of your shows except if I'm on the road. How's your mama and daddy? Did your brother David come too?" All was said while still embracing Ricky.
>
> Nelson turned crimson, then beet red, then a big grin broke out from ear to ear. But he was speechless.
>
> It was Elvis who rambled on. "Why I can't believe it. Rick Nelson at my party …" As he talked he walked back towards the living room still hanging on to Rick.

Finally finding his voice, Ricky told Elvis how much he enjoyed his show and how much he admired him. While the other guests milled around, the two singers spent more than a half hour in a corner of the room talking to each other. Ricky later told Borie that Elvis gave him "some great tips about things to do on my tour." From where she sat on a sofa, Borie kept her eyes on Ricky and Elvis. "The King of Rock'n'Roll standing head to head with the Prince Charming who some said was trying to dethrone him," Borie recalled. "It was truly a remarkable sight to see."

Most of the reviews in the L.A. papers the next morning were noncommittal or, in some cases, slightly positive. In the *Herald-Express*, George H. Jackson called the evening "electrifying," adding, "Another page, a fantastic page, in the growing Elvis Presley legend was written last night." Margie Montgomery of the *Hollywood Citizen News* predicted that the "Pan Pacific Auditorium should still be rockin' on its foundation after last night's Elvis show." She called his performance of "Jailhouse Rock" a "powerful piece" and the "high point of the evening."[13] Of Presley's fans, Wally George wrote in the *Times,* "Musically speaking, it was not the music that sold them. It was his hips. They wiggled, they bumped, they twisted … he yelled and his army of faithful yelled back. With the flashbulbs and spotlights it was exactly like a battlefield."[14]

Hedda Hopper, who the year before had declared herself "appalled by the whole Presley disease," found seeing Presley's act for the first time an illuminating experience. "Now I understand why 9000 people lost their minds over him," she wrote in her October 31 column. "He's a split personality, young, likable, wanting to please; but when he went into his act, it was very much like a neighbor of mine in Altoona who had fits, fell down and writhed on the sidewalk." Of Presley's rolling finale, Hopper insisted, "His performance isn't sickness. He knew what he was doing and the effect it was having on 9000 screaming people." In the end, she concluded, "Elvis' audience got the emotional workout of their lives and screamed their undying love for the greatest phenomenon I've seen in this century."[15]

All of these reviews of Presley's October 28 concert were completely submerged by the one that appeared in the *Mirror-News*. Entertainment Editor Dick Williams had long thought Elvis had a slapdown coming, and in his column the next day he gave it to him.

> Sexhibitionist Elvis Presley has come at last in person to a visibly palpitating, adolescent female Los Angeles to give all the little girls' libidos the jolt of their lives ...
>
> They screamed their lungs out without letup as Elvis shook, bumped and did the grinds from one end of the stage to the other until he was a quivering heap on the floor 35 minutes later.
>
> With anyone else the police would have closed the show 10 minutes after it started. But not with Elvis, our new national teen-age hero.
>
> If any further proof were needed that what Elvis offers is not basically music but a sex show, it was provided last night. Pandemonium took over from the time he swaggered triumphantly on stage like some ancient Caesar, resplendent in gold lame tux jacket with rhinestone lapels until he weaved off at the end of his stint ...
>
> The whole panorama, from the frenzy on stage to the far reaches of the jammed bleachers which seemed a mile back at the rear, looked like one of those screeching, uninhibited party rallies which the Nazis used to hold for Hitler ...
>
> He wiggled, bounced, shook and ground in the style which strip-teasers of the opposite sex have been using at stag shows since grandpa was a boy ... He played up to the mike stand like it was a girl in a gesture which is expressly forbidden by the police department in every burlesque show in Los Angeles County.
>
> The wilder Elvis got in his pelvic gyrations, the more frenzied his audience became. Inevitably, he announced midway, sweat pouring

down his face, that he was "all shook up." ... The madness reached its peak at the finish with "Hound Dog."

I do know this is corruption of the innocent on a scale such as I have never witnessed before. For these are children to whom Elvis appeals, pre-conditioned, curious adolescents, who are artificially and unhealthfully stimulated. Their reactions would shock many a parent if he or she could see this display. They are not adults who can take his crudities and laugh or shrug them off ...

The same lesson in pornography will be repeated tonight, barring any interruption by the Police Department, which is unlikely, in view of the fact that they might have a riot on their hands.[16]

What Williams wanted amounted to no less than censorship, and he openly called for it. "As one who has long argued against any form of censorship but public opinion," he avowed, "I confess that there is a limit reached when there is no other answer. In my opinion this was a time for censorship." Williams wasn't the only one outraged by Presley's antics. The columnist claimed several days later that the response to his dressing down of Presley revealed a "tremendous undercurrent of resentment against Elvis surges through a sizable portion of the public."[17] The *Mirror-News* received a letter from a twenty-eight-year-old L.A. mother with two daughters. "We pray our girls will marry boys with something besides sex on their minds," she wrote. "Isn't there any way to ban Elvis Presley and others like him to teen-agers?"[18] A number of other parents, including some celebrities, who witnessed Presley's show at the Pan Pacific were equally incensed and complained to the police and the newspapers.

Of course there were plenty of police officers at the Pan Pacific to witness Elvis' display on stage first-hand. Allowing that Presley's performance may have been of "questionable taste," city officials found the show did not violate city obscenity laws and no action against the singer was planned. Still, Dick Williams' column characterizing the show as "pornography," combined with some citizen complaints, caused police officials to take action to calm things down during Presley's performance the next night. The police department warned Colonel Parker that Elvis needed to moderate his suggestive body movements during his Tuesday night show to avoid violating the city's public decency laws. Parker passed the warning to his client, along with the information that the police vice squad would be filming the performance to use as evidence if needed.

This resulted in what was arguably Elvis Presley's wildest stage performance of the year being followed the next night by one of the calmest, least provocative shows of his career. Before another near-capacity crowd of 9,000, the subdued rocker came on stage conservatively dressed without his gold lamé jacket for one of the few times that year. The RCA dog replica, implicated in Presley's floor-rolling finale the night before, was nowhere to be seen on the stage. Under police censure Elvis "stripped his act of most of his burlesque-show-type pelvic gyrations," disclosed *Mirror-News* staff writer Roger Beck. "He did few bumps and grinds," Beck added. "Presley himself seemed to get quite a kick out of the response he could command by merely wobbling his knees or tossing his head."[19]

Seeming to take the whole thing as a joke, Elvis at times played to the police motion picture camera more than the crowd. Frequently glancing at the camera, he seemed to want the crowd to know he was performing under restraints. Thrusting his arms out with wrists touching, he showed them his imaginary handcuffs. "You shoulda been here last night," he told them. Several times he used his hands to form virtual halos over his head.

In addition to the police camera, the crowd's makeup added to its restrained reaction to Elvis' performance. The audience that second night contained a large number of adult couples and fewer of the excitable teenagers that had filled the auditorium the night before. A number of Hollywood celebrities were scattered throughout the arena. Actor Nick Adams and actresses Valerie Allen and Venetia Stevenson sat in the fifth row.

As usual, Elvis ended the Tuesday night show with "Hound Dog," but this time a calmer version that didn't include rolling across the stage. Socialite Judy Spreckels, who dated Presley at times, could be seen crying after the show. "That's the worst he's ever been," she sobbed. Captain Floyd Hayes announced that Presley had behaved. The vice squad declared Presley's show "acceptable" and that no obscenity laws had been violated. The police film would confirm that judgment, according to Captain Hayes. In his *Mirror-News* review the next day, Beck wrote, "Police and ushers who worked both nights said last night's show was far less frantic, but the crowd seemed to enjoy it just as much."

Presley's voluntarily toning down his suggestive stage movements did not put an end to the controversy surrounding him in Los Angeles. For several weeks, long after he had left the city, its newspapers continued to carry comments of support and condemnation. Hedda Hopper reported that she had "rarely seen a madder man than Yul Brynner" when she visited the actor on the set of *Buccaneer*, his latest movie. "I hold no brief for Presley; I've never seen him," Brynner told Hopper. "But when police are allowed to set up cameras and be judge, that's an invasion of an artist's rights and should be looked into mighty carefully by every artist and actors' agency in our business."[20]

Elvis also drew support from journalist Wally George, whose defense of Presley in the *Times* was clearly critical of Dick Williams' comments in the rival *Mirror-News*.

Elvis Presley's appearance this week was received with mixed emotions—as usual. He enraptured his fans and enraged the critics. It's the usual score for the course and one he's resigned to.

What seemed foolish to us was the way some observers went into a tantrum of holiness at his antics.

Gee, fellas, he's only been wiggling his way around the country for two or three years now. Not to mention movies and television. So now he comes to L.A. for his first local personal appearance and we find he's different.

Granted, his style may not appeal to all. But since when is this an excuse for viciousness? And some of the remarks penned his way were nothing more than that.[21]

While Presley found defenders in some areas, Williams' *Mirror-News* brought out all its artillery to enfilade Presley with a barrage of criticism. On October 31, two days after Elvis' offending performance, the newspaper went after the singer on its editorial page. Declaring itself a "Family Newspaper," the *Mirror-News* editorial staff put the blame for Presley's popularity on "heedless parents."

Frankly we wonder what ails parents who let their teen-age youngsters—mostly daughters—attend these Presley orgies. Papa would take daughter across his knee with a hairbrush if he caught her sneaking into a Main St. burlesque joint.

But the Presley "concert" is even more disreputable and far less honest than the simple strip tease.

If Elvis Presley is a Pop Age phenomenon, so are the lackadaisical parents who allow their offspring to join the crazy mob of his juvenile admirers.[22]

That same day Paul Coates contributed to the *Mirror-News'* Elvis bashing in his "Confidential File" column. Coates didn't attend either of Presley's shows at the Pan Pacific, but nevertheless responded to what he read in the papers. "Let me admit at the outset that I don't like Elvis Presley," Coates confessed. "He's the kind of a child that other children are traditionally 'not allowed to play with.' He's a sullen, ill-kempt-looking youth. If he was my kid (and I was in a helluva lot better shape than I am), I'd smack that sneer off his face and send him out for a haircut. In all, I consider him a very distasteful individual."[23]

However, Presley's "convulsive behavior" on stage didn't concern Coates as it had Williams. "Watching him gives me the same uneasy feeling I get watching somebody get sick in public," Coates confided. "You feel terribly embarrassed for

him. You wish he were able to go somewhere and not be seen until he felt better."
Aside from causing a temporary queasy feeling, though, Coates saw no lasting
effect in Elvis' stage show. "I hardly can believe that he will be responsible for making salacious, lascivious wantons out of our younger generation," he concluded.
He did feel Elvis corrupted teenagers in another way, though. "Instead, he's guilty
of cruel and unwarranted attacks on the English language," he wrote. "He's not
impairing the morals of minors. He's just ruining their grammar." Coates gave an
example of how one of his own kids had been infected by Presley's "incoherent
drawl." The child asked, "Daddy, how come we cain't stay up an' watch TV 'nut-
hah hour? They h'ain't no reason us got to rush off to bed." That was bad enough,
according to Coates, "But I'm waiting for the day they call me Big Daddy. Then
I'm gonna belt them."

While Coates and others weighed in on the Presley debate, Dick Williams
clearly reveled in the controversy he had created with his incendiary column after
Elvis' initial L.A. show. The day after he wrote the column, *Variety* reprinted it.
ABC-TV's Los Angeles affiliate station invited Williams on to discuss the controversial review. The columnist commended the police for quickly moving in
to investigate Monday's show and preventing a repetition of Presley's "salacious"
performance on Tuesday night.

On the East Coast, the *New York Journal-American's* Jack O'Brian, another per-
sistent Presley critic, picked up on the story. In his "TViews" column on November
8, O'Brian, who had not attended the L.A. concert, extensively quoted Williams
and referred to what O'Brian called his "informants" in the crowd. Of Presley in
L.A., O'Brian wrote, "His performance was absolutely frightful in its cynical pan-
dering to the most violent sexuality, not too far short of Sodom and Gomorrah."
He called Presley a "pliable hip bone with a monotonous voice attached." O'Brian
praised the police for filming Elvis' second show, explaining that they were "simply trying to record a terrible public display" and "keeping young folks free of
such performing pornography." Calling Yul Brynner a "bleeding heart," O'Brian
termed his protest "ridiculous."[24]

Clearing savoring the notoriety that knocking Presley down a notch had
brought him, Dick Williams continued blasting Elvis in his column. The day
after Presley's second, toned-down show, Williams asked the community to consider the hold the rock 'n' roll singer had on their children.

> There can be no doubt that Presley exercises a hypnotic hold on one
> segment of the public (and let us not minimize its size). As another
> newsman commented to me amid the shrieking pandemonium Monday
> night, "If Elvis asked them to hang Col. Parker from the nearest rafter,

they'd do it. That's how he has them wrapped up." To me it's a frightening form of brainwashing in America.

Probably no one can accurately assess the damage or nondamage which such a Presley performance has on young, growing minds. One mother snapped that her 11-year-old daughter at the show was made simply happy from seeing it and appreciated his "wonderful rhythm."

But to me the reaction was better epitomized by a feverish-eyed boy of 16 or 17, dashing out the door at the windup of the performance. "Man, that's sheer sex," he shouted to his companions.

Over the next few weeks, the public responded to the controversy with a horde of letters to L.A. newspapers. The *Times* printed several letters praising Wally George for his support of Elvis. "Thanks for being fair," wrote a housewife, "instead of grabbing a whip and joining the aging male critics who believe female personalities are the only ones whose wiggle is appealing."[25] Another writer, identifying herself as a "Middle-Aged Housewife," revealed that "Wally George's column of November 2 struck a harmonious note to which I listened with enthusiasm. When I first saw Elvis Presley on television I was astonished, then slightly repelled. But the critics have placed me firmly on Elvis' side."

The *Mirror-News* printed nearly two dozen letters from the flood of mail that came in. Dick Williams revealed that a late surge of letters from Elvis defenders evened the response he had received for and against Presley. The columnist downgraded the pro-Presley mail, however, by noting that much of it had come unsigned. "While they are eager to defend their idol," the columnist wrote of Presley's supporters, "they prefer to cloak their feelings in comfortable, safe anonymity." In fairness to Williams, though, he printed without further comment an equal number of letters "For Presley" and "Against Presley," excerpts from some of which follow.[26]

Being the mother of three young daughters, I too, pray they grow up and marry boys without just sex on their minds. But why always pick on Elvis Presley? Certainly the boys don't get "ideas" from Elvis but more from the low cut dresses and hip-swinging Marilyn Monroes and Jayne Mansfields.—Mrs. Pat Frank, Downey

Thank you, Dick Williams, for your column on Elvis Presley. When you told of the crowd that had gathered to see him it makes me wonder about the seriousness parents stake nowadays in the challenge of raising good children and wholesome future citizens. Maybe your column will make parents of teen-age girls, especially, take stock of their indifferent leniency and do something about this menace to their children's moral attitudes.—Parent, Venice

I am a mature businesswoman, a mother of two married children, a teen-age daughter and two grandchildren. I like and admire Elvis Presley and his performances very much. I am glad my teen-age daughter admires him … I witnessed Elvis' gestures and I saw nothing wrong in them … Every singing performer has a gimmick of some kind.—Mrs. Edward J. Miller

One wonders how many adults who laugh at the Elvis craze have seen him. There would undoubtedly be much less laughter and a little more concern if all adults were forced to sit through one of his "concerts."—Mrs. F. A. McNeil, Glendora

It didn't hurt him one bit when he rolled on the stage floor. Elvis was only doing a hula. I suppose you approve of burlesque shows. They never say anything against them. They are worse and trashy. There is nothing wrong with a hula and it's cleaner.—A Fan

I was there to see this jerk and you are so right. I am considered a fine girl of 16 and I love music but this idiot is too much and should be in jail. (He) is dangerous, believe me. If I were a man I would tar and feather this animal and send him on a rail.—M.

It was real sweet when Elvis made love to the dog. And you would pull up your pants if yours were falling.—Connie Pann, Westwood Village

Elvis said Marilyn Monroe did it, so could he. But I doubt if she or any other of our sexy ladies would make an exhibition of themselves as Elvis did. I am certainly glad someone can stand up against the cheap degrading show Elvis Presley makes of himself. If only the mothers of the world would boycott him.—May Ross, Los Angeles

Why, o why, do you adults always downgrade every singer or person we like? Elvis Presley can't even move his toe, arm or finger without you adults with your dirty minds thinking up something awful to say about it.—Presley Fan, Los Angeles

You must admit that his emphasis on "wiggle" is the idea of his advisers (older men) and I do hope that Elvis will wiggle out of his contract with them and depend on his talents.—Mothers for Elvis Committee, Los Angeles

I was thoroughly disgusted when I read in the Mirror-News, his speech; "you shoulda been here last night." The handcuff and halo acts just go to prove the type of person he really is. Obviously, he is not the pure-minded person he says he is, because this is just a money-making process, nothing more.—Leslie Newman Los Angeles

He was making fun of the song "Hound Dog," and if you had a decent seat you would have seen him laughing at the whole idea himself.—Disgusted Reader

Why don't you write about the strippers who do their gyrations in the nude? ... Now along comes one male who wiggles on a stage with his clothes on and practically every other male in the country becomes holier than thou with their cries of indecency.—Disgusted

It took only a few days in L.A. for the Presley uproar to reach its peak, and about ten days after his performances there, the subject had run its course in the city's newspapers. Then, on November 28, exactly a month after the controversial concert, Dick Williams again featured Presley in his column. This time he printed a lengthy letter, which Williams termed an "articulate, intelligent self-analysis," by Karen Forsberg, a sixteen-year-old Pasadena girl, who explained how she was lured into Elvis' world and eventually escaped from it. "She has gone through the Elvis coma and has now outgrown it," Williams affirmed before presenting the girl's testimony as evidence that recovery was possible for all Elvis addicts.

Karen explained that she had been slowly drawn into Elvis' world the previous year. "I worshipped him with wild abandon," she admitted, "buying all his records, reading every magazine article about him and spending the entire summer living, breathing and defending Elvis Presley." She shared her addiction with her best friend. "We suffered it out together," Karen said.

Her road to recovery began when she saw her idol perform at the Pan Pacific Auditorium. She wanted to scream, but instead she couldn't stop laughing. Suddenly, she couldn't take him seriously. "'Greater than Ever' Elvis left me cold," she noted. With the passion gone, Karen found herself able to analyze why she had fallen for Elvis and the long-term effect of the ordeal.

Let me get to the point. At 14, Elvis struck me at a very vulnerable and impressionable age. I found his sexy looks and voice tricks, combined with his swaying movements, aroused feelings in me which I had never been aware of before.

It was exciting to have one person to vent all these newly discovered emotions upon and be able to fall into a dream world with just the use of a phonograph record and a picture cut out of a magazine.

Now the question is, did these much-aroused feelings that Elvis gave me then give me a lot of twisted ideas and ruin my morals? Of course not!

Elvis' movements are a symbol of age, a way to escape the inexperience of beginning adolescence. It's a phase to go into one year and come out of the next. So what's the difference if he shakes his legs and jumps around?

As they mature, the same bunch that screamed will soon realize that a pair of waving hips is a pretty ridiculous thing to yell about and sit back and relax to watch the next batch of kids go into action …

Let the cycle go on if it must. An idol is the most natural thing in the world for a teen-age girl, and whether he sings through a megaphone, croons into a microphone, shakes his legs or stands on his head makes little difference when the realization strikes you that it doesn't make much sense to scream over somebody else and waste a lot of energy that you could be using to further your own goals and ambitions.

And then you've passed out of the Elvis Presley stage. And, I sincerely believe, with no damage done.[27]

Of course, Karen's story belied Dick Williams' public warnings that a gyrating Elvis Presley threatened to do permanent damage to the moral fiber of impressionable young girls. Still, Williams remained firmly convinced that he had done his city a favor by exposing the danger that Presley presented. "I'm sure of one thing," Williams wrote in his column. "He will build no more fires in L.A." Williams' conviction was a bit shaken by the realization that, while his criticism of Elvis was warranted, it might have resulted in an unintentional boost to the singer's career. A Presley fan club officer pointed out to Williams that Elvis' career had been languishing and that the L.A. controversy could be just what he needed to jumpstart it again.

In the end, though, the incident at the Pan Pacific turned out to be just another episode in the legend of "Elvis the Pelvis." The 1950s portion of the King of Rock 'n' Roll's career was about to come to a sudden end. Less than two months after leaving L.A., he received his draft notice. Elvis Presley would build no more fires in L.A., or anywhere else, for more than two years. But before he left there was a trip to paradise on the horizon, and one last fling on stage.

Final concert of the 1950s at the Conroy Boxing Bowl, Schofield Barracks, Hawaii, November 11, 1957. (U.S. Army photo)

Chapter 20

Hawaii

Prelude

Located along Kaneohe Bay on the windward side of Oahu, Kaneohe is a large residential community within the city limits of Honolulu. In the fall of 1957, seventeen-year-old Barbara Wong was president of the Kaneohe Elvis Presley Fan Club. The pony-tailed honor student at James B. Castle High School was arguably Elvis' number one fan in all the islands. For two years she had written him a letter every week; one was even answered. When Presley's first movie, *Love Me Tender,* opened in Honolulu, Barbara made a special dress, appliquéd with black profiles of Elvis, to wear when she went to see it.

When word broke on Monday, November 4, that her idol was actually coming to Hawaii to perform at Honolulu Stadium the following Sunday, Barbara had some planning to do. Elvis would be arriving in only five days and would be in Honolulu for four days. She would see Elvis; she knew that. But more than that, she would see him every day. And more than that, she would meet him, touch him, give him gifts, talk with him, and, yes, even kiss him. Barbara didn't have all the details worked out yet, but she would make it happen. For now she only knew that while Elvis was in town, her commitment to him would be the highest priority in her life.

Honolulu Stadium
Sunday, November 10, 1957, 3:00 pm and 8:15 pm
Schofield Barracks Conroy Boxing Bowl
Monday, November 11, 1957, 8:00 pm

Originally the late October shows in Los Angeles were to end a quick, four-day California stage tour. Fortunately for his Hawaiian fans, though, Presley had nothing scheduled until January, when shooting on his fourth movie, *King Creole,* would begin. So when tour promoter Lee Gordon pitched the idea of a Hawaiian trip to Colonel Parker, there was room on the calendar to extend the tour.

Throughout his career Elvis had kept up an exhausting pace on the road. His spring 1957 tour of the Midwest and Canada was a good example. Traveling by night and working nearly every day, he did fourteen shows in eight cities in just ten days. In contrast, the side trip to Hawaii would be leisurely. It would take two full weeks just to put on three shows.

Colonel Parker told the *Honolulu Star-Bulletin* that the Hawaii show schedule had been worked out "in 30 minutes over lunch" on Thursday, October 31, two days after Presley's last appearance at the Pan Pacific in L.A. During a shipboard press conference a week later, Presley explained the sudden decision to play Hawaii. "It was a real rush deal," he said. "We were in Hollywood to make a picture, but it was postponed until the first of the year. We weren't doing anything, so Mr. Parker asked if we'd like to go to Hawaii. I said, 'Huh!' and was packed right away."[1]

Parker flew immediately to Honolulu to oversee arrangements, but Elvis, honoring his promise to his mother and his own fear of flying, made the trip by ship. In 1957 commercial airline flights to Hawaii were still relatively new, and many passengers still traveled to and from the islands aboard a small fleet of ships that plowed the route across the Pacific. On November 5, Elvis boarded one of those ships, the USS *Matsonia*, for the leisurely four-and-a-half-day, 2,500-mile journey to Honolulu.

The next day Colonel Parker and his assistant Tom Diskin sat down to lunch in Honolulu with *Star-Bulletin* columnist Cobey Black. Parker told her he had received over thirty phone calls, mostly from "kids," asking if Elvis was really coming. "He's really coming on the Matsonia with a party of ten friends and relations," the Colonel confirmed. "Boy, will they be all shook up when they land."[2]

"He won't fly, you know," Parker explained without being asked. He then went on to embellish the story of Elvis' scary flight from Amarillo to Nashville the year before. "We once chartered a plane in Texas and two motors went out. We ditched in a field." (The truth was that the Colonel was not on the plane, which landed safely on the runway in Nashville.) "And that cured him?" Black asked. "Cured him, honey? It scared the living daylights out of him," Parker declared. "The only thing he was sure of was his safety belt and it was so tight it nearly cut him in two."

On board the *Matsonia*, Elvis mingled openly with his fellow passengers in a way he could never have done on land. His traveling companions were mostly his friends from Memphis. The Jordanaires and the band had decided to fly over a few days later. It was a leisurely crossing for Elvis. The first day out he and his buddies joined in the daily ship bingo game. "He was always polite, a real gentlemen," remembered forty-three-year-old Velma Fisher, who with her four children was quartered a few doors from Presley's cabin. "Every day at cocktail time in the lounge, he played the piano for everybody."[3] Another passenger later told the *Honolulu Advertiser* that Elvis was a pleasant traveling companion. "He spent a lot of time posing for movies with the waitresses so they could show their children."

At the midpoint of the voyage on Friday, Elvis sent a ship-to-shore telegram to the *Star-Bulletin,* which printed it on the front page of their afternoon edition that day. It read, "ALOHA VERY ENJOYABLE TRIP SUNBATHING SWIMMING TENNIS READING I KNOW I WILL ENJOY YOUR ISLANDS LIKE TO SURF AND SWIM GETTING GOOD TAN ON BOARD HAVE READ ABOUT HAWAIIAN HOSPITALITY AND AM EAGERLY LOOKING FORWARD TO SAME BEST OF LUCK—ELVIS PRESLEY.

As the *Matsonia* neared Honolulu, the ship company and city police officials prepared to execute the security plan they had been working on for days. Tom Diskin had met with Matson company representatives to come up with what Diskin termed the "best plan of operation because we don't want anyone hurt in any kind of unnecessary confusion." Diskin even floated the possibility that Elvis might be brought to shore on a smaller craft before the *Matsonia* docked.

Assistant Police Chief Dewey O. Mookini estimated that several thousand teenagers would be at the dock to greet Presley. "In addition to the normal complement of officers assigned to handle traffic at the pier," said the chief, "we'll have a bodyguard squad on hand to make sure those teen-agers don't pull him apart." The goal, he added, was to get the singer safely from the ship to the car that would take him to his hotel. Asked if Presley would receive a police motorcycle escort to his hotel, Mookini answered brusquely, "He's no hero."[4]

An hour before the *Matsonia's* nine o'clock Saturday morning docking at Pier 10, Elvis held a shipboard press conference for reporters who had ferried out to the ship for the occasion. Wearing a white knit sweater, a maroon sport coat, black pants, and well-shined black loafers with checkered socks, Presley quickly won over the dubious writers, according to Orman Vertrees of the *Star-Bulletin.* About his attire, Elvis confessed, "I'm pretty green when it comes to clothes. I don't pay over $7 for a shirt and $10 for a pair of shoes. But I do plan to stock up on a Hawaiian outfit while I'm here."

"What do you think of being called 'Elvis the Pelvis'?" one reporter asked. "It's very immature and childish," Presley responded. "Like a kid trying to find something to rhyme with Elvis."

His nine traveling companions were mostly friends from high school and around Memphis, Elvis explained. "I like to have my friends along," he told the reporters. "It gives me a little touch of home. Anyway, it's more fun to see things together." He had a long waiting list of friends who wanted to go on trips with him, he said, adding, "In fact I've heard from lots of so-called old friends from years ago who always say, 'You remember me, don't you?'" Elvis brought only three pieces of luggage, but estimated the total for his whole group at about forty bags.

As for coming over by ship, Elvis asserted, "I don't like airplanes. I'm scared stiff of them. In fact, we could've been on this one missing now." He was referring to a Pan American commercial flight that had gone down the night before in the Pacific with forty-four passengers and crewmembers. When Elvis first heard about the lost plane, he feared the Jordanaires and his band were on it, but they had taken a later flight and arrived safely.

As the *Matsonia* entered the harbor, Elvis embraced a hula girl and posed for photos. "Take your time," he told the photographers. "This is the best part of the trip." A little later fifteen-year-old Snookie Skoglund of Minneapolis squirmed through the crowd to slip a lei around his neck. After giving her a kiss, Elvis warned her, "Honey, it's been five days since I've seen a girl. You better watch out." Meanwhile, a small outboard craft had approached the *Matsonia*. Three teenagers stood in it holding up a banner that read, "Elvis Go Home."

Teenagers began showing up at 6:30 AM to see Presley arrive. By the time the ship nestled toward the dock for its 9:00 AM arrival, over four thousand screaming fans crowded the wharf area. When the ship was ready for disembarkation, Elvis stopped briefly at the top of the gangplank to brush back his hair and kissed a few more hula girls for cameramen. Surrounded by his traveling companions, Elvis hurried down the gangplank. Aided by a security force of thirty men, Presley's guards formed a flying wedge in front of him, and the whole gang trotted down a set of stairs to a waiting limousine and drove away. No one within the assembled multitude got within ten feet of the singer. No other person arriving there had ever been accorded such tight security, according to Chief Mookini, not even ex-president Harry Truman.

Elvis and his entourage were driven to the Hawaiian Village Hotel, where they took over all of the $82-a-day top floor rooms for a four-day stay. With most Presley fans left behind at the pier, arrival at the hotel went relatively smoothly. Only a few teenage girls were there when the Presley party arrived. One of them, Bobby Andre, walked up to Elvis and put a lei around his neck, accompanying the gesture with the customary gentle kiss. Elvis responded with a more fervent kiss, sending Bobby away in a haze.

At fourteen stories, the hotel was the tallest building along Waikiki Beach at the time. Its sprawling grounds presented a problem for security forces trying to control Presley fans intent on meeting their idol. A five-man hotel security force normally patrolled the eighteen-acre site, which was open to foot traffic on all sides. Hotel security chief Al Pinoli boosted the staff for Presley's stay to a dozen men to guard entrances, elevators, and staircases twenty-four hours a day. The two side entrances were blockaded and guarded, diverting all in-and-out traffic through the main entrance. Pinoli explained that all teenagers wandering around by themselves would be confronted and only guests would be allowed to go upstairs. If guests invited friends they would have to come down to the lobby and escort them up to their rooms. "Absolutely no one will be allowed to go up to see Presley," Pinoli declared. "Teen-agers may as well forget about seeing him up close. They aren't going to have a chance. This place is teen-aged proof."[5] Protecting Presley, however, was not the goal of the hotel staff, according to one official. "Presley brings his own guards," he explained, "and that's fine for him. What we're concerned about is the other guests and the property."

Police officers patrolling the grounds augmented the hotel staff. Chief Mookini said their job was to make sure the teenagers "don't try to tear the place down." The officers were not there to escort Presley, the chief asserted, but "for the protection of life and property." He said he hoped the teenagers would behave themselves. "I have a lot of faith in them," he said, but on second thought added, "I don't know. This boy seems to be a little different than the rest."

Of course, many teenage girls came to the hotel on a mission to find Elvis anyway. The *Star-Bulletin* unintentionally aided their efforts by printing a diagram showing the location of barricades and guards around the hotel grounds. The only fan known to get near Elvis that first day was Barbara Wong, who came to the hotel with a sixty-three-foot plumeria lei she had made for Elvis. When she discovered her idol was not answering his phone, she tearfully asked the hotel manager if he could take the lei up to Elvis. "Sorry, there's nothing I can do," he told her. Somehow Colonel Parker learned of Barbara's plight and sent someone to the lobby to escort the girl to Presley's room. There she met Elvis and wrapped the lei around his neck. Parker also gave Barbara a credential to attend Presley's press conference the next day.

Meanwhile, amidst all the hubbub of Presley's arrival in Honolulu, ticket sales for his two Sunday concerts moved quickly. The shows, one a matinee and the other an evening show, were booked into Honolulu Stadium, located at the intersection of King and Isenberg Streets. Tickets, priced at $2.50 and $3.50 for reserved seats and at $1.50 for general admission, went on sale at 8:45 Monday morning, November 4, at the stadium and at Thayer Piano Company on South Hotel Street. The thirty-one-year-old Honolulu Stadium accommodated about 24,000, most on three sides of its vast, square-shaped playing surface. Having the stage set up facing just one side of the grandstand allowed all 14,963 who attended the two shows a good view of Elvis. The gate gross totaled about $32,000, but tour promoter Lee Gordon refused to reveal Presley's guarantee. "I can't tell you how much," he told the press, claiming Elvis' contract with local promoters kept the amount confidential.

The Honolulu community lived up to its friendly reputation in welcoming Elvis to the islands. Missing from the city's newspapers entirely were articles about community groups calling for an Elvis boycott of the kind so often seen in other cities he visited in 1957. Two days before Elvis arrived, the *Star-Bulletin* printed a letter from Brenda Matsuda asking Honolulu citizens to receive Presley with open arms.

> The controversial Elvis Presley is coming to our Hawaii. It is a great privilege for the people of Hawaii to welcome this rare talent combined with a personality that spells solid entertainment.
>
> With the coming of Mr. Presley, some people will find it a chance to learn what makes him "tick." Others will prepare themselves to ridicule him and spoil the show for many who sincerely appreciate the music that made him so famous and loved by his many fans.
>
> Anti-Presleyites find it impossible to understand the pro-Presleyites because the latter find it a blessing just to listen to the Presley sounds. But toleration should be expressed instead of obstinacy. What impression will Mr. Presley have of the people of Hawaii if he is confronted with adversity?
>
> I hope that the people will give a warm aloha to Elvis Presley.[6]

On Saturday and Sunday after Elvis' arrival, a full-page advertisement ran in the *Star-Bulletin*. Under a large headline reading, "Aloha Elvis—Hawaii Welcomes You," many of Presley's records were pictured, along with a list of RCA Victor neighborhood dealers on the islands of Oahu, Hawaii, Kauai, Maui, and Molokai. The ad also plugged Elvis' Sunday concerts and his new movie, *Jailhouse Rock*, soon to open at the Waikiki Theatre. An "Elvis Special Souvenir Extra" edition of the *Star-Bulletin*, featuring a huge headshot of Presley on the cover, was sold at the stadium on Sunday. A half-dozen articles about Presley accompanied the paper's coverage of his two shows.

Tom Moffatt and Ron Jacobs, two young DJs at KHVH, Honolulu's top rock 'n' roll station, took advantage of Presley's presence to pull a stunt using a phony Elvis. On Saturday, the day before Elvis' shows, they dressed up a station employee to look like Presley, put him in the back of an open convertible, and sent it driving around the city. At the station, Moffatt began getting calls from listeners reporting Elvis sightings all around town. The car even pulled into Honolulu Stadium and circled the track during warm-ups for a football game. KHVH's studios were in the Hawaiian Village Hotel, and later that afternoon Moffatt and Jacobs were summoned to Colonel Parker's suite. Moffatt recalled what happened when Parker confronted them. "We went down, scared to death. He was wearing a straw hat and a string tie. He looked at us for a minute. He wasn't smiling. Then he said, 'You boys got a fair sense of humor. Now, I heard your little stunt. And you know what? It should sell some tickets.'"[7] Parker introduced them to Elvis, and the two DJs agreed to introduce him at his two shows the next day.

Sunday, November 10, dawned cloudy over Honolulu, with scattered, light rain forecast for the afternoon and evening. Wind in the stadium played havoc with the juggling act of Chicago comedian Howard Hardin, emcee of the opening portion of the program. Except for Hardin and the Jordanaires, the opening acts were local. Ray Tanaka and his eleven-piece orchestra played an opening medley and backed Elvis after intermission. Other local acts on the bill included "the hula cop," Sterling Mossman; dancer Kaui Barrett; singer Phyllis Brooks; Eddie Spencer's Queen's Men from the Queen's Surf floor show; and knife 'n' fire dancer Kul Lee. *Variety's* review of the event credited the Jordanaires with lifting the show into a rock 'n' roll pace, but censured the quartet for its weak comedy efforts and the repeated plugging of its own records. "They're good enough to get by on their own singing wares alone," concluded *Variety's* reviewer.[8]

Tom Moffatt was chosen to introduce Elvis at the afternoon show, and Rob Jacobs would do the same at the evening performance. Moffatt, wearing a white jacket, walked out on the field to the cheers of the crowd that sensed Elvis was near. "The Colonel told me to get up on the stage and introduce Elvis," Moffatt remembers. "'Where is he?' I said. 'Don't worry about it,' the Colonel said, '—just introduce him.'" As usual when he played open-air stadiums, Elvis arrived at the stage in a limousine.

Wearing his gold jacket with black shirt, slacks, and shoes, Elvis trembled slightly, as if to test the crowd. The teenagers answered with an explosion of screams. "From then on the concert resembled some kind of primitive religious ceremony," noted the *Advertiser's* Bob Krauss, "with the audience gradually working itself into a greater and greater frenzy." A girl behind Krauss kept up a continual clamor, shouting, "Oh, Elvis, you're killing me. I can't stand it, I can't stand it."[9]

Elvis' finale convinced Krauss that Presley was an expert at creating mass hysteria. "Presley threw his hips around," noted Krauss, "wobbled his knees, flopped his shoulders and shook all over until girls in the stands were hopping up and down with excitement." When Elvis sat down on the edge of the stage, the teenagers began pressing forward, and when he jumped down to the grass, they jumped up on their seats to get a better view of him. Presley leaned over the barricade between him and his fans to kiss a girl. He took a coconut hat from another fan and put it on his head. Finishing his song, Elvis jumped into his waiting car and disappeared into the mist. Despite the mayhem, Krauss saw nothing objection-able in Presley's act. "He was loose but he wasn't lewd," Krauss concluded.

Presley's energetic exit also impressed Tom Moffatt. "He did this slow, sexy version of 'Hound Dog,'" the DJ explained. "He jumped off the stage and sang to the audience. And the barriers were nothing like they are today, just a piece of fencing. So you could see Elvis through the fencing, and he was down on his knees singing ... Of all the rock-and-roll shows I did, that was the one Rock-and-Roll Moment."

After the matinee show, Elvis held another press conference in the Carousel Room of the Hawaiian Village Hotel. Cobey Black was there to get a story for her "Who's News" column in the *Star-Bulletin*. Elvis arrived fifteen minutes late, and that gave Cobey time to talk with Barbara Wong, who had arrived an hour early to assure herself a front-row seat. With a sixty-three-foot lei and a set of binocu-lars in her lap, she told Cobey she hadn't slept in four days. "OHHHH," sighed Barbara when Cobey asked what she saw in Elvis. "His dreamy looks. His voice. His southern accent. He's just a livin' MAN!"[10]

At that point Presley entered the room, dressed conservatively in a gray sport jacket over a black, open-necked shirt with light beige slacks and black shoes and socks. As Elvis stepped into the room, Barbara "threw herself on him like a meringue pie," according to Cobey Black. "The members of the press shifted uneasily as Elvis, powerless as Laocoon in the coils of Miss Wong and her lengthy lei, attempted to extricate himself. Finally he lifted her bodily and carried her to her front-row seat."

Retreating a few steps to a desk, Elvis sat on top and dangled his legs as he faced the crowded room. "Any questions?" he asked. "Yes, Elvis," Barbara responded quickly. "Did you get my letters, and the teddy bear?" He answered softly, "I got the teddy bear," and then quickly changed the subject. "I want to say my recep-tion in Hawaii was one of the most well behaved in my career," he announced. "I've been on stage long enough to tell if an audience has manners and today I could have safely leapt off the stage into the midst of them." Cobey heard Barbara whisper, "If only you had, Elvis."

The questions then came fast and were answered just as quickly.

"Do you like Hawaii?"

"I love it. If I move, I'll move here ... if they'll ever deport me."

"How often do you have a haircut?"

"Not often, and when I do, it doesn't look like a haircut."

"How about southern cooking?"

"I don't like fried chicken. I like pineapples and coconut."

"What's your ancestry?"

"Irish, I reckon. And some Italian. Never gave it a thought."

"Has success affected your life?"

"Of course. I never realized anything like this was possible, that I'd ever be in Hawaii—or Las Vegas, or Hollywood. It's quite a change to jump into this stuff. If you're not careful, you'll crack up."

"Do you feel an obligation to your public?"

"I do feel an obligation. I'm very careful not to do anything that would disappoint my fans. I behave myself. People have preconceived ideas about me. It's natural. I've often said, 'I won't like that person,' and then found out he's a nice guy."

Barbara piped up again. "What's your reaction to those older people who don't like you?"

"Honey, I can't please everybody. Maybe they're Pat Boone fans."

Sitting farther back in the crowd was Lynn Clausen, a women's page writer for the *Star-Bulletin*. Not a real Elvis fan, she had come to see if Elvis could "send" a girl of his own age. "I went, I saw—and I was really impressed," she admitted. "To begin with, he's good looking, much more so than his pictures—tall, broad-shouldered, and slim-hipped, with deep-set dark blue eyes fringed with long lashes." She went on to discuss his pleasing mannerisms. "Elvis is really charming ... He has a slow, almost hesitant smile, which matches his way of speaking. And he has a rather appealing trick of giving you a side-long, questioning glance before he answers you. At all times, he's tactful, hurting no one and stepping on no one's toes."[11]

Unlike Lynn Clausen, who took a young woman's measured assessment of Elvis, Barbara Wong saw him only through a veil of adoration. After he had been presented with a six-foot-long scroll from his fans on neighboring islands, Barbara begged to ask one more question before the press conference ended. "What is your reaction to this paragraph from a fan magazine?" she asked. Cobey Black thought she noted a tremor in Barbara's voice as she started to read. "'Elvis takes his date home and drives to a secluded spot, where he gives her the love-me-tender kind of kiss a girl won't fight ...'" Colonel Parker stood up and broke in, "That's enough. Will the radio people now come forward to record their questions." Undeterred, Barbara, taking a chain from around her neck, beat the DJs to Elvis. "I've been wearing this necklace all week," she told him as she reached around with both hands to fasten the clasp behind his neck. "I want you to have it, Elvis. It's my lucky ivory fang."

Lynn Clausen's favorable impression of Elvis was reinforced when she asked for his autograph. "He obliged quickly and graciously," she reported, "even inscribing my name at the top. And before I could thank him, he thanked me for asking." She came away concluding that Elvis could indeed "send" a young woman like her. "He's really just a very nice boy, this soft-spoken, good looking idol of the younger set. In fact, minus pompadour and side burns, he's something even a young lady his own age wouldn't mind taking home to mother."

At the evening show, "Presley had 'em eating out of his pinkies from the moment he bounced onstage," according to *Variety.* "Presley's casualness belies all the rules of show biz but his devotees squeal in delight with every gesture and every movement—even when he turned his back on the audience." Walt Christie covered the evening show for the *Star-Bulletin.* He judged Elvis as a "pre-sold" attraction and predicted that once his "fanatical following abates, Presley can emerge as a mighty competent 'straight' singer." Those closest to the stage had to shield their eyes from several banks of field lights aimed directly at them. The crowd's enthusiasm seemed undiminished by the field lights, the poor stage lighting, a weak sound system, two rain flurries, and a whirl of dust. Christie described Elvis' stage antics.

> He scratched his ear—and squeals of joy echoed through the uninhibited audience that jam-packed the Makai side of Honolulu Stadium.
>
> He shrugged a shoulder of his sparkling metallic-threaded jacket— and the girls literally bounced up and down in their seats ...
>
> Elvis, it appears, enjoys this mass hero worship. Indeed there are times when you wonder how he can keep a straight face as he watches his audience.
>
> Presley had 'em rockin' if not rollin' to the tempos of many of his best-known songs ... Surprisingly, he spent more time at the piano than he did with his guitar.
>
> It's not only teenagers who were "oohing" and bouncing and shrieking to his beat and loose-legged gyrations. Many of the teenagers' mothers were too. And a 7-or-8-year-old girl sitting near this writer was equally responsive.[12]

After his evening performance that Sunday, Elvis retreated to his suite at the Hawaiian Village Hotel. He had one more show planned the next night for military families. While he relaxed on the fourteenth floor, hotel officials dealt with his fans' never-ending efforts to contact him. Guards turned back about three hundred teenagers who tried to reach his penthouse stronghold. Using the service elevator, some invaders even reached the forbidden floor before being nabbed by hotel guards. The hotel operator fielded hundreds of calls for Elvis, some of them coming from neighboring islands. About a thousand letters were waiting for Elvis when he arrived at the hotel, and hundreds of others poured in over the next few days.

Monday, November 11, was Veterans Day, and appropriately, Elvis, soon to be in the military himself, gave his last stage show of the 1950s that evening at Schofield Barracks, a 17,725-acre Army post located in central Oahu in the hills north of Pearl Harbor. The venue was the large, open-air Conroy Boxing Bowl. Elvis' appearance there was the first step in a plan by Schofield Special Services to bring first-class entertainers to the post. Negotiations were underway to bring in Nat King Cole, Fats Domino, and Sammy Davis Jr. Although Presley's show was intended primarily for military personnel and their dependents, it was also open to the general public. With all tickets priced at $1, a huge contingent came up from Honolulu to help fill the Conroy Bowl to its capacity of 10,000. The throng was larger than either crowd the day before in Honolulu Stadium.

A couple of Schofield acts helped open the show. The Lightningaires Band provided the background music, and a five-member vocal group, The Lucky Charms, performed a couple of numbers. When Elvis came on stage for his final stage show of the decade, he was dressed in a pearl gray suit with black shirt, striped socks, and dark shoes.

Neither of the Honolulu papers covered Monday night's concert, and the only known review of it appeared three days later in Schofield's post paper, the *Hawaii-Lightning News*. The unidentified writer made Presley's final concert review of the 1950s a positive one.

> You gotta give it to him—he's a great showman.
> Elvis Presley, the one man hurricane who took the rhythm and blues and turned it into a multi-million rock'n'roll rampage, literally wiggled his way into the Post Bowl Monday night and shook up the some 10,000 squealing, screaming fans.
> The hottest thing to hit this post since the Honest John, Elvis led his audience, majority teen-age girls, into a state of mass hysteria ...
> His rendition of "Jailhouse Rock" brought the house down. He threw his hips, wobbled his knees, flopped his shoulders then shook and rolled. The more he rolled—the more the audience screamed.[13]

Years later, one nineteen-year-old sailor at the time remembered being there to see Presley's farewell show. "There was a notice that Elvis would be doing a concert for military personnel," he recalled. "I asked my girlfriend (now my wife) if she wanted to go with me to see him. She did not really care for Elvis so I went alone. The admission price was $1.00 ... The venue ... was a rather small showroom so most everybody would have a good seat. I think I was about 10 rows from the stage. It's been a while so I can't remember much of the show but he did all his songs that are now classics."[14]

Elvis wasn't due to sail for the mainland until Wednesday, so Tuesday was a free day for him. It had become obvious by then, however, that he was not going to be able to do much swimming and surfing, as he had expressed a desire to do in his telegram from the *Matsonia*. Presley took all of his meals in his room as groups of teenagers swarmed around the hotel grounds and the adjoining beach all hours of the day and night. Clearly, Elvis could not expect to be left alone to enjoy time on the beach like other tourists. Once during the afternoon, Elvis responded to the familiar chant of "We want Elvis" coming from a group of teenage girls on the beach below his room. (Barbara Wong was there, of course.) Going out on his balcony, Elvis began tossing things to the girls below. Among the items that went down were records, album covers, two ties, a beach towel, and a handkerchief. There weren't enough items for all the girls, so they broke the records into pieces, ripped the album covers apart, and cut the ties and handkerchief into sections so that all could have some souvenirs.

Late on his last full day in Hawaii, Elvis finally made an appearance on the beach. Gordon Stoker remembers what happened.

> He wanted to come down to the beach with us, and we encouraged him to "come on down." So he did, with his hair pretty as always. There were not many people on the beach at the time he came down with us. At first no one came over, but then the old ladies started to come over and ask him to "sign this for my kids, not for me, but for my kids." You know the bit. So, he had to leave soon.[15]

Stoker thought that had Elvis come down in disguise, say with an old hat and dark glasses, he might have not been recognized. Later, though, Stoker thought Elvis might actually have wanted to be recognized that night, and that he would have been disappointed had no one approached him. It was an example of the paradox of Presley's life, that he became a willing prisoner of the fame he always craved.

The next day Elvis was scheduled to leave Hawaii at 4:00 PM aboard the USS *Lurline*. Security for the departure was minimal, with only the regular force of police officers patrolling Pier 10. "We haven't had any requests for extras," said Chief Mookini. Colonel Parker explained that the reduced security was due partly to his faith in Hawaiian hospitality and partly to the fact that school would be in session until 3:00 PM that Wednesday. One student who had no intention of going to school that day, however, was Barbara Wong. She had already made and given Elvis three sixty-foot leis, and she planned to skip school so she could make another one for his departure.

As it turned out, an estimated five thousand fans turned out to see Presley off. That was a thousand more than had greeted him upon his arrival four days earlier. Completely filling the top and bottom of the pier's veranda, the crowd alternately chanted, "We want Elvis!" and "Elvis, Elvis, yea Elvis!" The *Star-Bulletin* reported that the singer "signed autographs and planted moist kisses on many a-quivering lips as a steady stream of fans heaped him with leis."[16] As many of the teenagers as space allowed were permitted on board the ship until thirty minutes before sailing time. Flanked by two of his traveling bodyguards, Elvis greeted fans in the aisle in front of his cabin.

After the liner was cleared of visitors, the Elvis faithful remained on the pier, hoping for one last look at their idol. As the ship pulled away from the pier to the sounds of the band playing "To You Sweetheart Aloha," Elvis appeared at the railing near the captain's bridge. Wearing a brightly colored aloha shirt, he threw flowers and kisses to the slowly disappearing throng at the dock.

Barbara Wong was among those fans who got to say their farewells to Elvis outside his stateroom on the *Lurline*. It was the culmination of a magical four days for the seventeen-year-old fan club president. She had seen her idol close-up every day—in his hotel room, on stage, at his press conference, on the beach, and aboard ship. Her stock of souvenirs included a pink beach towel, pieces of ties and records thrown from his hotel balcony, and a blue and white shirt that Elvis himself put on her.

There was a price to pay, though. For skipping school on the day of Elvis' departure, Barbara faced disciplinary action from Castle High School principal Clarence Watson. At home her punishment was having to miss the Castle-Kailua High School football game, an important social event for students attending the two schools. "I couldn't help myself," Barbara explained. "It was almost as though it wasn't me doing these things. I did it for Elvis and I'd do it again." Her parents seemed to understand. "The girl was wrong to play hooky," her stepfather James McGinley said, "but her mother and I are rather proud that our quiet little Barbara was able to accomplish all she started out to do."[17]

As for Elvis, after a short vacation in Las Vegas, he returned home to Memphis, where on December 20, one month after returning to the mainland from Hawaii, he received his draft induction notice. Tour promoter Lee Gordon, who stayed behind in Honolulu for a few days after Elvis left, told the press that Elvis "really liked it here" and that he would always have a soft spot in his heart for Hawaii. Indeed, Elvis would often return to the islands during the remaining twenty years of his life. Soon after leaving the army, he came back for a concert to benefit the U.S.S. Arizona Memorial Fund. Three of his movies during the 1960s were shot on location in Hawaii, as was his worldwide satellite TV concert special in 1973. In addition, Hawaii would be his favorite vacation destination through the years.

All of that, however, came in a different life. After emerging from the army in 1960, Elvis performed on stage only twice before settling into the comfortable, secluded life of a Hollywood movie star. Even when he returned to the concert stage in 1969, he appeared in some ways to be a mere caricature of himself. The years quickly separated him from the dynamic stage phenomenon he had been in the 1950s. As he stood at the railing watching the island of Oahu slowly sink below the western horizon that November morning in 1957, Elvis Presley faced an uncertain future. He would take one day at a time, as he had during the past year of unfathomable success. It's doubtful he thought much about his legacy then, or about the impact his 1957 stage shows had on the quarter million people who saw them.

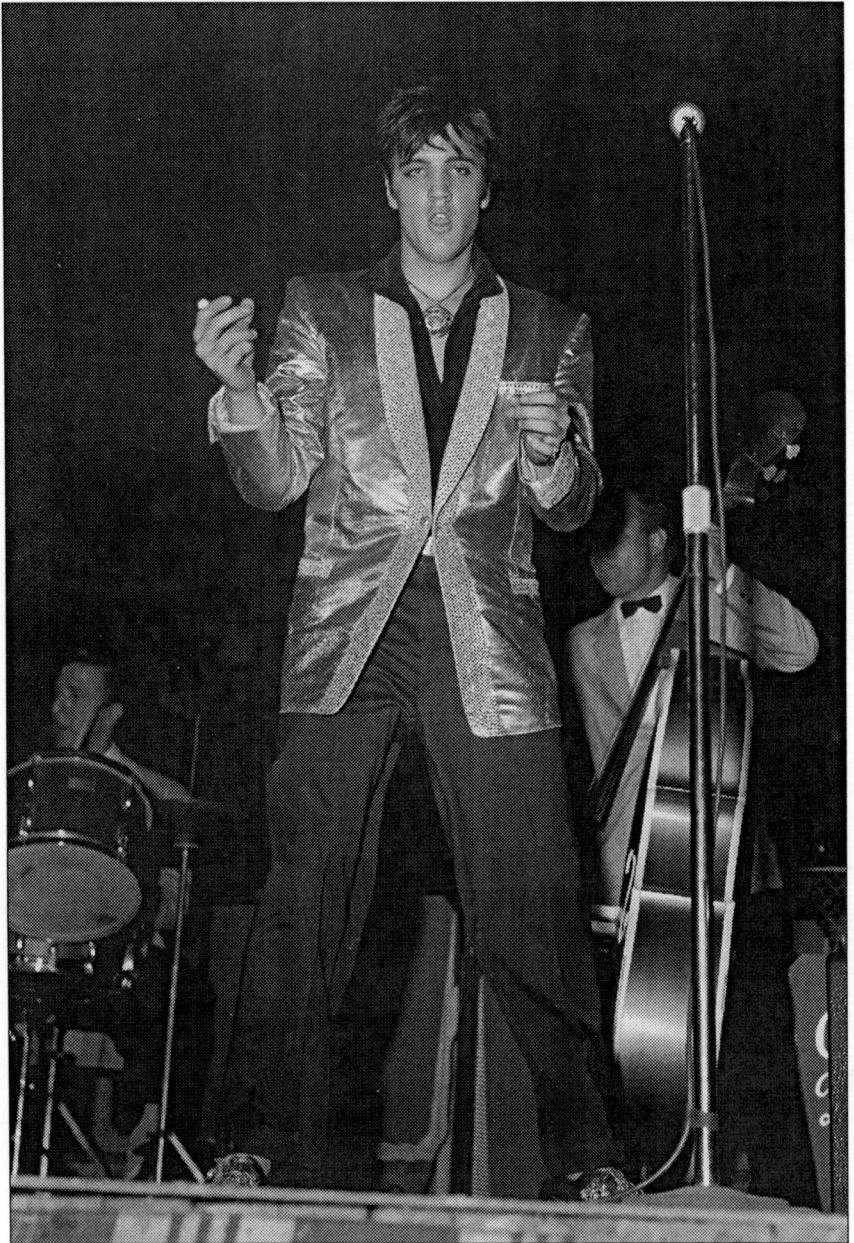

Ottawa, April 3, 1957. (City of Ottawa Archives, Andrews Newton
Collection, AN 49378 #110)

Chapter 21

Legacy

"It might be a stretch to say that Portland was a different place when he left than it was before he arrived, but it is no exaggeration to say that no one who saw him will ever forget it."[1] So observed the *Oregonian's* Jeff Baker in his 1999 retrospective article about Elvis Presley's 1957 appearance in his city. He continued, "The secret of Presley's appeal is elusive, a mystery that is powerful and immediate but not quite tangible, like a song or a dream. You can hear it in his voice and see it in the way he moves across a stage, but you can't easily put it into words." There is the challenge—how to assess and express the impact of Presley's final stage shows of the 1950s.

His personal appearances in 1957 were so limited that, on the surface, it seems unlikely that they could have had any lasting effect. That year Presley was on the road only twenty-one days, appearing in just eighteen cities. During the twenty-eight concerts he gave, he was on stage an aggregate of only about eighteen hours. Yet, during that time over 250,000 people paid over $600,000 to see him perform. For many of them, contact with Elvis during those last fifties tours had a lasting influence on their lives. In preparing his article, Baker sifted through over four hundred replies to his request for *Oregonian* readers to share their memories of having seen Elvis in Portland, both in 1957 and later in the 1970s. Baker noted, "All but a handful were positive, and the overwhelming majority were delighted to talk about what it was like to see the King in Portland. They repeatedly said how happy Elvis made them and how seeing him was a highlight of their lives, something they would tell their children and grandchildren."

Of course, when Presley left the stage at Schofield Barracks in Hawaii on the evening of November 11, 1957, he didn't realize that it had been his last stage performance of the decade. He still had hopes of escaping the draft and continuing to tour the following year. In fact, Colonel Parker already had five personal appearances arranged for Elvis in 1958. Those dates had to be cancelled when the deferment granted by the Memphis Draft Board only allowed Presley enough time to film *King Creole.*

So Elvis Presley's stage appearances in eighteen American and Canadian cities in 1957 can be viewed as a farewell tour, as he was to leave behind not only his fans, but also his fifties image as an outrageous rock 'n' roller. He would return in 1960 a more subdued entertainer, leaving his cutting-edge rock music status behind. His final 1950s appearances solidified his icon status in the eyes of the quarter of a million people who saw those shows. They matured along with him during the next two years, so his popularity continued unabated during the 1960s despite the softening of his style.

Just as important as his 1957 stage shows to his successful career shift were the press conferences he gave in conjunction with his concerts during the year. At each of those press gatherings, Elvis endeared himself to most of the reporters and columnists present. His courteous demeanor and thoughtful approach to questions disarmed and impressed those journalists who had previously judged him only on his wild stage gyrations.

Writing in the *Detroit Free-Press* in March 1957, disc jockey Clark Reid explained the importance of an entertainer's ability to relate to the public and the press in that era when young performers who shot to the top quickly could drop from sight equally as fast. "Many singers in the recent past have bungled a chance for lasting fame," Reid alleged, "by not knowing how to handle the upheaval in daily living that stardom brings. By snubbing a reporter, DJ, movie reviewer or photographer, the great golden castle can go tumbling down—in a hurry ... There is more to being a star than singing ability, sex appeal or a lucky record. It's too bad that some entertainers find this out too late." In Reid's judgment, Presley was one singer who had learned the value of public relations. "In spite of his critics," noted Reid, "Elvis Presley has managed to maintain an unusually stable composure. I have yet to read or hear of any instances of high-hattedness in his press relations. He tirelessly shakes hands, answers questions and smiles (especially to girls) to the point where he even gets a plug from evangelist Billy Graham."[2] Reid wrote his column before Presley's first tour of 1957, but the way the singer answered all questions put to him, signed thousands of autographs, hugged and kissed hundreds of young girls, and patiently posed for countless photographs during his press conferences that year only confirmed Reid's judgment that Elvis had the ability off stage, as well as on it, to support a lasting career.

When he went back on the road in the 1970s, Elvis appeared in or close to all of the American cities that he visited in 1957. (Toronto, Ottawa, and Vancouver, B.C., were left out, however, as Presley never again performed outside the U.S.) By that time, though, both Elvis and his fans had grown older and less animated. While many of those concerts, nearly all held in indoor auditoriums, were sold out, they bore no resemblance to the explosive Presley shows of 1957. The excitement of that time could only be recalled, not relived, through an Elvis who had long since slipped comfortably into the pop mainstream.

However, the fallout from the final fifties tours of "America's Only Atomic Powered Singer" has outlived the army years, the movie years, and the Las Vegas years. The impact has even outlived Presley himself and can still be felt thirty years after his death and fifty years after the tours that spawned it.

In some ways, the Elvis faithful of that era shared the impact of their idol with the rest of the nation. A case can be made that Presley, through his music, had a discernible role in the country's civil rights movement, the opening acts of which were playing out simultaneously with Presley's rise to fame. In merging black rhythm and blues music with traditional white pop and country sounds, Elvis helped break down culture-based racial barriers, particularly among the country's young people.

In October 1957, just a month after Elvis finished his tour there, a rock 'n' roll touring show came to the Pacific Northwest. It included black performers Fats Domino, Clyde McPhatter, LaVern Baker, Frankie Lymon, Chuck Berry, and The Drifters. They shared the same stage and billing with white performers such as The Everly Brothers, Buddy Holly, Paul Anka, Buddy Knox, and Eddie Cochran. The show must have validated what the overwhelmingly white teenage population already intuitively felt—that the segregated policies existing in the South were wrong. As teenagers throughout the country grew into adulthood, many threw their political power behind the movement that ultimately brought about the civil rights legislation of the mid-sixties.

Presley is less often credited with the impact he had on the women's liberation movement. Newspaper accounts of his 1957 appearances routinely dismissed his predominantly adolescent girl audiences as masses of mindless, screaming banshees. From a cultural viewpoint of fifty years later, even more disturbing are some specific reports then of male domination, such as that of the young wife in Portland who secretly went off to see Elvis against her husband's wishes, and the *Vancouver Sun* reporter who vowed he'd "kick her teeth in" should his daughter try to see Presley.

Granted, it was a different era then—a man's home was his castle and his women were expected to stay at home and accept his decisions. However, Elvis Presley and rock 'n' roll helped give young women courage to test those gender limits. The change is subtly evident in the stories told today by the then teenaged girls who saw Elvis perform in the fifties. Often they tell of how they were allowed to see Presley only after an understanding mother prevailed over the objections of an apprehensive father.

The case for Presley's influence on women's liberation was made by B. G. Welch in the following letter printed in the *Tacoma News Tribune* on September 12, 1957, just eleven days after Elvis performed there.

To the Editor: What's wrong with the women of today? Are they afraid to like Elvis Presley because the men won't approve of him?

It seems most men are either jealous of Elvis or else they don't want the papers, TV, radio, magazines and theaters to have Elvis take time and space which would otherwise be used for hundreds of near-naked women, clad only in bikinis, flimsy evening gowns, etc., to shake, rattle and roll, plus "wiggle" out with TV, theater, newspapers and magazines.

Elvis can't even wink without someone getting all worked up over it and say he's "disgraceful and vulgar." Now, even though he's completely dressed, they've cut him off from shoulders down on TV! Why? Because he "wiggles"! It's about time the women get a chance to watch a man do more while he sings than open and shut his mouth!

Half-dressed women on TV, theaters, magazines and newspapers leave nothing to the "imagination"!

Are women afraid to say how they really feel? Have they listened too long to the old tales of what women should or shouldn't see because it's supposed to be "bad," while their men are in "clubs" and "business meetings" watching burlesque!

Why don't women wake up? It's time they watched and heard about something more than recipes, laundry soap and breakfast cereal. They've as much right to see all of Elvis on TV, etc., as men have Marilyn Monroe and hundreds of other one-fourth dressed women "wiggle" their way onto stages.[3]

In addition to impacting race and gender relations, Elvis also had a role in changing the country's live concert business, the beginnings of which can be traced back to one man who attended Presley's Seattle concert in 1957.

Pat O'Day has been called the "Godfather of Northwest Rock." First as a disc jockey, then as a program director and concert promoter, O'Day ruled over rock 'n' roll in the Puget Sound area for over a decade starting in the late fifties. In 1958 entertainers Frank Sinatra and Danny Kaye formed a partnership and bought radio station KJR in Seattle. The following year O'Day settled in behind the mike at KJR and soon became the Emerald City's highest-profile DJ. He went on to run the station for a decade, building and expanding it into an entertainment empire. In 1964 and 1965 he was named top program director by the national radio industry, and the following year he was voted "Radioman of the Year." KJR's listener ratings under his leadership completely overwhelmed the competition in the Seattle area, giving O'Day power to expand his operations beyond the station. He produced recordings for many top local bands, such as The Wailers, The Dynamics, The Casuals, and The Viceroys. But the most profitable part of his operations was the teen dance circuit he controlled across the Northwest under the banner of O'Day and Associates. During the mid-sixties the company sponsored over fifty teen dances a week throughout Washington State. In 1967 O'Day was sued over allegations of payola and kickbacks at KJR. Although exonerated of all charges in a three-year legal battle, O'Day's stranglehold on Seattle radio had been weakened, and he quit KJR in 1974 to concentrate on his concert business.

All of this was ahead of Pat O'Day, however, on the Labor Day weekend of 1957. At that time he was a rookie disc jockey working at KLOQ in Yakima, Washington. On Saturday, September 1, he drove over the Cascade Mountains to see Elvis Presley perform in Sicks' Seattle Stadium. He went to see and judge Elvis for himself.

Like most Americans, O'Day had developed his image of Presley from watching the singer's appearances a year earlier on *The Ed Sullivan Show*. His instincts for promotion already emerging, however, O'Day did not share the disappointment of so many American teenagers when Sullivan shot Presley from waist up, but rather saw the ploy as adding to the excitement created by Elvis. In his 2002 autobiography, *It Was All Just Rock'n'Roll*, O'Day wrote, "His upper body projected its own fair share of sexuality and inspired those watching to fantasize about what was going on below his belt ... How the human imagination loves to fill in blanks. Given the chance, we conjure up mental pictures far more graphic and shocking than any reality we have been denied seeing."[4]

In Sicks' Stadium in 1957, Pat O'Day couldn't hear Elvis, as the singer's voice was completely obliterated by the screaming of young girls in the stands. In fact, none of Presley's 1957 concerts could be considered musical events due to the crowd noise. Along with the screaming fans, another factor worked against those fans who came hoping to hear Elvis sing. The technology of the age was incapable of capturing and projecting the volume of sound needed to reach such large and distant audiences. In Spokane, Dick Baker, a drummer in a local rock 'n' roll band, blamed the sound equipment more than the screaming for the inability to hear Elvis. "I think it was more the bouncing and the echoing, not having enough power for that big a place," he explained. "I mean, if we had a thirty or forty watt amp then, that was a lot."

Although Pat O'Day couldn't hear the music, he still found that being at the Presley concert in Seattle was a mind-blowing experience.

> Like everyone else in attendance that night, I was overwhelmed. Not so much by his songs, though I knew all of them by heart. Nor by his dancing or singing, great though they were. But rather by the grand theater, by the spectacle of it all. In my mind, I silently saluted Colonel Parker: Sir, you are a genius! This was a presidential address, a professional wrestling match, a Billy Graham revival, a heavyweight

championship fight and a World Series game—everything exciting a person could imagine—all wrapped up in one package. Years passed before anyone duplicated Presley's and Parker's feat.[5]

O'Day realized that music was irrelevant at an Elvis concert in those days. The people came to see Presley, not hear him. Elvis, then, literally made a personal appearance tour of the Northwest, not a concert tour. O'Day sensed that it was the magnetic force of Presley's personality rather than his voice that drew the huge, excitable crowds. In 1957 Elvis was the only entertainer able to attract such large, emotional throngs. But as the son of a fundamentalist minister, Pat O'Day could see a parallel between Presley's drawing power and that of another popular figure of the day.

> Twice I attended Billy Graham crusades in outdoor stadiums with 50,000 others and was spellbound by the thousand-voice choir, the emotional upswelling and the galvanizing sermon. I noticed that the electricity charging the atmosphere at such gatherings arose from more than just the message delivered. With Graham, it rapidly gained strength as the size of his audience grew, and the same math applied with Elvis. The pulsating force did more than match the audience in growth; it squared itself, it expanded exponentially. The larger the crowd, the deeper are the emotions, the greater the spiritual experience. Vast crowds can bring tears when matched with powerful music and oratory—most especially with music. When the music packs the right emotional punch, this combination delivers a highly personal experience, one with a narcotic-like effect, one that's sometimes euphoric, other times exhausting, and always genuine and meaningful. Rather than dangerous, emotional trips like these are a vital part of life, something which individuals should be encouraged to embrace and not be denied. Sounding like a shrink, I believe that such emotional experiences serve as a natural release. They can soothe anger, lessen frustration, soften disappointment and cure disillusionment—all of which life offers in generous quantities.[6]

On the evening of September 1, 1957, Elvis Presley opened the mind of Pat O'Day to the possibilities of large-venue rock concerts. O'Day knew the music world would have to wait until large auditoriums were built and the technology was developed to create the necessary powerful sound systems. But his foresight came with the determination to see it through. "Seeing Elvis perform live for the first time," he wrote, "I felt a magical genie lived in that rock'n'roll bottle, and I intended to set it free." Eleven years later in 1968, with the backing of Danny Kaye and financier Les Smith, O'Day helped form Concerts West, which quickly grew into a huge promotion and management company. It handled the concert appearances of Jimi Hendrix, Led Zeppelin, Chicago, The Beach Boys, Bob Dylan, The Moody Blues, Credence Clearwater Revival, Three Dog Night, Frank Sinatra, and Elvis Presley after he returned to the concert circuit in the 1970s. Watching Elvis on stage for just forty minutes in 1957 planted a seed in the imagination of Pat O'Day that, a decade later, grew into the largest concert promotion company in the world.

Some dispute the far-reaching influence of the Elvis Presley of 1957 on the social movements of civil rights and women's liberation, and on economic endeavors like Concerts West. It's an intellectual argument in which many scholars and fans have engaged over the past fifty years. However, the impact Presley had on the 250,000 people who saw him during his three 1957 tours was much more emotional than intellectual.

As Jeff Baker wrote in the *Oregonian,* none of those thousands who saw Elvis perform live that year will ever forget it. And many, perhaps most, have stories to tell, ones that speak not only to the excitement caused by seeing Elvis on stage, but also to the lasting influence that experience produced for years to come. For many there was an emotional tie, sometimes hard to explain, that has lasted.

One of those is Red Robinson, the Canadian disc jockey who spent a few hours with Elvis before his appearance in Vancouver, B.C., on August 31, 1957. Robinson has often acknowledged Presley's role in making his hall of fame radio career possible, but on hearing of Presley's death in 1977, Red responded on an emotional level. "I treasure my personal memories of meeting Elvis and they will live with me the rest of my life," he stated. "Big events never leave you. When I close my eyes I can still see the stage ... I see the Jordanaires—Bill Black, Scotty Moore, D.J. Fontana, the other supporting musicians, and, of course, Elvis in person."[7] On August 31, 1977, just two weeks after Presley's death, Robinson, along with Harold Kendall of station CKWX, placed a floral wreath on the spot where Elvis had performed in Empire Stadium exactly twenty years before. To show their respect, Robinson and Kendall stood silently before the wreath for half an hour. Seated in his Vancouver office in 2005, Robinson, then approaching seventy years of age, declared, "I was a fan then, and I'm a fan now."[8]

Many times through the years, in interviews, books, and speeches, Red Robinson has publicly retold the story of his connection with Elvis. However, most of the thousands who saw Presley perform live fifty years ago were not public figures like Robinson. Their stories of seeing Elvis, when told at all, have been related only to family and friends. For many, though, their connections to Elvis have been every bit as personal and lasting as Robinson's.

One of those is Judith Zenk, who saw Elvis in Tacoma during his afternoon appearance at Lincoln Bowl on September 1, 1957. She was only thirteen at the time, but still remembers the event well. "Seeing Elvis in 1957 really was the beginning of great years as a teenager," she reported. "I enjoyed all of his music and can still sing most of the songs. Many of us had his records and played them at parties and loved to dance to them. His music and that of others at that time was and are still favorites among my friends and me. I think he probably did a lot of pioneering for us by introducing a different style of music which we were all very open to receiving. It was a great time and I enjoyed every moment of it. I can tell you that upon hearing of his death in 1977, I felt a sense of loss. Does that seem weird?"9

Cassandra Tate was twelve the summer Elvis came to Seattle in 1957. Her story of seeing him then is not only one of vivid memory, but also one of rite of passage. Oblivious to communism, the civil rights movement, and other forces causing major changes in the world around her, Cassandra spent her days that summer exploring her expanding personal world in Seattle's Columbia City neighborhood. But when her friend Frances Bragg introduced her to Elvis Presley, it "changed my life forever," she declared decades later.

> It was on Labor Day weekend, the actual if not the official end of summer, when Frances spotted the advertisement that promised "TOMORROW Will Be Seattle's Most Exciting Day!" Elvis Presley "and his all-star stage show" would be appearing Sunday, the next day, "IN PERSON," at Sicks' baseball stadium, tickets $1.50, $2.50, and $3.50. We had been planning to go to a movie, and were looking at the newspaper to see what was playing at the Columbia Theater. Elvis won out over a double feature ...
>
> I dressed carefully for my meeting with Elvis: gray felt circle skirt with a pink poodle appliquéd on one side; enough crinoline petticoats to make the skirt stand out almost perpendicular to the ground; pink sweater, enhanced with the strategic use of tissue paper; new loafers with shiny pennies in the flaps; my hair in a ponytail. It pleased me to think that I looked like any other teenage girl, walking down the street on her way to someplace interesting.10

The best seats Cassandra and Frances could get on the day of the show were $1.50 seats at the top of the bleachers. They couldn't see the stage well from there, but the huge crowd impressed Cassandra. It was the most people she had ever seen in one place in her young life. The girls didn't pay much attention to the opening acts as they waited for Elvis to appear. "We entertained ourselves meanwhile,"

Cassandra recalled, "with walking up and down the aisles, going back and forth to the restrooms, and looking over the things we could have bought if we had any money: Elvis Presley hats, Elvis Presley buttons, Elvis Presley souvenir books, Elvis Presley photographs, and Elvis Presley ice cream bars, among other things."

When Elvis finally did appear on stage after 10:00 PM, a girl sitting next to Cassandra promptly fainted. As the girl was put on a stretcher and carried away, Frances screamed and held on to her friend. By the end of the show, Cassandra was screaming too, "having become a full-fledged acolyte in the Church of Elvis," as she put it. Later that evening the two girls realized the full impact of the experience on their lives.

> Frances and I walked back to Columbia City along Rainier Avenue, a good half-hour walk from the stadium at Rainier and McClellan Street. We sat on the curb in front of Tradewell for a while, not saying much of anything. The evening had been an untrammeled success. We had seen a rock and roll star, and a car full of boys had honked at us as we walked home. We took it as a sign of validation. We had crossed over a bridge, and left our childhoods behind.

To those of us who were not around or, if we were, were not old enough to have fallen under the spell of Elvis Presley in the fifties, it is hard to fully understand the effect he had on the lives of Cassandra Tate and others like her fifty years ago. Most of his fans today know Elvis best in one of his later incarnations, as the neatly groomed singing Hollywood star of the sixties or the jump-suited Las Vegas headliner of the seventies. Even then he had enough charisma to lure devoted followers into his world. But for those of us who came to him in those later years, Elvis was invariably a life-enhancing force, rarely rising to the level of a life-changing one, as he was to many who saw him perform in the 1950s. There is a true disconnect there. Subsequent generations of fans can never really understand the power that was Elvis Presley in his youth.

In 2002 Earl McRae wrote an article in the *Ottawa Sun* recalling Elvis Presley's 1957 appearance in that Canadian city. In that article, McRae tried to explain the inexplicable influence of Elvis Presley on America's youth in that crucial year when the nation's innocence was dissolving.

> You had to have been there.
> If not, it is impossible for you to know.
> You can read and you can hear and you can surmise, but you simply cannot know all that was Elvis Presley and all that he was about. You had to live it, you had to feel it. There has not been a greater magic, a

greater musical force, a greater pop culture phenomenon. Not Sinatra, not the Beatles, not Dylan, not Springsteen, not any you can name.

Elvis changed the times. He changed the way young people dressed, the way they talked, the way they thought, the way they regarded themselves ...

Elvis Presley means this, and always will: A young, lean, electrifyingly energetic, impossibly-handsome, southern rebel prince with twitchy hips, pouty lips, long, greased-back hair, jutting pompadour, trademark sideburns, and a boyish, sexy sneer of a smile that exploded the hearts of adoring females.[11]

About the Author

Alan Hanson grew up in Spokane, Washington. After high school, he attended the University of Washington, from which he graduated magna cum laude in 1971 with a bachelor's degree in history. The following year he was an honor graduate of the Defense Information School and spent the next four years writing feature articles for military newspapers.

After leaving military service in 1975, he began a thirty-year career teaching English, history, and journalism at North Central High School in Spokane. During his years as a teacher, he wrote dozens of articles, which were published in various fan magazines, newspapers, and books.

In 2005 he left the field of public education and began giving full attention to his writing and publishing efforts. He is the author and publisher of *A Tarzan Chrono-log: A Chronicle of Lord Greystoke* (Waziri Publications, 2003). He is also publisher and co-editor of *Heritage of the Flaming God* (Waziri Publications, 2000), a collection of essays on the mythical cities of Opar and Atlantis. Primarily for those two volumes he received in 2006 a Lifetime Achievement Award from The Burroughs Bibliophiles, an organization dedicated to preserving the works of Edgar Rice Burroughs.

As a teenager in the early 1960s, he first took an interest in the music of Elvis Presley. He twice saw Elvis perform in concert, first in Seattle in 1970 and again in Spokane in 1976. His article on Elvis' 1957 Spokane concert was published by the *Spokesman-Review* in 2002.

He still lives in Spokane with his wife of twenty-five years, Christine, and their two college-age daughters, Katie and Beth.

Ottawa, April 3, 1957. (City of Ottawa Archives, Andrews Newton Collection, AN 49378 #112)

Notes

Introduction

1. Hugh Jarrett, telephone discussion with author, June 16, 2004.
2. Gordon Stoker, e-mail message to author, August 6, 2003.

Chapter 1: Transition

1. Jerry Osborne, *Elvis Word for Word,* (New York: Harmony Books, 1999) 69.
2. Ibid.
3. David Carmichael, "He's In Chips But Elvis Sorry Learnin' Poor," *Toronto Telegram,* April 2, 1957.
4. "Elvis Tops at Selling Corn," *Detroit Free Press,* March 23, 1957.
5. Red Robinson and Peggy Hodgins, *Rockbound,* (Surrey, British Columbia: Hancock House Publishers, 1983) 65.
6. Gillian G. Gaar, "Guitar Man: How 1968 brought Elvis a King-sized comeback," *Goldmine,* January 9, 2004, 16.
7. Ben Metcalfe, "A set up from word go," *Vancouver Province,* September 3, 1957.
8. Doc Lawrence, "The Day the Music Happened," *North Carolina Journal,* winter 1998, 18.
9. Gordon Stoker, e-mail message to author, August 20, 2003.
10. Bob Heiss, *An Interview With George Klein,* The King in Concert, http://www.thekinginconcert.com/

Chapter 2: Chicago

1. Eugene Gilbert, "Presley Fad on the Skids," *Philadelphia Inquirer,* March 22, 1957.
2. Richard Gehman, "Pat Boone—easy-going rock 'n' roller," *American Weekly Magazine,* March 17, 1957, 8.
3. Fred Danzig, "Belafonte Passes Presley," *Toronto Telegram,* March 22, 1957.
4. Mervin Block, "Elvis—Talent or Musical Freak?" *Chicago American,* March 22, 1957.
5. "Catholics Deny 'Ban' On Presley," *Chicago Daily News,* March 28, 1957.
6. Tony Weitzel, The Town Crier, *Chicago Daily News,* March 26, 1957.
7. Irving Sablosky, "Teens Love Elvis … But Not Tender," *Chicago Daily News,* March 29, 1957.
8. John Berhl, "'Sir' Every Sentence John Finds Presley Regular, Soft-Spoken," *Toronto Daily Star,* March 29, 1957.
9. Ann Marsters, "Elvis Stirs Teen Bedlam, Off-Stage He's Calm, 'Nice Guy' " *Chicago-American,* March 29, 1957.
10. Mervin Block, "Dozens of Teens Faint," *Chicago-American,* March 29, 1957.

11. Irving Sablosky, "Teens Love Elvis … But Not Tender," *Chicago Daily News,* March 29, 1957.
12. Louise Hutchinson, "Elvis Rolls and 12,000 Teen-Age Fans Rock," *Chicago Daily Tribune,* March 29, 1957.
13. Mervin Block, "Dozens of Teens Faint," *Chicago-American,* March 29, 1957.
14. Hugh Watson, The Early Bird, *Vancouver Province,* September 3, 1957.
15. Tony Weitzel, The Town Crier, *Chicago Daily News,* March 30, 1957.
16. Tony Weitzel, The Town Crier, *Chicago Daily News,* April 8, 1957.
17. Bob Hughes, "The Night That Elvis the Pelvis Came to Rock the Whole Town," *Chicago Tribune,* April 28, 1985.
18. Irving Sablosky, "Teens Love Elvis … But Not Tender," *Chicago Daily News,* March 29, 1957.
19. Hugh Jarrett, telephone discussion with author, August 24, 2003.

Chapter 3: St. Louis

1. "Elvis Presley at Auditorium March 29," *St. Louis Post-Dispatch,* March 17, 1957.
2. Hal Humphrey, "Young Hopefuls Go Presley," *St. Louis Globe-Democrat,* March 17, 1957.
3. "Elvis Sings Here, but Squeals of 11,000 Often Drown Him Out," *St. Louis Globe-Democrat,* March 30, 1957.
4. Ibid.
5. Bob Goddard, In Our Town, *St. Louis Globe-Democrat,* April 4, 1957.
6. Ken Beaver, "10,000 Teen-Agers Squeal for Elvis Here," *St. Louis Globe-Democrat,* March 30, 1957.
7. "Elvis Sings Here, but Squeals of 11,000 Often Drown Him Out," *St. Louis Globe-Democrat,* March 30, 1957.
8. Ibid.
9. Ken Beaver, "10,000 Teen-Agers Squeal for Elvis Here," *St. Louis Globe-Democrat,* March 30, 1957.
10. Ibid.
11. Phyllis Van Damme, letter to the editor, *St. Louis Post-Dispatch,* April 2, 1957.
12. Letter to the editor, *St. Louis Post-Dispatch,* April 2, 1957.

Chapter 4: Fort Wayne

1. George E. Sokolsky, "Really Daft Over Elvis," *Fort Wayne News-Sentinel,* March 14, 1957.
2. George E. Sokolsky, "Elvis Fans Speak Up," *Fort Wayne News-Sentinel,* March 28, 1957.
3. "Cardinal Stritch Bans 'Rock, Roll' as Tribal Rhythm," *Fort Wayne News-Sentinel,* March 1, 1957.
4. "'Pelvis Contortionist' Flayed," *Fort Wayne News-Sentinel,* April 13, 1957.

5. Marjorie Barnhart, "Presley Show's Police Ready for Teen-age TNT," *Fort Wayne News-Sentinel,* March 30, 1957.

6. Marjorie Barnhart, "Elvis' Entrance Would Have Scared Savages," *Fort Wayne News-Sentinel,* April 1, 1957.

7. Kathy Bohnke, letter to the editor, *Fort Wayne News-Sentinel,* April 12, 1957.

8. "Elvis Presley To Try to Set Records Here," *Fort Wayne News-Sentinel,* March 9, 1957.

9. Marjorie Barnhart, "Presley Show's Police Ready for Teen-age TNT," *Fort Wayne News-Sentinel,* March 30, 1957.

10. "10,003 to See Show With Presley," *Fort Wayne News-Sentinel,* March 29, 1957.

11. Marjorie Barnhart, "Presley Show's Police Ready for Teen-age TNT," *Fort Wayne News-Sentinel,* March 30, 1957.

12. "Elvis Target in Tirade at City-Council," *Fort Wayne News-Sentinel,* March 27, 1957.

13. Mrs. Alan Howenstine, letter to the editor, *Fort Wayne Journal-Gazette,* April 7, 1957.

14. Mrs. Everette Pippinger, letter to the editor, *Fort Wayne News-Sentinel,* April 5, 1957.

15. Marjorie Barnhart, "Presley Show's Police Ready for Teen-age TNT," *Fort Wayne News-Sentinel,* March 30, 1957.

16. William Disbro, "Enjoying Popularity While It Lasts," *Fort Wayne Journal-Gazette,* March 31, 1957.

17. Marjorie Barnhart, "Elvis' Entrance Would Have Scared Savages," *Fort Wayne News-Sentinel,* April 1, 1957.

18. Anita De Armond, Susan Holmes and Jo Ann Perry, letter to the editor, *Fort Wayne Journal-Gazette,* April 7, 1957.

19. Jerry Kelly, "Elvis (Shriek!) Wows 'Em, Fells 'Em (Young Ones, Anyway) in Coliseum," *Fort Wayne Journal-Gazette,* March 31, 1957.

20. Marjorie Barnhart, "Elvis' Entrance Would Have Scared Savages," *Fort Wayne News-Sentinel,* April 1, 1957.

21. Helen Maxim, letter to the editor, *Fort Wayne News-Sentinel,* April 8, 1957.

22. Harold Heffernan, "Teen-Ager Latest Crooning Sensation," *Detroit News,* March 12, 1957.

23. Don Carlson, "'Girls Like Me to Look Sullen' Presley's View," *Toronto Daily Star,* April 2, 1957.

24. Ibid.

25. "Fort Wayne's Presley Tired of Answering Calls on Elvis," *Fort Wayne News-Sentinel,* April 8, 1957.

Chapter 5: Detroit

1. Jane Schermerhorn, "Elvis Lights Up a Switchboard," *Detroit News,* March 29, 1957.

2. Mark Beltaire, The Town Crier, *Detroit Free Press,* March 29, 1957.

3. Bob Campbell, letter to the editor, *Detroit News,* April 10, 1957.

4. Mark Beltaire, The Town Crier, *Detroit Free Press,* March 20, 1957.

5. Jane Schermerhorn, "Elvis Lights Up a Switchboard," *Detroit News,* March 29, 1957.

6. Frank Beckman and Carter Van Lopik, "28,000 Go Wild at Presley Shows," *Detroit Free Press,* April 1, 1957.
7. John Finlayson, "Elvis Wiggles and Wails as 24,000 Scream and Sob," *Detroit News,* April 11, 1957.
8. Frank Beckman and Carter Van Lopik, "28,000 Go Wild at Presley Shows," *Detroit Free Press,* April 1, 1957.
9. "Presley Fans Keep Condon Up All Night," *Detroit Free Press,* April 2, 1957.
10. Mark Beltaire, The Town Crier, *Detroit Free Press,* April 8, 1957.
11. Mark Beltaire, The Town Crier, *Detroit Free Press,* April 2, 1957.

Chapter 6: Buffalo

1. Margaret Wynn, "14,000 Scream for Elvis," *Buffalo Courier-Express,* April 2, 1957.
2. Eylvan Fox, "Elvis Sings, Swings, Leaves Thousands in Teens Hoarse," *Buffalo Evening News,* April 2, 1957.
3. Eugene Sochor, "Prof Ponders Presley's Pelvic Pyrotechnics," *Buffalo Courier-Express,* April 3, 1957.
4. Margaret Wynn, "14,000 Scream for Elvis," *Buffalo Courier-Express,* April 2, 1957.
5. "This Music Fan Missed Both Elvis and Armstrong," *Buffalo Evening News,* April 2, 1957.
6. Dick Hirsch, "Elvis' Grin Enthralls Girl Fans," *Buffalo Courier-Express,* April 2, 1957.
7. Ibid.
8. Jerry Evarts, As I See It, *Buffalo Courier-Express,* March 31, 1957.
9. Letter to the editor, *Buffalo Evening News,* April 8, 1957.
10. Editorial, *Buffalo Evening News,* April 3, 1957.
11. Letter to the editor, *Buffalo Evening News,* April 8, 1957.

Chapter 7: Toronto

1. Wessely Hicks, "In Elvis' Car—With a Doll on His Shoulder," *Toronto Telegram,* April 3, 1957.
2. David Carmichael, "He's in Chips But Elvis Sorry Learnin' Poor," *Toronto Telegram,* April 2, 1957.
3. Jerry Osborne, *Elvis Word for Word,* (New York: Harmony Books, 1999) 102.
4. Mark Beltaire, The Town Crier, *Detroit Free Press,* March 20, 1957.
5. Leon Kossar, "Elvis Gittin' Tuh Come Tuh Canada," *Toronto Telegram,* March 20, 1957.
6. "Where Is Presley? Can't Locate Him," *Toronto Daily Star,* April 2, 1957.
7. Ibid.
8. "Elvis Arrives Alone Now 4 Bodyguards," *Toronto Telegram,* April 2, 1957.
9. Dr. Charles Peaker, "In His Dreadful Finery," *Toronto Daily Star,* April 3, 1957.
10. Angela Burke, "She Likes Elvis But Not Pelvis," *Toronto Daily Star,* April 3, 1957.
11. "'Mind Men' Not Scared by Elvis," *Toronto Telegram,* April 3, 1957.

12. Colin Murray, "Groans, Weeping, Moans of Ecstasy For Elvis," *Toronto Telegram,* April 3, 1957.

13. Dr. Charles Peaker, "In His Dreadful Finery," *Toronto Daily Star,* April 3, 1957.

14. Joe Scanlon, "23,000 See Elvis Late Show 15,000 His Largest Ever," *Toronto Daily Star,* April 3, 1957.

15. "Disguise Makes You Look More of Oddball Than You Are—Elvis," *Toronto Daily Star,* April 3, 1957.

16. Ibid.

17. "'Mind Men' Not Scared by Elvis," *Toronto Telegram,* April 3, 1957.

18. Ibid.

19. Patricia Coxon, letter to the editor, *Toronto Telegram,* April 11, 1957.

20. Hugh Thomson, "All Too Plainly Visible Elvis Is Barely Audible," *Toronto Daily Star,* April 3, 1957.

21. Editorial, *Toronto Telegram,* April 3, 1957.

22. Dr. S. D. Clark, "Youth Have It Too Soft," *Toronto Daily Star,* April 3, 1957.

23. Eric Geiger, "Elvis Thinks 'Houn' Dog' Jazz, Experts Annoyed," *Toronto Daily Star,* April 3, 1957.

24. Hugh Thomson, "All Too Plainly Visible Elvis Is Barely Audible," *Toronto Daily Star,* March 30, 1957.

25. Barbara Bromley, "Fears Army Barber Will Ruin Presley," *Toronto Daily Star,* April 3, 1957.

Chapter 8: Ottawa

1. "Discourage Presley Attendance," *Ottawa Citizen,* March 29, 1957.

2. World of Wayne and Shuster, *Ottawa Journal,* March 30, 1957.

3. Helen Denny, letter to the editor, *Ottawa Citizen,* April 6, 1957.

4. "Ask Girls Stay Away From Elvis," *Ottawa Journal,* April 3, 1957.

5. Jerry Osborne, *Elvis Word for Word,* (New York: Harmony Books, 1999) 99.

6. "Presley Battles Belafonte for Top," *Ottawa Journal,* March 23, 1957.

7. Keith Sterling, Sterling's Hot Pops, *Ottawa Journal,* April 6, 1957.

8. Harold Lewis, "Overwhelmed By Police Control," *Ottawa Journal,* April 4, 1957.

9. Eng Hardy, "Riding The Elvis Special Was Weird And Wonderful," *Ottawa Citizen,* April 4, 1957.

10. Robert Stewart, "400 Montrealers On Presley Special" *Ottawa Journal,* April 4, 1957.

11. "Montreal Teenagers Started for School, But …" *Ottawa Journal,* April 4, 1957.

12. "The Police Kept It Peaceful," *Ottawa Citizen,* April 4, 1957.

13. "Only 37 in Commons Rest at Elvis Presley?" *Ottawa Journal,* April 4, 1957.

14. Bob Burgess, TV and Radio, *Ottawa Journal,* April 4, 1957.

15. Bob Blackburn, "Elvis Every Bit a Pro," *Ottawa Citizen,* April 4, 1957.

16. Paul Cantin, "Radio host fondly recalls day legend came to Ottawa," *Ottawa Sun,* August 15, 1996.

17. Jerry Osborne, *Elvis Word for Word,* (New York: Harmony Books, 1999) 99.

18. "The Police Kept It Peaceful," *Ottawa Citizen,* April 4, 1957.

19. Richard Jackson, "16,000 See Elvis in Ottawa Shows," *Ottawa Journal,* April 4, 1957.

20. "Nobody Got Near His Prize," *Ottawa Citizen,* April 4, 1957.

21. Richard Jackson, "16,000 See Elvis in Ottawa Shows," *Ottawa Journal,* April 4, 1957.

22. Helen Parmelee, "Elvis Fans Gave Helen a Headache," *Ottawa Journal,* April 4, 1957.

23. "Cultural Invasion," Canada: A People's History, http://history.cbc.ca/histicons/

24. "Convent Suspends Eight Elvis Fans," *Ottawa Citizen,* April 8, 1957.

25. W. L. Farmer, letter to the editor, *Ottawa Citizen,* April 11, 1957.

26. George Phoenix, letter to the editor, *Ottawa Citizen,* April 10, 1957.

27. Wilfrid Lefebvre, letter to the editor, *Ottawa Citizen,* April 12, 1957.

Chapter 9: Philadelphia

1. Frank Brookhouser, Man About Town, *Philadelphia Evening Bulletin,* April 8, 1957.

2. Jerry Gaghan, "2,300 Fans, 130 Cops Turn Out for Elvis Here," *Philadelphia Daily News,* April 6, 1957.

3. "Elvis Rocks, His Fans Roll," *Philadelphia Enquirer,* April 6, 1957.

4. James Smart, "Hysterical Mob Drowns Out Elvis' Rock 'n' Roll Songs," *Philadelphia Evening Bulletin,* April 6, 1957.

5. Joseph P. Barrett, "Tossed egg Misses Elvis," *Philadelphia Sunday Bulletin,* April 7, 1957.

6. "Elvis Assailed As Golden Calf," *Philadelphia Daily News,* April 9, 1957.

7. "Dear Elvis: We Foiled a Hair Raid," *Philadelphia Daily News,* April 5, 1957.

8. Gordon Stoker, e-mail message to author, August 20, 2003.

9. Joseph P. Barrett, "Tossed Egg Misses Elvis," *Philadelphia Sunday Bulletin,* April 7, 1957.

10. "Elvis Egged at Arena—'Gittar' Gets the Yolk," *Philadelphia Inquirer,* April 7, 1957.

11. Joseph P. Barrett, "Tossed Egg Misses Elvis," *Philadelphia Sunday Bulletin,* April 7, 1957.

12. "Elvis 'Yeggs' Land Sunny Side Up," *Philadelphia Inquirer,* April 8, 1957.

Chapter 10: Car 312

1. Jim White, "'Anita Is No. 1,' Elvis tells Sendoff Gathering," *Memphis Press-Scimitar,* Aug. 28, 1957.

2. Letter to the editor, *Vancouver Sun,* September 10, 1957.

3. L. A. Bach, "Apparently Deputy Sheriff Only One to Get Presley Autograph," *Havre Daily News,* August 29, 1957.

4. Peggy Ahenakew, letter to the editor, *Spokesman-Review* (Spokane), September 2, 1957.

5. Jerry Osborne, *Elvis Word for Word,* (New York: Harmony Books, 1999) 114.

6. "Mystery Surrounds Elvis Presley Arrival," *Spokesman-Review* (Spokane), August 29, 1957.

Chapter 11: Spokane

1. Bob Hough, discussion with author, July 21, 2003.
2. Dick Baker, discussion with author, July 15, 2003.
3. Dorothy Powers, Our Town, *Spokesman-Review,* (Spokane), August 22, 1957.
4. "Well-Guarded Elvis Arrives Safe," *Spokesman-Review* (Spokane), August 30, 1957.
5. Kevin Taylor, "Davenport is site for 100th birthday," *Spokesman-Review* (Spokane), July 8, 2002.
6. "Maximum Security Safeguards Singer," *Spokane Daily Chronicle,* August 30, 1957.
7. Dorothy Powers, Our Town, *Spokesman-Review* (Spokane), August 30, 1957.
8. "Mystery Surrounds Elvis Presley Arrival," *Spokesman-Review* (Spokane), August 29, 1957.
9. Marlene Moeller, written communication with author, July 2002.
10. Lavette Carpenter, telephone discussion with author, July 2002.
11. "Fan of Presley Slashes Wrists," *Spokane Daily Chronicle,* August 31, 1957.
12. Editorial, *Spokane Daily Chronicle,* August 30, 1957.
13. Hugh Jarrett, telephone discussion with author, June 16, 2004.
14. David Carmichael, "He's in Chips But Elvis Sorry Learnin' Poor," *Toronto Telegram,* April 2, 1957.
15. Dorothy Powers, Our Town, *Spokesman-Review* (Spokane), September 3, 1957.
16. "Presley Whips 12,000 Into Near-Hysteria," *Spokesman-Review* (Spokane), August 31, 1957.
17. Ilah Black, "Elvis Gives Interview; Is Sincere, Gracious," *Lewis and Clark Journal,* September 18, 1957.
18. Jim Spoerhase, "Same Old Thing–Presley Wows 'Em," *Spokane Daily Chronicle,* August 30, 1957.
19. Gary Pinkley, discussion with author, July 2002.
20. Linda Stephens, telephone discussion with author, February 3, 2006.
21. Mac Reynolds, "Kick Her in the Teeth!" *Vancouver Sun,* August 31, 1957.
22. Edwin Howard, "'I Told You So, Baby,' Elvis Says to Anita," *Memphis Press-Scimitar,* August 31, 1957.
23. C. E. Hertzog, letter to the editor, *Spokesman-Review* (Spokane), September 6, 1957.
24. William Weitzman, letter to the editor, *Spokesman-Review* (Spokane), September 13, 1957.
25. Editorial, *Spokane Daily Chronicle,* September 6, 1957.
26. Editorial, *Spokesman-Review* (Spokane), September 3, 1957.
27. Gottfired S. Ehrenberg, Gottfried, letter to the editor, *Spokesman-Review* (Spokane), September 13, 1957.

Chapter 12: Vancouver, B.C.

1. Brandon Yip, "King of the Empire," *Vancouver Courier On Line,* http://www.vancourier.com/issues02/082202/news/082202nn1.html
2. Letter to the editor, *Vancouver Sun,* August 14, 1957.
3. Ian Smith, A Teenager's Views, *Vancouver Province,* August 30, 1957.
4. Red Robinson and Peggy Hodgins, *Rockbound,* (Surrey, British Columbia: Hancock House Publishers, 1983) 65.
5. Red Robinson, discussion with author, September 28, 2005.
6. Jack Wasserman, About Now, *Vancouver Sun,* September 10, 1957.
7. Sandra Sheppard, "He's Shook Up With Success!" *Vancouver Sun,* September 3, 1957.
8. "Haircut Doesn't Faze Elvis, As Long as It Grows Back," *Vancouver Sun,* September 3, 1957.
9. Red Robinson, discussion with author, September 28, 2005.
10. "Haircut Doesn't Faze Elvis, As Long as It Grows Back," *Vancouver Sun,* September 3, 1957.
11. Judy Root, "Elvis is still the most—but, oh, those fans!" *Vancouver Province,* September 3, 1957.
12. Les Wedman, "Elvis takes his box—and $20,000 in cash," *Vancouver Province,* September 3, 1957.
13. Ibid.
14. Brandon Yip, "King of the Empire," *Vancouver Courier On Line,* http://www.vancourier.com/issues02/082202/news/082202nn1.html
15. Ibid.
16. Red Robinson and Peggy Hodgins, *Rockbound,* (Surrey, B.C.: Hancock House Publishers, 1983) 65.
17. Red Robinson, "Elvis Presley: A Personal Memory," *Vancouver and Victoria TV Week,* September 24, 1977, 22.
18. Scotty Moore, *That's Alright, Elvis,* with James Dickerson, (New York: Schirmer Books, 1997) 143.
19. D.J. Fontana, *The Beat Behind the King,* (Thousand Oaks, CA: Elvis International Books, 2002) 44.
20. Peter Guralnick, *Last Train to Memphis: The Rise of Elvis Presley,* (Boston: Little, Brown and Company, 1994) 430.
21. Jack Wasserman, About Now, *Vancouver Sun,* September 3, 1957.
22. John Kirkwood, "Presley Fans Demented," *Vancouver Sun,* September 3, 1957.
23. Red Robinson, discussion with author, September 28, 2005.
24. Jerry Hopkins, *Elvis: A Biography,* (New York: Warner Books, 1971) 178.
25. Gordon Stoker, e-mail message to author, August 20, 2003.
26. Albert Goldman, *Elvis,* (New York: Avon Books, 1981) 315.
27. Jerry Hopkins, *Elvis: A Biography,* (New York: Warner Books, 1971) 178.
28. Gordon Stoker, e-mail message to author, August 20, 2003.
29. Gordon Stoker, e-mail message to author, August 25, 2003.
30. Jerry Hopkins, *Elvis: A Biography,* (New York: Warner Books, 1971) 165.

31. John Kirkwood, "Presley Fans Demented," *Vancouver Sun,* September 3, 1957.

32. Brandon Yip, "King of the Empire," *Vancouver Courier On Line,* http://www.vancourier.com/issues02/082202/news/082202nn1.html

33. Peter Guralnick, *Last Train to Memphis: The Rise of Elvis Presley,* (Boston: Little, Brown and Company, 1994) 430.

34. Jerry Hopkins, *Elvis: A Biography,* (New York: Warner Books, 1971) 178.

35. D.J. Fontana, *The Beat Behind the King,* (Thousand Oaks, CA: Elvis International Books, 2002), 44.

36. Brandon Yip, "King of the Empire," *Vancouver Courier On Line,* http://www.vancourier.com/issues02/082202/news/082202nn1.html

37. Ibid.

38. Letter to the editor, *Vancouver Sun,* September 5, 1957.

39. Letter to the editor, *Vancouver Province,* September 9, 1957.

40. Dr. Ida Halpern, "A frog injected with strychnine," *Vancouver Province,* September 3, 1957.

41. Hugh Watson, The Early Bird, *Vancouver Province,* September 3, 1957.

42. Jean Stuart, letter to the editor, *Vancouver Sun,* September 4, 1957.

43. M. Morrison, letter to the editor, *Vancouver Province,* September 5, 1957.

44. Letter to the editor, *Vancouver Province,* September 10, 1957.

45. Ann Archibald, letter to the editor, *Vancouver Sun,* September 7, 1957.

46. Archibald Beavan, letter to the editor, *Vancouver Province,* September 10, 1957.

47. P. Rowley, letter to the editor, *Vancouver Province,* September 13, 1957.

48. "Court raps Presley's Show Here," Final Edition, *Vancouver Sun,* September 10, 1957.

49. Red Robinson, "Test Coming Up For Elvis Presley," *Vancouver Sun,* September 6, 1957.

Chapter 13: Seattle–Tacoma

1. Richard F. Perkins, letter to the editor, *Tacoma News Tribune,* September 12, 1957.

2. Bart Ripp, "In '57, Tacoma was all shook up by the king," *News Tribune* (Tacoma) August 10, 1997.

3. Don Duncan, "The day Elvis wowed 'em in Tacoma," *News Tribune,* October 6, 1974.

4. Bart Ripp, "In '57, Tacoma was all shook up by the king," *News Tribune* (Tacoma) August 10, 1997.

5. Judith Zenk, e-mail message to author, November 8, 2005.

6. Lexi Arick, letter to the editor, *Tacoma News Tribune,* September 7, 1957.

7. Don Duncan, "Presley Rocks 'n' Rolls Tacoma Teenagers Into Frenzy at Bowl," *Tacoma News Tribune,* September 2, 1957.

8. Bart Ripp, "In '57, Tacoma was all shook up by the king," *News Tribune* (Tacoma) August 10, 1997.

9. Don Duncan, "elvis nice to press, dazzler with girls," *Tacoma News Tribune,* September 8, 1957.

10. John Voorhees, "Presley Fan Club Head Screams," *Seattle Post-Intelligencer,* August 21, 1957.

11. John Voorhees, Look and Listen, *Seattle Post-Intelligencer,* August 18, 1957.

12. John Voorhees, "15,000 Here Attend Elvis Presley Show, *Seattle Post-Intelligencer,* September 2, 1957.

13. Royal Brougham, The Morning After, *Seattle Post-Intelligencer,* September 3, 1957.

14. Patrick MacDonald, "Elvis Touched It!" *Seattle Times,* August 16, 2002.

15. Laurie Warshal Cohen, letter to the editor, *Seattle Times,* August 25, 2002.

16. Marjorie Jones, "Presley Enraptures Squealing Fans," *Seattle Times,* September 2, 1957.

17. Hugh Jarrett, telephone discussion with author, June 16, 2004.

18. Arjan Deelen, "D.J. Fontana Interviewed," Elvis Australia, http://www.elvis.com.au/presley/interview_djfontana.shtml

19. "Ernst Jorgensen discusses the 'Summer Festival' FTD, Elvis Information Network, http://www.elvisinfonet.com/interview_ernst_on_Sirius.html

20. Charles S. Hadley Jr., letter to the editor, *Seattle Times,* September 5, 1957.

21. Hugh Jarrett, telephone discussion with author, August 24, 2003.

22. Leonard Butcher, letter to the editor, *Seattle Post-Intelligencer,* September 12, 1957.

23. Grace O'Dell, letter to the editor, *Seattle Post-Intelligencer,* September 15, 1957.

24. Charles R. Cross, *Room Full of Mirrors,* (New York: Hyperion, 2005) 53.

Chapter 14: Portland

1. Nancy Ramsden, e-mail message to author, November 11, 2005.

2. Bob Blackburn, telephone discussion with author, November 7, 2005.

3. Dorothy Lois Smith, Stage and Screen, sec. 1, *Oregon Journal* (Portland), August 26, 1957.

4. William Moyes, "B. Mike's Lowdown: People Still Ask Why Elvis Isn't in Service," sec. 2, *Oregon Journal* (Portland), August 29, 1957.

5. Dorothy Lois Smith, Stage and Screen, sec. 1, *Oregon Journal* (Portland), August 9, 1957.

6. Dorothy Lois Smith, Stage and Screen, sec. 1, *Oregon Journal* (Portland), August 20, 1957.

7. Dorothy Lois Smith, Stage and Screen, sec. 1, *Oregon Journal* (Portland), August 26, 1957.

8. Dorothy Lois Smith, Stage and Screen, sec. 2, *Oregon Journal* (Portland), September 2, 1957.

9. William Moyes, "B. Mike's Lowdown: People Still Ask Why Elvis Isn't in Service," sec. 2, *Oregon Journal* (Portland), August 29, 1957.

10. William Moyes, Behind the Mike, sec. 3, *Portland Oregonian,* August 30, 1957.

11. Editorial, *Portland Oregonian,* sec. 1, August 28, 1957.

12. Arnold Marks, "Elvis Presley's popularity here never diminished," sec. 3, *Oregon Journal* (Portland), August 17, 1977.

13. Cáit Curtin, *The Grand Lady of Fourth Avenue,* (Portland, OR: Binford and Mort Publishing, 1997) 53.

14. Jeff Baker, "Love Me Tender," *Portland Oregonian,* sec. L, January 17, 1999.

15. William Moyes, Behind the Mike, sec. 3, *Portland Oregonian,* September 5, 1957.

16. Arnold Marks, "Elvis Presley's popularity here never diminished," sec. 3, *Oregon Journal* (Portland), August 17, 1977.

17. Holly Johnson, "Teener Tells Elvis Story," sec. 1, *Portland Oregonian,* September 3, 1957.

18. "14,600 Fans Squeal, Jump As Elvis Shakes, Gyrates," *Portland Oregonian,* September 3, 1957.

19. Phyllis Lauritz, "Critic of Elvis Convinced He Must Have Something," sec. 1, *Portland Oregonian,* September 3.

20. Holly Johnson, "Teener Tells Elvis Story," sec. 1, *Portland Oregonian,* September 3, 1957.

21. Don Horine, "Portland Teenagers Frenzied Over Elvis," sec. 1, *Oregon Journal,* (Portland), September 3, 1957.

22. Dorothy Lois Smith, "Stadium Shakes Here," sec. 1, *Oregon Journal* (Portland), September 3, 1957.

23. Jeff Baker, "Love Me Tender," *Portland Oregonian,* sec. L, January 17, 1999.

24. Ibid.

25. "Elvis Eats Burnt Bacon," *Oregon Journal,* (Portland), September 4, 1957.

Chapter 15: Changes

1. Alana Nash, *Elvis Aaron Presley: Revelations from the Memphis Mafia,* with Billy Smith, Marty Lacker, and Lamar Fike, (New York: Harper Collins, 1995) 114.

2. Jerry Hopkins, *Elvis: A Biography,* (New York: Warner Books, 1971), 76.

3. Ibid., 77.

4. Ibid.

5. Joe Esposito and Elena Oumano, *Good Rockin' Tonight,* (New York: Simon and Schuster, 1994) 100.

6. Robert Johnson, "Two of Elvis' Musicians Quit Him," *Memphis Press-Scimitar,* September 13, 1957.

7. "Elvis Is 'Shocked' At Musicians Quitting," sec. 2, *Memphis Press-Scimitar,* September 14, 1957.

8. Scotty Moore, *That's Alright, Elvis,* with James Dickerson, (New York: Schirmer Books, 1997) 145.

9. Gordon Stoker, e-mail message to author, August 25, 2003.

10. Hugh Jarrett, telephone discussion with author, June 16, 2004.

11. Alana Nash, *Elvis Aaron Presley: Revelations from the Memphis Mafia,* with Billy Smith, Marty Lacker, and Lamar Fike, (New York: Harper Collins, 1995) 115.

12. Peter Guralnick, *Last Train to Memphis: The Rise of Elvis Presley,* (Boston: Little, Brown and Company, 1994), 445.
13. Barbara Bromley, "Fears Army Barber Will Ruin Presley," *Toronto Daily Star,* April 3, 1957.
14. "On Thinking It Over," *Ottawa Citizen,* March 29, 1957.
15. William Moyes, "B. Mike's Lowdown: People Still Ask Why Elvis Isn't in Service," sec. 3, *Portland Oregonian,* August 29, 1957.
16. "Drafting Elvis Cause Of Woe For His Board," *Memphis Commercial Appeal,* January 5, 1958.

Chapter 16: Tupelo

1. David Carmichael, "Owns 6 Cars Elvis Can't Explain Why," *Toronto Telegram,* March 30, 1957.
2. David Carmichael, "He's in Chips But Elvis Sorry Learnin' Poor," *Toronto Telegram,* April 2, 1957.
3. David Carmichael, "Owns 6 Cars Elvis Can't Explain Why," *Toronto Telegram,* March 30, 1957.
4. Robert Johnson, "Elvis to Appear at Tupelo Fair. No Charge!" *Memphis Press Scimitar,* March 22, 1957.
5. Editorial, *Tupelo Daily Journal,* September 27, 1957.
6. James F. Page Jr., "Burp Adds to Act and 12,000 Scream and Cry," sec. 2, *Memphis Press-Scimitar,* September 28, 1957.
7. Ibid.

Chapter 17: The Parker Propaganda Machine

1. Editorial, sec. 1, *Portland Oregonian,* August 28, 1957.
2. Phyllis Lauritz, "Fetch Me My Teddy Bear Perfume, Lipstick For I've a Date With Elvis Presley Monday," *Portland Oregonian,* August 31, 1957.
3. Leon Kossar, "Elvis Gittin' Tuh Come Tuh Canada," *Toronto Telegram,* March 20, 1957.
4. John Voorhees, "Presley Virtual Unknown Until Colonel Parker Got Him," *Seattle Post-Intelligencer,* August 29, 1957.
5. Gordon Stoker, e-mail message to author, January 29, 2007.
6. Emmett Watson, This Our City, *Seattle Post-Intelligencer,* September 3, 1957.
7. Frank Beckman and Carter Van Lopik, "28,000 Go Wild at Presley Shows," *Detroit Free Press,* April 1, 1957.
8. Mark Beltaire, The Town Crier, *Detroit Free Press,* March 20, 1957.
9. Jerry Hopkins, *Elvis: A Biography,* (New York: Warner Books, 1971) 146.
10. Dick Baker, discussion with the author, July 2003.
11. Peter Guralnick, and Ernst Jorgensen. *Elvis Day by Day,* (New York: Ballantine Books, 1999) 62.

12. Les Wedman, "Elvis takes his box—and $20,000 in cash," *Vancouver Province,* September 3, 1957.
13. Jack Wasserman, About Now, *Vancouver Sun,* September 3, 1957.
14. Dorothy Lois Smith, "Stadium Shakes Here," sec. 1, *Oregon Journal* (Portland), September 3, 1957.
15. Hugh Jarrett, telephone discussion with author, August 24, 2003.

Chapter 18: The Bay Area

1. Daily Knave, *Oakland Tribune,* June 5, 1956.
2. Hortense Morton, "'Jailhouse Rock', With Presley, at Warfield," *San Francisco Examiner,* sec. 2, October 31, 1957.
3. Eugene Gilbert, "Hero Worshipping Youth Go for Ike, Grace Kelly," *Oakland Tribune,* October 10, 1957.
4. Don Steele, Going Places ..., *Oakland Tribune,* October 26, 1957.
5. Daily Knave, *Oakland Tribune,* October 25, 1957.
6. Herb Caen, Baghdad-by-the-Bay, *San Francisco Examiner,* sec. 2, October 23, 1957.
7. Terrence O'Flaherty, column, *San Francisco Chronicle,* November 14, 1957.
8. Terrence O'Flaherty, column, *San Francisco Chronicle,* October 1, 1957.
9. Terrence O'Flaherty, column, *San Francisco Chronicle,* October 21, 1957.
10. Carolyn Anspacher, "Presley Here—Hip, Hip Hooray," *San Francisco Chronicle,* October 27, 1957.
11. Dwight Newton, Day and Night, *San Francisco Examiner,* sec. 1, November 2, 1957.
12. Daily Knave, *Oakland Tribune,* June 6, 1956.
13. Dwight Newton, Day and Night, *San Francisco Examiner,* sec. 1, November 2, 1957.
14. Carolyn Anspacher, "Presley Here—Hip, Hip Hooray," *San Francisco Chronicle,* October 27, 1957.
15. "Elvis Ducks Frenzied Teen Fans," *Oakland Tribune.* October 28, 1957.
16. Herb Caen, Baghdad-by-the-Bay, *San Francisco Examiner,* sec. 2, October 25, 1957.
17. Terrence O'Flaherty, column, *San Francisco Chronicle,* October 25, 1957.
18. Dennis Lewis, letter to the editor, *Oakland Tribune,* October 30, 1957.
19. Pat Droke, letter to the editor, *Oakland Tribune,* November 4, 1957.
20. Marilyn C. Rushmer, letter to the editor, *Oakland Tribune,* November 11, 1957.
21. M. Lopez, letter to the editor, *Oakland Tribune,* November 5, 1957.
22. Louise Bevitt, letter to the editor, *San Francisco Examiner,* sec. 2, November 9, 1957.
23. Ronnie Kleinhammer, letter to the editor, *San Francisco Chronicle,* November 5, 1957.
24. Dwight Nelson, Day and Night, *San Francisco Examiner,* sec. 1, October 29, 1957.

Chapter 19: Los Angeles

1. Howard Williams, "Public Ignored by Disc Jockeys," *Los Angeles Mirror News,* part 2, November 19, 1957.

2. "Rock-Roll's for 'Goons,' Sinatra Tells French," *Los Angeles Mirror News,* October 28, 1957.

3. Dick Williams, "Presley's Manager Steals the Show," *Los Angeles Mirror News,* part 3, October 4, 1957.

4. Dick Williams, "Friends and Foes of Elvis Take Firm Stand," *Los Angeles Mirror News,* part 3, November 4, 1957.

5. "Disguise Makes You Look More of Oddball Than You Are—Elvis," *Toronto Daily Star,* April 3, 1957.

6. "Sinatra Swoons For Pat Boone as Cream of New Singing Crop," *Variety,* June 5, 1957.

7. George H. Jackson, "New Page for Elvis Legend," *Los Angeles Herald Express,* October 29, 1957.

8. Dick Williams, "6000 Kids Cheer Elvis' Frantic Sex Show," *Los Angeles Mirror News,* part 2, October 29, 1957.

9. Gordon Stoker, e-mail message to author, November 6, 2006.

10. Byron Raphael, "In Bed with Elvis," with Alanna Nash, *Playboy,* November 2005, 66.

11. Dina Angus, "Update: From a Fan That Was There," Elvis Presley News.com, http://www.elvispresleynews.com/ElvisBanned.html

12. Marcia Bore, "Rick Nelson's Special Memory of Elvis," *A Photoplay Tribute,* 1977, 104.

13. Margie Montgomery, "Elvis Makes Their Lives Complete, Dreams Fulfill," *Hollywood Citizen News,* October 29, 1957.

14. Wally George, "Elvis Wriggles, Fans Scream at Pan-Pacific," *Los Angeles Times,* October 29, 1957.

15. Hedda Hopper, "Elvis' Performance Called Shattering," *Los Angeles Times,* October 31, 1957.

16. Dick Williams, "6000 Kids Cheer Elvis' Frantic Sex Show," *Los Angeles Mirror News,* part 2, October 29, 1957.

17. Dick Williams, "Elvis Review Stirs Furor of Comments," *Los Angeles Mirror News,* part 1, October 31, 1957.

18. Letter to the editor, *Los Angeles Mirror News,* part 1, November 4, 1957.

19. Roger Beck, "Elvis Tones Down Act When Police Move In," *Los Angeles Mirror News,* October 30, 1957.

20. Hedda Hopper, "Angry Man," *Los Angeles Times,* November 4, 1957.

21. Wally George, Strickly Off the Record, *Los Angeles Times,* November 2, 1957.

22. Editorial, *Los Angeles Mirror News,* part 1, October 31, 1957.

23. Paul V. Coates, Confidential File, *Los Angeles Mirror News,* part 1, October 31, 1957.

24. Jack O'Brian, "L.A. Outraged at Presley," *New York Journal-American,* November 8, 1957.

25. Mrs. H. V. Bossche, letter to the editor, *Los Angeles Times,* November 6, 1957.

26. Dick Williams, "Friends and Foes of Elvis Take Firm Stand," *Los Angeles Mirror News,* part 3, November 4, 1957.

27. Dick Williams, "Ex-Fan of Elvis Now Wonders Why," *Los Angeles Mirror News,* part 3, November 28, 1957.

Chapter 20: Hawaii

1. Orman Vertrees, "Presley Descends to Comanche yells of 4,000 Admirers As Matsonia Docks," *Honolulu Star-Bulletin,* November 9, 1957.
2. Cobey Black, "He's a Promoter and a Gentleman," *Honolulu Star-Bulletin,* November 7, 1957.
3. Jerry Hopkins, *Elvis in Hawai'i,* (Honolulu: The Bess Press, 2002) 4.
4. "Singer May Switch to Boat Offshore," *Honolulu Star-Bulletin,* November 6, 1957.
5. "Teen-agers Will See but Not touch Elvis," *Honolulu Star-Bulletin,* November 8, 1957.
6. Brenda Matsuda, letter to the editor, *Honolulu Star-Bulletin,* November 7, 1957.
7. Tom Moffatt, *The Showman of the Pacific: 50 Years of Radio and Rock Stars,* with Jerry Hopkins, (Honolulu: Watermark Publishing, 2005) 47.
8. "Honoluluans Dig Up High $3.50 Top to Dig Presley for 32G in 2 Sun. Shows," *Variety,* November 20, 1957.
9. Bob Kraus, "Hipster Hexes Hysterical Hepsters," *Honolulu Advertiser,* November 11, 1957.
10. Cobey Black, "Love Him Tender Like a Tiger," *Honolulu Star-Bulletin,* November 11, 1957.
11. Lynn Clausen, "Elvis Is 'The Most' Says New Presley Fan," *Honolulu Star-Bulletin,* November 12, 1957.
12. Walt Christie, "Presley Proves He's 'King' To Squealing Teen-Agers," *Honolulu Star-Bulletin,* November 11, 1957.
13. "Elvis Rocks the Bowl," *Hawaii-Lightning News,* November 14, 1957.
14. "Have You Seen Elvis Presley in Concert?" Elvis Presley In Concert, http://www.elvisconcerts.com/concert/concert01.htm
15. Gordon Stoker, e-mail message to author, November 7, 2006.
16. "Pony-Tail Set Rocks Pier 10 As Idol Presley Sails Away," *Honolulu Star-Bulletin,* November 14, 1957.
17. Shirley Hutton, "Elvis Is Gone but the Memory—And Troubles—Linger for No. 1 Fan," *Honolulu Star-Bulletin,* November 15, 1957.

Chapter 21: Legacy

1. Jeff Baker, "Love Me Tender," *Portland Oregonian,* sec. L, January 17, 1999.
2. Clark Reid, "It Takes Plenty of Character To Be a Star—and Stay One," *Detroit Free Press,* March 2, 1957.
3. B. G. Welch, letter to the editor, *Tacoma News Tribune,* September 12, 1957.
4. Pat O'Day and Jim Ojala, *It Was All Just Rock'n'Roll,* (Seattle: Rock'n'Roll Press, 2002) 46.
5. Ibid., 47.

6. Ibid.
7. Red Robinson, "Elvis Presley: A Personal Memory," *Vancouver and Victoria TV Week,* September 24, 1977, 22.
8. Red Robinson, discussion with author, September 28, 2005.
9. Judith Zenk, e-mail message to author, November 8, 2005.
10. Cassandra Tate, "Elvis and Me," HistoryLink.org: The Online Encyclopedia of Washington State History, http://www.historylink.org/essays/output.cfm?file_id=3218
11. Earl McRae, "The day Elvis came to Ottawa," *Ottawa Sun,* August 16, 2002.

Selected Bibliography

Listed here are only the book titles that have been of use in the making of this volume. This bibliography is not intended to be a complete list of all the book titles and other sources I have consulted. All newspaper articles, personal interviews, and Internet sources cited in this book are listed in detail in the endnotes.

Cotton, Lee. *Did Elvis Sing in Your Hometown?* Sacramento: High Sierra Books, 1995.

Cross, Charles R. *Room Full of Mirrors,* New York: Hyperion, 2005.

Curtin, Cáit. *The Grand Lady of Fourth Avenue: Portland's Historic Multnomah Hotel,* Portland, OR: Binford and Mort Publishing, 1997.

Esposito, Joe, and Elena Oumano. *Good Rockin' Tonight,* New York: Simon and Schuster, 1994.

Fontana, D.J. *The Beat Behind the King,* Thousand Oaks, CA: Elvis International Books, 2002.

Goldman, Albert: *Elvis,* New York: Avon Books, 1981.

Guralnick, Peter. *Last Train to Memphis: The Rise of Elvis Presley,* Boston: Little, Brown and Company, 1994.

Guralnick, Peter, and Ernst Jorgensen. *Elvis Day by Day,* New York: Ballantine Books, 1999.

Hopkins, Jerry. *Elvis: A Biography,* New York: Warner Books, 1971.

Hopkins, Jerry. *Elvis in Hawai'i,* Honolulu: The Bess Press, 2002.

Moffatt, Tom, with Jerry Hopkins. *The Showman of the Pacific: 50 Years of Radio and Rock Stars,* Honolulu: Watermark Publishing, 2005.

Moore, Scotty, with James Dickerson. *That's Alright, Elvis,* New York: Schirmer Books, 1997.

Nash, Alanna, with Billy Smith, Marty Lacker, and Lamar Fike. *Elvis Aaron Presley: Revelations from the Memphis Mafia,* New York: Harper Collins, 1995.

Oberst, Stanley, and Lori Torrance. *Elvis in Texas, 1954-1958,* Plano, TX: Republic of Texas Press, 2002.

O'Day, Pat, and Jim Ojala. *It Was All Just Rock'n'Roll,* Seattle: Rock'n'Roll Press, 2002.

Osborne, Jerry. *Elvis Word for Word,* New York: Harmony Books, 1999.

Robinson, Red, and Peggy Hodgins. *Rockbound,* Surrey, B.C.: Hancock House Publishers, 1983.

Ottawa, April 3, 1957. (City of Ottawa Archives, Andrews Newton
Collection, AN 49378 #105)

Index

978-0-595-43122-9
0-595-43122-4

Lightning Source UK Ltd.
Milton Keynes UK
UKOW040036110613

212050UK00001B/57/A